Displacement and Dispossession in the Modern Middle East

Dispossession and forced migration in the Middle East remain even today significant elements of contemporary life in the region. Dawn Chatty's book traces the history of those who, as a reconstructed Middle East emerged at the beginning of the twentieth century, found themselves cut off from their homeland, refugees in a new world with borders created out of the ashes of war and the fall of the Ottoman Empire. As an anthropologist, the author is particularly sensitive to individual experience and how these experiences have impacted on society as a whole from the political, social, and environmental perspectives. Through personal stories and interviews within different communities, she shows how some minorities, such as the Armenian and Circassian communities, have succeeded in integrating and creating new identities whereas others, such as the Palestinians and the Kurds, have been left homeless within impermanent landscapes. The book is unusual in combining an ethnographic approach that analyzes the everyday experiences of refugees and migrants against the backdrop of the broad sweep of Mediterranean history. It is intended as an introduction for students in Middle East studies, history, political science, and anthropology and for anyone concerned with war and conflict in the region.

Dawn Chatty is a University Reader in Anthropology and Forced Migration at the Refugee Studies Centre Department of International Development, University of Oxford. She is a Fellow of the American Anthropological Association, the Society for Applied Anthropology, the Middle East Studies Association, the Royal Anthropological Institute, and the Association of Social Anthropology. Most recently she has edited (with Gillian Lewando-Hundt) *Children of Palestine: Experiencing Forced Migration in the Middle East* (2005) and *Nomadic Societies in the Middle East and North Africa: Entering the 21st Century* (2006).

The Contemporary Middle East 5

Series editor: Eugene L. Rogan

Books published in *The Contemporary Middle East* series address the major political, economic, and social debates facing the region today. Each title comprises a survey of the available literature against the background of the author's own critical interpretation, designed to challenge and encourage independent analysis. While the focus of the series is the Middle East and North Africa, books are presented as aspects of a rounded treatment, which cut across disciplinary and geographic boundaries. They are intended to initiate debate in the classroom and to foster understanding amongst professionals and policy-makers.

1 Clement M. Henry and Robert Springborg, *Globalization and the Politics of Development in the Middle East*
2 Joel Beinin, *Workers and Peasants in the Modern Middle East*
3 Zachary Lockman, *Contending Visions of the Middle East: The History and Politics of Orientalism*
4 Fred Halliday, *The Middle East in International Relations: Power, Politics and Ideology*

Displacement and Dispossession in the Modern Middle East

DAWN CHATTY

University of Oxford

CAMBRIDGE
UNIVERSITY PRESS

32 Avenue of the Americas, New York NY 10013-2473, USA

Cambridge University Press is part of the University of Cambridge.

It furthers the University's mission by disseminating knowledge in the pursuit of
education, learning and research at the highest international levels of excellence.

www.cambridge.org
Information on this title: www.cambridge.org/9780521521048

First published 2010

A catalogue record for this publication is available from the British Library

Library of Congress Cataloguing in Publication data
Chatty, Dawn.
Displacement and dispossession in the modern Middle East / Dawn Chatty.
    p.   cm. – (The contemporary Middle East ; 5)
Includes bibliographical references and index.
ISBN 978-0-521-81792-9 – ISBN 978-0-521-52104-8 (pbk.)
1. Forced migration –Middle East – History.   2. Refugees –Middle East – History.
3. Middle East – Emigration and immigration – History.   I. Title.   II. Series.
HV640.4.M628C53   2010
362.870956–dc22

                                                                2009054138

ISBN 978-0-521-81792-9 Hardback
ISBN 978-0-521-52104-8 Paperback

In Memory of Dia Eddine

Contents

List of Tables

List of Charts and Maps

Acknowledgements

I owe Eugene Rogan and Marigold Acland a huge debt of appreciation. It was Marigold who first suggested this project to me over lunch in Oxford one day. I was not very keen at first; dispossession, displacement, forced migration, and exile are topics that eventually burn you out. After some reflection and further discussion with Eugene, we agreed I might take a fresh perspective and supplement secondary historical material with contemporary interviews conducted with surviving members of dispossessed and displaced groups in the Middle East.

A Leverhulme Major Research Award and a Large British Academy grant gave me two years free from teaching and a modest budget to travel and conduct interviews. I spent most of 2005 to 2007 travelling back and forth between the UK and Lebanon, Syria, Jordan, and Egypt. In each country I found a research assistant who helped me to identify possible informants and conduct my interviews. I am grateful to Mariz Tadros and Nora Kolyan for all their help in Egypt; to Arda Dergarabedian in Jordan; to Hovig Etyemezian in Lebanon; and to Jihad Darawza and her sister, Watfa, for their expert assistance and hospitality in Syria. Also I would like to thank Sarab Atassi, the Scientific Director at the French Institute for Near Eastern Studies in Damascus (IFPO), for all her support.

I am also grateful for the cooperation which I received from the Zoryan Institute in Toronto; from the Haigazian University and the American University of Beirut librarians; and from the IFPO librarians in Damascus.

In Oxford I owe a great debt to Nigel James for his cartographic assistance; Nadia Abu Zahra for her reference searches; and Mastan Ebtehaj, librarian at the Middle East Centre, St. Antony's College Oxford. Judy Mabro sub-edited and generally searched out infelicities in style. I would also like to thank my anonymous reader who offered excellent advice on improving the manuscript, particularly the Palestinian chapter. To Sarah Green at Cambridge University Press, my deep admiration for locating a suitable photograph for the front cover, something I failed to do after months of searching. To Amanda Hellenthal and an unnamed copy editor, my thanks for their patience and general sympathy with my overloaded schedule.

I would also like to express my thanks to Miranda Mylne for her patience as she helped me through the mysteries of Endnote. And finally to Nicholas Mylne, my deepest gratitude for the fortitude with which he accepted the late nights and weekends taken up with this project as well as frequent travel abroad at the expense of normal family life.

Dispossession and Forced Migration in the Middle East: Community Cohesion in Impermanent Landscapes

> The problem today is that scholarship has had thrust upon it the necessity of partisan practice, and about this I would like to be very exact. When power of any sort, be it political, professional or institutional takes a hostile stance toward certain directions of study and the results of such study, then scholars can no longer pretend to escape political consequences. Antigone might wish only to give her brother decent burial, but Creon has ruled otherwise and, like it or not, she is forced to perform her private duties within a context defined by the king. This is what I mean by "political intrusion" by now a nearly universal affliction in private as in public lives, for men and women dedicated to knowledge no less than for men and women committed to action. The curse is general, and scholars are neither immune nor exempt.
>
> (Des Pres 1988:11)

Although academics seek to be objective in their research, I can think of few fields of study more affected by partisanship than forced migration. The very nature of the phenomenon cries out for moral positioning; that a people's dispossession and ensuing suffering should be recognized and, whenever possible, made less painful. Such a stand leaves to one side any judgements regarding the causes of the dispossession, the rights and wrongs of the events leading up to the forced migration, and the national and international politics which often underwrite these events. The Middle East in particular has been the scene of continuous forced migration over the past 150 years. Inevitably, a shadow of political correctness has been cast over some of these tragic and violent events; observers have taken sides and given primacy to certain interpretations and positions. I am as much affected by such bias as the next researcher or reader. That, however, is not the concern of this study and I make a concerted effort to put my political positioning to one side. My primary interest in this work is to convey to the reader an understanding of how various peoples, forced to migrate into or within the Middle East, have survived, founded new communities, integrated, and generally exhibited remarkable coping strategies and resilience. Integration of minorities without assimilation has led to exceptional cultural diversity, which I believe is derived from a particular historical context. Unlike many other parts of the world where culturally diverse communities often face a stark choice between assimilation into dominant cultures or general exclusion, the Middle East strikes me as unique in that it seems to provide a framework whereby different peoples can successfully find a place for themselves without either being assimilated or excluded. It is an approach to 'multi-culturalism' or perhaps a form of 'local cosmopolitanism' that we in the West could do well to understand (Zubaida 1999).

Commonly, when we think of dispossession, forced migration, or exile, our minds turn to the plight of the Palestinian people. At a stretch of the imagination, we might also consider what has come to be called the 'Kurdish problem'. This study seeks to situate both the Palestinian and Kurdish involuntary migrations of the twentieth century into the wider dispossessions and forced movements of populations, which have indelibly marked the region throughout the last hundred years. Furthermore, it aims to locate the dispossession of peoples in the Middle East as part of the policy of empire, carried further by the colonial encounter and then revitalized in the Arab socialist awakening of the mid-twentieth century.

By drawing on the individual narratives of forced migrants and their descendants, an understanding of their coping strategies and mechanisms emerges. Neither solely victims nor totally political actors, the lives of the dispossessed and often involuntary migrants are drawn out to portray the communities that have been shaped and redrawn by the significant migrations of the recent past (Barber 2002; Chatty & Lewando Hundt 2005; Farah 1999; Sayigh 1988; Sayigh 1994). Finally, this study sets out to contextualize the dispossession, statelessness, and forced migration in the Middle East. Whereas some communities, which have been forced to move within the region, have succeeded in physically assimilating and creating new identities as minorities (e.g., Armenian, Circassian, and Chechnyan), many others have been left stateless (e.g., Palestinian and Kurds), some of whom have had their attachments to their land erased from under their feet without even moving.

RESEARCH METHODOLOGY

I have mainly relied on secondary sources to write the historical background to the dispossessions and forced migrations in the Middle East. The narratives and oral histories, which I quote extensively in the study, are derived from interviews I collected between 2005 and 2007 in Lebanon, Syria, Jordan, and Egypt. I set out to interview the oldest surviving members of the social groups who had been forced into the Arab Middle East over the last 100 years. Using research assistants from the communities themselves, I was able to identify a representative sample and negotiate permission to interview a total of thirty-six key informants from among the Circassian, Kurdish, Palestinian, and Armenian communities. I developed a topic guide which sought to stimulate interviewees' memories of their childhood and youth, their memory of forced migration or those of their parents, their recollections of places where they sought refuge, the institutions and networks in their new places as well as their perceptions and aspirations regarding home and homeland. All interviews were taped and digitally recorded in order to accommodate requests for copies of the interviews by family members. The tapes represented a tangible 'memory' which the extended family could listen to repeatedly in the future. At many of these meetings the interviews became occasions for significant family gatherings with grandparents or great-grandparents opening up and talking about a past that had never before been shared. For some of the oldest subjects who were very frail or terminally ill, there was the added pressure of knowing that this was possibly the last opportunity to gather such memoirs. There would be no repeat visits to clarify points or elaborate on others. The interviews were poignant but not sad, often wise and tinged with cynicism, but in essence warm and reassuring of the human spirit for recovery. To protect the privacy of these individuals, some names have been changed and, unless otherwise indicated, interview dates and places appear in the bibliography.

SCOPE OF THE TERM MIDDLE EAST IN THIS STUDY

For the purpose of this study the Middle East includes the Arabian Peninsula or the Arab East (Egypt, Palestine/Israel, Jordan, Syria, Lebanon, and Iraq) and Turkey. The justification for limiting the study to these states is that they encompass what was once the Ottoman Empire and still share a dominant religious and cultural tradition formed and shaped by Islam. It is also similar to geographical boundaries used by

Roger Owen (1981b) and proposed by Joel Beinin (1998). Some stimulating parallels could be drawn from North African material on the involuntary movements of communities as well as the dramatic refugee flows in southwestern Asia. These, however, deserve to be independent studies based very much on French language sources in France and North Africa, and Persian and Pashto sources in Iran and Afghanistan.

ORGANIZATION OF THE BOOK CHAPTERS

The study naturally falls into two parts: the first theoretical and historical and the second grounded in contemporary case studies, which link to the past through the oral testimony and narratives I collected. The first two chapters set the stage by laying out the debates, issues, and concepts surrounding the term *migration,* both voluntary and involuntary, as well as aspects of what I call *local cosmopolitanism.* It moves on to set the historical background and context for the waves of dispossessions which characterized the Middle East as the greatest producer of unassimilated forced migrants in the twentieth century. It presents the migration of discrete, ethnic communities in the late Ottoman period as the direct outcome of Great Power struggles between Imperial Russia, the Austro-Hungarian Empire, and the rapidly declining Ottoman Empire. The movement of populations in the face of defeat, shrinking borders, and purposive situating of some of these communities by the state for internal security (Abkhazian, Circassian, Chechnyan, Dagestani, and Albanian) are examined, with a particular eye to the way in which the communities maintained their social and cultural cohesion and separateness as part of a larger 'virtual' whole. The efforts at integration without assimilation and of the creation of new age *millet*s (semi-autonomous cultural communities organized and administered on the basis of common religious faith) in the last days of the Ottoman Empire are an important focus of this section.

The second, and major, part of the book examines contemporary communities who faced dispossession and involuntary migration as the result of lines drawn on maps at the end of the nineteenth and early twentieth centuries, or who were already isolated and set apart as 'others' as a result of earlier identification with the Ottoman period *millet* status (*dhimmi*). Chapter Three looks at the Circassian, Chechnyan, and other Muslim communities expelled from the Caucasus and the Balkans. The earliest groups to be forced out of their homelands on the borderlands of the Ottoman and czarist Russian empires were mainly Muslim forced migrant groups (and also some Jewish communities), who were moved or fled to Syria and Jordan. Some were attracted to land packages provided by Ottoman decree to establish border settlements to fight off Bedouin incursions; others gathered on the Jaulan Heights and further south in the area that became known as Greater Amman. These European Muslims maintained their cultural uniqueness – their languages, customs, and traditions – while achieving significant economic successes nationally in the following decades.

Chapter Four examines the formerly protected Christian minorities: the Armenians along with the Copts, Greek Orthodox, and Christian Nestorians. These special communities (often previously the *dhimmi* communities of the Ottoman period) were recognized by the interwar years mandate authorities and experienced a chequered existence in the Middle East over the twentieth century. These non-Muslim minorities were coerced to leave and, in some cases, expelled as a whole by governments seeking to create homogenous nation-states or searching for scapegoats to blame for their modern ills. In Egypt, the wealthy, mainly Greek Orthodox and Christian Copts, were targeted for land and property confiscation. In Iraq, it was the Nestorian Christian community. The continuing oppression of some of these minority groups at the close of the twentieth century – particularly in Iraq, Syria, and Turkey – has resulted in the steady flow of people out of the region seeking refuge, asylum, and new lives in diaspora communities in the West. This chapter, however, is concerned with those that remained in the Middle East. Oral testimony and narratives of members of the Armenian communities in Lebanon, Syria, Jordan, and Egypt, particularly regarding their sense of loss, their feelings of social and community cohesion, and also their complex feelings of nationalism form the underpinning of this chapter.

Chapter Five turns to the Palestinian dispossessions. It looks at the forced migration of Palestinians throughout the Middle East and not just in the UNRWA field sites. It draws back to nineteenth-century colonialism and the neocolonial projects in the southern Ottoman *sanjaks* (administrative districts) to get a sense of the social and cultural dimensions of Palestine before the 1948 *Nakbah* or 'catastrophe' which saw the end of the existence of the political state of British-mandated Palestine. The chapter focuses on the life stories of Palestinians, some refugees, some exiles, some living in refugee camps and others in middle-class neighbourhoods in the major cities of the Middle East. It integrates the stories of the landless Palestinian labourers, the nationalist elite reformers, and the members of the Palestinian middle class in an effort to understand the resilience and cultural survival coping strategies of a people still wishing to return to villages and towns of origin often less than 100 miles away.

Chapter Six examines the Kurdish forced migrations, the dispossessions, later political recognition, and finally abandonment. If one can measure suffering on a scale, then perhaps one can say that the Kurds suffered most by the fall of the Ottoman Empire. With their mountainous homeland once an integral part of the Empire, the Kurds were dramatically undermined by the setting out of four state boundaries – Turkey, Iran, Syria, and Iraq – through the middle of their homeland. Although promised a state of their own – and actually seeing a Kurdistan exist for a period of one year in the late 1940s – the Kurds have struggled for self-determination and, in some cases, the mere rights of citizenship for decades. Some Kurds are well integrated in the states that have been created underneath their feet. Others, however, have been ignored, persecuted, stripped of citizenship, and declared stateless. Kurds in the Middle East continue to maintain their cultural, social, and linguistic heritage. But for some of them, the recognition of their human rights and the cessation of state-sponsored persecution are goals for which they continue to strive.

Chapter Seven then concludes with a reexamination and summary of the thesis 'Community Cohesion in Impermanent Landscapes'. The history of dispossession and forced settlement in the Middle East has been mediated by a shared Ottoman history and League of Nations Mandate experience, both of which, ironically, have given strength to small minority communities. Survival in shifting landscapes has resulted in numerous communities existing as islands in a sea of 'others'. Identity formation, social cohesion, and sense of community separated from territoriality give many of the dispossessed communities in the Middle East the means to survive and transcend the limitations of political boundaries and geographical isolation. It is an adaptation to history and geography that has given rise to a special kind of cosmopolitanism. The Kurds, Palestinians, Armenians, Circassians, and the numerous social, linguistic, and religious communities bound together by a shared Ottoman and Mandate history have been forced to move innumerable times over the last century. Most have re-created themselves across borders, transcending the limitations placed on them by political boundaries and geographical isolation, to become coherent social communities bound together by radio, television, telephone, email, aeroplane, and the other trappings of global and local culture. They are becoming the transnational communities of the twenty-first century, setting an example for other similar communities in the region and elsewhere.

I

Dispossession and Displacement within the Contemporary Middle East: An Overview of Theories and Concepts

We came in carts – big carts – we didn't stop. Eating and drinking were all done in the carts – all the way from Abkhazia to Sham [Syria]. What can I say? Death would have been much better. When a person dies, he is rested. But those grandfathers of ours suffered a lot, as no other people ever did. They came from Abkhazia in carts, as I told you, all the way through Turkey to the Jaulan. In the Jolan, you know, it was like implanting a piece of wood in a member of your body. If a piece of wood were inserted in your arm, would your arm accept it? It has been continuous tragic mishaps and suffering. Then, just when we started to belong, to become rested, and as if to make things worse, the Jews took over and we were driven out. We left the Jolan empty-handed with nothing but the clothes on our backs.

Abdul-Salam (2005)

INTRODUCTION

Abdul-Salam was 93 years old when he recalled the story of his parents' and grandparents' dispossession, eviction, and forced march out of the Northern Caucasus at the end of the nineteenth century during one of the many Russian–Ottoman wars. The Russian Imperial Empire, determined to expand south and west, had conquered the Ottoman Empire's borderlands in Abkhazia, sending hundreds of thousands of Muslim peasant and Jewish artisanal and trader families south and west into Anatolia and the Syrian provinces of the Ottoman Empire. Surrounded by his many sons and daughters, as well as grandchildren, Abdul-Salam told, for the first time, the stories he had heard from his parents about their involuntary march out of their 'homeland' and then his own story of dispossession and migration as a result of the Six-Day War in June 1967.

Now living in a suburb of Damascus where many other Abkhazi families had resettled, he was the 'paterfamilias' of a kin group of sixty or more people. My interview session with Abdul-Salam had been anticipated by the family for some time; most of his children, grandchildren, and nieces and nephews wanted to know more about their family history and this was an occasion, they felt, not to be missed. He had been recently diagnosed with cancer and, although still appearing very hearty and fit, no one expected him to live for much longer.

Most human beings reside somewhere near their place of birth. Willingly leaving home to live and work elsewhere or being dispossessed and forced out seems, for many, to be more the exception than the rule of human existence. Yet migration is the story of human life. It is the story of population movement across the face of the earth. Migration has seen the planet conquered and societies and cultures shaped and reshaped by successive waves of human movement. Forced migration is one part of the migration history of humanity. Forced migration is generally big, sudden, violent, dangerous, painful, and compelling. It is documented in religious texts, in folk tales, and in oral narratives of peoples around the world. It is detailed in ancient myths such as Gilgamesh, in the Old Testament story of the Hebrew Exodus, in Homer's *Iliad* and *Odyssey*, in Virgil's tale of the Trojan refugees, in the *Aeneid*. It is the tale of the Han people in China who colonized non-Han regions to the south and west to create a vast empire. It is the story of the Central Asian Turkic people who migrated to Anatolia and founded the Ottoman Empire and then the Turkish state. It describes the Viking colonization of Normandy and then the Norman invasion of Britain in 1066. It is also part of the legacy of the end of imperial and colonial empires and the coming of age of the nation-states of the nineteenth and early twentieth centuries. The late twentieth and the early twenty-first centuries have continued to see waves of forced migrants; four million people in five waves fleeing from Kuwait in the 1990s (Van Hear 1993); another two and a half million people, if not more, escaping Iraq since 2006.

Forced migration in the contemporary Middle East is most often associated with the Palestinian people's dispossession from their lands and homes in the 1947–8 war that brought the modern Israeli state into existence. Perhaps next on the list of forced migrants in the Middle East one might consider the Kurdish people, whose homeland has been divided across four modern states: Turkey, Iran, Iraq, and Syria. Given the significance and enormity of these two cases, this book aims to situate both the Palestinian and Kurdish dispossessions and forced migrations of the twentieth century into the wider range of involuntary movements of peoples, which has indelibly marked the region throughout the last 150 years.

The Fertile Crescent of the Middle East, that highly contested stretch of land, has been the focus of centuries, if not millennia, of movements of people. Invading hordes from the East, mounted fighting forces from the Arabian heartland, and colonial armies from the West have resulted in the terrified flight of communities and the opportunistic entrance of others as land was appropriated and new states created. Then, for much of the last five hundred years, the largely involuntary movement of peoples in the Middle East declined as a system of government emerged, which encouraged pluralism and tolerated diversity among peoples under its rule; the drawing out of differences between neighbours, and the encouragement of unique identities based on cultural, linguistic, or religious grounds prevailed. However, the empire upon which such identities were based – the Ottoman Empire – came to an end with World War I.

Amid the rubble left behind in the grab for land and new nation-making out of the Russian, Austro-Hungarian, and Ottoman empires were the discrete communities of people sharing common beliefs about their identities based on ideas of ethnicity (Barth 1969; Eriksen 1993; Gellner 1983; Richmond 1994) and, as often, religious variation. In the Middle East heartland of the Ottoman Empire, belonging was based not on a physical birthplace alone, but specifically included the social community of origin (Humphrey 1993; Kedourie 1984). It was rooted in the connections and links between and among a specific group of people as much as, if not more than, in a territory.

The twentieth century saw an array of involuntary movements of communities once rooted in the shifting borders disturbed by the ending of empires. This included communities on the Russian–Ottoman borderlands such as the Armenian, the Circassian, and other Northern Caucasus peoples (Barkey & Von Hagen 1997; Brubaker 1995). Much of this region has remained deeply contested, even at the beginning of the twenty-first century, as we have seen between Georgia and Russia over the disputed territory of South Ossetia in 2008. Other dispossessions had their origins in the lines drawn on maps by the Great Western Powers to create new nation-states (Bocco et al. 1993; Chatty 1986; Gelvin 1998; Helms 1981; Morris 1987; Wilkinson 1983). These included the Palestinians, the Kurds, the pastoral Bedouin, and a variety of 'stateless peoples'. Other cases of forced migration, such as those of the Yazidis, the Assyrians, and some Armenian groups, were closely linked to the regional repercussions of pan-Arab, socialist, and Islamic political movements (Al-Rasheed 1994; Khalidi 1997; Lerner et al. 1958).

Given such competing forces, many communities of single identities were deprived of their land base and forced to move, seeking security elsewhere in the region (and abroad). In the Arab Middle East, I contend, they set about restoring their social cohesiveness and cultural identity but without the tie to territory which largely had been the cause of their earlier undoing.

THEORETICAL BACKGROUND

This study sets out to understand not just the broad historical context within which the dispossession of communities in the Middle East has taken place, but also the anthropological context, that is, the individual and social group life experiences of home and imagined homeland, of single and mixed identities, of spaces and places. By focusing, whenever possible, on individual narratives of forced migration, resettlement, integration, and compromise, this work seeks to humanize and lay bare the significance of such experiences while also celebrating the unique adaptive quality of human social life and its resilience. In addition, the study addresses the on-going pressures on marginal societies – minority groups, ethnic and religious communities – to change, adapt, and conform to the practices and identifying features of mainstream communities or to migrate out of the region altogether. Such an understanding may go some distance in helping to comprehend the relationship between politics and identity formation, forced migration, globalization, and localization in the Middle East. The study does not seek to explore the international and legal implications of such movement but rather to give this phenomenon a significance that has resonance in the imagination and life experience of the reader.

Although contemporary Middle Eastern society has been the focus of detailed scholarship, the substantive topic of forced migration has not seen much research. In part, this may be related to the seriously limited research capacity in the region, with the general lack of baseline studies and databases, the limited funding and sponsorship opportunities, as well as the generally inadequate training in academic institutions in the region. In spite of a wealth of particular case studies, the Middle East has been under-represented in comparative studies of displacement, refugees, and forced migration; one exception is Shami's excellent analysis of causal factors of forced migration in the region (Shami 1994:4). There were two important survey works in the 1980s and 1990s: Hansen and Oliver-Smith (1982) did not include any discussion of the Middle East; although

Zolberg et al. (1989) did include a short discussion of the more than four million Palestinian refugees – nearly 20 per cent of the world's total – in their work. But even more recent works tend to marginalize or pay token recognition to the region (Gibney 2004; Hopkins & Donnelly 1993) as a major site of dispossession, forced migration, and creation of refugees and asylum seekers. Even the production of more than two million Iraqi refugees in recent years has tended to be treated as a fleeting phenomenon that will be reversed shortly. Hence the area remains largely silenced and much neglected in scholarship, and therefore has contributed little to development of theory in this field.

Migration theory

Most of what has been written about the Middle East in migration studies relates to labour migration and contributes descriptively to the growing body of work on international migration (Castles & Miller 2003; Cohen 1997; Richmond 1994; Weiner 1995). As Castles and Miller write, migration is a process which affects every dimension of social existence, making research on migration intrinsically interdisciplinary (2003:21). Almost all theories of migration focus on the voluntary migration of individuals. In most cases, economic factors are assumed to be predominant in determining the flow of populations and in interpreting the experience after the migration (Richmond 1994). Few writers express an interest in involuntary or politically motivated migrations, it being taken for granted that, while there might be some regularity in the movement of economic migrants, the flow of refugees as a result of political crisis or disaster is assumed to be spontaneous and unpredictable. Opposing this position is the work of Agamben and other theorists and philosophers who regard the forced migrant personified in the refugee, asylum seeker, or illegal migrant as a harbinger of a universal condition (Agamben 1994). Agamben's investigations into the nature of the state and the 'state of exception', which can strip individuals of their rights and turn them into mere *homo sacer* (individual with no rights of citizenship), show how widespread this is in our era as modern totalitarianism comes to characterize greater segments of our political world. It is such action which connects the concentration camps of the twentieth century to the detention centres of the twenty-first century, including Guantanamo Bay and the numerous immigration detention units on US and European soil. Here, states of exception proliferate and certain categories of people are imprisoned in entire zones of exception where the application of law is itself suspended. Although

Agamben's work is not directly focused on theories of migration, it sets out a powerful argument for recognizing the figure of the refugee or forced migrant as a trope for contemporary interstate politics.

The phenomenon of migration is underpinned by two major theoretical approaches; the first is largely grounded in a neo-classical economic perspective and the second in a historical-structural approach (Castles & Miller 2003). The first general set of theories, also known as the 'push-pull' theories, regards people as following certain predictable actions. For example, people generally move from sparsely to densely populated regions, and from low- to high-income areas. Pull factors are those that attract people to certain areas, such as access to jobs, land, and opportunity, while push factors are generally those negative aspects that drive people away, such as low living standards or lack of economic opportunities. The alternative approach to understanding migration, developed in the 1970s, had its historical roots in Marxist political economy and world systems theory. This approach recognizes the unequal distribution of power in the world economy and sees migration as a way of mobilizing cheap labour for capital. Unlike the 'push-pull' theories, which tend to look at individual voluntary migration, the historical-structural approach looks at mass recruitment of labour by capital. In this approach, the availability of labour can be seen as a legacy of colonialism, armed conflict, and other regional inequalities, and thus integrates involuntary as well as voluntary migration into its frame of reference. However, both of these explanatory sets of theories – the neo-classical perspective and the historical-structural approach – have, in recent years, come to be perceived as inadequate to the great complexity of contemporary migration. The first neglects historical causes of movement and the second sees the interests of capital as predominant, giving little attention to the actions and motivations of individual migrants (Castles & Miller 2003:25–26). Castles and Miller instead propose that 'migration systems theory' undertakes to deal with both these weaknesses and focuses instead on the experiences between two or more countries that exchange migrants with each other. It operates at two levels: the macrostate system and the microinformal social networks of the migrants themselves. As an explanatory tool for understanding migration it has both the historical dimension of earlier theory as well as that based on capitalism and global inequalities of later theory.

An offshoot of migration systems theory is the rise and gradual theoretical sophistication of transnational theory or transnationalism. Partially an outgrowth of the rapid improvement of technologies of transport and communications, migrants are increasingly able to maintain close links with their homeland and places of origin. In many parts of the world, but particularly noticeable between Europe and North Africa, migrants regularly visit their places of origin by scrimping on monthly wages earned in Europe (Crivello 2003). Transnational communities are made up of people who migrate regularly between a number of places where they have social, economic, and political links. With globalization and increased international migration, such communities are likely to grow in size and impact locally and regionally. Remittances from migrants back to the home community are recognized as making a significant contribution to the nonmigratory group. Transnational communities are not new. The term, however, is. It reflects our global nation-state system. In earlier times, the term *diaspora* was used to describe a people dispossessed, displaced, and dispersed generally, but not always, by force. We speak of the Jewish Diaspora, the Armenian Diaspora, and the Palestinian Diaspora, but there are also the African American descendants of slaves, Greeks in Western Asia, and the Arabs in West Africa and South East Asia. The new diasporas include contemporary flows of involuntary and often temporary migrants (Van Hear 1993, 1998). In the 1990–1 Gulf War, two million fled and then returned in one year; most transnational and diasporic communities have members who regularly move back and forth. Migration is no longer a one-way road.

One of the few scholars in recent decades to attempt a diagrammatic explanation of migratory movements is Anthony Richmond. In his book *Global Apartheid* (1994), he derides the inability or unwillingness of sociological theoreticians to explain the scale, direction, and composition of population movements that cross state boundaries; the factors that determine decisions to move or stay; and the choice of destination. As he sees it, studies of international migration have not attempted such an agenda, preferring to focus instead on such specific aspects as the demographic characteristics of immigrants, migrant decision making, economic and social adaptation in receiving countries, the policies of sending and receiving countries, or global trends in population movements (Richmond 1994).

Early efforts to tease out types of migrations and set up typologies included the work of Fairchild (1925), who distinguished invasion, conquest, and colonization (and hence dispossession) from immigration. Later scholars made distinctions between voluntary and involuntary movements. Among the voluntary movements were those of seasonal, temporary, or permanent workers and nomadic pastoralists, while involuntary movements characterized those of slaves and others fleeing war, violence, or political pressure (Price 1969). Others elaborated on this basic distinction between voluntary and forced movement, developing more descriptive categories drawing in factors such as ecology and nature, state migratory policy, and aspirations and freedoms as well as social momentum. Hansen and Oliver-Smith (1982) put forward the idea that voluntary and involuntary migration should be seen not as dichotomous but as distinct phenomena on a continuum of population movement. More recent work attempting to bring together the literature on voluntary and involuntary migration has tried to stress the similarities between, for example, 'refugees' and 'people ousted by development projects' (Cernea 1993). The effort to draw up distinctions between voluntary and involuntary, or forced versus free, migration never really gained a strong foothold as the convergence between these forms was often identified and depended upon relationships to the state (Hein 1993), particularly the modern entity of the nation-state.

As Richmond points out, most theories concerning migration address voluntary migration, the assumption being that economic factors predominate in determining the movement of people on a global scale. Many writers explicitly state that they find the movements of politically motivated migrants, or refugees, to be too spontaneous and unpredictable for empirical study; the movements and flows of economic migrants, however, are assumed to be more regular and thus amenable to analysis. Other researchers recognize that in the study of international migration the reality of a global, political, and social system must be recognized (Richmond 1988: 1–27). Most migration is of people from poorer to richer areas of the world, although the most industrial, Western societies also have high rates of exchange emigration. Even those who focus their attention on the study of refugee movements recognize that there is a relationship between economic and political factors in the decision to move or remain. As Soguk writes, 'Enormous political, social and technological changes and transformations are triggering mass movement of people in search of "better" and "safer" places. Suffering or affected by poverty, famine, natural disasters, military coups, civil wars, or slow-working societal disjunctures, or enamoured with the imagined possibilities of the "homelands" in distant places, a steady flux of people is expanding the world's "refugee population"' (Soguk 1999).

Involuntary migration

What is obvious in seeking a conceptual understanding of the difference between voluntary and involuntary migration is that it is largely built upon descriptive characteristics. With war and civil upheaval, political unrest, revolution, terrorism, expulsion of ethnic minorities, ethno-religious and communal conflict, or large-scale human rights violations in oppressive state regimes, come large 'refugee movements'.[1] Yet even in these extreme cases, economic, social, and political factors are interdependent. Zolberg et al. (1986) clearly show that the movements of refugees 'do not constitute a collection of random events' but rather form distinct patterns that are related to political transformations, such as the break-up of former colonial empires and the creation of nation-states. Even the levels of development aid and refugee policies of the wealthy developed countries of the North are largely defined by economic and political interests at home. As Dowty clearly points out, 'So-called economic migrants are often responding as much to political repression as to material deprivation' (1987:183). Among the many recent examples he cites are the refugees fleeing Haiti, where political repression and economic underdevelopment go hand in hand, and Ethiopian refugees fleeing both famine and war. In such situations, Dowty makes clear, the distinction between 'economic' and 'political' refugee becomes meaningless (1987:236). For contemporary social sciences, however, such distinction is important, as it is the basis upon which mainly Western countries agree or refuse to grant asylum. Being determined a 'Convention refugee' allows a political victim to gain asylum. Others found to be 'economic migrants' in the determination process are generally excluded from entry into the Western state and sent back. These concerns regarding asylum ultimately are of little interest for the Arab Middle East, where forced migrants and other dispossessed and displaced peoples have sought refuge. By and large, such peoples have been welcomed in the new nation-states where they have found themselves and have been allowed to settle and integrate, if not assimilate. Only the Palestinians (see Chapter Four) have faced 'eviction' in such places of refuge as Lebanon and Libya.

The question, which is perhaps of more interest here, is why some people move in situations of war and extreme political coercion and others choose to remain, or go underground or face political imprisonment, torture, or even death. Forced migration or flight is just one option out of many

---

[1] Refugee status is determined through the *de jure* definition of a refugee (Convention refugee) used by the United Nations and adopted by many countries in determining eligibility for admission into that state. It is a post-World War II invention setting out to deal with the millions of Europeans displaced by the war and seeking resettlement and assimilation in third countries. It is based on the individual claimant 'outside their own country, owing to a well-founded fear of persecution for reasons of race, religion, nationality, membership of a particular social group or political opinion' (UNHCR 1951).

(Van Hear 2000). A number of social psychologists have addressed the questions of motivation and the decision to move. They recognize that it is generally in consultation with family members or others in close-knit communities. Implicit in most microlevel studies, especially those based on theories of motivation, is the element of 'rational choice', followed by a considered evaluation of the options available. Here a distinction is generally made between push and pull factors; push factors are generally understood to be economic and political insecurity in the sending country, while pull factors are seen as perceived opportunities for economic benefit, family reunion, or political asylum. However, as neatly as this polarity suggests, push and pull factors are not necessarily independent.

The relationship between social and political constraints and individual choice is an important problem in the study of forced migration. It is a fundamental concern in philosophy, sociology, and political science. It brings together the question of free will and agency as opposed to behavioural determination by forces over which we have no control. Talcott Parsons, the most eminent of American sociologists, grappled with these issues in much of his work, starting with *The Structure of Social Action* ([1937] 1964). Parsons used the term *voluntaristic action* to mean, among other things, free will or the capacity to make choices despite constraints. Giddens grapples with similar ideas when he distinguishes between various forms of constraint and the nature of structural properties that the individual is unable to change and that limit the range of options (1984:174). Giddens' concept of structuration replaces the static view of social structures with one that emphasizes the process by which social structures are created and changed through the exercise of freedom of action. This theoretical leap is important to the understanding of theories of motivation that might account for the behaviour of migrants and refugees.

The implications of such theory are complex and beyond the scope of this book. However, as Richmond points out, there are a few key points to consider with regard to migratory decisions. Such decisions, even those made under conditions of extreme stress, do not differ from other kinds of decision-governing social behaviour. Also, the distinction between free and forced or voluntary and involuntary is misleading. All human behaviour is constrained to some extent. Choices are never unlimited because we live in groups and our behaviour reflects our need to remain part of a group. Thus our decisions are determined by the forces that hold the society together, the *structuration process* (Richmond 1994:55). In an effort to understand why people move, Richmond attempts to integrate features of constraint and enablement, of unequal distributions of power, of naked force and physical coercion, material rewards, threats of deprivation, and various forms of persuasion and inducements. He introduces two new terms to the literature, *proactive migration* and *reactive migration*, largely as replacements for the terms *voluntary* and *involuntary*.

What Richmond sets out to do is to identify the complexity of both proactive and reactive migration and to link them on a continuum between the extremes of an axis. This creates a grey area between the two but also allows for some descriptive categorization between who will migrate out of 'relatively unconstrained choice' while others, like refugees, react to circumstances almost entirely beyond their control. The choices facing proactive migrants include whether to move at all, when to move, how far to go, and whether to cross an international border. These tend to be motivated by socioeconomic considerations. On the other hand, reactive migrants – a person or group of persons expelled from their home, a stateless person, slave, or forced labourer – have little control over their environment, and their degree of choice over when and where to flee is severely restricted. The motivation to move or flee will most often be due to political considerations. Between these two extreme positions are the large proportion of people who cross state boundaries, motivated by a combination of economic, social, and political pressures and exercising some element of choice in determining where and when to move.

Certain events, such as sudden changes in economic, political, social, or environmental situations, may result in marked reactive migration. The outbreak of war or revolution, ethnic cleansing, terrorist activity, or other violent conflicts will result in a sudden and large-scale flight of people. When people feel that they and their families are at serious risk or that their food supply, housing, or livelihood are threatened, they will reactively migrate (Richmond 1994:65).

The topic of dispossession and resulting involuntary migration has not been rigorously examined, though ground-breaking studies do exist in the fields of history, for example, in the work of Michael Marrus and his tracing of the emerging European consciousness of the refugee phenomena during the pre-World War II era (Marrus 1985); and in the work of Justin McCarthy presenting a revisionist view of the rise of the Turkish state at the close of World War I (McCarthy 1983). In law, there are a number of excellent studies especially in relation to the rights of refugees in international humanitarian and refugee law (Falk & Bâli 2006; Goodwin-Gill 1996; Hathaway 1991); in sociology, important contributions have emerged especially with regard to global diasporas, mass exodus, dispersal, and regrouping of migrant communities (Cohen 1995; Van Hear 1998); and

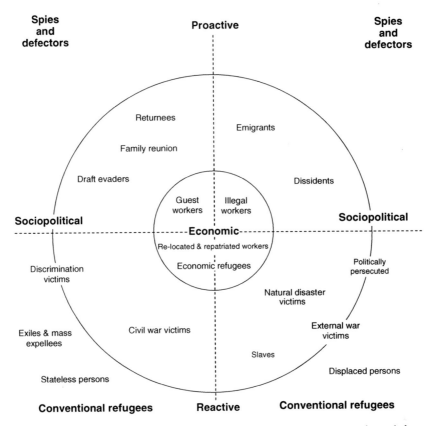

CHART 1. Paradigm of Voluntary and Involuntary Migration (adapted from Richmond 1994)

in demography, particularly with regard to political turmoil and international migration in the Middle East (Russell 1992).

Political science has made a particular contribution to understanding forced migration (Soguk 1999; Weiner 1995; Zolberg 1983; Zolberg et al. 1986). Weiner documents the sources and growth of refugee flows and what this has meant for the international world order: a growing moral crisis in receiving countries. After examining detailed case studies of the principal refugee flows generated in Asia, Africa, and Latin America from approximately 1960 to 1985, Zolberg and his colleagues find that international factors often impacted on the major types of social conflict that triggered refugee flows. In their analysis, refugees were also produced by conflicts that were not only manifestly international, but which often related to international social conflicts among the antagonists. The authors concluded that any frameworks for the analysis of the causes of refugee movements must therefore reflect the transnational character of the process involved. Weiner, for example, considers that most of the world's population movements, certainly since World War II, did not just happen, but were made to happen in order to serve a variety of political purposes in the sending countries. He regards much involuntary migration as being derived from the interest of a state to achieve some cultural homogeneity or, at least, of asserting state dominance and control over particular social groups. He cites historical examples of European state action to eject religious communities that did not subscribe to the established religion, and ethnic minorities that did not belong to the dominant ethnic community. For example, the Spanish crown expelled Muslims and Jews in the fifteenth century; the French expelled the Protestant Huguenots in the sixteenth century; the British Crown induced Protestant dissenters to settle in the colonies in the seventeenth and eighteenth centuries; and in the nineteenth and twentieth centuries, Greek, Bulgarian, Turkish, and Romanian minorities in eastern and southeastern Europe were driven out (Weiner 1995; Zolberg 1983; Zolberg et al. 1986).

Throughout most of the twentieth century, governments have been active in their goal of cultural homogeneity within their nation-state. At mid-twentieth century, international support for ideals of assimilation in order to bolster the newly independent state was at its peak, as exemplified by the wide adoption by member states of the United Nations of the International Labour Organization's (ILO) Convention 107, which supported assimilation of traditional and tribal peoples. However, by the 1980s world opinion and informal international law had changed and national assimilationist policies came to be considered as undermining the cultural and social rights of traditional and indigenous peoples protected in a number of international legal instruments. In 1989 the ILO replaced its Convention 107 with the nonassimilationist Convention 169 regarding the treatment of traditional and indigenous peoples. Still, nation-states have continued to expel minorities or make conditions so harsh for them that these ethnic groups have left of their own accord: the Chinese in Vietnam, Indians and Pakistanis in East Africa, Vietnamese in Cambodia, Tamils in Sri Lanka, Kurds in Turkey and, of course, the Serbs, Croatians, and Bosnians at the disintegration of the Yugoslavian state. In some cases, states have expelled or pushed out whole social classes, such as the middle-class Cubans at the start of Castro's socialist regime, or the Haitian boat people encouraged to leave for foreign policy reasons – both in Haiti and in the United States at various times. From this perspective, Weiner sees forced migration as very much a foreign policy tool used to force recognition, to destabilize a neighbour, or to extend cultural interests through decolonization or external colonization (1995:33). It is thus a part of the rise of nations and nationalism and, as a corollary, significant in the identity politics surrounding concepts of ethnicity, ethnic communities, and ethnic minorities. Taking this argument further, Soguk argues that, historically, refugee presences have had surprising impacts on state sovereignty that have been both disruptive and 'recuperative', becoming both a problem and a resource to the practices of representation that constitute the realities of the sovereign territorial state (Soguk 1999). He argues that although the refugee does not properly belong to the state, the site of the refugee, conceived in a variety of activities, becomes a site of modern statecraft. The figure of the refugee has become instrumental in the formulation of a specific imagination of the world [of the modern territorial states] and international regime practice. Thus he argues that the history of the practices of statecraft is closely bound up with the history of specific refugee 'problematizations' (Soguk 1999).

Nationalism, boundaries, minorities, and majorities

The concepts of nationalism and ethnicity are closely intertwined and take up a significant place in understanding how majority and minority groups are created and how, often as a result, minority groups end up being dispossessed and expelled. Anthropology has long studied ethnic groups and ethnicity. It was part of the central focus of the discipline: the study of small bounded groups being the 'Other' as opposed to 'Us'. For many years the terminology used to define the 'other' was the 'tribe'; in recent years the term *tribe* has gradually been replaced by *ethnic group* as anthropology began to run out of simple bounded groups to study at the far reaches of the earth and turned to study more complex unbounded cultures amongst ourselves. By studying others, we learn about ourselves: 'The boundary mechanisms that keep ethnic groups more or less discrete have the same formal characteristics in a London suburb as the New Guinea highlands, and the development of ethnic identity can be studied with largely the same conceptual tools in New Zealand as in Central Europe' (Eriksen 1993:98).

The study of nationalism, however, has for many years been the preserve of political scientists and historians. Only in the 1980s and 1990s has the study of nationalism become a topic within anthropology. In earlier periods, anthropologists used the term *nation* as a way to designate a large category of people or societies of more of less uniform culture. I. M. Lewis, for example, regarded nations, tribes, and ethnic groups as being of the same kind, only differing in size (Lewis 1985:358). In the past decade, however, anthropologists have made more effort to distinguish nations from ethnic categories because of their relationship to the modern state. I will pursue this discussion further because it becomes particularly relevant in the later chapters to understand how particular ethnic communities of forced migrants, such as the Armenians, were able in recent times to negotiate particular positions vis-à-vis the nation-state in places like Lebanon, Egypt, and Syria.

Ernest Gellner is perhaps best known for his work on nationalism. In his landmark book he defines *nationalism* as 'primarily a political principle, which holds that the political and the national unit should be congruent ... In brief, nationalism is a theory of political legitimacy, which requires that ethnic boundaries should not cut across political ones' (Gellner 1983:1). In other words, as Eriksen points out, this definition of nationalism set out by Gellner and adopted by many social scientists refers to a peculiar link between ethnicity and the state. From this perspective, nationalisms are the same as ethnic ideologies that hold that their group should dominate a state. The 'nation-state', then, is the state dominated by one ethnic group and whose 'ethnic markers' (such as language or religion) are frequently embedded in the official symbolism and legislation of the state.

Another important theoretical contribution to the understanding of nationalism comes from the work of Benedict Anderson, who proposed the following definition of *nation:* 'It is an imagined political community – and imagined as both inherently limited and sovereign' (Anderson 1991:6). This imagining is not the same as the primordialist invention of 'ethnicity' for the sake of specific political hegemony. For Anderson, this imagined community of people who define themselves as members of a nation 'will never know most of their fellow-members, meet them, or even hear of them, yet in the minds of each lives the image of their communion' (1991:6). Anderson is interested in understanding the extraordinary force of national ideology or nationalism such that some people are willing to die for it. Gellner, on the other hand, is more interested in understanding the political aspects of nationalism. Both approaches stress that nations are ideological constructions seeking to forge links between a self-defined social or cultural group and the state. These links are based neither on ideas of dynastic rule nor kin-based associations. For Anderson, the very strength and persistence of nationalism into the twentieth and twenty-first centuries is curious. The age of nationalism, he writes, should be over. It should not have survived in the individualist post-Enlightenment world, and yet he sees it as the most universally legitimate value in the political life of our time (1991:3). Why it acquired such force in the past two centuries, and continues to do so in contemporary life, is a question that is beyond the scope of this book.

Identity formation, ethnicity, and nationalism

Contemporary research on ethnic identity formation and boundary maintenance does help to understand the anomaly Eriksen pointed to earlier, regarding the link between ethnicity and the state. As the work of Barth (1969) and others reveals, ethnic identities tend to become most important in situations of flux, when there are sudden or profound changes underfoot, when resources or boundaries are being threatened. It should not be surprising, therefore, that societies undergoing rapid change or modernization would be characterized by political movements based on ethnic or cultural identity. What is striking is that the theories of nationalism as propounded by Gellner and Anderson are congruent with anthropological theories of ethnicity.

In addition, the 'new' nationalism and the 'new' ethnicities emerge from contemporary diaspora studies (e.g., Cohen 1997; Van Hear 1998) that are described and articulated in the work of Voutira (2006). Beyond critiquing the traditional anthropological concepts of kinship and membership with a place or territory, as scholars have increasingly done since the 1990s, Voutira explores the way in which displacement no longer merely refers to people moving across borders (the conventional view of diaspora) but of borders moving across people. Here, she refers to a kind of border redrawing or displacement that results in the radical dispossession of those who are found not to 'belong' within the newly determined territorial boundaries emerging from the collapse of the Soviet Union (e.g., Russians in the new states of the former Soviet Union). Her case study is a longitudinal one of the Soviet Greeks. What she reveals is that the post-Soviet diaspora – the Greeks of the former Soviet Union – are new because they are doubly displaced and ethnicized. They claim an ethnic European historical homeland. As this is largely recognized and accepted by Greek society, they can enter Greece with special rights and privileges granted to members of the nation-state. However, for some, this membership requires negotiating a 'Greekness' they do not necessarily feel, and thus they either choose to remain in diaspora or they retreat into ethnic enclaves where they are able to reconstruct lives according to the Russophone identities that they also carry. For the older generation, family stories of their dispossession and memories of the homeland are important elements in creating and maintaining their ethnic identities. For the younger generations, family socialization is no longer the primary mover in whether they remain in diaspora, or go. Rather, it is a matter of having the funds to travel back and forth to recognize the historical homeland and to feel part of it, but from a distance. The process of dispossession, migration, and resettlement and further displacement, over time, results in some elements of incorporation or hybridization, so that the group on the move is no longer exactly like that of those left behind or resettled in other near or distant places. Through different mechanisms than those described by Hannerz (1987) but with similar outcomes, groups dispossessed and either cut off from their cultural moorings or affected by adjacent cultural practices and ideas become new hybridized entities. Thus, whether the transformation is the result of centre–periphery interaction in a global system, as elucidated by Hannerz in Nigeria, or the result of physical distance and time spent away from the mythical homeland, the result is the same: a culture affected and somehow changed by new experiences and by the void and loss of contact with the mother country.

Displacement, space, and place

Anthropological debate regarding the relationship of land with culture has occupied the discipline for several decades. There is the common assumption of a fixed relationship between a nation-state and its culture and society, which also touches upon the understanding of the nature of change, particularly cultural change. The common representation of the world is as a collection of countries with diverse national societies, each rooted in its proper place (Malkki 1992). Thus we have the notion that each country has its own distinctive culture and society: for example, when tourists visit India it is to understand Indian culture, or they visit Australia to get a glimpse of Australian culture. Here, the geographic spaces are taken to be the same as the cultural places they contain. Such mapping of cultures onto places fails to account for the existence of cultural differences within a single locality or space as well as internal differences within cultures. Lebanon is one example of the way in which multiple cultures may share the same place, however uncomfortably. 'Multiculturalism' is thus, as Gupta and Ferguson comment, 'both a feeble acknowledgement of the fact that cultures have lost their moorings in definite places and an attempt to subsume this plurality of cultures within the framework of a national identity' (Gupta & Ferguson 1992:7). The idea of 'subcultures', also common in this context, is an attempt to explain the existence of distinct cultures while also acknowledging the existence of a dominant culture sharing the same geographical space. Both notions of 'multiculture' and 'subculture' attempt to link identity with place rather than simply geographic space.

Ideas and concepts regarding displacement assume a natural correspondence between people, geographic space, and place, which anthropologists such as Malkki (1990; 1992) have questioned for some time. As Malkki shows, there is an abundance of 'botanical metaphors', largely derived from nineteenth-century nation-state ideologies, through which both anthropological and nationalist discourses have rooted people in the 'soil' of the nation or 'ethnic territory'. Yet despite this theoretical preoccupation with 'roots', historical research has consistently shown that migration is not the exception in human history, but rather more of a constant.[2] Even more popular postmodern metaphors like 'grafting', 'transplanting', and 'hybridization' continue this 'mother-earth' imagery. Contesting this popular conceptualization, Malkki makes clear that 'people are chronically mobile and routinely displaced and invent homes and homelands in the absence of territorial national bases …. through memories of, and claims on, places that they can or will no longer corporeally inhabit' (Malkki 1992:24).

In a region like the Middle East, where dispossession and forced migration and diasporic flows have indelibly marked the landscape, the mass movements of people into the region over the past one hundred years, if not millennia, make the attempt to regard the area as a set of homelands or cultural regions – bewildering, to say the least. The Assyrian Arabs, once largely found in pre- and postcolonial Iraq, have reappeared in Chicago, just as the pre-Revolutionary Iranians of Tehran have arisen phoenix-like in Los Angeles. The 'here' and the 'there' have become blurred in such transnational or diasporic situations and the cultural certainty of the 'centre' becomes as unclear and as uneasy as that of the periphery. Thus the experience of displacement is not restricted to those who have moved to the periphery but also affects those in the core (Bhabha 1990:66). This undermining of the connections between peoples and places, which are imagined to be natural, has not led to cultural homogenization (Clifford 1988). Instead, what has tended to happen with this blurring of places and localities is that ideas of cultural and ethnic distinctions are becoming more prevalent. What we see is the imagined community striving to become attached to imagined places

---

[2] As Voutira remarks, despite the long trail of empirical studies which show the extent to which humans have migrated, the 'collective awareness of this fact' appears unique each time it is asserted (1994:25).

(Anderson 1983). Dispossessed people everywhere remember their imagined homelands in a world that increasingly denies such firm identification of 'place' with 'geographic space'. Remembered places have often served as symbolic anchors for forced migrants and other dispersed people. Thus 'homeland' is one of the most powerful unifying symbols for the dispossessed, even though the way in which that place is constructed in the social imagination may be quite different among the far-flung members of the imagined community. Geographic space, as anthropology has long argued, is made meaningful by people. The experience of space is always socially constructed. Spatial meanings are thus established by those with the power to make places out of spaces.

The contestation of these places then often lies on the periphery with those who have been dispossessed or have become minorities in a dominant cultural sphere. It is clear that nationalism plays an important role in the politics of 'place-making' out of territorial spaces. Thus, the creation of 'natural links' between places and people is largely dominated by the strongest cultural group that controls the state. However, contestation or opposition to these 'natural links' is common among the dispossessed and those in diaspora, as evidenced in the emergence of ethnic 'counter-nations' such as the Circassians, Palestinians, and Armenians. Palestinians, for example, express a deeply felt relationship to the 'villages of origin' and the 'land', in general. This geographic space and imagined 'place' is the fundamental inspiration for the Palestinian struggle for self-determination.

For many of the dispossessed, the imagined 'homeland' acquires a mythical status and image. It is assumed to be unchanged by the departure and relocation of its dispossessed. Yet the way in which the representation of the imagined community is drawn and fixed rests largely with the people themselves. The past is smoothed out, preexisting differences and ambiguities are often covered up or cleaned up, and members of the dispossessed group often assign a primordial being to the society and homeland. This imagery is now being challenged by anthropologists and geographers, among others, and is becoming the 'current orthodoxy' in the social sciences.[3] Yet, as David Turton and others point out, those who write on

---

[3] Anthropology has had a special interest in this area as the practice of fieldwork, so central to the discipline, has long revolved around the idea that cultures are spatially located, which fits perfectly with the conception of the nation-state model that nations are 'naturally-rooted' in the native soil of their people (Olwig & Hastrup 1997:4). It is perhaps because anthropology realizes it must abandon this idea of the natural, demarcated link between culture and nation, that there has been so much effort in the last decade or so to find ways of

the subject of forced migration and displacement pay little attention to 'social and cultural constructions of the ... places occupied by refugees and other forced migrants, preferring instead to concentrate on the physical and productive properties of these places' (Turton 2004). It is an irony, then, that anthropological theorizing about 'place' and 'place-making' (emplacement) has not made more of a mark on those who study displacement. It is as if the recognition of places as imagined and contested, de-couples or 'de-naturalizes' the link between people and territorial space. This somehow is regarded as entering a minefield by those who seek to help or protect people such as refugees. Such conceptualizations, especially those which question and contest the 'natural' link between people, culture, and space, may be feared to play into the hands of governments and others who may wish to diminish or ignore the suffering of those who have been forced out of their homes. As we move ever more into a deterritorialized world, we are coming to recognize that questions of space and place are very much more central to the concerns of both the dispossessed in their new resting places and those who remain.

Ethnic and national ideologies

Ethnicity can be generally defined as a sense of belonging to a group, based on shared ideas of group history, language, experience, and culture. Arguably, everyone belongs to an ethnic group, although the popular meaning in current language is seen as an attribute of a minority group. Commonly in this sense, nationality and ethnicity are frequently interchangeable, while some anthropologists see nationalism as a variant of ethnicity (Eriksen 1993:99). There are several theoretical positions regarding the rise of ethnicity. Clifford Geertz, for example, regards ethnicity as being a 'primordial attachment', something presocial, something one is born into. It is developed from 'being born into a particular religious community, speaking a particular language, or even a dialect of a language and following particular social practices' (Geertz 1963:109).

Fredrick Barth, on the other hand, sees ethnicity as socially constructed or created and emerging from the recognition of difference from

'constructing' the field in 'unbounded' territory or multi-local and transnational milieus. As Malkki writes 'There has emerged a new awareness of the global social fact that now, more than perhaps ever before, people are chronically mobile and routinely displaced, and invent homes and homelands in the absence of territorial, national bases – not in situ, but through memories of, and claims on, places that they can, or will, no longer corporeally inhabit' (1992:24).

neighbouring groups (1969). This is sometimes called a situational ethnicity as it derives from a specific group's recognition that it needs to mark out a differentiated self-identity to create social and physical boundaries. The differentiating markers are generally cultural characteristics such as language, shared history, religion, and customs. Occasionally, the differentiation is made on the basis of some perceived physical attribute, skin colour, nose shape, mouth size, and hair qualities. Ethnicity can thus be determined on the basis of some perceived cultural difference or phenotypical distinction.[4] Other anthropologists and sociologists see ethnicity as derived from instrumental need. These ideas have their roots in the work of Max Weber, who identified organizational efforts by status groups to establish rules which exclude others (Weber 1968).

Whichever explanatory model of ethnicity appeals to the reader, what is important for us here is that ethnicity is often linked to political processes of boundary drawing between dominant groups and minorities. Becoming an ethnic minority – rather than simply an ethnic community – is a mechanism of marginalization, which can have profound effects on how a community creates and maintains its social stability and cohesion. Being regarded as an ethnic community in a multicultural society is generally seen as a positive attribute. At the other extreme, however, is the ethnic minority in a dominant majority state, whose presence is regarded as undesirable and divisive. The concept of ethnic minority always implies some degree of marginalization or exclusion leading to situations of actual or potential conflict (Castles & Miller 2003:32).

Like ethnic identities, national identities are constituted in relation to others; the very idea of the nation presupposes that there are other nations, or at least other people, who are not members of the nation. It is the fact of the 'Other' that feeds the growth of a 'single' unified 'Us'. This differentiation is the basis for wars between nation-states. Though not as common in the second half of the twentieth century as in the first half, such conflicts have nonetheless been responsible for much of the refugee flows across borders. The problems of identity and of boundary maintenance have usually been studied in relation to minorities or otherwise 'threatened' groups in situations of rapid social change. Most of the world's territory has been divided into sovereign states. The borders

---

[4] Phenotypes in human groups (skin and hair colour, facial features, etc.) are popularly understood as 'race'. However, as most social scientists agree, there are greater genetic variations among one population group than the differences between groups; there are no grounds upon which to determine any classifications into 'races'. Race is therefore nothing more than a social construction.

between these states, as shown on internationally recognized maps, do not reveal the often distinct disjunction between effective state control and the territorial aspirations of state leaders and others (Rabo & Utas 2005:91). Border disputes remain major sources of conflict between states and between nonstate actors and governments.

Nationalism and ethnicity are similar concepts and the majority of nationalisms are ethnic in character (Eriksen 1993:118). More simply put, a nationalist ideology is an ethnic ideology which demands a state on behalf of the ethnic group. Some states, such as Mauritius, have poly-ethnic or supra-ethnic nationalism, which does not detract from the underlying principle of commonality between nationalism and ethnicity, but leads us to a brief discussion of minorities and majorities. The notion of 'majority' and 'minority' is derived from political institutions and concepts which evolved in medieval Europe around the notion of representation and council. The majority in a council or representative assembly represented the general interest or consensus. Thus, the decision of a majority was binding not only on itself but also on the minority. This notion of representative governance with fluid majority and minority constituents operated on the presumption of consensus (much like the Muslim notion of *ijma'* introduced in the Muslim world from the *Hadith* or Traditions of Mohammed) (Kedourie 1984:278). These assumptions were, however, overturned by the rise of Western notions of nationalism, which defined 'the nation' as being a natural entity with a historical, religious, and linguistic character shared by every member of the nation. There followed the transformation of the fluid majority and minority in governance into national majority and national minority, thus undermining government by consensus.

In the Middle East in the nineteenth and early twentieth centuries, the introduction of majorities and minorities played havoc with the balance long established in an area that was religiously and ethnically heterogeneous. For centuries, authority had been derived not by any particular form of representation but rather from war, invasion, conquest, and religious supremacy/warrant. The Ottoman rulers' base of authority was derived from Islam. However, the Ottomans recognized the vastly heterogeneous religious and ethnic character of their empire by setting up and managing the *millet* system. This form of governing allowed those who did not belong to the dominant religion of Islam to run their communal affairs under the authority of their own ecclesiastic or religious heads. Thus the Jews and Christians of the Middle East – who at times represented as much as 25 per cent of the total population – were formed into numerous *millets*, which were largely self-governed and dealt with all the important moments of an individual's life, from birth through marriage to death (Shaw 1978:334). These *millets* were based not on geographical facts but on belief systems and thus their membership could be far-flung depending upon where co-religionists and those sharing the same denomination were located. It was only with the demise of the Ottoman Empire that those who had been considered members of *millets*, with well-defined and recognized subordinate status in the Muslim body politic, were suddenly transformed into minorities dispersed in small pockets throughout the region.

As it happened, it was within these non-Muslim *millets* that the Western idea of nationalism first spread. The Rum *millet* (the common reference to the Greek orthodox millet) came to see itself as the Greek nation followed by the Serbians, Armenians, and Kurds (Kedourie 1984:280). The description of the rapid transformation of these *millets* into nationalist minorities at the end of the nineteenth century and the beginning of the twentieth century, along with the ensuing dispossession and forced migration, will follow in Chapter Two.

An ethnic minority can be defined as a group that is numerically inferior to the rest of the population in a society. These are generally nondominant ethnic, religious, and linguistic communities; they can include indigenous and tribal peoples, migrant communities, and refugees (Minority Rights Group 2008). By the same definitional features, we can say that an ethnic majority is a group which is numerically superior to the rest of the population in a society; it is politically dominant and is reproduced as an ethnic category.

In Western nation-states largely premised on the idea of cultural and political unity, and also in many new postcolonial nation-states, the existence and growing presence of migrant ethnic minority communities that are not assimilating and adopting the main common language, history, and cultural traditions of the majority community are often viewed as threatening to the ideas of the state. Such peoples, who do not assimilate, take on the common language of the state, and internalize the historical myth of the state, become citizens but not nationals in that they remain outside the framework of the national culture. The maintenance of such ethnic diversity is regarded as a threat to many in these nation-states in Europe and elsewhere, except where the myth of national origin is based on ideas of absorbing immigrants (Canada, the United States, and Australia). Countries which hold a common culture to be at the heart of the nation have found it very difficult to deal with ethnic minority presence and respond by adopting quite restrictive rules of naturalization and citizenship (Castles 2000:279). National debates regarding the importance of integration and assimilation of the minority ethnic migrant groups have occupied most liberal democratic states in the West for the past decade if not longer. In many cases, a distinction is not drawn between assimilation and integration (Gibney 2004:174–175).

Multicultural spaces and hybridized places

Some regions – in the Middle East in particular, but elsewhere too – entertain conflicting notions of the existence of any singular sense of majority culture. With multiple ideas prevailing regarding the notions of cultural identity, as well as competing power struggles between which notion is predominant, the assimilation or integration of a cultural or ethnic group becomes a recognition of the power relationship between one community and those more powerful or running the state. If assimilation is taken to mean the process by which one cultural group is absorbed by another, it can also be taken to the extreme to mean the complete disappearance of a minority culture into the mainstream ethnic group. It can be regarded as the failure of the weak to be recognized by the powerful (complete cultural loss or cultural genocide would be the extreme).[5] Integration, on the other hand, can be interpreted to mean the process whereby a group becomes part of the prevalent or majority society. This can take many forms, such as economic, political, religious, or social integration. The integration can be passive or active – the latter seeking to influence change and modify the course of changes to maximize benefits and minimize disadvantages, the former requiring only adaptation and acceptance of change and its consequential impacts.

In many of the states of the region, Syria being just one case in point, the sense of national unity was created through the struggle for independence (Brandell & Rabo 2003). Beginning in 1920 with the awarding of the League of Nations mandate to the French administration, the territory was divided into a number of states. Through common cause and hostility, the

---

[5] This is perhaps the case for the Cretan Muslims who were moved to Damascus under special dispensation of Abdul Hamid II. Housing in Muhajiriin (migrants, largely groups of forced migrants) was designed, built, and funded from the Caliph's purse. For several generations, these migrants remained in this quarter maintaining their 'Cretan' Ottoman identity and Greek language. For several generations they continued to send their young to Athens for study – as did other Cretan village communities along the coast of Syria near the Lebanese border. By the time of the French Mandate in the 1920s, the quarter had sunk into poverty and many of the original Cretans had moved elsewhere. The French administration was initially interested in promoting the separateness of this small cultural group, but they had largely assimilated or migrated out (Tsokalidou 2006).

population of the territory rebelled and continues to fight the French policy of 'Divide and Rule'. However, it was not until 1936 that the French reunited the territory administratively into a single state. The exceptions were the areas that had been attached to Mount Lebanon to create the new state of Greater Lebanon and the *Sanjak* of Alexandretta. With independence in 1946, the Arab Republic of Syria had to build a functioning state and integrate territorially. None of its borders followed any geophysical boundaries but rather were created by the Great Powers. The postindependent state-led efforts to create a specific Syrian nation, however, have been ambiguous. This is partially the reaction of Syrian political actors to the historical factors that emerged from the protracted dismemberment of the Ottoman Empire. The idea of the Arab nation, as opposed to a Syrian nation, remained strong and the Arab Cause as opposed to specific Syrian Cause, was what largely has provided Syrian regimes with legitimacy (Hinnebusch 2001:141).[6] A glance at the Syrian constitution shows a continuing ambiguity with regard to the Syrian Arab Republic's place in the Arab homeland and Arab nation. With such ambiguity, the essential requirement for a single-majority cultural hegemony within the nation-state is not quite as pronounced as in many Western liberal democracies or new postcolonial nation-states. In Syria the idea of the nation or state, the glue which keeps the modern territory and the people within it together, is perceived to be as the defender of the Arab Cause. Thus, the numerous minorities, many of them forced migrants from the demise of the Ottoman Empire, form discrete unassimilated ethnic communities that are not perceived as a threat to the state, because by and large they buy into the state sponsorship and prioritization of the Arab nation and its cause.

Placing the Other ('Us' and 'Them')

Anthropological studies on refugees have begun to appear regularly; on the Sudan (Harrell-Bond 1986), in Kenya (Horst 2005), in Tanzania (Malkki 1995), and in Greece (Hirschon 1998). Each study has added to our understanding of such basic concepts as ethnicity and nationalism, belonging, territoriality, agency, space, and place. Each of these authors, working often at a micro level within the framework of common anthropological conceptual tools such as kinship and social networks, has made significant

---

[6] Article 1:2–3 states: 'The Syrian Arab republic is a part of the Arab homeland. The people in the Syrian Arab region are part of the Arab nation and work and struggle to achieve the Arab nation's comprehensive unity' (Official translation).

contributions to our understanding of dispossession and forced migration as well as their impact on the displaced community and host. The application of a general anthropological perspective to the dispossessed communities of the Middle East has not yet been attempted. Nor has a study emerged which reexamines the assumptions concerning identity formation, social cohesion, integration, and assimilation in the context of dispossession, forced migration and, often, statelessness.

In much of the Middle East, integration without assimilation can be regarded as the working model for state support and continuity. Economic and political integration of previous forced migrant communities is common throughout the region, with social integration arguably not as well delineated. The latter, however, is not perceived as threatening to the state, nor is the lack of any effort to assimilate. Recent settler ethnic communities in the Arab landscape – people recently dispossessed and resettled – continue to maintain a cultural coherence through their adherence to an imagined homeland and an emphasis on maintaining their language as well as their religion or religious denomination/school. These practices do set such groups apart, but in the contextual background of numerous such groups sharing the same space and thus creating a mosaic of 'Others', the 'Us' becomes defined by the very diversity of its surroundings. For some researchers, this supports an 'everyday cosmopolitanism' in a sociological sense rather than a normative, philosophical one where individuals and groups are aware of, tolerate and, in some cases, celebrate the mix of 'others' in their daily relations and social networks (Bayat 2008; Hannerz 1990; Zubaida 1999).

As the doctrine of ethnic exclusiveness and ethnic nationalism (other than 'Arabness') does not largely define the Arab world, the image of a singular closed and primordial group, as defining the state, does not emerge with such clarity. In fact, the reverse may be truer. Out of the remains of the former Ottoman Empire and as a result of neocolonial rule of various lengths in the region, multiple ethnicities are largely accepted as partners in the contemporary states of the region. As Rosel (1997:156) writes, there is nothing preordained about ethnic conflict. Majority and minority groups can and do live side by side without the spectre of primordial rights necessarily being raised. There will always be specific thresholds to be crossed before ethnic conflict emerges as inevitable, and political profiteers – ideologues and warlords – who exploit opportunities for gain at the expense of political failure. In this view, Rosel argues that ethnic conflicts are not tragic confrontations between primordial groups but the result of bad politics. Lebanon presents a case in point: a complex nation borne out of the French neocolonial exercise of power between two world wars. Lebanon was set out as an elected sectarian state with an imagined equal sharing of power among rival groups. In reality, one traditionally dominant but minority ethnic group (the Maronites) held the image of the nation in its hands. A sophisticated game of politics saw the state weave from one crisis to another, often avoiding all-out warfare only through the timely intervention of Western powers. Occasionally, however, outside intervention is not enough to prevent one sectarian group from trying to defend its hegemony under new political circumstances and civil war does break out. But the political basis of the state built upon numerous nations or ethnic minorities juggling their demands amongst each other, does not necessarily lead to inevitable conflict. Ethnic diversity can also be acknowledged and accommodated, resulting in long periods of power sharing in terms of how the nation-state is governed.[7] This national model based on ethnic diversity need not be restricted to democratic government. Nondemocratic regimes in the Middle East have shown great capacity to adapt to ethnic diversity and to control ethnic conflicts despite firmly entrenched ethnic loyalties. The Syrian Arab Republic is a case in point.

Community and social cohesion

The terms *community, identity,* and *social cohesion* are used throughout this work and need to be defined – as possible – so as to maintain a coherent set of meanings for the purposes of this study. In this volume, I follow Cohen's definition of community as a symbolic rather than structural construct: 'Community exists in the minds of its members and should not be confused with geographic or sociographic assertions of "fact"' (Cohen 1985:98). The distinctiveness of communities and the boundaries they recognize are in the minds of the members and in the meanings people attach to them. This reality is most often expressed symbolically and through culture. A community often expresses its unity through a shared

---

[7] The Lebanese state is built upon the recognition of its ethno-religious minorities. Its parliament is divided into a number of seats which must be filled by representatives of its ethnic minorities. This sectarian form of government is a legacy of the French Mandate period, when Greater Lebanon was created by carving out areas of Syria. From 1932 until 1972, 54 parliament seats were allocated for Christians and 45 for Muslims. After the 1975–90 civil war, 64 seats were allocated for each (34 Maronite, 14 Greek Orthodox, 8 Greek Catholic, 4 Armenian Orthodox, 1 Armenian Catholic, 1 Protestant, and 1 other Christian; as well as 27 Sunni, 27 Shi'a, 8 Druze, and 2 Alawite). Choucair (2006:5) writes that 'distribution of power is still based on the 1932 census, which no longer reflects the religious makeup of the population.'

past, through shared beliefs of past events which unite them, and through other common experiences. These in turn are frequently expressed through rituals or traditions that are often under threat in contemporary circumstances.

Just as community exists in the mind, so too does identity. In both cases, there is a process of understanding and constant transformation based on new experiences and shared ideas. Defining identity means confronting basic questions such as 'Who am I'? and 'Where am I going'? For the individual in a group of dispossessed people sharing ideas of an imagined nation, homeland, and community often in the context of competing claims to place and nationhood, the answers to such questions are complex and often multiple. Many refugee youth who have lived in limbo present themselves as going through what Erik Erikson (1968) defined as 'identity crisis' as they actively question who they are, their imagined homeland, and what successes they might have in exploring alternative identities. Thus, Palestinian refugee youth living in camps in Syria and Jordan often suggest that they hold multiple identities; they are Palestinian but the imagined homeland or village of origin means little to the reality of their lives; they are also, de facto, Jordanian or Syrian even if they do not hold formal citizenship papers. Identification with a community is reinforced with intergenerational contact and assembly; the more intense the contact, the greater the sense of rootedness and identity. Sometimes this is created by physical space being heavily colonized by a single community. A community, whose roots have been cut by dispossession and forced migration, creates new roots in imagined places in order to maintain and sustain social coherence. The narratives of the past and the creation of new symbolic traditions tied to the homeland take root and are infused with timelessness. Such efforts imbue the community with a symbolism particularly effective in maintaining cohesion during 'periods of intensive social change when communities have to drop their heaviest cultural anchors in order to resist the currents of transformation' (Cohen 1985:103).[8]

---

[8] Communities dispossessed and reconnected in diaspora often select particular elements of their 'cultural baggage' to focus upon as a core identifying trait. A particular practice such as herding or mobility in a formerly pastoral society can then become a 'fundamental referent of identity' (Cohen 1985:103). During intense periods of social change, of which forced migration is perhaps paramount, such core referents of identity become compelling bases for stabilizing social identity. 'It is then the very impression of these references to the past – timeless masquerading as history – which makes them so apt a device for symbolism or for expressing symbolically the continuity of past and present and re-asserting the cultural integrity of the community in the face of its apparent subversion by the forces of change' (Cohen 1985:103).

Such symbolic rootedness commonly emerges from within the dispossessed community. An unintended, if ironic, consequence of contemporary states' preference to place the dispossessed in especially demarcated and often isolated camps, as opposed to self-settlement as a way to contain the disrupting and perhaps politically dangerous influences of refugees in bordering states, is that these very localities tend to reinforce the sense of community and cohesion among the dispossessed. As Malkki has so clearly shown in her work among the Hutu refugees in Tanzania, those refugees who settled in a rigorously organized, isolated refugee camp 'saw themselves as a nation in exile, and defined exile as a moral trajectory of trials and tribulations that would ultimately empower them to reclaim their homeland' (1992:35). They saw their refugee status as valued and protected and a sign of the ultimate temporariness of exile. Their identity as refugees and association with their imagined homeland was firmly in place. The true nation was also the moral community these refugees inhabited. Those Hutu who self-settled in the nearby town did not construct such a categorically distinct collective identity. Instead, they spoke of multiple identities or borrowing from the social context of the town, and tended to seek ways to assimilate into their surroundings. They were more individualistic, cut off from intense reaffirming contact with other Hutu. They tended not to see themselves as refugees first, nor did they see their exile in moral terms. Rather, they saw their 'homeland' as a place they might return to one day, though many were unsure whether they would ever return to Burundi, even if political changes were ever to permit it. What they had done was to create lives located in the present circumstances of the town they live in, not in the past of their homeland in Burundi.

For many, rootlessness is somehow seen as a morally challenging status, as if the loss of bodily connection to the homeland were somehow a loss of moral bearing. This psychological turn to the analysis of rootlessness or loss of homeland has resulted in the growth of a school of enquiry in the study of forced migration that is medicalized or pathologized. Refugees or other dispossessed peoples are regarded as 'the victimized sick', and psychological and psychiatric studies and therapies to heal and resolve the sicknesses of refugees have a large presence in the field of refugee studies. International humanitarian aid funding commonly focuses on the problem within the refugee community rather than on the political condition or processes which produced these massive territorial displacements of people. Although Barbara Harrell-Bond is best known for having established the subdiscipline of refugee studies in the 1980s and for her groundbreaking work that identified the demoralizing effects of aid on the capabilities and agency of refugees, her research has also had another potent impact. Some of her work promoted the rise of this pathologizing type of study by citing evidence of breakdown of families and erosion of social behaviour, mental illness, psychological stress, and clinical levels of depression and anxiety (1986). Such focus has contributed to the prominence of psychology and psychiatry in contemporary refugee studies. Perhaps the outcomes of such study more readily play into aid agencies' and governments' agendas to do 'good' and alleviate pain and suffering. Thus we have the now long-established tradition of looking at refugees and the dispossessed as helpless victims in need of humanitarian aid (something which Harrell-Bond consistently challenged), rather than seeing them as active agents who might one day challenge the economic power systems and international politics which originally set their displacement and forced migration into place.

The twentieth century has seen a surge of forced migration, people displaced, uprooted, and forced out of spaces they had occupied for decades if not centuries. For many scholars and aid specialists, it was the peculiar

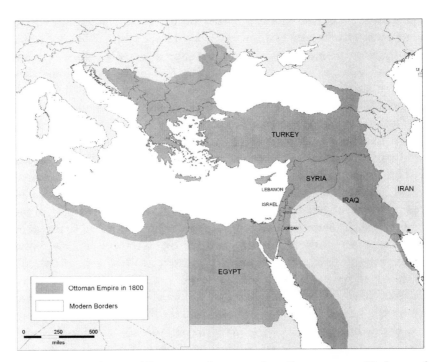

MAP 1. The Modern Middle East (modern states from Egypt across to Turkey, and Iraq superimposed on 19th-century Ottoman Empire)

psychological effects arising from prolonged refugee status which attracted study and ameliorating concern. The refugee world was somehow strange and unfamiliar and contrary to the natural/national order of things. Forced migrants, cut off from their homeland and thus deracinated, were regarded as lacking some of the qualities that made the rest of us human. For some it went as far as assuming a loss of culture also accompanied the loss of the homeland. The refugee came to be objectified, denoting a category of people without homelands, torn loose from their culture (assumed to be grounded in a territory or particular space). The forced migrant or refugee came to be generally regarded as an aberration to the way the world was meant to be organized and hence requiring therapeutic intervention, in the first instance the carefully laid out and spatially delimited refugee camp. Hannah Arendt, writing about post-World War II refugees and forced migrants in Europe, summed up these strange perceptions quite eloquently. 'Mankind, for so long a time considered under the image of a family of nations, had reached the stage where whoever was thrown out of one of these tightly organized closed communities found himself thrown out of the family of nations altogether' (1973:294).

The close link between culture and national identity with territory – which has been so characteristic of European nation-states and which has largely determined the perception of refugees and other dispossessed people in the West – does not translate as easily to the contemporary states comprising the territory once part of the Arab provinces of the Ottoman Empire. Here, perhaps because of the large percentage of the population which has experienced both voluntary and involuntary migration in their lifetimes and in those of their parents and grandparents, the acceptance of mobility as normal rather than an aberration is widespread. Furthermore, the tradition of overlapping heritages and homelands, imagined and rooted, sometimes in the same spaces, has meant greater acceptance of the portability of culture and national identities, a kind of local cosmopolitanism. Perhaps the Ottoman Empire, for all its faults and weakness, did leave one valuable heritage for all those who once inhabited its territorial spread: the integration of ethnic or national communities as important groups in the running of the Empire, the recognition that frontiers were often best protected by the creation of buffer communities of one national or ethnic group or another, and the willingness to allow such communities, though often widely dispersed, to be nonassimilated and culturally self-governed.

2

Dispossession and Forced Migration in the Late Ottoman Empire: Distinct Cultures and Separated Communities

> The fall of the Ottoman, Habsburg and Russian empires ... generated about thirty new states. ... One can reasonably place Ottomans, Habsburgs, and Romanovs into the same pigeon-hole; all were obsolescent political entities in an era of nation-building, to which they offered no alternative. All were weak (relative to their official size and resources) and therefore endangered players in the international power game. All were regarded as doomed, or at least as on the slide, for many decades before they actually fell.
>
> (Hobsbawm 1997:13)

The sentiment expressed in the Hobsbawm quote, which places the end of the Ottoman Empire in the same 'pigeon-hole' as the Habsburgs' Austro-Hungarian Empire and the Romanovs' Russian Empire, broadly outlines the generally accepted features of the terminal decline of these states. The ending of these empires at the beginning of the twentieth century was marked by the distinct disruption of state structures. Single states were divided into several, and each of these non-national, multi-ethnic entities had to be transformed into a number of notionally national but often, in fact, still multi-ethnic states. More important, the 'End of Empire' broke what had been a coherent web of internal relations within the single states, into unintelligible fragments. It automatically set people onto forced journeys of migration seeking others with whom they might take refuge and so mass movements of mainly ethno-religious communities defined the moment. Where the parallels between the Ottoman, Habsburg, and Romanov empires end is in the scale of the migration into the formerly Ottoman Middle East as well as the receptions of these forced migrants. Some found new spaces to settle and created imaginary or mythical homelands; others found kindred settlements to join, yet others remained dispersed, stateless, and doubly marginalized, and some eventually left the region altogether to become part of various diasporas or assimilated into new nation-states.

DISPOSSESSION, BANISHMENT, EXILE, AND REFUGE IN EUROPE

Dispossession, banishment, and granting of refuge to strangers in need are practices recorded throughout history. They are part and parcel of conquest, of the creating of civilizations and maintaining power. The expulsion of religious minorities, in particular, was a common feature of the European landscape going back five hundred years or more. Much of this casting aside was part of efforts to build states of common ethno-religious background. Minorities deemed threatening to the dominant group in the territory were rejected, and religious communities who did not subscribe to the established religion were driven out. Although France had been gradually exterminating heretical religious groups for several centuries before (e.g. the Cathari or Albigensians of the Languedoc in southwest France during the thirteenth and fourteenth centuries) in its bid to create a united Christian state, the first large-scale expulsion of religious minorities took place on the Iberian peninsula in the late fifteenth century. In 1492, the Catholic Spanish crown, united under Isabel and Ferdinand, succeeded in defeating the last stronghold of the Moorish King Boabil at Granada. This ended nearly seven hundred years of Moorish and Arab rule, including the Ummayid Caliphate at Cordoba established in 756 by Abdul Rahman I, the only survivor of the Abbasid massacre of his family in Damascus in 750 (Fletcher 1992; Harvey 1990). Although the Muslim inhabitants of Granada had at first been granted religious freedom in the January 1492 terms of surrender of Boabil, this was rescinded in the Alhambra Decree of 31 March in the same year (Lane-Poole & Gilman 1888). Approximately 200,000 people – Jews and Muslims – left Spain in 1492 and sought refuge mainly along the southern Mediterranean rim, settling in a wide arc of towns and cities from Tangiers and Oujda [Morocco], Cairo [Egypt], Damascus and Aleppo [Syria], and Istanbul [Turkey] to Thessalonica [Greece].[1] Another 275,000,

---

[1] Zolberg (1982) estimates that 150,000 of the 200,000 Iberians banished from Catholic Spain were Jews. Some made their way clandestinely into neighbouring France (from which Jews had been officially expelled at the turn of the fourteenth century); others moved to the 'Low' countries and still others moved to Portugal whose sovereign saw an opportunity for economic promotion. But most scattered among the Muslim states of North Africa and the Middle East, where they joined established communities of their co-religionists and where they were welcomed for the wealth and skills they brought with them.

mainly Muslim converts to Christianity [Moriscos] and Jews, were expelled and deported between 1609 and 1614 (Harvey 1992; Mackay 1992).

In 1573 the term *refugee* first appeared in European sources in the context of granting asylum and assistance to foreigners escaping persecution.[2] The date suggests that this was probably referring to the flight of Calvinists from the Low Countries [the Netherlands], a region where the Protestant Reformation had gained a strong foothold, but whose Spanish rulers, having instituted the Roman Catholic Inquisition a century earlier, were engaged in a full drive to repress any religious dissent.[3] A hundred years later, the term *refugee* was used in English with reference to the Catholic French majority powers' persecution of Calvinists (Huguenots) from France who were fleeing into England immediately before and after the revocation of the Edict of Nantes by Louis XIV in 1685 (Zolberg et al. 1989).[4]

Throughout the sixteenth and seventeenth centuries, minorities fled across Europe and across the English Channel. German Catholics and Lutherans were involved in a series of population exchanges of religious minorities as the result of political compromises at the end of the Thirty Years War. These movements of people took place within the principalities making up the Holy Roman Empire where the convention was that the religion of the ruler determined the religion of the people he ruled over. Irish Catholics, especially in the mid-seventeenth century, began to flee to Spain and France in the face of Oliver Cromwell's attempts to deport them to western Ireland or send them off as indentured plantation labourers to Barbados. This was followed by the various Protestant minorities in the

---

[2] The term is found in *Le Petit Robert* (1978:1641).

[3] Between the 1540s and 1630s approximately one-fifth of the population of the southern part of the region – contemporary Belgium – under Spanish rule relocated to the northern part, which gained its independence in 1609 – contemporary Netherlands (Zolberg 1982).

[4] France had been unusual among the European states in having a fairly peaceful accommodation between a Catholic majority and a Protestant minority, which was based on the Edict of Nantes enacted in 1598. After four decades of civil war, the edict had been enacted as a political compromise between Catholics and Protestants, predominantly Calvinist nobles. This nobility made up about one-quarter of the French aristocracy. The edict re-established Catholicism as the state religion, but the Protestants were granted some political autonomy – including their own courts of law and military forces – in their fortified cities. Gradually over the years, these 'freedoms' were suspended so that by the mid-seventeenth century, French Protestants were reduced to a mainly bourgeoisie minority of between 6–8 percent. The revocation of the Edict of Nantes in 1685 was the capstone of a twenty-year-long attempt to force the Calvinists to return to the Catholic fold. It is estimated that between 1691 and 1720 nearly one-fourth of the Protestants fled, mainly going to England and the Netherlands, Switzerland, and the British colonies of North America (Bertier de Sauvigny & Pinkney 1983).

British Isles who were pushed to leave and relocate to the relative wilder-nesses of the New World and other far-flung colonies (Marrus 1985).

These movements of religious minorities slowed down and came to an end by the early eighteenth century, when most of the states concerned had achieved a high degree of religious homogeneity and the Catholic–Protestant divide no longer held such emotional or theological significance. The relative absence of religious persecution came to be seen as a hallmark of the civilized European state. This did not mean, however, that there were no longer flows of people exiled or banished from one place or another. Eighteenth- and nineteenth-century Europe was marked by a drive to preserve particular regimes and status groups. The nature of the flow of exiles and refugees during the revolutionary conflicts of the late eighteenth century was based on individual exclusion rather than on group identity. For example, during the French Revolution, repression was direc-ted at individuals deemed undesirable or dangerous because of their polit-ical opinion. The total number of refugees produced by the French Revolution has been estimated at 129,000 out of a population of 25 million. Of these, a quarter were members of the clergy; the others were primarily members of the nobility (Palmer 1959).

By the nineteenth century, the comings and goings of political refu-gees – marking confrontations between revolutionaries and counter-revolutionaries as well as between national independence movements and imperial authority – became commonplace in Europe. Michael Marrus notes that these politically determined migrations were 'generally exiles, individu-als who had chosen their political path, rather than large masses of people torn loose from their society and driven to seek refuge' (1985:15).[5]

The mid-nineteenth and early twentieth centuries marked the beginning of a new political crisis and ensuing large-scale involuntary population movements across the continent. The European, Russian, and Ottoman empires faced pressure to transform themselves into nation-states, and Germany was embarking on a period of expansion. The result of this activity was the creation and recognition of new nation-states and sponta-neous and involuntary population exchanges. The first to emerge was Greece in 1832, which became a client state of Russia and Britain, both of whom were intent on reducing Ottoman power. Greece then steadily

---

[5] Marrus noted, furthermore, that 'the world of political exiles was that of the relatively well-to-do or, at least, of the once well-to-do' as 'national politics and the long-term investment in the business of revolution was not generally possible for the ordinary European' and furthermore that 'it took some measure of affluence to flee' in the first place (1985:20).

encroached on Ottoman territory and each of these gains precipitated the flight of part of the local Muslim population.[6] There followed the establishment of Bulgaria, Serbia, and Montenegro. Each new state sought to 'unmix' their nationalities as their minorities came to be regarded as obstacles to state building.[7] As a result of the nationalist movements of the nineteenth century and the unmixing of peoples, Greek, Bulgarian, Romanian, and Turkish minorities generally moved from what had become a new state in which they constituted a minority, to another where their nationality was dominant. Muslim refugees largely resettled in Asia Minor (Kulischer 1948). In a number of cases the populations were equally distributed between Christian and Muslim before the unmixing; in the extreme case of Bulgaria, the newly established state-supported nationality actually represented a minority of the population. Consequent to the establishment of these nation-states, millions of people fled or were expelled, many of them Muslims and Jews who moved south seeking refuge in the Ottoman heartlands where some were further dispersed along the distant frontiers of the Empire.

DISPOSSESSION AND REFUGE IN THE OTTOMAN LANDS

These same five hundred years of social and political transformation in Europe witnessed the rise and fall of Ottoman hegemony over the Muslim caliphate in the Middle East. Throughout this period of time, the dispossession and forced migration of peoples within the region did not emerge primarily as a drive to homogenize its lands, but as a response to international pressures resulting from lost expansionist bids or failed attempts to repulse competing claims to borderlands. What was remarkable about the Ottoman Empire was the way that its organizing ethos was not based on ideas of ethnic superiority of one community over another, but rather on the superiority of Islam. Its tolerance of its Jewish and Christian communities was based on religious tenets as well as economic and political realism. European mercantile interests in their co-religionists in the Middle East as well as Ottoman principles of self-governance for these ethno-religious groups resulted in the establishment of protected community millets whose religious and social affairs were organized from within the structured and

---

[6] Greece acquired Thessaly in 1881, Crete in 1908, and Macedonia in 1913. These locations were largely evenly divided between Greek Orthodox and Muslims, resulting in a massive flight of the Muslims to the remaining Ottoman territories.

[7] The term *unmixing of peoples* was attributed to Lord Curzon in his reflections on the Balkan Wars (Marrus 1985:41).

specific mechanisms of the church or synagogue.[8] It was the legacy of these millets that shaped the way in which the great forced migrations of the nineteenth and twentieth centuries were absorbed into the fabric of the societies and cultures of the Middle East.

As the three great empires of Europe and the Middle East fell, the massive and involuntary movement of people into and within the Middle East far surpassed that of those fleeing the region. The history of Ottoman tolerance for minorities is part of the explanation of this great inflow. However, the fact that Muslim refugees from the borderlands of the three great empires had no welcome either in Europe or in the new Soviet Union also determined that the first – and perhaps only – choice of movement was south and then west. This chapter will examine the historical background to much of the movement of peoples in the Middle East. After a brief examination of the rise of the Ottoman Empire in the Arab heartland and the establishment of the millet system of managing its ethno-religious minorities, it will look at European expressions of interest in their largely minority co-religionists. It will then focus on the last century of Ottoman rule and the mainly internal dispossession of peoples within the empire as its borders began to cave in. It will look for clues to explain the by-and-large successful re-rooting of these previously dispossessed and forced migrant communities from the northern frontiers of the empire who continued to maintain a separateness of identity and sense of social cohesion while promoting a commonality of political aspirations within the state.

THE RISE OF THE OTTOMAN EMPIRE

The Ottomans were the last of the Turkic tribes to move west into Anatolia from central Asia and Iran. They were the descendants of the central Asian Ghuzz tribe and followed in the footsteps of the Seljuk Turks before them, who had set up their capital in Isfahan, in their struggle against the Byzantine Empire. For some time the Seljuks had promoted the development of military emirates along the borders with Byzantium. The most successful of these was the emirate ruled by Osman, the Ottoman founder. From its power base in Anatolia, the Osmanli ruling family defeated the Byzantine Empire and governed the western region of the Middle East

---

[8] The term *millet* was used by the Ottoman administration to identify and designate Ottoman non-Muslims. It dates back to the reign of Sultan Mahmud II (1808–39). Before the nineteenth century the term meant Muslims within the empire and Christians outside it (Quataert:2000:173).

including northern Arabia, North Africa, and much of southeast Europe. The Empire expanded steadily from 1300 to 1699 and held sway over most of this vast territory until the beginning of the twentieth century (Shaw & Shaw 1977). It was perhaps one of the most successful of cosmopolitan sultanates to emerge in the Islamic world, reigning coherently over this enormous territory for an unprecedented length of time (Lindholm 2002). The Ottoman rulers were able to maintain their power and longevity over the centuries as a result of the particular circumstances of their entry into Anatolia, as well as the earlier Byzantium pacification of the tribes of their region. As was the case with the previous Turkic emirates, the Ottoman rulers depended upon warfare and military expansion more than trade to maintain their supremacy. By maintaining a war-based economy, the Ottomans found it possible to press into Europe for hundreds of years, thereby building an internal sense of unity on successful martial successes. In 1529 the Ottomans laid siege to Vienna, marking the highpoint of their expansion north and suffering their major defeat 150 years later in the Battle of Vienna in 1683. Until that point, the Ottomans had made little attempt to control or patrol their frontiers to the south and west, which were generally Muslim but also tribal-based hinterlands. Except for Anatolia [which had been largely subdued by the Byzantines] and the major trade cities of the Levant and North Africa, the empire contained many largely independent semi-autonomous, tribal confederations difficult to manage, let alone control.

The military base of the Ottoman Empire was enhanced by the development of an exceptionally effective slave army, the *Janissaries*, which they used alongside their less dependable tribal allies. These soldiers were said to ideally live in isolation and remain celibate until their retirement. They were also largely associated with Sufism [Bektashi and Melewi]. Their recruits were often Christian children taken from their parents at a very young age, converted to Islam, then rigorously trained to become members of the Ottoman court, warriors, and high-level administrators.[9] Like the Muslim sultanates that preceded them, the Ottomans used slaves to man their army. The principal organizing concept was extraordinarily paternalistic. The household of the sultan and his immediate entourage were seen as cared for by a slave army, which was set off from the rest of the people by

---

[9] During the fifteenth and sixteenth centuries, the Christian child levy or *devşirme* method of recruiting solders and administrators was an important source of manpower for the state, and many such Christian child recruits became important officials. The child levy was abandoned by the end of the seventeenth century.

background and practice. Many of these slaves were drawn from Christian Europe, where on-going Ottoman military expansion afforded a continuous supply of loyal slave soldiers and administrators (Lindholm 2002:123).

The Ottomans had a number of factors in their favour which promoted the successful evolution and longevity of their empire. They were able to build a strongly hierarchical society despite their own origins as a tribal-based society. This was in contrast to the largely egalitarian and kin-bound, but competitive, individualism of the pastoral nomadic tribal confederations on the frontiers of the empire's agricultural hinterland.[10] The Ottomans had a comparatively easily controlled peasant population – particularly on the Anatolian plateau, which the Byzantine Empire before them had successfully subdued – and a good food supply. They had also learned from the legacy of the highly centralized Byzantine state and adapted their regime accordingly (Lindholm 2002; Shaw & Shaw 1977). They had an expanding and successful war economy along with an easily available supply of slaves who could be trained to be loyal soldiers and administrators. Furthermore, apart from a raiding mentality [*ghazzu*] that enthusiastically supported the struggles against the Christian societies of the north (Lindholm 2002), the Ottoman Empire's longevity was aided by the divisions amongst its enemies. The Habsburgs, the most dangerous of their seventeenth- and eighteenth-century antagonists, were generally kept busy by the religious wars in Europe, particularly conflicts with France and dissension within what is now known as Germany (McCarthy 2001:9).

THE ESTABLISHMENT OF THE MILLET (RELIGIOUS COMMUNITY) TO GOVERN THE NON-MUSLIM (DHIMMI) PEOPLES

The Ottoman administration adapted and formalized the protected status of non-Muslim peoples within their empire through the Islamic concept of

---

[10] These nomadic pastoral tribes along the southern and western edges of the Anatolian Plateau were mainly Kurds and Bedouin. The theory of Ibn Khaldun, as articulated in the *Muqaddimah*, placed the notion of *asabiyyah* [social solidarity, group solidarity, blood tie] at the heart of the organizing principle of tribal society. Asabiyyah is the foundational principle by which the great desert tribes are able to conquer settled society, take it over, and then once they have adopted the trappings of civilization, begin to decline. In their decline they lose some of their asabiyyah and as a result are taken over by a younger, more vigorous, and cohesive tribe emerging from the desert fringe. This cyclical theory of the rise and fall of civilizations was derived specifically from his own knowledge of the waves of desert tribes which came out from the Maghreb and took over Andalucian Spain over a number of centuries [e.g. Al-Moravids, Al-Mohads, and Al-Murabitin] (Ibn Khaldûn 1958).

dhimmi (the free, non-Muslim subject living in Muslim society). The dhimma, by extension, was the covenant of protection and safety awarded the non-Muslim in return for paying certain taxes. This covenant was extended to Christian and Jews as *Ahl-il Kitab* (People of the Book [Old Testament], e.g. Christian and Jews) and later to Sikhs, Zoroastrians, and Mandeans. The origin of this practice was attributed to Mohammed as he conquered Arabia and extended the first Islamic Empire into North Africa and southwest Asia. It was said that he offered those he was about to fight three options: convert to Islam, pay tribute, or fight. The first to accept the second option – keeping their own religion but paying tribute – were the Jews of Khaybar. In the early Ottoman era, the dhimmi communities were found throughout the empire living side by side with other dhimmi as well as Muslims, sometimes making up whole villages. Governing such widely scattered and dispersed peoples was an administrative challenge.

The Ottomans established the institution of the millet (which comes from the Arabic *milla*, a religious community or denomination) as a way of managing the internal affairs of their empire. Ottoman law did not recognize notions of ethnicity or citizenship. A Muslim of any ethnic background enjoyed precisely the same rights and privileges as any other Muslim. The various sects of Islam such as Shi'a, Alawi, and Yazidi had no official status and were all considered to be part of the Muslim millet.[11] Christian and Jewish minority groups of all denominations and sects were spread across the empire, with significant minorities in most of the major cities. Even as late as the nineteenth century, the population of Istanbul, for example, was 56 per cent Muslim, 22 per cent Greek, 15 per cent Armenian, and 4 per cent Jewish (Levy 2000). While Muslims represented a large majority in the Asiatic provinces and a significant one in the empire's European areas, most regions had significant Christian and Jewish minorities.

The term *millet* originally meant both a religion and a religious community. Although it had its origins in the earlier Umayyad and Abbasid empires, the Ottomans regulated and institutionalized the millet system, setting up mechanisms for its proper operation in the nineteenth century. All Ottoman population records were maintained by religion, not ethnic or linguistic categories. Thus, for example, Muslims might be ethnically and linguistically Turks, Arabs, Kurds, Albanians, Bosnians, Circassians, and others. Jews, especially in the northern provinces, were mainly Sephardic, the

---

[11] Only the syncretic Druze of the Syrian Jebel Druze and Lebanon enjoyed a type of autonomy. Druze are regarded as heretics by both Sunni and Shi'a Muslims. Their religion is an offshoot from Shi'a Islam, with its own sacred book and law (Makdisi 2002).

descendants of those who had been given refuge after being expelled from Spain and Portugal; but there were also many *Mizrahi*, or Oriental Jews. The Christians were mainly Orthodox and comprised Greeks, Serbs, Bulgarians in the Balkans, and Arabs in Palestine and Syria (McCarthy 2001:3). The actual living patterns of peoples varied widely. In some areas, ethnic groups were fairly homogenous. Few non-Albanians, for example, lived in Albania. But there were Muslim, Catholic, and Orthodox Albanians. Most of west and central Anatolia was Turkish; the southeast was Kurdish while the Levant and Arabia were mainly Arabic. Yet these regions also had significant Muslim, Christian, and Jewish adherents. Many other areas, especially in Ottoman Europe, contained a thorough mix of ethnic groups and religion. Sometimes it was villages of one ethnic group or religion adjacent to another ethnic group or religion. In other cases, single villages and small towns had a number of ethnic and religious groups. Thus it was impossible to manage these widely dispersed peoples on the basis of territoriality.

The millet system was, in effect, an extension of Ottoman general administrative practice, and allowed for the centralization of government along strong hierarchical lines. It devolved to the millet community to self-govern its internal affairs. These were directed and managed by the community's leadership. Except for taxation and security, the Ottoman government adopted a laissez-faire attitude toward the internal affairs of these minority communities. In practical terms, the millet system meant that the minority communities were permitted to 'establish and maintain their houses of worship, often with the help of tax-exempt religious endowments. The minorities also operated their own educational institutions. The curriculum and language of these schools were determined by the community. Each community could also set up its own welfare institutions which depended on its own financial resources. To support their institutions, the communities were permitted to collect their own internal taxes' (Levy 2000:2). These communities also had considerable judicial autonomy. They had their own courts to adjudicate on a wide range of family and civil matters, such as marriage, divorce, inheritance, and financial transactions. Members of minority millets could also bring their cases before Muslim courts, which they often did, perhaps recognizing the greater executive authority needed for certain kinds of legal disputes. Life under such a system was one of relative segregation whereby language, customs, and culture were promoted in separate schools. But there was also significant acculturation and borrowing through the regular professional and commercial interactions between communities and in the service of the Ottoman elite (physicians, bankers, merchants, and craftsmen were especially well-represented among the minority professions). Intercommunity relations gave rise to multi-lingualism, especially among the professional and commercial classes (Levy 2000).

This system of governance, however, was inherently biased. There was fundamental inequality between Muslims and non-Muslims. Christians and Jews paid higher taxes than their Muslim neighbours, as emerged from the original concept of paying taxes in order not to be pushed to convert. Non-Muslims were kept back from holding higher government positions though they often made up for such injustices by developing close professional links with the ruling elite. In general, in the fifteenth and sixteenth centuries, when the Ottoman administration was at its peak and well run, inter-communal relations were good. But there was always some sentiment of rivalry, distrust and even hostility by one millet toward another. As Roderic Davison points out, Christians were looked down upon as second-class citizens both by the Muslim public and by the government. 'They suffered unequal treatment in various ways. Their dress was distinctive, and if Christian or Jew wore the *fez* (felt cap distinctive of a Muslim subject), he was required to sew on it a strip of black ribbon or cloth, not to be concealed by the tassel' so as not to conceal his religious affiliation (Davison 2003:62). These negative attitudes and attributes rarely erupted into inter-ethnic violence. In the seventeenth and eighteenth centuries, however, as the Ottoman Empire became more marginal economically to Europe, life became more difficult and inter-ethnic group relations showed signs of deterioration. Still, throughout this entire period, there were no incidents of wide-scale inter-ethnic violence.

THE EUROPEAN INTERFERENCES IN OTTOMAN AFFAIRS REGULARIZED IN THE CAPITULATIONS OF THE OTTOMAN EMPIRE

The Capitulations were first developed between a strong Ottoman Empire in the fourteenth and fifteenth centuries and its 'friendly states'. They were in origin perceived as a gesture of good will by the sultan to those states that had good relations with the empire. They were regarded, at first, as unilateral acts of generosity, friendship, or favour. They could be viewed as a sort of favoured-nation status granted by the Sublime Porte to last the lifetime of the sultan on the throne. The first of these capitulations was to the Italian trading cities and France.[12] The first capitulation agreed

---

[12] Although it is generally assumed that the first capitulation was to King Francis I, they date back to 1352 with the sultanic capitulation to Genoa (Quataert 2000:77).

between the Ottoman ruler, Sulayman the Magnificent, and Francis I of France in 1528 allowed Francis' subjects to travel in Ottoman lands and remain under the French king's own laws, outside of the legal jurisdiction of the Ottoman ruler. This capitulation, which was to benefit the Ottoman state in some way, lapsed on the death of the sultan granting it. By the middle of the eighteenth century, however, the limited character of the capitulations changed and the French capitulations were made permanent in gratitude for previous diplomatic assistance provided to the Ottoman court. In general, a capitulation meant that the subjects of a foreign monarch remained under the laws of their king or republic once the capitulatory favour had been granted. A person with capitulatory status was exempted from Ottoman taxes and customs duties. Not surprisingly, these agreements were popular and frequently requested by other monarchs after Francis I. Although originally simply gestures of good will between two ruling monarchs, they later came to be dangerously abused and threatened to undermine the sovereignty of the Ottoman state in later centuries.

For example, through further similar capitulations over the following centuries, France came to see itself as the protector of all Catholics throughout the Ottoman Empire. French demands started simply as capitulations in regard to the protection of Catholic pilgrims, of free entry into places of worship and other similar religious advantages. Eventually, after the development of Catholic missions of various religious orders (Capuchin, Carmelite, Dominican, Franciscan, and Jesuit), chaplains, ambassadors, and consuls were established in the major Ottoman cities (Istanbul, Smyrna, Aleppo, Damascus, Beirut) and eventually included the establishment of Catholic schools for foreign nationals as well as local Catholics.

By 1673, Louis XIV of France had persuaded the Ottoman Mehmet IV to confirm the earlier capitulations regarding the safety of pilgrims and the guardianship of the Church of the Holy Sepulchre. He also negotiated further conditions giving the French Catholic Church greater freedoms and latitude with regard to Catholicism in general in the Ottoman Empire. These arrangements greatly worried the local Greek and Armenian non-Uniate patriarchs. They complained to the sultan about the great privileges of the Catholic French missions, especially the Franciscans, as they were seeing portions of their congregation abandon them for the Roman Church.

Other European states followed suit, negotiating capitulations and expanding their significance. By the eighteenth century, large numbers of foreigners within the Ottoman Empire were exempted from taxes as a result of these capitulations. A century later, the capitulations gave the signatory European states the right to customs dues averaging 5 per cent. This was often less than the taxes paid by Ottoman merchants. Thus, instead of assisting domestic manufactures, the customs laws often hurt local producers. Furthermore, many Ottoman, non-Muslim subjects were also able to obtain certificates (*berats*) allowing them the tax privileges and benefits of Europeans who had capitulatory status, including exemption from the jurisdiction of the Ottoman courts. There was little the Ottomans could do about this distorted and parasitic state of affairs, for although the capitulations had begun as a good gesture to friends, they were now backed up by European diplomacy – gunboat or otherwise.[13]

OTTOMAN IDENTITIES AND SOCIAL TRANSFORMATIONS IN THE NINETEENTH CENTURY

In the Ottoman Empire of the early nineteenth century, religion provided a man with a label, in his own eyes as well as those of his neighbours and those who governed his life. He was a Muslim, Greek Orthodox, Gregorian Armenian, Jew, Catholic, or Protestant before he was a Turk, Arab, Greek, or Bulgar, and also before he saw himself as an Ottoman citizen. The empire itself was governed by Muslims on laws based on Islam. The numerous Christian and Jewish communities had their partial autonomy, with millets' ecclesiastical hierarchy supervising the community's religious, educational, and charitable affairs. In practice, this meant that Christian and Muslim lived side by side in the same state under the same sovereign, but were subject to different laws and different officials. Law was personal rather than territorial.

With the growing influence of the French among the Christian minorities, the transformative and revolutionary ideas of equality and liberty (nationalism) emerged. From America had come the proclamation that 'all men are created equal' and from France the 'Declaration of the Rights of Man and the Citizen'. The early nineteenth century saw growing acceptance of these ideas among the Christian millets in particular, through their close contact with France and the French mission schools. This was coupled with the rapid spread of separatist movements in the Balkans supported by both the Habsburg and the Russian empires, sending shock

---

[13] Although Ottoman policy makers tried over and over to suspend the capitulatory regime and its abuses, they were unable to do so in the face of opposition from Europe. Only during World War I were the Young Turks able to suspend the capitulations unilaterally, despite protests from German allies.

waves throughout the Ottoman governing elite. As a result, sweeping reforms called the *Tanzimat* were introduced between 1839 and 1876 to modernize the administration of the empire, the economy, education, public health, and all aspects of public life. A building programme to modernize the infrastructure of the major cities was set up and great strides were made in turning the empire into a modern rival to its European contemporaries (by the end of the nineteenth century Damascus, for example, had been restructured with its major roads widened and extended, a tram line connected the old city with its outlying suburbs, and telegraph and railroad connected it to a string of other cities, making it as modern as many European cities of similar size at the time, such as Glasgow (Khoury 1984:508–511; Sauvaget 1934). More important was the Ottoman government's effort to reassure its minorities that their future lay within the Ottoman Empire rather than with a small separated, national successor state.

The Ottoman leadership elite began to issue a series of decrees to reshape and redefine the nature of Ottomanism. Whereas the traditional concept of the state was essentially Muslim with unequal membership by non-Muslims, an attempt was made to add two further elements: pluralism and equality before the law. In 1830 for example, Sultan Mahmud II (1808–39) declared: 'I distinguish among my subjects, Muslims in the mosque, Christians in the church and Jews in the synagogue, but there is no difference among them in any other way. My affection and sense of justice for all of them is strong and they are indeed my children' (Karal 1982:388). The idea was to blur the traditional perception of Ottoman society as divided between a ruling people, Muslims, and non-Muslim subjects even though by the time these pronouncements were being made in the nineteenth century, the basic tenet of Ottomanism – Muslim superiority – no longer held in practice. By this point in their history, many Ottoman Christian and Jewish subjects held powerful positions in government and commerce and formed a growing and thriving middle class in some ways more privileged than their Muslim counterparts (McCarthy 2001). As these Christian groups absorbed the Western ideas of liberty and nationality, and as education and literacy increased among them [thanks to the Catholic and also largely American Protestant missions], they began to complain frequently and loudly about their lack of equality. They also found ready supporters among the Great Powers who traditionally acted as protectors of Christians in the Middle East [France and Russia].

The early nineteenth century saw the Ottoman leadership make the decision to press for changes, modernize the state, and stop its territorial disintegration. They embarked on a programme to reorganize the empire along Western lines, which inevitably brought them up against the same problems of equality that had faced the Western states. However, the question of the Christian, Muslim, and Jewish equality was not the major question facing these reforming statesmen (Davison 1954:63). Nonetheless, it was significant in that it ran like a thread through many phases of the overall conceptualization and implementation of Ottoman reform and modernization. It could be traced in the government debate and discussion concerning whether Christian students should be given equal opportunity in the reformed education system. Should they be allowed to serve in a rejuvenated army? Should they be admitted to the highest government administrative posts? Should the revision and codification of law apply equally to Christian and Muslim?

What is perhaps most significant in nineteenth-century Ottoman history is that the doctrine of equality did, in fact, become official policy. Sultan Mahmud II took a number of steps to make clear this creed of equality of all his subjects. In 1829 a clothing law attempted to do away with the sartorial order based on differences between class, religion, and occupation. In previous centuries, such clothing laws had sought to maintain the class, status, ethnic, religious, and occupational distinctions between men and women.[14] The 1829 law sought to eliminate the visual difference among males by requiring all male subjects to wear identical headgear, the fez. With this action, all state servants looked the same: the different turbans and robes of honour were gone. The only exceptions were for religious clerics, Muslim and non-Muslim alike. By appearing to dress the same, the presumption was that all men would become equal. However, it was in the later era of the Tanzimat reforms (1839–76) that the doctrine of equality between Christian and Muslim was most categorically put into place.

This era of reform was opened in 1839 with an imperial decree which included a commitment to equal justice for all Ottoman subjects, regardless of religion (*Hatt-i Sherif* or Imperial Decree). The stated purpose of the decree was to promote each individual Ottoman's loyalty to the state (*devlet*), the religious community (millet), and the country (*vatan*). Bringing the millet into the equation represented a significant step by the Ottoman leadership to promote the loyalty of Ottoman subjects to their state and country. By 1840, the Ottoman state introduced legal reforms modelled on European codes of law to implement the principle of equality

[14] Such clothing laws were common not only in the Ottoman Empire, but in western Europe and also China (Quataert 2000:65).

of all before the law. By mid-century, minority groups were represented in municipal, provincial, and state councils. This trend culminated in 1876 with the promulgation of the first written constitution in Ottoman history, establishing a limited monarchy all of whose subjects were considered 'Osmanli whatever religion or creed they hold'. The constitution, furthermore, affirmed that 'all Osmanli are equal before the law ... without distinction as to religion'.[15] The representatives at the first Ottoman Parliament of 1876–7 came from a range of religious backgrounds. Out of 125 deputies, there were 77 Muslims, 44 Christians, and 4 Jews – diversity perhaps unique in the history of multi-ethnic empires.[16]

In 1856, another decree, the *Hatt-I Humayun,* promised equal treatment for followers of all creeds in the empire. More extensive than the decree of 1839, it specifically mentioned equal educational opportunities, appointments to government posts, and the administration of justice as well as taxation and military service.[17] Throughout the period of the Tanzimat, these decrees and edicts as well as their application in law did raise the status of Christians in the empire. They were accorded better access to education, to government, and military service, but the advance was slow and piecemeal and was not always accompanied by a change in attitudes. Many would argue that equality among Christians and Muslims was never actually attained despite the good will and intention of Ottoman statesmen and lawmakers.

MILLETS, NATIONALISM, AND THE TANZIMAT RECONSIDERED

Many European writers of the time, as well as contemporary historians, have examined the Tanzimat period and the question of equality that ran through it to try to understand why it ultimately failed. Some have looked at it as part of a European effort to deal with the Eastern Questions (the Ottoman Empire). They regarded the era from the perspective of the European statesmen and diplomats who were constantly reminding and prodding a less-than-committed Ottoman government to live up to its

---

[15] These relate to articles 8 and 17 of the Ottoman constitution (see Davison 1954:64).

[16] The rapid changes in the composition of the empire are reflected in the 1908 Parliament, where there were 234 Muslims (147 Turks, 60 Arabs, and 27 Albanians), 50 Christians, and 4 Jews (see Shaw & Shaw 1977:278).

[17] These decrees and edicts were known by a number of different names in French and also in Turkish; for example, the 1839 edict was also known as *the Hatt-i Sherif* or *Tanzimat Fermani* while the 1856 *Hatt-i Humayun* is also known as the *Islahat Fermani.*

promised reforms regarding equality and citizenship. These European statesmen expected to see results carried out as they would have been in Europe. Others looked at this period as a phase in the ongoing internal decay of the Ottoman Empire, all efforts to restore health to the 'sick man of Europe' having failed. Some have gone as far as to judge the promises of equality as largely hypocritical with no real effort made to overcome the oppressive rule over 'downtrodden Christians'.[18]

Many competing and contested explanations have been offered in academia to explain the decline and fall of the Ottoman Empire. Some perspectives are coloured by nationalist mythologizing and others by the theoretical or philosophical attachment of the author (e.g. Hobsbawm and Marxist theoretical interpretation). Çağlar Keyder, reflecting on these various accounts of the decline and fall of the Empire, nevertheless questions one of the dominant versions of history, which adopts the perspective of the nation-state. This interpretation sees the collapse of the Ottoman Empire as the inevitable fulfilment of the destiny of a nation (1997). In an exercise of academic exploration, he sets out alternatives to the nation-state at the moment of collapse of empires. From this 'optimist' reading of imperial history, he considers that 'a constitution providing universal and equal citizenship combined with ethnic and territorial autonomy might just have saved the empire and avoided the excesses of nationalism and the nation-state' (1997:30). It might also have saved millions of deaths and forced marches in the un-mixing of populations which followed. Keyder

---

[18] At the time, Edward A. Freeman published *The Ottoman Power in Europe* (1877), a 300-page anti-Turkish tirade, especially regarding the promised reforms. This work marked a high point in Europe's about-face with regard to the Ottoman Empire. During the fifteenth and sixteenth centuries, at a time when Ottoman military strength and expansion into central Europe remained unchecked, it was regarded as an exotic but mysterious place. However, by the late eighteenth and early nineteenth centuries, many of the same things that had earlier been regarded as signs of Ottoman superiority and virtue came to be seen as defects and signs of degeneracy. This view is taken up by Lucette Valensi in her study, *The Birth of the Despot* (1993). She shows the clear negative transformation among Venetian ruling elite of their formerly admired trading partner, the Ottoman Empire. This transformation was reflected throughout Europe and was as much a response to the decline of Ottoman military strength as to Europe's evolving self-image after centuries of religious wars and profound social and economic changes. European thinkers came to see their own societies as based on freedom and law whereas Ottoman society came to be regarded as despotic. See, for example, Montesquieu, *The Spirit of the Laws* (1748), which had a significant impact on European and American political thought with its typology of government into three main forms – republic, monarchy, and despotism. The first two represented European and American government, while the last was represented by the Ottoman Empire. As Lockman points out, Montesquieu's depiction of Ottoman despotism had more to do with European anxieties and debates than with Ottoman realities (2004:48–49).

concludes that the combination of patrimonial crisis, with the use of non-hereditary tax-collecting administrators controlling peripheral areas and second, the ideology of national separatism, doomed the Ottoman Empire.[19]

The impact of European ideas of national separatism via the wealthy and educated Christian elite is also taken up by Roderic Davison, in his reassessment of the Ottoman materials from the Tanzimat period (1954). Davison goes further to show that such ideologies weakened the feasibility of the Tanzimat reforms ever actually taking hold. More importantly, he shows that the commonly held views regarding the inevitable decline of the Ottoman Empire were based on inadequate understanding of the aims of the Ottoman government and the results actually obtained as well as the truly formidable obstacles to reform and modernization at the time. What Davison sets out to do in his seminal piece 'Turkish Attitudes concerning Christian-Muslim equality in the Nineteenth Century' is to understand the attitude of Ottoman statesmen on the subject of Muslim–Christian equality and thereby understand why the official programme was only partially realised. Furthermore, he sets out to understand the traditions and experiences that shaped the basic attitude of Ottoman Muslims towards Christians and what attitudes were current among them at the time of the proclamations of Christian equality with Muslims.

Davison examines the records of the four Ottoman statesmen who initiated and carried out most of the reform measures during this period – Reshid, Ali, Fuad, and Midhat.[20] He considered that each of the four, in their efforts to manage the administration of the Ottoman Empire, came to

---

[19] Such patrimonial crises were generally overcome by recentralization efforts. In the nineteenth century, the Ottoman Empire embarked on a relatively successful recentralization project. Only in Egypt did it fail. There, Muhammad Ali, originally from Macedonia, had been appointed by the Ottoman authority to govern Egypt. He soon established his own independent administration and converted himself into a local 'ruler' or *khedive* independent from Istanbul.

Before the Tanzimat reforms could take root, Keyder maintains, differentiation and class formation had already gained momentum, especially in Ottoman Europe. This growing wealthier, newly educated middle class came into being in proximity with the European mainland. That most of these groups were non-Muslim meant they also attracted the protection, encouragement, and support of various European powers that were promoting the case of nationalism and ready to lend both diplomatic and military assistance. This was the story of Greek, Serbian, and Bulgarian nationalisms (Keyder 1997:33).

[20] The lives of these four Ottoman statesmen and 'viziers' spanned most of the nineteenth century, with Midhat living until 1884. They all had a fairly sound understanding of Western political and cultural ideas and practice. According to Davison, three of them were Freemasons and it may have been that Midhat was as well, though this is not certain from the sources.

believe that a degree of Westernization was necessary to strengthen the empire. They also believed that a basic reform, which demanded that all subjects of the empire be treated alike regardless of creed, was required. These four basically saw that in order to save the Ottoman Empire, a new egalitarian citizenship and concept of patriotism, *Osmanlilik* or 'Ottomanism', had to be created to break through the boundaries of the millet system. In Davison's analysis of the work of these four statesmen he suggests that, although they knew the concept of Osmanlilik represented a break with the past, they may not have fully realized what a revolution in traditional views was involved. They were not trying to undermine the dominant position of the Muslim in the Ottoman state. But by promoting an egalitarian citizenship and attempting to blur the demarcation lines between millets, they were taking great strides towards a secular concept of state and citizenship. When the 1876 Constitution specified that all people of the empire were to be called Osmanli, the understanding was that from that time on, their primary allegiance was to be to the state and only secondarily to their Muslim, Jewish, or Greek (Orthodox) millet (Davison 1954:68).

Davison goes on to argue that the largely unrealized programme of equality between Christian and Muslim in the empire lay not only with bad faith on the part of some Ottoman statesmen but also with Christian Ottoman leaders who wanted it to fail. He points to the demand in Crete for autonomy or union with Greece, but not for equality within the Ottoman Empire. The same was true for other Greeks still part of the Ottoman Empire. He describes a banquet held in 1862 on the Bosporus with five thousand Greeks all agitating for the extension of Greek rule to Macedonia and Thessaly.[21] The Serbs, in the same vein, were not seeking equality within the Ottoman Empire, but rather union with the – at that

---

[21] Most of Greece had been part of the Ottoman Empire from the fourteenth century. The Byzantine Empire – which had ruled most of the Greek-speaking world for more than a millennium – had been fatally weakened by the sacking of Constantinople by the Crusaders in 1204. A century later the Ottomans, having defeated the Bulgarians in 1371 and the Serbs in 1389, advanced south into Greece and captured Athens in 1458. In 1571 Cyprus fell and in 1670 Crete [ruled by the Venetians] also fell. The Ottomans established their capital in Constantinople in 1453 and appointed six '*sanjakbeys*' to administer the six *sanjaks* that Greece was divided into. The sultan regarded the Ecumenical Patriarch of the Greek Orthodox Church as the leader of the Greek millet. The patriarch controlled the courts and the schools as well as the church throughout the Greek communities in the empire. On their part, the patriarchs regarded the tolerant rule of the Ottomans as preferable to the rule by Roman Catholic Venetians, who threatened the Orthodox faith in a way the Ottomans did not. In fact, when the Ottomans fought the Venetians, the Greeks sided mostly with the Ottomans.

time – autonomous principality of Serbia. When, in 1872, Midhat Pasha began a scheme to convert the Ottoman Empire into a federal state like Bismarck's new Germany with its Bavarian and Prussian state, both Romania and Serbia – still part of the Ottoman Empire – declined to take up the suggestion. They were not interested even in a sort of corporate equality within the empire; they wanted national independence. Even the ecclesiastical heads of the Christian millets were opposed to equality. As they saw it, Osmanlilik would both decrease their authority and make it more difficult for them to collect religious taxes. This was especially true of the Greek Orthodox hierarchy, which had the most extensive set of privileges and the largest number of followers. When the Imperial Decree of 1839 (*Hatt-i- Sherif*) was taken out of its red satin pouch and read at a public meeting, it was reported that the Greek Orthodox patriarch, who was present among the notables, said, 'Inshallah – God grant that it not be taken out of this bag again' (Davison 1954:69).[22]

Whether the Muslim Ottomans would have accepted a fusion in which Christians were their equal remains an unanswered and unanswerable question. For many, there was the inherited religious tradition of tolerance for 'People of the Book', those who, like Christians and Jews, possessed a book of divine revelation and paid tribute to the Muslim government. There was also the remarkable degree of religious syncretism across Anatolia and the Balkans (with mysticism and Sufism, particularly the Bektashi order with its many heterodox notions), which could have provided a climate sympathetic to Christianity and Christians. But despite the tolerance and syncretism, there remained among many Muslims an intense feeling of the superiority of Islam, the true religion of which Christianity was only a partial revelation. Therefore, in their eyes Christians were not their equal. Along with this religious dogma came the slow but nevertheless shocking recognition that the Tanzimat reforms implied that somehow the traditional Ottoman way of life did not compare favourably with the way some things were done in Christian Europe. This dawning revelation among Muslims coincided with an era of pronounced Christian sectarian friction within the Ottoman Empire; squabbles were over privileges in the Holy Places, over whether the Greek hierarchy should include the Bulgars, over the shifting of individuals from one millet to another in order to gain some small political

---

[22] A similar response was recorded at another important pronouncement in 1856 by the Archbishop of Nicomedia. The Greek religious hierarchy's opposition to a democratization of its own millet structure was understandable as such reform would have meant that lay participation in the millet's administration would have had to increase.

advantage or greater foreign protection. Furthermore, the actual Christian rebellions along the European borders of the Ottoman Empire generally antagonized Muslim sentiment. During this period of reform and search for federated governance, many largely Christian regions were in general revolt. In 1867, Crete rebelled, forcing the sultan to remove the Muslim Cretans from the island and offer them safe haven on the Syrian coast as well as in the Muhajiriin quarter of Damascus (Khoury 1984:514; Tsokalidou 2006). The forced withdrawal of the Ottoman garrisons from Belgrade, uprisings in Bosnia, Herzegovina, and Bulgaria in 1875–6, and the open war against the Ottoman government in Serbia and Montenegro resulted in mounting anger amongst Ottoman Muslims against both the Christian rebels and what seemed to be the weakness of the government in dealing with such rebellion.

It was, however, the continuous interference of the European powers in Ottoman affairs that angered Muslims most. As Davison remarked 'These powers were all, of course, Christian by profession, if not in conduct. Russia, an enemy of long standing, was in a category by itself. But England and France also, despite the fact that they had assisted the Empire with their armies in the Crimean War, at other times with diplomatic pressure, were often detested because these services were overshadowed in the Turkish view by frequent and often high-handed interference' (Davison 1954:71–72). Foreign meddling was particularly irksome when it was based on the capitulations with the European powers, which had been stretched and abused over the centuries. Many Muslim Ottomans became aware of this when they saw the support given by Christian diplomats to the thousands of appellants, mainly Ottoman Christians, who were then shielded from the taxes and courts of their own state (sometimes even granted foreign passports) without ever having even seen their new 'protecting country'. Given this background of innate Muslim convictions of superiority, Christian religious leaderships' unwillingness to give up power or authority, and the unfortunate experience of most Muslim Ottomans with Christians, the official state doctrine of Muslim–Christian equality was not likely to find full acceptance. Some in the Ottoman bureaucracy accepted it at least superficially, but wholehearted acceptance was rare. There were no great uprisings against the reform edicts. There may have been some mutterings or resentment but, by and large, the response was muted. Finally, as a purely political concept of the allegiance of peoples of all creeds to a ruler who treated them equally, the Osmanlilik was unrealistic. The foundational ideology of the Empire was Osmanli (belonging to the Osman) and this had always carried strong implications of Muslim orthodoxy as well as loyalty to the Ottoman state.

In his sampling of Ottoman opinion regarding the Tanzimat reforms, Davison also looks at the New Ottoman Committee. This group, composed mainly of writers and would-be reformers, coalesced for a short time in the 1860s into something like a political party, influential far out of proportion to the size of its membership. Its members were unusual individuals – often quarrelling with each other, but united in their fervent desire to preserve the Ottoman Empire. Occasionally called the 'Young Turks', they were the spiritual fathers of the Young Turks of 1908 who went on to create the Turkish national republic. The New Ottomans believed the empire could be reformed and revived within the framework of Muslim tradition and religious law. Most of them seem to have believed – somewhat contradictorily – in Muslim superiority among a united people in a united empire. They supported the Edict of 1839, as they saw it setting the empire on the road to progress and self-preservation. But they regarded the later edicts (such as that of 1856) as harmful because they saw them as basically concessions to Christians in response to pressures exerted by European powers and by domestic rebellion. This, to the New Ottomans, was not about equality, but rather inequality. It was about special privileges and injustice to Muslims. As one of the New Ottomans, Ziya wrote in the newspapers of the day that equality could never be attained so long as Christians within the empire could have recourse not only to Ottoman government, but also to their millet representative and their foreign protectors.[23] For example, Ziya is quoted as saying 'if a guilty Christian is jailed, he is suddenly released without cause because someone influential has intervened. But if an innocent Muslim falls into the toils of justice and be imprisoned without cause, who is there to help him? Is this equality?' (Davison 1954:77).[24]

The period of reform in the nineteenth-century Ottoman Empire faced extraordinary difficulties. The great four Tanzimat statesmen's hope in a salvation by creating a new bond among its peoples of equal citizenship as a first step in modernization and westernization was begun too late and faced too many obstacles, some from unexpected sources.[25] The Muslim Ottomans were not ready to accept either absolute equality or the granting

[23] See, for example, the 'Manifesto of the Muslim Patriots' of 9 March 1876, *Le Stambou*, 2 June 1876. Also see Davison (1954:77).

[24] In *Hürriyet*, no 15 (5 October 1868) as quoted in Davison (1954).

[25] There were many other obstacles – such as land tenure and reform – to the realisation of a doctrine of equality during the Tanzimat era other than those discussed here. But the originality of Davison's article is the focus on trying to understand attitudes of the time. See also Davison (1963) and Mardin (1962).

of special privileges to Christians in the empire. Many of the Christian minorities, on the other hand, were pushing for separation. In the end, the idea of Ottoman equality so earnestly sought by the Tanzimat statesmen was discredited both by Muslims and Christians. Instead of equality of Muslims and Christians within a heterogeneous empire, there emerged – at great personal expense for millions of people both within the empire and on its borders – a different kind of equality. It was an equality of sorts amongst newly emerging national sovereign states but at great cost, with massive loss of life and much suffering.

EUROPEAN AND RUSSIAN IMPERIALISM AND THE DIMINUTION OF THE OTTOMAN STATE

European imperialism constantly undermined Ottoman reforms. No matter how much the Europeans criticized the Ottomans and called for reforms, none of these powers wanted to see the Ottomans succeed. Nor did they want to see the total collapse of the empire, at least not in the

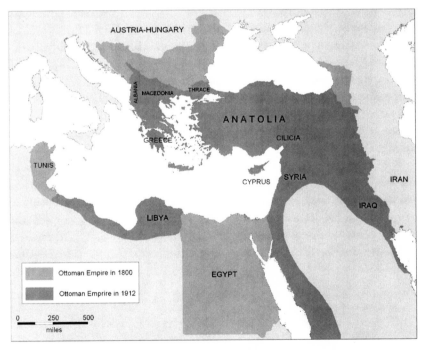

MAP 2. Ottoman Empire in the 19th Century (adapted from McCarthy 2001:10–11)

nineteenth century. Great Britain, France, Germany, and Austria sold more to the Ottomans than they bought. Ottoman purchases of textiles and other finished goods helped to keep the mills of Europe working, so a reformed Ottoman Empire with a revived manufacturing base was not in the interests of European powers.

The Russians, however, wanted Ottoman lands. Unable to expand further into Europe – or, for that matter, into Asia – they saw the Ottoman Empire as their natural route to expansion. Specifically, they wanted the Dardanelles, the Bosporus Straits, and Istanbul in order to gain access to the Mediterranean.

The European states were also influenced by their own internal agendas. Prime among these were the domestic sympathies of their constituents for the Christian minorities in the Ottoman Empire. Such public opinion led to European military intervention in the creation of an independent Greece, Serbia, and Bulgaria, all the while maintaining diplomatic support for the territorial integrity of the Ottoman Empire. But more striking, and certainly a mindset repeated in the twentieth and twenty-first centuries, the European powers and the growing media callously disregarded the reports of murder and forced migration of the millions of Muslims caused by the creation of those very states (McCarthy 2001:21).

It was the Russian imperial agenda which caused the most damage to the Ottoman Empire. The Russians repeatedly invaded the empire, capturing lands both in Europe and Asia. They forced the creation of an independent Bulgaria, Serbia, and Romania by defeating the Ottomans in wars they themselves initiated. In victory, the Russians demanded reparations for their wartime losses. These demands were often mediated by the European powers to soften the blow to the 'Sick Man of Europe'. The Russians, as detailed by Justin McCarthy, dispossessed and ejected the native populations of Circassia and Abkhazia in the Caucasus, forcing the Ottomans to take in more than 800,000 Caucasian peoples at great human and civil costs. The Russians also forced an additional 900,000 Turks into the Ottoman Empire, which then had to find food and shelter for them when the existing population was already poor (McCarthy 2001:21). Many of the economic and military disasters that constantly threatened the Ottomans in the nineteenth century were due to the Russian czars.

The whole of the nineteenth century was a period of growing nationalist unrest amongst the European Ottoman provinces. To comprehend this particular nationalism would seem to require an understanding of the factors giving rise to such violence among Ottoman communities that had previously co-existed fairly well for centuries. However, so many competing mythologies encrust these histories that it is not easy to come to single explanations. Some of the explanatory tales, however, can be discredited. One popular myth has it that the Balkan economies were dying under oppressive Ottoman mismanagement and that, in order to survive, these regions had to free themselves. Recent scholarship has shown just the opposite to be the case; Ottoman state policies and economic reforms had produced positive results. In Ottoman Bulgaria, for example, the reforms had regularized and reduced the tax burden, bringing about greater internal stability and making life more secure for the peasantry. The Bulgarian economy was actually expanding during the mid-nineteenth century just before the breakaway from Ottoman rule (Quataert 2000:70).[26] The use of economic decline to explain the rise of separatist movements in the Balkans therefore is not justified (Palairet 1997). This is not to say that economics was an unimportant factor in explaining the rise of the violent nationalism that emerged in the Balkans. However, closer examination of much more complicated sets of factors – economic, cultural, political, and other variables at particular points in time – need to be generally appreciated.

Powerful factors such as increasing economic growth and closer trading partnerships with Europe had an impact on the growth of Balkan nationalist movements. As Keyder clearly points out, the link with Europe was derived not only from political ideologies which had previously swept across the continent and were now influencing the Balkan region, but also mercantile interests in Austria, Russia, France, and Britain created a gravitational pull for Greek, Serbian, and Bulgarian nationalists (1997). It was during this period that a new group of communal leaders emerged, transforming the relationship between the state and its subjects.

In the Arab lands of the empire these were the *ayyans,* or notables, which have been studied and fully documented by Hourani (1968) and his students (Khoury 1983, as well as others). Ayyans or *eşraf* were either court-appointed notables or recognized as such by individual communities. Some ayyans were descendants from Ottoman provincial governors or other state functionaries who managed to put down roots – a marked violation of central state regulations. Others consisted of prominent notables whose families had been among the local elites before the Ottoman era. And others, particularly in the Arab provinces, were slave soldiers,

---

[26] As the account of the Bulgarian uprising shows, efforts to foment uprising of the peasantry initially failed repeatedly (Quataert 2000).

Mamluks, whose origins went back to medieval Islamic times.[27] Whether these notables originated from central government appointments, pre-Ottoman elites, or Mamluks, they built and maintained strong ties with the local religious, merchant, and landholding community. They generally held considerable wealth and power in their provincial areas. They were an authority not in rebellion against the Ottoman central state. Rather, local ayyans recognized the sultan and central authority in general, collecting and forwarding taxes as well as sending troops for imperial wars. By the end of the eighteenth century, many ayyans had become semi-independent. It is not far-fetched to imagine them making an effort to break away from Ottoman rule. But accounts of early nineteenth-century negotiations between the ayyan and the sultan suggest, on the contrary, that provincial notables and the central elite had an on-going reciprocal and mutually profitable relationship (Quataert 2000:49).

A different pattern emerged with respect to leadership among the inhabitants of the European Ottoman provinces (Karpat 1972:245). This was due in part to the transformation in the nature of trade relationships with Europe. These changes emerged out of proximity – the growing trade with adjacent European states as well as the impact of the industrial revolution in the West, its growing urbanization, and change in consumption habits. The trade transformations were largely against the interests of the Ottoman state, which saw its strong export trade of manufactured items die off in the nineteenth century. By the second half of the century, the Ottoman Empire was basically exporting agricultural commodities only. From about 1850 to 1914, imports greatly exceeded exports and much of this was tied to an Anglo–Ottoman commercial agreement (1838), which gave Great Britain undisputed competitive superiority with regard to domestic manufactures.[28] These developments particularly disrupted the internal trade within the empire whereby one region supplied the other with raw materials or manufactured goods. Instead, these regions became economically attached to France and England while maintaining their formal political ties to the Ottoman administration (Karpat 1972:247). Nowhere was this more strongly felt than in the empire's southeastern European provinces.

---

[27] Ahmet Jezzar Pasha, who ruled Sidon and Acre (1785–1805), began as a *Mamluk* in the service of Ali Bey in Egypt.

[28] The transformation of the Ottoman Empire's trade relationship with Europe is well documented in Issawi (1966b). These transformations had a profound impact on the rise of local leaders who in turn sought governments shaped in accordance with their interests, aspirations, and cultures.

By the end of the eighteenth century, in the largely Christian and European parts of the Ottoman Empire, a different leadership had emerged that was, as Karpat puts it, conspicuously absent among Muslims. These groups became 'the torch-bearers of Balkan nationalism, and eventually the backbone of the Serbian, Greek and Bulgarian nation states' (1972:248). The first group was made up of the leading merchants and manufacturers, whose origins could be traced back to the development of intense trade with Europe beginning in the early part of the century.[29] The second group was made up of the non-Muslim intellectuals whose origins could be traced back to the schools established or supported by the local church and who took to heart the ideas of the French Revolution. The third group of leaders was made up of romantic figures called *haiduk,* or *klephte.* These were popular figures, half highwaymen, half military leaders who often served in Western armies and then also fought as guerrilla leaders in their respective national revolutions.

The social stratification, from which this leadership emerged in the Balkan region, supported and fed the nationalist uprisings that commenced with the Serbian revolt in 1804, and culminated with the Bulgarian revolt of 1875. As one Bulgarian scholar put it, the profound antagonism between a de facto bourgeois land-ownership, a capitalist system of production, and a feudal type of authority at the government level was a formula for dissolution (Karpat 1972:249). The dominating political group was almost exclusively composed of the Ottoman bureaucracy, while the leaders in the towns and villages, as well as the community leaders in non-Muslim villages, were Christians. The Christians came to see the government administration as an exploitative alien group. They began to call the Ottoman bureaucracy 'Turkish', reflecting their own nationalist political outlook. In the eyes of many of the Balkan nationalist leaders, the Ottoman state was already a national Turkish state.

At the same time, the Turkish–Muslim peasant, throughout most of the rest of the Ottoman Empire, was not undergoing a similar social transformation as was occurring in the European regions of the empire. The Ottoman Muslim peasant became increasingly more isolated from the world and was relatively being pushed down the social scale by the growth of a more prosperous Christian peasantry; the latter was bolstered economically and ideologically by a middle class of its own kind and religion. The Muslim–Turkish craftsmen who had formed the backbone of the

---

[29] Greek merchant colonies in Vienna, Venice, Trieste, and Odessa were the active revolutionary vanguards of their ethnic groups under Ottoman rule. See Stoianovich (1960).

manufacturing groups in the Balkan towns were steadily pushed to less important trades and eventually to ordinary menial jobs. By the middle of the nineteenth century they had ceased to be a meaningful economic force. Politically these Turkish–Muslim peasants, recognizing their declining social position in the Balkans, turned to religion as a basis for group solidarity and thus identified themselves with the Ottoman political elite. This identification was eventually to lever support from the lower strata of society for Muslim or Turkish nationalist and political solidarity in the nation-state. In the view of some scholars, the Turkish–Muslim segment of society did not have a middle class (of merchant intellectuals or clergy) who could compete politically with the Christian one. The leaders in the Muslim countryside were the ayyans, generally men who had been appointed by the court or had inherited their social position and wealth. They were often landlords, but not traders or manufacturers.

The situation of the Turkish–Muslim and non-Muslim groups in the Balkans is described by T. G. Vlaykov in his memoirs of 1860s Bulgaria as one of peaceful, if segregated, coexistence.

Compared with the life of the Turks, our life was patently on a higher level. Take livelihoods. For the Bulgarians, these were so varied – there were indeed hardly any trades, hardly any manufacture or fields of commerce in which they did not deal. As for the Turks, their agriculture was all they knew. And our leading people, our merchants and *chorbajii* [heads of Bulgarian villages] – how much higher they stood in alertness of spirit, in national consciousness as well as in monetary wealth than the Turkish leading folk ... Yet for all this, we Bulgarians felt a subconscious fear of the Turks ... The fear of all our folk for the Turks arose from the fact that although we lived in the village unoppressed by them, we felt nevertheless that they were the masters; the governor in the *konak* [mansion] was a Turk ... then the prefect and the judge in the citadel also were Turks. Turkish was the whole power. Turkish was the kingdom. And we Bulgarians were their subjects.[30] (Warriner 1965:235–236)

DISMEMBERMENT OF THE EMPIRE (AND THE GROWING DISPOSSESSION OF MUSLIMS FROM OTTOMAN EUROPE)

The groundwork of national separatism had been laid throughout the Balkans as a result of the particularly Euro-centric socioeconomic trans-formations and restructured trade relations with the rest of the Ottoman Empire. The development of particular middle-class leaderships in the Balkans also contributed to the growing independence movements. The

---

[30] Fragments of these memoirs (Vlaykov 1934–42) were reproduced in Doreen Warriner (1965:235–236).

first three-quarters of the nineteenth century were marked by unrest, rebellion, and resistance, particularly in the European regions of the empire. However, the massive dispossessions and forced movements of peoples, mainly Muslim, did not occur until the last quarter of the century.

GREEK NATIONALISM

Greek nationalism first surfaced in the late eighteenth century, partially through the development of an educated and well-travelled class of wealthy Greeks (Pharnariotes) and through the meddling of the Europeans and, especially, the Russian Empire. Catherine the Great, the Orthodox ruler of the Russian Empire, was believed to have sent agents to stimulate a Christian rebellion against the Ottomans. However, in the Russian–Ottoman War, which broke out in 1768, the Greeks did not rebel, disillusioning their Russian patrons. The key moment in the Greek war for independence came in 1814 in Odessa, when a secret Greek nationalist organization called the 'Company of Friends' (*Filiki eteria*) was formed. Its members planned a rebellion with the support of sympathizers in Europe and Russia. On 25 March 1821, the Orthodox Bishop Germanos of Patras proclaimed a national uprising, with simultaneous uprisings planned across Greece, Crete, and Cyprus. Attacks were launched against tax collectors and all things Muslim. In southern Greece, nearly 25,000 Muslims were killed in Morea. The only ones to survive had escaped to Ottoman military fortresses or fled the area altogether.[31] The Ottoman authority retaliated with a massacre and mass deportations on the island of Chios.

Although the British and French suspected that the uprising was a Russian plot to seize Greece and possibly Constantinople from the Ottomans, the news of this massacre and other atrocities resulted in further sympathy for the Greeks in western Europe. The Europeans did not see the realities of the rebellion as being as much about hatred of tax collectors and murderous acts against Muslims as concern with nationalistic ideals. The elite intellectuals and politicians of Europe, who had recently conducted their own struggle for independence, freedom, and democracy, read the Greek struggle as a war between Christianity and Islam and came down on the side of Christianity. Inconclusive fighting between Greek separatist militias and the Ottoman military continued for

---

[31] The following year, the Greek revolution had spread to Ottoman Romania and once again the character of the rebellion was primarily religious in character, Christians against Muslims (McCarthy 2001:45).

a number of years. Finally in October 1827, the British, French, and Russians intervened, without a declaration of war, attacking and destroying the combined Egyptian and Ottoman fleet (sent by Muhammad Ali Pasha of Egypt in support of the Sublime Porte) at the Battle of Navarino. In 1828, the French landed troops in the Peloponnese to protect and help the Greeks to regroup and form a government of their own. In the same year, Russia invaded the Ottoman Europe, defeating the Ottomans in the War of 1828–9.

Thus the Ottomans were forced to recognize an independent Greek kingdom.[32] In March 1829 in London, European powers held a conference to define the independent Greek state and delimit its northern border and island holdings. But it was not until the Convention of 11 May 1832 that Greece was recognized as a sovereign state. However, due to the constant bickering and unpredictability of Greek national leadership, the European powers again imposed their will. They decided that Greece would be a monarchy and the Bavarian Prince Otto, rather than someone of Greek origin, was chosen as its first king (Hobsbawm 1962:181–5).

ROMANIAN SEMI-INDEPENDENCE

In the mid-nineteenth century, another war erupted: a harbinger of things to come. This was the Crimean War (1854–6). Its direct root cause could be traced back to the 1851 coup d'état in France. Napoleon III had his ambassador at the Ottoman court insist on the recognition of France as the 'sovereign authority' in the Holy Land. Despite two earlier treaties with Russia (1757 and 1774) granting Russian sovereign authority over the same lands, Ottoman sultan Abdul Majid I agreed with the French ambassador. Russia quickly protested this change of authority. After much prevaricating, as well as a show of force by the French navy in the Black Sea, the Ottoman sultan transferred control over the various Christian holy places – as well as the keys to the Church of the Nativity – from the Greek Orthodox Church to the Catholic Church.

Russian czar Nicholas I regarded this as an act of injustice towards the Greek Church and set about finding a remedy to these wrongs. That remedy was ultimately the Russian takeover of Moldavia and Wallachia (the Danubian principalities) coupled with a naval battle at Sinope in 1853 in which Russia destroyed the Ottoman fleet. The heavy casualties alarmed

---

[32] They were also pushed to grant Serbia and Romania (Wallachia and Moldavia) semi-autonomous status as vassals or principalities of the Ottoman Empire.

Great Britain and France, and after issuing an Anglo-French ultimatum to Russia to withdraw from the Danubian principalities, both France and Great Britain entered the war on the side of the Ottoman Empire. At the conclusion of the Crimean War in 1856, the Treaty of Paris returned the Danubian principalities briefly to the Ottomans under a shared tutelage with its allies Great Britain, France, and Austria. During the peace negotiations, Nicholas I's successor Alexander II agreed not to establish a naval arsenal on the Black Sea because of the threat it would pose to the Ottomans. Moreover, the European powers pledged to respect the independence and territorial integrity of the Ottoman Empire. The Treaty of Paris stood for nearly a decade, but one by one, each treaty commitment unravelled. In 1859 the principalities of Moldavia and Wallachia merged to become the precursor of what is now Romania.[33] Once the European powers had begun to quarrel and fight amongst themselves, the Russians quietly reestablished a naval presence on the Black Sea (Napoleon III was deposed and the French republic established in 1870 during the Franco-Prussian War of 1870–1). Moldavia and Wallachia (Romania) began to distance itself ever more assuredly from its former Ottoman masters. The European undertaking to respect Ottoman territorial integrity as one of its allies in the successful campaign against Russia began to come apart. The Ottoman Empire continued to shrink territorially as one European Ottoman province after another, with European interest and support, rebelled and withdrew from the Ottoman Empire.

Clearly Europe was concerned about its Eastern Question – how to deal with the continuing erosion and unrest of the Ottoman Empire. On the one hand, many European leaders came to perceive grave risks to general peace in the event of a total Ottoman collapse. Thus they agreed to maintain its integrity (as in the 1856 Treaty of Paris) and this resulted in the Ottoman Empire being admitted into the 'Concert of Nations'. Russia had a more complicated agenda. It did not want to see the state collapse entirely, but it did not want to have too strong a neighbour on its southern borders so as to be able to continue to pick away at its frontier.[34] The European powers

---

[33] In 1866, Prince Carl became leader of this semi-independent state. In 1881 Romania was declared a kingdom under Prince Carol I.

[34] After the Russian, French, and British defeat of the combined Egyptian and Ottoman fleet at Navarino, the Ottoman Empire was threatened internally by Muhammad Ali Pasha, who perhaps thought that he should be rewarded for having sent a fleet to Navarino to help the Ottoman Sultan. Muhammad Ali sent his son Ibrahim Pasha against the Ottoman Empire in 1832 taking over Acre, Damascus, Aleppo, and Konya in central Anatolia. He seemed poised to capture Istanbul. The Russians, perhaps fearing the rise of a powerful

felt they should help preserve and maintain a tottering, but intact, state because of the dangerous vacuum that might emerge.[35] Yet through their own internal wars and their support for the separatists' goals of numerous rebellious Ottoman subjects, they were aiding the very processes of fragmentation that they feared. In 1850, approximately 50 per cent of all Ottoman subjects lived in the Balkans, yet by 1906 the remaining European provinces made up only 20 per cent of the Ottoman population (Quataert 2000).

SERBIAN INDEPENDENCE

Serbia's separation from the Ottoman Empire was a long struggle compared to that of Greece. In the northwest corner of the Ottoman Empire, Serbs rebelled in 1804. Originally, as with uprisings in previous centuries, it was not so much a secessionist movement as an appeal to the sultan to correct what they regarded as abuses at the hands of the local Ottoman administration and the *Janissaries* (the Ottoman slave army) who were behaving more as an occupying army of plunderers than an efficient military force. Serbian Muslims, Jews, and Christians alike shared this hatred of them. Not getting a satisfactory response from the Ottoman sultan, the Serbs appealed to Russia for aid. There followed a complex struggle between Russia and the Ottoman state with Serbs in the middle. A second uprising took place in 1815. By 1817, both Russia and the Ottoman Porte had agreed to the establishment of hereditary rule by a Serbian prince. From that point on, Serbia became a semi-autonomous principality. From direct rule, it was now under a form of vassalage. Its full

new dynasty, landed troops between Muhammad Ali's army and Istanbul and thus saved the Ottoman sultan from defeat.

In 1838 Muhammad Ali, controlling much of the Arab provinces, threatened to declare his own independence and was attacked by the Ottoman army in Syria. They were defeated and then rescued, this time by a coalition of Russia, Prussia, Britain, and Austria. This defeat stripped Muhammad Ali of his earlier gains – Crete and Syria and the holy cities of Mecca and Medina – leaving him only with hereditary control over Egypt. The Western powers were unwilling to allow the emergence of a new strong and powerful Egyptian who would threaten the stability of the Ottoman Empire, and thus the international order. There is much debate over this issue. See Marsot (1984) and Gelvin (1998) for differing views.

[35] Throughout the century, when revolt would meet with success or Russia would drive deep into the Ottoman southern Balkans, a troubled international community – the Great Powers – would gather and try to undo the worst, fearful of Ottoman disintegration or Russian success. In 1829, for example, after Russian major victories against the Ottomans in eastern Anatolia and elsewhere, the international community agreed the Treaty of Adrianople whereby Russia gave up nearly all its conquests, settling for an actual – if not formal – Ottoman withdrawal from Moldavia and Wallachia (Quataert 2000:57).

independence would eventually come about at the conclusion of the later Russian–Ottoman War of 1877–8.

BOSNIAN REBELLION (1875–6) AND THE
RUSSIAN–OTTOMAN WARS OF 1877–8

Whatever the internal economic, political, and military decline within the Ottoman Empire, there is little doubt that European military power created an independent Greece and certainly a semi-independent Serbia and Romania. In both Serbia and Greece, the struggle was for more than independence; the rebels had intended to eject local Muslims from their new states. In Serbia this had been managed with limited bloodshed as a result of the conditions of treaties imposed by Russia. But in Greece, killing took place on a massive scale in an effort to cleanse the new state from its Muslim residents. In the end, both Greece and Serbia were to become relatively ethnically homogenous states in which nationalist sentiment would be strong. The same pattern was to emerge in the civil wars of 1875–6 in Bosnia and the Russian–Ottoman Wars of 1877–8. Orthodox Russia would defeat the Ottomans. The defeat would result in the creation of a new state, Bulgaria, as well as the enlargement of Greece and Serbia. Local Muslims would again be killed or forced from their lands.

In 1875, rebellion erupted in Ottoman Bosnia. It too began first as a protest against local landlords and the high rate of taxation. Most of the rebels were Bosnian Serbs, but they had sympathy from other communities as most groups, whatever their religion or ethnic background, had little love for tax collectors. The nature of this rebellion soon changed character: guns, money, and men began to arrive from Serbia and Montenegro supported by Russia, which pursued a 'pan-Slavic' ideology. Instead of attacking government officials (tax collectors), these nationalists began to attack Muslim villages. This was a significant change: instead of fighting their perceived oppressors, the government representatives, Serbian nationalists turned against those whom they perceived might possibly be agitators for another nation in their midst. The Muslim villagers, who had little if any nationalist sentiment, responded with equally vicious revenge attacks on Serbian villages. Bosnia was now caught up in its own civil war. By the end of that year, the European powers entered into the fray and demanded that the Ottomans make concessions to the Bosnian rebels. Russia, Austria, and Germany demanded that the Ottomans end tax-farming, lower taxes in general, and make other reforms. The Ottomans agreed to these conditions, thus meeting the initial demands of the rebels, but by then the movement had become a nationalist revolt that went far beyond any straightforward economic reforms. The Serbian rebels wanted Bosnia to be joined to the Serbian kingdom and so continued their revolt. The Ottoman army responded by putting the rebellion down by force. Serbia declared war on the Ottomans in July 1876 and was defeated two months later. At this point Russia intervened and threatened to invade the Ottoman Empire if it continued its attack on Serbia. The Ottomans withdrew.

Meanwhile in Bulgaria, another group of nationalist rebels attempted to revolt, taking advantage of Ottoman military efforts elsewhere in Bosnia. Guerrilla bands in Serbia and Romania crossed into Bulgaria and attacked Ottoman posts in an effort to create a nationalist revolt among the Bulgarian peasants. These efforts all failed because of lack of popular support in the countryside and also the renewed strength of the Ottoman military – recently reformed during the Tanzimat era. In May 1876, fighting occurred in three towns in Bulgaria, instigated mainly by local nationalists from the merchant class. There was as yet little support from the local peasantry. These initial actions led to ever increasing levels of violence and eventually Russia intervened. At first the rebels killed about 1,000 Muslim villagers in the surrounding region. The Ottomans, with most of their regular troops tied up in Bosnia, called upon local Muslims and also resettled Circassians to put down the revolt.[36] This they did with ferocity, killing the rebels as well as many innocent Bulgarians. From an initial massacre of 1,000 Muslims, it was now reported that between 3,000 and 12,000 Bulgarians had died (McCarthy 2001:46). Eventually the regular Ottoman army was moved out of Serbia and Bosnia and placed in Bulgaria to put an end to the unrest.

The Ottomans were successful in putting down rebellions in Bosnia and Bulgaria. They also defeated the Serbian kingdom. These internal rebellions and civil uprisings were within the ability of the Ottoman military machine to manage. However, European public opinion was no longer on the Ottomans' side. For a long time, Britain had been a diplomatic ally of the Ottoman Empire (taking its side in the Crimean War along with France a few decades earlier). But the events in Bulgaria and Bosnia, as reported in the European press, made this position difficult for Great Britain to justify to its public. British newspapers reported – and some say greatly

---

[36] The Circassians, who had earlier been expelled with great brutality and mortality from their homelands by the Russians, were especially violent and resisted Ottoman orders to stop.

exaggerated – the deaths of Bulgarians, which the press called the 'Bulgarian Horrors'. Muslim deaths, however, went unmentioned. The same was true for Serbian attacks against Muslim Bosnians, which also went largely unreported. William Gladstone, at the time opposition leader in the British House of Commons, held strong evangelical Christian convictions. He organized a mass campaign against the Ottomans, helping to turn British public opinion against them. Prime minister Benjamin Disraeli wished to side with the Ottomans against the Russians, but was held back from taking any action by this growing negative public opinion.

In Russia too, public opinion, unusually, held some sway at this time. Pan-Slavic sentiments were fashionable among the Russian intelligentsia. These beliefs ranged from a general but vague idea of Slavic brotherhood to the more ideological notion that all Slavs were really one nation to be led by Russia. The losses in Serbia and Bosnia greatly strengthened the Russian belief that they needed to support the Serbs and so the czar was expected to do something for the Slavs.

Just as total Serbian defeat was imminent, the Ottomans gave in to Russian demands regarding the Slavs and agreed to sign an armistice with Serbia in October 1876. The Serbians would have accepted most plans for reforms in Bulgaria as they already had in Bosnia, but the Russians wanted more. It seems they wanted to divide up this part of Ottoman Europe into autonomous Christian states protected by Russia. They wanted the dissolution of the Ottoman Empire in Europe. The Ottomans naturally refused these demands and Russia declared war against the Ottoman Empire.[37]

In April 1877, Russia crossed the Danube and invaded the European Ottoman region. By July, Russia held all of northern Bulgaria, then Thrace, and by January 1878 had taken Edirne, leaving Istanbul now virtually undefended. In the east Russia had taken Kars and surrounded the Ottoman garrison in Erzurum. Surrounded on two flanks, the Ottomans were forced to capitulate and in January 1879 they signed an armistice. Two months later, in the first round of negotiations, Russia forced the Ottomans to sign the Treaty of San Stefano. Under these terms, a Greater Bulgaria was created, stretching from the Black Sea to Albania and south to the Aegean. In effect, it created a gigantic zone of Russian puppet states in the Balkans. These terms would, in effect, vastly increase Russian

---

[37] Before the declaration of war, however, Russia covered its side. In January 1877, it acceded to the Budapest Convention whereby Austria agreed to remain neutral in the coming Russo-Ottoman war. In return, Russia would give her Bosnia (Gauld 1927:561–567).

domination and influence and destroy the European balance of power. British public opinion now turned against Russia, which was seen as threatening British interests in the Middle East. Austria, too, was upset by this creation of a new Balkan rival. German chancellor Otto von Bismarck, probably the leading politician of the age, proclaimed himself an honest broker and stepped in to offer his 'good offices' as mediator. This resulted in the Congress of Berlin. The negotiated Treaty of Berlin then took away most of the Russian gains parcelling out Balkan territory. Russia was forced to accept a much smaller Bulgaria – a Bulgarian kingdom in the north – one-third the original size of the 'Greater Bulgaria'. The rest remained under qualified Ottoman control. Serbia was granted a small area of land (the region of Niş from which all but 10 per cent of the Muslims were evicted or died). Montenegro received some small territory, Greece as well (Thessaly and Epirus). Russia was force to settle with only the land in northeast Anatolia and southern Bessarabia, from which all Muslims were dispossessed and expelled to Muslim lands.

These wars in the Balkans led to massive dispossession and forced migration of peoples – it was to become the characteristic mark of nationalism. Unknown numbers of Bulgarians left Macedonia for Bulgaria when Macedonia was returned to the Ottomans. But by far, the Muslims of the Balkans suffered most from the Russian conquest.

Surprisingly, civilian losses in Bulgaria were relatively small as few of the scenes of battle were in the cities; nevertheless, 17 per cent of the Muslims of Bulgaria – 262,000 people – died during and immediately after the 1877–8 war. Some 515,000 Muslims, almost all Turkish speaking (generally now called Turks), were driven out of Bulgaria into other parts of the Ottoman Empire. They were the victims of a kind of state-sponsored programme of rape, plunder, and massacre by Bulgarian revolutionaries, Russian soldiers (especially Cossacks), and Bulgarian peasants. In the end, 55 per cent of the Muslims of Bulgaria were either killed or evicted. In Bosnia, which had been formally handed over to Austria, the mortality during the 1875–6 civil war resulted in a decline in the Muslim population from 694,000 to 449,000, a loss of 35 per cent (McCarthy 2001:48).

The Russian–Ottoman War of 1876–7 and the ensuing treaties of San Stefano and Berlin of 1878–9 resulted in the loss of most of the European areas of the Ottoman Empire – the territories south and southeast of the Danube and the Caucasus. These regions were populated by large numbers of Muslim Turkish-speaking people. The dispossession and forced migration of more than one million people, which began during this period, was referred to by successive generations as the ''93 disaster' [1877 being 1293 in the Muslim calendar] or the 'unweaving of '93'. The decades that followed saw the Ottoman Empire lose additional European territory and the dispossession and forced migration of many more thousands of Muslim Turks into Thrace, Anatolia, and Syria. The Christian–Muslim balance of the Ottoman Empire disappeared as Muslims became an overwhelming majority in the remaining areas. And the ideas of the Muslim–Christian equality (promulgated in the Imperial Decrees of the Tanzimat era) in terms of common citizenship in a multi-ethnic state, lost their practical significance as the state became predominantly inhabited by Muslims.

JEWISH IMMIGRATION TO PALESTINE

Initially, the Jews of Europe did not greet with much interest the 1857 Ottoman government decree opening immigration into the Ottoman state to anyone willing to respect the country's laws and recognize the sultan as sovereign.[38] But it was the poor treatment of Jews in Russia and their possible resettlement in Palestine which interested important Jewish personalities at the time as well as the British government. In 1846, for example, wealthy French merchant Isaac Altarass and British financier Moses Montefiore had discussed the settlement of persecuted Jews from Russia in Palestine. As Russian persecution of Jews increased, small groups began to flee, some into Romania [Moldavia and Wallachia, which were still part of the Ottoman Empire until 1878] and others into Anatolia and the Syrian provinces of the Ottoman Empire. Individuals and small groups of Jewish settlers were generally welcomed. However, Ottoman authorities – whose policy was to disperse both Muslim and Jewish migrants fleeing Russia – generally turned down larger groups requesting the right to settle in Palestine. Starting in Macedonia and spreading south, the Ottomans wanted to maintain the multi-ethnic and multi-national basis of their state and thus insisted that newcomers spread out over its long frontier zone.

Jewish interests, however, were very much focused on immigration to Palestine. Karpat cites one of many letters he found in the Ottoman

---

[38] Several decades earlier, the British Consulate in Jerusalem had opened [in 1839] and made numerous efforts to settle Jews in Palestine as a check to the Russian influence among the Orthodox Christians and the French influence among Maronite Christians (Karpat 1974). In 1847, the British consul in Jerusalem put forward a plan to transfer Russian Jews in Palestine who had already outstayed their 'one year Russian permit' to British consular protection. This plan was rejected by the Russians who anticipated that such a scheme would result in mass Jewish emigration from Russia to Palestine.

archives from Rabbi Joseph Natonek of Budapest, dated 21 October 1876 and addressed to Sultan Abdul Hamid (quoted in Karpat 1974; Ottoman Archives F. M. (I) 47646/183). Natonek demands permission to settle Jews in Palestine, arguing that such settlement would rejuvenate the area. He makes the claim that if a substantial contingent from among the 3 million European Jews were to settle in Palestine, it would result in a major economic boon for the Ottoman state. The Jews, he argued, would not be dependent on the Ottoman state but would rather enrich the coffers of the state by buying land and reviving the economy. The Ottoman government rejected Natonek's demand, stating that almost all lands in Palestine were now occupied and that the 'autonomy' he proposed for the Jews was not compatible with the administrative principles of the Ottoman state (quoted in Karpat 1974; Ottoman Archives F. M. (I) 346 and 6078/183 1891).

The Ottoman position was clear. Individuals of any religion or nationality could immigrate, but there were restrictions on mass settlement – that is, the state would not permit one ethnic or religious group to establish its numerical superiority in any one specific area. The ideal of a multi-ethnic and multi-national state remained supreme in Istanbul.[39] Decrees were issued to this effect in 1884, 1887, and 1888. However, proposals for mass settlement of Jews from Europe and Russia continued to flow in.[40]

By the 1890s, Jewish requests for permission to immigrate had turned into facts on the ground. Large groups of Russian Jews began arriving at Ottoman ports without passports or visas. In 1891, one group of sixty-five Russian Jews were issued with visas at Odessa and travelled directly to Palestine. The Ottoman Foreign Ministry issued a stern rebuke to its consulate in Odessa and sent a circular to its representatives in St. Petersburg and Athens, reminding them that individual immigration was permissible but not mass immigration. Despite these restrictions and regulations, a few Jewish groups found their way around them. Many of

---

[39] As early as 1877, the Jewish colonies at Jaffa and St Jean d'Acre aroused the concern of the Ottoman authority for the way in which they had isolated themselves 'religiously and ethnically' from the local population and were more like communes than integrated settlements in the district (Karpat 1974).

[40] For example, Dr. Alfred Nossig of the Jewish Committee in Berlin made a request for an ambitious resettlement scheme in Palestine. Alexander Lederbaum of St Petersburg requested boats and land to transport Jews to Palestine from the Russian empire. The Ottoman authorities replied that at present they were occupied with resettling large groups of Muslims from Russia. Afterwards, if land was left they would also take on the care of the Russian Jews (Karpat 1974; Kerr 1971:355).

these immigrants settled in Jerusalem, transforming the ethnic character of the city by the end of the nineteenth century.[41]

By the turn of the century, the original open policy of immigration to the Ottoman Empire had been transformed. Non-Muslims (Jews) were allowed to immigrate only as individuals. And although mass immigration of Jews into Palestine had been greatly discouraged, some groups did manage to find their way there, as population figures revealed. In 1868 the Jewish (Arab and European Jewish settler) population of Palestine was between 12,000 and 15,000. In 1882 the number had nearly doubled to between 23,000 and 27,000 and represented about 6 per cent of the total population. By 1900, after the period of intensive Jewish emigration from Russia (1881–1900), the total Jewish population of Palestine had reached, by some estimates, as much as 50,000 out of a total population of 500,000.[42] With the Jewish population of Palestine now estimated at between 6–10 per cent, the stage was now set for the concerted Zionist drive to create a homeland in Palestine for the persecuted Jews of Russia and increasingly in Europe as well.

ARMENIAN NATIONALISM

The other Christian nationalism to emerge during this era had an even smaller demographic profile than Greek Orthodox or Balkan Christians. As with most facts and figures regarding nineteenth-century Ottoman history, the exact number of Armenians in the empire is disputed. Some European travellers and missionaries put their number at 2 million. Stanford Shaw, using Ottoman Census Department figures, put the number at closer to 1,125,000 (1977:200). There was general agreement that Armenians only made up between 5 to 6 per cent of the total population of about 21 million people in the Ottoman Empire.[43] But there were simply not enough of them in any one place in the Ottoman Empire. Armenians were spread out far and wide and thus did not make up a majority or even significant minority in any

---

[41] In medieval times, Jews formed a very small portion of Jerusalem's population. Their numbers gradually increased over the centuries. By the middle of the nineteenth century Jews represented about half the city's total population. By the end of the century, Zionist immigration from Russia and eastern Europe had produced a Jewish majority in Jerusalem (Kerr 1971).

[42] Karpat derives these figures from a number of sources, including Margolis and Marx (1969) and Margalith (1957).

[43] Even in Istanbul, known to have the highest concentration of urban Armenians, they made up only 18 per cent of the total population in the 1897 census (Shaw & Shaw 1977:201).

one place. The only exceptions were perhaps Van (making up 25 per cent of the population at the beginning of the twentieth century) and Bitlis (making up perhaps 30 per cent of the total population at this time). Armenians had lived in southeast Anatolia for millennia. The Greek Orthodox Church considered the Armenian Church (Apostolic or Gregorian Church) heretical. This tight ethno-religious community was recognized by the state and had its own patriarchate and millet within the Ottoman Empire. By 1850 Armenians also had a Protestant and Catholic millet as American and European missionaries converted some of their dissident members.

Dispersal of Armenians from their largely mountainous homeland had been going on for centuries. Although the appearance of various conquering Turkic tribes in the eleventh and twelfth centuries, accompanied by Kurdish tribes who generally settled in the same mountainous regions, may have been a factor, more likely economics was a prime mover. Armenians dispersed to many of the major cities of the Middle East over the intervening centuries. They had always played an important role in Ottoman trade and industry specializing in money changing, foreign trade, medicine, and working as goldsmiths and jewellers. After the withdrawal from Anatolia of Ottoman Orthodox Christians to become part of the newly created Kingdom of Greece in 1832, Armenians filled many of the high government administrative positions left open. Because of their knowledge of foreign languages, Armenians rose high in particular ministries such as Finance, Interior, Foreign Affairs, Education, Justice, and Public Works.

The real Armenian tragedy in the making, however, came from imperial Russian meddling. One view is that Russia, frustrated in its hopes of creating large satellite states like Greater Bulgaria in southeast Europe, turned its expansionist attention to Transcaucasia and the eastern frontier with the Ottoman Empire (Shaw & Shaw 1977). Here it sought out a minority that had not revolted against the sultan – the Armenians – and cultivated their incipient nationalist interests and cultural distinctiveness. However, the Armenian Gregorian millet was well integrated into the Ottoman Empire and opposed these nationalists' aspirations. As Russia expanded into Transcaucasia, it annexed Georgia in 1800 and between 1804 and 1829 took over areas that today are the republics of Azerbaijan and Armenia. Local Armenian militias imbued with a sense of nationalist struggle aided these campaigns, perhaps feeling that Christian Russia would be more likely to help them to create their own independent Armenian homeland than would the Muslim Ottoman state.

This was perhaps the Armenian nationalists' greatest miscalculation. In 1855 and 1877, Ottoman Armenians helped the Russians invade

Anatolia. When European powers forced Russia to return some of those areas to the Ottoman Empire, tens of thousands of local Armenians withdrew with the Russian troops. Into the vacuum came the Muslims, who had been forced out earlier by Russia. An unscripted forced 'exchange' of peoples was taking place in areas that held Armenian minorities, creating tension, hatred, and fear in the newly resettled and returning population. These hatreds were worsened by the arrival of more than 1.2 million Muslims – the Circassians and Abkhazians – expelled by Russia from the western Caucasus in the 1860s (McCarthy 2001:68).

In the 1860s and 1870s Armenian revolutionary groups began to appear in Istanbul and further east. These groups attempted to gain Russian support for their communities, especially in Van and Zeytoun, but they had little success. Although Russia had conquered much of the region called Armenia, there was no accommodation of the Armenian national claims in the treaties of San Stefano or Berlin in 1878. Between 1878 and World War I, Armenian nationalist groups set about organizing a revolution in order to draw the attention of the European powers to help them create an Armenian state for their nation. During this period Armenians made some headway and found increasing support in the international media through reports from European missionaries, if not with the Allied powers themselves.[44] Young Armenians founded the Armenakan Party in Van in 1885. In Europe, Russian students and émigrés formed the Hunchakian Revolutionary Party (Hunchaks), and Armenian students in Russia founded the Dashnaktsuthian Party (Dashnaks). Some Armenian revolutionaries believed the Bulgaria model – in which a small group of revolutionaries killed large numbers of Muslims, causing massive retaliation and Russian intervention, forcing Bulgarian Muslims out of the region and creating a new Bulgarian state – would work in Anatolia. The problem, however, was that 'there was not a single large area in the Ottoman Empire where the Armenians were in a clear majority' and where a claim to statehood could be entertained (Shaw & Shaw 1977).

---

[44] American Board of Commissioners for Foreign Missions sent its first missionaries to the Middle East in 1819. Conversion of Muslims and Jews to Protestantism proved very difficult. Orthodox Christians were also largely unwilling to consider leaving Catholicism. Only the Armenians accepted conversion in any large number, despite the disapproval of the Armenian Gregorian Church. It was the schools set up by the missionary churches that proved popular to all. As the Ottoman government was willing to accept foreign schools, the missionary presence grew rapidly. In 1819 the American Congregationalists had two missions; by 1845 they had 34; by 1880 there were 146 and by 1913, 209. In total, they were educating 26,000 students in 450 schools, mainly for Armenians in Anatolia (McCarthy 2001:69).

THE MACEDONIA PROBLEM 1912-3

The rebellions in Greece, Serbia, and Bulgaria set the standard for nationalist revolts in the Balkans. The new states were to be ethnically – that is, religiously – homogenous. This required the deportation and expulsion of Muslims, in some cases more than 50 per cent of its population.[45] Once the Muslim peoples had been expelled, the Christian nationalists sometimes turned upon each other in a secondary Christian sectarian-based effort of cleansing in order to create states of 'one people' alone, that is, members of a single ethno-religious group. The example of Macedonia is complicated but fairly typical. In order to grasp some of the fundamental issues behind this secondary Christian sectarian conflict, it is necessary to briefly return to the administration of the Christian millets in Istanbul.

The Orthodox patriarchate in Istanbul did not support these nationalist sentiments in the European regions of the Empire. Perhaps it felt that, as men of God, the first allegiance was to religion and not to a secular faith. In Istanbul the Orthodox patriarchate and its bureaucracy were Greek and attempted to spread the Greek language and religious traditions among Orthodox Christians in the Ottoman Empire. The lack of support for these nationalist movements by the patriarchate may also have been derived from a fear that nationalist sentiments would eventually fuel a demand for national churches. Such a move would mean the creation of separate clergy and authority structures, thus undermining the Orthodox patriarchy. This is exactly what happened. For many of the nationalists, the patriarch of Constantinople was controlled by the Ottoman administration and was not truly independent. Greek nationalists were the first to break away and declare an autocephalous Greek Church in 1833 in the newly established Greek kingdom. For a long time, the Bulgarians in the Ottoman Empire had deeply resented the Greek Orthodox Church, which they felt dismissed and diminished their own interests. The Bulgarians wanted priests and bishops who spoke the same language as the people. After years of Bulgarian agitating within the system, the Ottoman government recognized a Bulgarian Church in Istanbul in 1848. Then in 1870, in an effort to quell nationalist sentiment in Bulgaria, Ottoman authorities recognized the Bulgarian Exarchate, an autocephalous Bulgarian church. This newly created church became a rallying point for Bulgarian Christians and after

---

[45] According to the population statistics presented by McCarthy, Muslims were the largest religious group of Ottoman Europe, making up 51 per cent of the total population of the region (2001:90).

TABLE 1. *The population of Ottoman Macedonia by religion, 1911*

Religion	Population	Proportion (%)
Muslim	1,012,000	42
Greek	514,000	22
Bulgarian	774,000	32
Other	84,000	4
Total	2,384,000	

Source: Adapted from Justin McCarthy, 'The Population of Ottoman Europe Before and After the Fall of the Empire', in Heath W. Lowry and Ralph S. Hattox (eds), *Proceedings of the Third Conference on the Social and Economic History of Turkey*, Istanbul, 1990, pp. 275–98.

1878, when European powers created an independent Bulgaria, the church was used to spread the message of Bulgarian nationalism.

The secondary sectarian infighting amongst Balkan nationalists occurred after the Russian Ottoman War of 1877–8 and led up to the Balkan Wars of 1912–3; it is best exemplified by what happened in Macedonia. This region was not a recognized single Ottoman administrative district. It was generally described as the Ottoman province of Selanik, the southern half of the Kosovo province, and the western Manastir province. Bulgarian, Greek, and Serbian nationalists each claimed all or part of Macedonia based on what they regarded as the Christian beliefs of the region's people. The question of 'who are the Macedonians' never arose in the Ottoman government as Ottomans were identified only by religion. But it was a very important question to Bulgarian, Serbian, and Greek nationalists. No one asked the Macedonians what they wanted. The only choice they had made for themselves was to join the Bulgarian Church in overwhelming numbers once Ottoman authorities created it in 1870.

Some historians have interpreted this move as a clear sign that the Macedonians absolutely did not wish to be Greek. However, it did not mean that they wished to be Bulgarian either, as there was no Macedonian church alternative. Although there was a rising Macedonian separatist movement growing at this time whose adherents claimed that they were neither Serb, Bulgars, nor Greeks but an entirely separate Slavic people, it was too weak to make any impact. Then, there was the largest group in Macedonia, the Muslims, with more than one million. Many of these were refugees from lands to the north conquered by Orthodox Christian Russia, who opposed any claim that would again place them under the control of Christians who had treated them so badly (Shaw & Shaw 1977:208).

TABLE 2. *The population of Macedonia: Bulgarian, Serbian, and Greek statistics*

	Bulgarian statistics	Serbian statistics	Greek statistics	Actual population
Turks (Muslims)	499,000	231,000	634,000	1,112,000
Bulgars	1,181,000	57,000	332,000	774,000
Greeks	229,000	201,000	653,000	514,000
Serbs	1,000	2,048,000	_[a]	

[a] Does not appear in Greek statistics.
Source: Adapted from McCarthy, 2001:59.

Bulgarian, Serbian, and Greek nationalists all wanted the same territory and produced conflicting statistics to show an ethnic population distribution based on religion and language. The Bulgarians claimed that anyone who was not Greek or Turk was automatically Bulgarian. Serbs recognized Macedonians (so as not to see them as Bulgarians) along with Serbs and Greeks. Meanwhile, the Greeks refused to recognize the heterogeneous nature of the region, which included Bulgarian, Muslim, Jewish, and Greek Orthodox. Instead they claimed that the Macedonians were actually Greeks whose language and customs had been forcibly changed over centuries of foreign rule.

In the European press and diplomatic corridors, the 'Macedonian Question' was always discussed as a matter concerning Greek, Bulgarian, and Serbian Christians, that is, which of these new states would get how much of Macedonia. Yet in all the diplomatic documents and media, there was no mention of the wishes of the people living in Macedonia, the largest majority of whom were Muslims.

While Serbia, Greece, and Bulgaria agreed that the Ottomans should be expelled from Europe, they could not agree on how the lands should be divided. This lack of consensus eventually led to the Balkan Wars (1912–3). Macedonia was an excellent example of this discord. Serbia, Greece, and Bulgaria each believed that Macedonia was its national patrimony. They could agree only that it did not belong to the Balkan Muslims who made up at least 51 per cent of the population. By 1913, much of the Muslim population had been expelled using tactics from earlier wars. The Bulgarians then attacked the Serbs in 1913. The Serbs and Greeks counterattacked and recovered. Taking advantage of the infighting among Greeks, Serbs, and Bulgarians, the Ottomans retook Edirne and recovered eastern Thrace. Ultimately, Bulgaria lost even more of Macedonia to the Greeks and Serbs.

The tactics used in the Balkan Wars were very much the same as those adopted in the 1877–8 Russian–Ottoman Wars. Here as before, Bulgarian, Greek, Serbian, and Montenegrin armies advanced, destroying Muslim villages in their path. Muslim peasants and villagers were raped and murdered. Fearing for their lives, Muslims in the adjacent villages fled, and soon an entire population was on the march trying to escape the pillage and death that accompanied the invading armies. For the forced migrants and refugees, flight was followed by starvation and disease. Often stripped of their possessions while walking towards imagined safety, Muslim refugees were overcome by hunger and cold. So many died that some reported piles of dead left by the road (McCarthy 2001:92). Those who did reach the few refugee camps in Ottoman-controlled territory often succumbed to typhus, typhoid, and cholera. Very little international assistance was available to these refugees until they reached the major cities and ports, where they were offered aid in the form of transportation by boat, train, and oxcarts. Forced migrants in the interior regions had to make their way over treacherous mountainous roads to ports or other places of refuge. Those who survived the fighting often found their villages destroyed or occupied by Greeks, Serbs, Bulgarians, or Montenegrins.

The final tragedy of the Balkan Wars came in the autumn of 1913. Albanians in Kosovo revolted against their Serbian army. The revolt was put down, the villages destroyed, and inhabitants killed or forced to flee to Albania, which had no resources and received aid from no one. These refugees succumbed to diseases and starvation. In all, 2.3 million Muslims once lived in the European Balkans. By the end of the wars, only 1.4 million remained. The Ottoman Refugee Commission recorded the number of refugees settled in the empire as 414,000 in total. Of these, most went to eastern Thrace and western Anatolia; some were placed as far afield as Syria. From 1921 to 1926, 399,000 others came to Turkey. All told, an estimated 632,000, 27 per cent of the Muslim population of Ottoman Europe, died in the Balkan Wars (McCarthy 2001).

THE ARMENIAN MASSACRES OF 1915–6[46]

Although the Ottoman Empire was largely characterized as having fairly good intercommunal relations, violence and intolerance did flare up from

---

[46] There is enormous scholarship on this subject presenting very different points of view. See, for example, Hovannisian (1997a), Dadrian (1997), McCarthy (2001), and Melson (1996).

time to time, and were quickly put down again – such as the religious disturbances in 1840 in Damascus and again in the 1860s in Mt Lebanon, Damascus, and Aleppo. However, towards the end of the nineteenth century, both the scale and the ferocity of such attacks against the Armenian population were unprecedented. These began with the massacres of Armenians in 1895–6 and again in 1908, 1909, and 1912. In 1912, Muslim refugees from the Balkans assaulted Armenian communities in towns such as Rodosto and Malgara on the northern shore of the Marmara Sea and also in Adapazari in western Anatolia. Massive numbers of Muslim refugees had fled to these places after being driven out of their own homes and took out their anger and frustration on innocent Ottoman Armenians.

But worse was to come in the 1915–6 massacres of Armenians driven from their homes in eastern Anatolia on forced marches to the Arab provinces. An estimated 600,000 to 1.2 million Armenians died during and after these forced marches.

There is considerable and passionate debate on this subject and on the intent of the Ottoman authorities, but this topic cannot be covered adequately here. The simplest outline of events is that in 1914 war erupted again between Russia and the Ottoman Empire along the eastern Anatolian frontier. In 1915, the Ottoman government – worried about the loyalty of the Armenian community – ordered the deportation of the entire Armenian population of eastern Anatolia out of the war zone southward into the Syrian Desert, claiming the need to guard the deportees and their property and assure their safety. Yet eyewitnesses, survivors, missionaries, and diplomatic observers report that Ottoman soldiers, bandits, and civilian officials murdered vast numbers of Armenian civilians – men, women, and children alike. It is not easy to reconcile the state orders to respect the life and property of the Armenian deportees with the actual slaughter of these Ottoman subjects. While some theories claim that circles within the government secretly sought to use the deportations as a guise for exterminating the Armenians, there are no records to establish such an explanation (Zürcher 1993). What should be kept in mind, however, is that Armenians outside the battle zone were not targeted for deportation. Armenians living in western Anatolia and in the southern Balkans were not included in these marches. In places like Istanbul and Izmir, the relatively large Armenian communities remained largely intact while hundreds of thousands of their co-religionists were slaughtered in the east.

THE END OF EMPIRE AND THE EMERGING TURKISH STATE

World War I began with the assassination in Sarajevo, Serbia, of Archduke Ferdinand of Austria. Once Austria declared war on Serbia, Russia was drawn in to defend its Serbian satellite state. The numerous other European alliances brought the rest of the continent into the war. Although the Ottomans remained neutral at first, this position was not tenable. Eventually, it joined the German and Austrian Axis, if for no other reason than the knowledge that, should Russia and its allies win the war, the Ottoman Empire would be completely dismantled. Russia had been eating away at the empire for at least one hundred years. Since the reign of Catherine the Great, Istanbul had been in Russian sights as had access to the Mediterranean. In both the Crimean and the 1877–8 Russo-Ottoman wars, Russia conquered large areas of the empire but had been stopped from keeping much of this territory in the ensuing peace negotiations by the actions of the European powers. For a long time England had supported the Ottoman Empire; but was Russia's ally in this latest war. For the Ottomans, it would have seemed that only Germany would be capable of stopping Russia.

By 1919 the Russian Empire was toppled and the Ottoman Empire defeated along with its allies Germany and Austria. The division of conquered land was taken up by a meeting of the Allied powers in a European capital, as was traditional. The Congress of Paris had ended the Crimean War, and the Congress of Berlin had divided up the Balkans. Now at the Paris Peace Conference in 1919, the victorious Allies set about deliberating how to divide up the territories of the defeated Germans, Austrians, and Ottomans. They had the difficult task of managing in this process the numerous promises – some secret and others not – they had made in order to gain support or keep potential troublemakers out of the conflict. Sometimes the same conquered lands had been promised to more than one recipient.

The Ottomans were not well represented in the peace conference. Their delegation's strategy was to be totally compliant so as to extract leniency from the Allies. They admitted to all the charges and claims made against them by the Allies – some true and others not. The Ottomans were sick of war. Many of their political leaders had friendly feelings towards the British and French. Furthermore, they were looking for principled decisions based on American espousal of self-determination and ethical treatment of conquered peoples. Their hope was to get the Allies to leave Anatolia to them and allow their Arab provinces some autonomy rather than putting them under mandates of the League of Nations. The Allies, however, had other plans for the Arab provinces negotiated in both the Sykes-Picot Agreement as well as the Balfour Declaration. They also had other partners to pay off.

The Treaty of Sèvres was signed in August 1920 but never enforced. The treaty's terms were exceedingly harsh, considering how previous treaties – such as that in Paris after the Crimean War or in Berlin after the Russo-Ottoman War – had sought to balance the interests of each of the major players. For the Ottomans, the proposed Greek spoils in Anatolia were not acceptable. What little was left of the Ottoman military structure stood up against these harsh terms, among which were the following:

- Greek administration was to be placed over the District of Smyrna only (the city of Izmir and its hinterland) in Anatolia. A plebiscite would then be held after five years to decide if the region should be annexed to the Greek kingdom.
- The borders between Armenia and the Ottoman Empire were to be determined by President Woodrow Wilson.
- In recognition of the previously secret Sykes-Picot Agreement between France and Great Britain, the Arab provinces of Syria and Mesopotamia [Iraq] were provisionally recognized as independent states subject to the 'rendering of administrative advice and assistance by a mandatory until such time as they were able to stand alone'. Britain was to take Palestine and Iraq, France to take what was to become Syria and Lebanon.
- The Balfour Declaration, creating a Jewish home in Palestine, was written into the treaty.

Although the Ottoman delegation signed the Treaty of Sèvres, it was not accepted at home. The year before, in May 1919, British, French, and American negotiators had agreed that Greek forces could be sent to occupy Izmir and its surrounding district – in advance of any treaty with the Ottoman Empire. This was in violation of the armistice agreement with the Ottomans. The Greeks had greater plans in mind and quickly moved out into the surrounding areas far beyond what had been allotted to them by the Paris Peace Conference. The remaining Ottoman forces recognized that they had a Greek invading force on their land, which they had to defeat or face total collapse.

In 1919, Ottoman Anatolia had been invaded, in effect, by the Greeks. To the south were the French and to the east, the Armenians. Squeezed between these three forces, the Ottoman Muslims became unified in a way they had not been able to do before. With their Arab provinces lost to the French and British, a new 'national' identity – solely Turkish – was coalescing, driven by their enemies. Between 1919 and 1922 the Turkish War for Independence raged. Before the war, Greeks had made up only 14 per cent of the population of western Anatolia, while Muslims, many of them Turks, made up 80 per cent. The only way the Greeks were going to be able to rule the territory was by dispossessing and evicting the Muslims. In May 1919, the Greek army landed at Izmir and quickly moved to the border assigned to it by the Allies. By June the Greeks had occupied all of the Aegean coast and inland areas; although these advances were beyond that agreed in the Treaty of Sèvres, they were largely ignored by the British forces and other diplomatic observers. More than a million Turkish refugees fled the advancing Greeks in Anatolia. The Greeks continued to take other cities where pillage and murder of Muslims and Jews regularly occurred.

Turkish resistance to the Greeks began immediately. At first it was weak and ineffective, but as the Greeks took more land, resistance increased. The first indication came in the city of Aydin on 30 June 1919, when Ottoman soldiers acted on their own authority to retake the city briefly and save Turks there from massacre. All over Anatolia, officers began to refuse to hand over their weapons to Allied control officers or to disband their units. Mustafa Kemal, the hero of Gallipoli, had returned from defeat in Syria to southern Anatolia with his army intact. With initial support from the government in Istanbul, he was able to pull together the political and military leadership of Anatolia based in Ankara to demand that the integrity of the regions inhabited by Turks be maintained and that Turks be politically independent. This Anatolian resistance movement set up its own parliament, the Grand National Assembly and elected Mustafa Kemal as its president. The Assembly then set about organizing war with the Greeks. By the summer of 1922 the Turks had defeated the Greeks all over western Anatolia and entered Izmir on 9 September 1922. The following year, the Treaty of Lausanne was signed, after which the British occupation force left Istanbul.

At the end of the war, nearly 1.2 million Muslims in western Anatolia had died. Of the Anatolian Greeks, more than 313,000 died. Nearly 25 per cent of the total Greek population in Anatolia had been lost – refugees as well as Greeks who died when forcibly removed from northern Anatolia (the Pontus region). In eastern Anatolia, mortality figures are less accurate but still reveal a level of death and mayhem that can only be likened to slaughter. Between 1912 and 1922 these provinces lost more than

1.4 million people – the original number of inhabitants minus the number of survivors. For Armenians, the statistics can only be given in terms of mortality of all Armenians of Anatolia. These figures show unimaginable inhuman suffering and death. More than 600,000 (40 per cent) of the Armenians of Anatolia were lost in World War I and the Turkish War of Independence.[47]

CONCLUSION

The late nineteenth and early twentieth centuries left a profoundly negative mark on the history of human settlement and political engineering. The Ottoman Empire, which had developed a largely successful multicultural and religious pluralism, was gradually dismantled by pressures from within as much as from outside. This demise came quickly, although it was prefaced by a nearly century-long reweaving of the peoples of the Balkans, eviction of the Muslim peoples in the Caucasus, and the remixing of the largely Muslim peoples in Anatolia with the departure of the Orthodox Greeks and Armenian Christians.

The numerous dispossessions and forced migrations that accompanied this era are too complex and also too contested to be dealt with in any great detail here. The Macedonian example given earlier provided only a taste of the elaborately contested nationalisms that emerged during this period, and which continue to plague the region even into the twenty-first century. Between about 1875 and 1925, several million people were uprooted from the Balkans – or, more specifically, from Bulgaria, Macedonia, Thrace, and western Anatolia. These forced migrants found their way to Anatolia where they largely assimilated and became part of the Turkish nationalist struggle. Others found their way further south to Syria, Lebanon, Jordan, and Egypt. These migrations radically simplified the ethnic demography of the regions left behind; greater homogeneity replaced a heterogeneity that, for a while at least, made it difficult for ethno-religious nationalism to take root. In 1879, for example, Muslims (Turks, Bulgarian, Circassians, and Crimean settlers from Russia) were at least as numerous as Orthodox Christian Bulgarians in what was later to become Bulgaria.[48] Similarly, between 1912 and 1924 the intricately intermixed population of Macedonia and Thrace – largely made up of Turkish-speaking Muslims, Greeks, and Slavs identifying themselves mainly as Bulgarians – were

[47] These figures are derived from McCarthy (1983).
[48] By 1920 Muslims comprised only 14 per cent of the population (also see Karpat 1985:50–51; Rothschild 1974:327).

shifted about to form relatively homogenous blocks corresponding to new state frontiers: northern Macedonia became Slavic, southern and western Macedonia predominantly Greek, and eastern Thrace and western Anatolia purely Turkish (Pallis 1925:316). The unmixing of peoples initially followed religious rather than linguistic lines. The Muslims moved south and east and the Christians moved north and west. Thus, it was not only ethnic Turks who retreated towards Ottoman core areas, but also other Muslims, Bulgarians, Bosnians, Circassians, and Crimean Tatars who had fled earlier from Russia to the Ottoman Balkans.

Until the final decades of the Ottoman Empire, peoples of different religions lived together who have been unable to do so since. The separation of people and religions, which brought down the Ottomans, was the legacy of nationalism and European imperialism. It has led to much strife in the modern Balkans and the Middle East. The expulsion of peoples and population exchanges on formerly Ottoman lands were sometimes peaceful as the result of treaties following exhausting wars, but sometimes these involuntary migrations were not peaceful at all. The exchanges following World War I were largely peaceful, if forcible. Turks and Greeks were exchanged in this manner, as were Greeks and Bulgarians. Peaceful or not, they were largely undertaken against the will of the individuals, families, and communities so dispossessed.

Believers in a traditional Hellenophobia–Turkophobia would have stared at the sight of the Mytilene Greeks spreading farewell meals for their departing neighbours, and later accompanying them to the quay, where Christians and Mohammedans, who for a lifetime had been plowing adjacently and even sharing occasional backgammon games at village cafes, embraced and parted with tears. Then, seated on their heaped up baggage, with their flocks around them – the women weeping, the children hugging their pets, the gray-bearded babas all dignity, as is their wont – the Mytilene Muslims set forth for unknown Turkey. (*National Geographic* magazine, November 1922, quoted in Clark 2006:21)

I was born in 1912, in a mountain valley where for many centuries, Greek-speaking Cretans made an excellent living from farming, trading and mining … During the first two decades of the twentieth century, Imera [fifty miles from the Black Sea port of Trebizond] was devoid of able-bodied men. My father and all his male contemporaries were away in Russia earning fortunes … We called ourselves Romioi – the old word for Greeks in the Ottoman world – but Greece itself was remote from our consciousness. The country that loomed in our imagination was Russia … Was I aware that a world war was going on? Did I know that our stretch of the Black Sea coast was taken over by the czar's forces in spring 1916 – and then abandoned, because of the revolution in Russia, in 1918? … After the Russian withdrawal in 1918, it was anybody's guess what would happen to us … One day in January 1923, all the Greeks who still live in Trebizond were rounded up and transported by sea to Constantinople. One of them was my older sister Sophia. She had married and lived well in a handsome two-story house in the port, though her husband was in exile. On the day of the expulsion order, she was given fifteen minutes to gather everything she could and go to the harbour. Of all my family, her story is the most tragic. Her infant child died in her arms during the voyage; and she remembered this until her death in Salonika, in March 2004, when she was 101. (George Siamanides, 92-year-old widower in 2005, quoted in Clark 2006:126–127)

This transfer of populations is made especially difficult by the fact that few if any of the Turks in Greece desire to leave and most of them will resort to every possible expedient to avoid being sent away. A thousand Turks who voluntarily emigrated from Crete to Smyrna have sent several deputations to the Greek government asking to be allowed to return. Groups of Turks from all parts of Greece have submitted petitions for exemptions. A few weeks ago, a group of Turks from Crete came to Athens to request that they be baptized into the Greek church and thus be entitled to considerations as Greeks. The government however declined to permit this evasion. (*The Times*, 5 December 1923, quoted in Clark 2006:158)

The earlier dispossession of Muslims during and after the Balkans Wars was accompanied by large-scale murder, as were the exchanges between the Armenians and Muslims in eastern Anatolia and Transcaucasia during and immediately after World War I. The last days of the war closed the book on a sequence of events in which millions were driven from their homes, millions more were killed and the victors divided the spoils with no regard for the Wilsonian ideals of self-determination or the wishes of the conquered peoples in the Balkans and the Middle East.

It is commonly believed that prior to the two Great Wars, the main casualties of armed conflict were soldiers who usually died as a result of infection or other injuries sustained on the battlefield (Goldson 1996:809). However, wars waged against and within the Ottoman Empire between the late nineteenth and early twentieth centuries impacted most heavily on civilians. In the nationalist wars of the Balkans, hundreds of thousands, if not more than a million, civilians were moved out or transferred internally. In the Crimea and the Caucasus regions at least 1.2 million Muslims were evicted and forced to move south to find new homes in Anatolia and the Arab provinces, and in the east, there was the slaughter of nearly a million Armenians, if not more. Beginning with the Russian–Ottoman War of 1877, intensifying in the Balkan Wars of 1912–3, and culminating with the aftermath of World War I, almost all the large-scale migrations were concerned directly or indirectly with military campaigns and the resulting inter-communal warfare. But it was the civilians who suffered most. It was a time of mass ethnic nationalism, undertaken by new states determined to shape their territories in the image of their imagined community. Their search was for making real the imagined homogenous nation-state. After the Turkish War of Independence, most of the Greeks and Armenians of Anatolia were gone, as were the majority of the Turks of Greece and Armenia. The Ottoman Empire had died in these wars and, with it, the society based on multiplicity of ethnic groups and religions. In its wake, millions of dispossessed peoples and other forced migrants had set out to find new spaces in which to live. They took with them the memory of a multi-ethnic and multi-religious empire as well as the singular remembered and partially imagined homelands that they hoped to cultivate and then nourish in new places. Two other peoples whose homelands were within the Ottoman Empire, the Palestinians and the Kurds, were shortly to become dispossessed and either forced from their native lands or have their lands politically transformed underfoot.

3

Circassian, Chechnyan, and Other Muslim Communities Expelled from the Caucasus and the Balkans

My parents came here when they were very young. My father was 7 years old and my mother was 6 years old. My mother was born in Anatolia in 1870. There had been a war in their homeland. The Circassians helped the Turks in the war against Russia, but they lost. Then they had to leave these conquered places. My parents used to tell me about their first impression of Damascus in Marjeh.[1] It was a vast green meadow. The oxcarts all stopped there and formed circles. Inside the carts, 15–20 families were squeezed in. They rested in Damascus for 10–15 days and then they carried on to the Jaulan. Their journey had started back in Caucasia and from Abkhazia. Abkhazia is to the east of the Black Sea and there is Abazin beyond the mountains. They came by sea. 5 million people were moved. Of the 5 million only 500,000 arrived in Turkey [Anatolia]. 4.5 million people died on the way, some overland, some in the sea. Most of them drowned. Whole ships sank. Only a half million made it to Turkey. Some people chose to stay in Turkey. Some of our relatives stayed there. Others chose to come to 'Sham Al-Sharif'.[2] Most people stayed in Turkey. Only some 20 per cent carried on and came here. Our ox-carts all passed through Aleppo, Homs, Damascus, Jaulan and then dropped down into Jordan, a few families stopping here and there. The Turks dispersed us in different places to protect various locations. For the Turks we were a weapon. It was like having pistols in their pockets which they used whenever they needed to protect an area. My family settled in Jaulan. They were part of 12 Circassian villages which were built there. Most villages had 150 families, but ours was very

[1] Marjeh used to be on the outskirts of the Old City in the nineteenth century, a vast meadow. In the early twentieth century, it became the locus of Ottoman and then French Mandate administration. Now it is a central square in the middle of the commercial district of the city.
[2] Sham Al Sherif (Damascus the Honourable) was the other name for Damascus, linking it religiously with Mecca as the city which Mohammed had refused to enter, considering it to be a paradise on earth (or because it was the starting point for one of the most important pilgrimage caravans to Mecca).

small it had only 50 houses. Our village was the closest to Qunaytrah. Even the French [during the French Mandate between 1920–43] admitted that our villages were the best in the area. All our Circassian houses had red tiles for roofs.

(Abdul-Salam 2005)

The term *Circassians,* as they are commonly called, refers to a collect of largely tribal peoples associated with the mountainous terrain of Caucasus; that region in Eurasia bordered on the west by the Black Sea, on the east by the Caspian Sea, on the south by Iran, on the southwest by Turkey, and on the north by Russia. The group itself uses the term *Adigye* [men] to refer to themselves. The Caucasus Mountains are commonly believed to be the dividing line between Asia and Europe. The northern portion of the Caucasus is known as the Ciscaucasus and the southern portion as the Transcaucasus. The entire region is one of great linguistic and cultural diversity: among the peoples of the region are the Circassians [Adigye], Abaza, Ossetians, Ingush, Chechnyan, Adjar, Azeri, Laz, Tatars, and Abkhaz. This chapter focuses on the Circassians and the Chechnyan forced migrants into the Middle East, but much of what befell them can also be generalized to the other peoples of the Caucasus. The differences among the Circassian tribes are of comparatively minor importance and are not dealt with here other than to acknowledge the tribal affiliation of various groups of Circassians as they arrived in the Middle East and went about the task of setting up their own distinct settlements. However, no one tribal community excluded members of another in these new home-lands; marriage within and between tribal groups was common, and social and cultural continuity very much focused on the larger group rather than on the tribal affiliation. The hierarchical nature of Circassian society as recorded in the Caucasus, it seems, did not translate to the settler society in the new Ottoman lands other than the slow unravelling of slavery due to Ottoman and western European pressure. In the early period of migration into the Middle East, the Circassian slave trade and agricultural slavery peculiar to Circassian society was a problem.[3]

---

[3] Ottoman government estimates in 1867 were that 150,000 Circassian immigrants were of slave status. Toledano considers that these figures were probably too high, but they do show that the number of slaves entering the Middle East was significant. The great majority of them were attached to their masters, commonly referred to as *emirs* or *beys*. In times of peace they cultivated the land of their masters and in war they fought under their masters' command. In their new homelands some slave families began to rebel and some poor families who had sold children to slave dealers in order to continue their journeys into

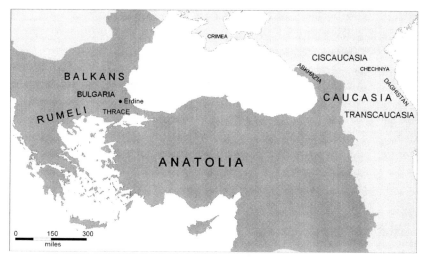

MAP 3. The Caucasus

As a crossroads between Asia and Europe as well as a frontier – especially during the last millennium – between a Christian Russian Empire to the north and a Muslim Ottoman Empire to the south, the Caucasus have been subjected to numerous invasions and migrations. Many Circassians converted to Islam when Ottoman rule was established in the western part of Caucasia in the beginning of the sixteenth century. The remaining population seems to have converted in the eighteenth and early nineteenth centuries as a result of the Nogai preachers from the northwest and also the Muridite movement from Daghestan (Karpat 1979:10). Muridism grew out of local resistance to Russian expansion into these lands. As a movement, it preached a doctrine of social equality and liberty as well as resistance to foreign occupation. This was translated into Muslim Circassian solidarity against Russian occupation. As a group, Circassians have long captured the historical imagination; the prowess and valour of their men, reinforced in the Mamluk warrior-slave tradition, have been referred to often in historical tracts as has the physical beauty of their

exile also began to protest. However, the traffic in young Circassian women for the harems of Istanbul and other cities continued with little protest. It was only in the 1880s that the slave trade went into decline as both the Ottoman and the British sought to finally suppress it (Toledano 1982:148–157).

women, both within and outside of the Ottoman sultan's seraglio, and captured in the paintings of the French romantics (Weightman 1970).

The last two centuries, however, have seen the wholesale dispossession and deportation of the Caucasus' Muslim inhabitants. It was perhaps the first full-scale ethnic cleansing, or genocide, of a region in our modern era. This came about in several stages as imperial Russia succeeded militarily in extending its rule and imposing its religion south and west into the diminishing and shrinking domain of the religiously more tolerant Ottoman Empire. The first wave of expulsion from the Caucasus region took place in the late eighteenth century, after the treaty of Kürçük-Kaynarca was signed at the end of the Russian–Ottoman War of 1774.

WAVES OF EXPULSION

Some 500,000 Tatars were reported to have left the Crimea in the 1780s for Ottoman lands. As was to be a pattern later, they settled first in the nearest Ottoman province at the time, Bessarabia, and only later were moved on when that land was also lost to Russia. From the original group of half a million, only 300,000 reportedly reached Anatolia. The loss of life on these journeys of exile were exceedingly high, reaching as much as 40 per cent. One can hardly imagine the hunger, thirst, and disease these migrants must have endured.

The second emigration from Crimea was in the nineteenth century after the Treaty of Edirne at the conclusion of the Russian Ottoman War of 1828–9. Many of these Tatars were first moved and settled in the southern European Balkans [in what was then known as Rumelia] and later, with the next Ottoman defeat, were expelled and forced to resettle in Anatolia (Tekeli 1994:209–210).

The next large-scale forced migration came forty years later as an outcome of the Crimean War of 1854–6, and was also of Crimean Tatars. It was estimated that 400,000 Tatars were forced to leave in this wave. Most sold their property and moved to the southern Balkans, as had the earlier group of Tatar forced migrants. Then, twenty years on, after the Russian Ottoman War of 1877–8, the Tatars who had settled in Rumelia just a few decades before, were moved on a second time and resettled on the Anatolian plateau with concentrations in and near Izmir, Ankara and Konya (Karpat 1985:66). The total number of Tatar forced migrants to Ottoman lands between the end of the eighteenth century and the beginning of the twentieth century is estimated to be about 1.8 million people.

The other significant waves of dispossession and flight in the nineteenth century came from the Caucasus. These started largely after the 1860s as Russia continued its expansion into Ottoman lands throughout the 1870s, 1880s, and 1890s. Many Circassians and Abazas who had been unhappy with the outcome of the Treaty of Edirne at the close of the Russian Ottoman War of 1828–9 stayed on in their lands and resisted the continuing Russian campaigns to occupy their homelands. These groups were finally defeated in 1865 a few years after the Russians captured their northern Caucasus leader Shaykh Shamil in 1859 (Tekeli 1994:210).[4] Few Circassians left their homeland during this thirty-year period of resistance to Russian incursions (1830s–1860s). Only in the 1860s did the emigration of Circassians become a mass movement. Russia had entered into a treaty with the Ottomans regarding the 'cleaning out' and transfer of peoples from these newly acquired lands.[5] Russia wanted to create a Christian majority on its newly conquered areas. Thus, the Greek Orthodox from the Eastern Black Sea region were to be sent to Russia and the Muslims in this frontier area were to be moved out and into the Ottoman heartlands. However, by 1865 as many as 520,000 Muslims had been forcibly moved into the Ottoman Empire while only several thousand Greek Orthodox subjects from the Ottoman Empire had agreed to migrate north to Russia. Many of these Greek Orthodox were reported to have returned to the eastern Black Sea region by 1869 [Sinop, Trabzon, & Samsun] unhappy with conditions in the Russian state (Tekeli 1994).

During the Russian Ottoman War of 1877–8, the Ottomans sent two Circassian units to help fight the Russian invaders in the Caucasus. Inevitably the local Circassian population also rose up against the Russians. In view of the Ottoman defeat and local Caucasian uprising,

---

[4] Sheikh Shamil, or Imam Shamil (1797–1871) was a political and religious leader of the Muslim tribes of the northern Caucasus. He was the third Imam of Daghestan and Chechnya (1834–59) and led the resistance to the Russian efforts to conquer his peoples.

[5] The transportation of these Circassians was so large an operation that the Ottoman and Russian governments had to cooperate to effect this mass clearing. The two governments had to employ war ships – after their guns had been removed – as well as hire numerous steam and sail vessels from other countries. The majority of Circassians being sent to Anatolia were landed at Trabzon and Samsun on the Black Sea. There the refugees were reported to be dying at the rate of two hundred per day as a result of typhus and smallpox. One contemporary observer estimated that the mortality for the entire emigration was 50 per cent. Those refugees headed for Bulgaria were landed at Constanta or Varna. Conditions there were no better. One observer estimated that 80,000 Circassians landed at Varna, destitute and suffering from fever, smallpox, and dysentery. Soon the beaches were covered with the dead. The Ottoman authorities had to bring in convicts to bury the dead or throw them into the sea (Pinson 1972:74).

Russia was able to insist in its treaty with the Ottomans at the close of the war that the Circassians on these newly acquired Russian lands had to be moved out and resettled far from the new Russian border. The Russians did not want troublesome Circassians to be settled in the adjacent areas of the Balkans. As a result, between 1859 and 1879, two million people were forced to leave the Caucasus for Anatolia in terrible conditions, travelling overland and by sea. Many died along the way from disease and starvation. It is estimated that only 1.5 million survived. These forced migrations of Muslim groups from the Caucasus regions carried on throughout the 1880s and 1890s (1881 through 1914) and increasingly included Chechnyan and Daghestani refugees from new areas of Russian conquests in the Caucasus. This last wave of forced migrants at the start of the twentieth century was estimated at another 500,000 people (Karpat 1985:67–70).[6]

The war of 1877–8 also resulted in the new nation-states of Romania and Bulgaria being carved out of the European Ottoman lands. A huge eviction of people ensued called by many Turkish sources simply the 'Big Balkan Migration'; a euphemism used by both historians and journalists of the time to describe these personal tragedies and large-scale dispossessions and evictions (Şimşir 1968; cited in Tekeli 1994). One million to 1.5 million people were driven from the Balkans to the Ottoman heartlands. About 300,000 people were reported to have lost their lives in these forced marches. Most of these migrants were then resettled on agricultural lands in Anatolia. Then between 1893 and 1902, another 72,000 Muslims and Jews were forced out of Bulgaria. Unlike earlier migrants, they were resettled in towns in Thrace as well as in rural areas of central and eastern Anatolia. During the 1912–3 Balkan Wars, a second large wave of Muslims and Jews fled the Balkans for Ottoman lands to the south. This specific further dispossession and involuntary migration was estimated to be of 64,000 persons (Tekeli 1994:210).

---

[6] James Meyer maintains, however, in his recent article 'Immigration, return and the politics of citizenship: Russian Muslims in the Ottoman Empire, 1860–1914', that except for the 1877–8 mass expulsions, return migration of Russian Muslims was also typical and that emigration was not always perceived (at least initially) as a one-way voyage, but rather as a temporary necessity. He maintains that following the massive emigration of Muslims from the Crimea in the mid-nineteenth century, the Russian state began to take measures to prevent such emigration from recurring and sought to convince Muslims to stay in Russia. He documents a certain regularity of cyclical migration for the close of the nineteenth century as Ottoman Muslims of Russian origin sought family reunion or trade (2007).

SURVIVING EXPULSION AND FORCED MIGRATION

The mid-nineteenth century and the early twentieth century were periods of terrible suffering for individuals caught up in the large-scale dispossessions and resettlements of Ottoman subjects. Unlike the expulsions of the Tatars at the end of the eighteenth century, these people had little time to sell off possessions and go into exile with some start-up capital. Instead, they often travelled with little more than the clothing on their backs and whatever they could pile onto their ox-carts. Their survival on the road depended upon the kindness of local people and municipal authorities as they made their way south. There was little if any official government organization to assist them. Many died on the road from starvation or disease. In time, these expulsions were accompanied by the development of special Ottoman organizations to assist and resettle the forced migrants. In the first half of the nineteenth century this was largely limited to some assistance from the municipalities and provincial administrations where they were being directed. As the sheer scale of the migrations grew, the need for a centralized organization also became clear to the Ottoman central authorities.

In 1857 the Ottoman government instituted the Refugee Code (also referred to in some texts as the Immigration Law) whereby 'immigrant' families and groups with only a minimum amount of capital were given plots of state land with exemptions from taxes and conscription obligations for six years if they settled in Rumeli and for twelve years if they settled in Anatolia. They had to agree to cultivate the land and not to sell or leave it for twenty years.[7] These immigrants were also promised freedom of religion, whatever their faith, and were permitted to construct their own places of worship. News of this decree spread widely both along the frontier zone and in Europe. To process the rising requests under this Refugee Code, a Refugee Commission (the Ottoman Commission for the General Administration of Immigration) was set up in 1860 under the Ministry of Trade; in 1861 it became an independent agency (Shaw & Shaw 1977:115). The commission was a belated response to the waves of forced migrants who had already arrived; among them Tatars and Circassians fleeing from the lands conquered by the Russians north and west of the Black Sea as well as thousands of non-Muslim immigrant

---

[7] The Ottoman countryside had been largely depopulated since the seventeenth century as a result of misadministration, war, famine, and the several pandemics of the plague (Shaw & Shaw 1977:115).

farmers and political and intellectual leaders from Hungary, Bohemia, and Poland.[8] The Commission on Immigration also oversaw the management of the rapidly expanding – mainly missionary – international aid coming into the Ottoman Empire. More importantly, it tried to coordinate in-country aid and the feeding, clothing, and sheltering of the forced migrants as they progressed through or near cities, towns, and villages, as well as the actual resettlement process.[9]

In eastern Anatolia and Cilicia as well as in the Syrian provinces, the Ottoman authorities set out greater incentives to lure refugees and immigrants to settle there. In line with the Ottoman Refugee Code/Immigration Law of 1857, these forced migrants-turned-settlers were given 70 donums (about 17 acres) to start farming.[10] They were also provided with seeds, draft animals, and money to buy farm equipment. They were expected to build their own houses – often in the style of their original homeland – or get local people to build for them. These new settlers were prohibited from selling their new land for fifteen years (though that was later dropped to ten years) so as to make sure these rural areas remained inhabited and to give the newcomers time to adapt and acclimatize. These generous settler-grants – both in materials and in land – were eventually cut back as more and more forced migrants appeared in the Ottoman heartland and Syrian provinces. Until 1878, migrants were resettled primarily in rural areas. Only after that year – when productive land or areas not associated with malarial disease became difficult to locate for migrant resettlement – did the Ottomans permit the construction of new migrant districts in the neighbourhoods of towns and cities.

The work of resettling these Muslim refugees was taken on by the Commission for Immigration following certain fundamental principles: create a frontier, resettle in environmentally similar areas, and prevent

---

[8] Also taking advantage of the Ottoman Refugee Code of 1857 were thousands of Cossacks who fled from the Russian army and settled as farmers in Macedonia, Thrace, and western Anatolia. Thousands of Bulgarians also came. Many of them travelled from the Crimea, where they had been forced to resettle by the Russians as replacements for the Tatars whom the Russians had expelled earlier (Shaw & Shaw 1977:116).

[9] It took some time before the receiving provinces of the Ottoman Empire were able to meet the basic needs of these newcomers. In February 1878, for example, the Wali of Damascus, where thousands of Circassians had arrived penniless and hungry, found that he had to levy a forced tax of four piasters per head on the registered male population of the Vilayet in order to feed and cloth these dispossessed migrants (Lewis 1987:99).

[10] Where the land was considered only relatively productive, the settler was given 100 donums (25 acres) and where it was considered poor, they received 130 donums (or 32 acres) (Tekeli 1994:211).

any one group from becoming a majority. Thus, the commission made efforts to settle the dispossessed Muslim population of the Balkans in unoccupied land in Thrace. In this way it could create a buffer zone between the border of the Ottoman Empire and the new Balkan nation-states. Second, it sought to settle these newly evicted peoples on land where the climate was similar to what they had become used to. And third, it sought to create new population mixes so that no one group would become a majority and try to dominate the others. In the case of the Circassians, it seems that their warrior ethos and popularly acknowledged ferocity was such that the Ottomans carried out a different policy and settled them in small discrete groups while dispersing their leaders to different parts of the country. After the Balkan Wars of 1912–3, the surge of multiple dispossession and eviction from the newly resettled areas of Thrace and adjacent areas was so great that the Ottomans created a General Directorate of Tribes and Immigrants in 1914 to deal with these huge numbers (Shaw 1980).[11]

The mass migration of Muslims primarily between the middle and the end of the nineteenth century resulted in the doubling of male Muslims in the Ottoman Empire from 1831 to 1882. As the Ottoman census counted males and not females, we can assume that these figures reflected a larger population rise in general of males and females. Furthermore, and as a result of this rapid doubling in Muslim numbers, the proportion of Muslims to non-Muslims radically changed in the Ottoman Empire. Where Orthodox and Gregorian Christians and Jews had been sizeable minorities particularly in urban settings, their numbers were decreasing and the percentage of the total population they represented was also declining rapidly. Between 1876 and 1895, official statistics compiled by the Commission on Immigration showed that more than one million – largely Muslim – refugees had survived their perilous forced marches and sea voyages and entered the Ottoman Empire.

However, with the deprivation, disease, slaughter, massacres, and further ethnic cleansings that occurred between 1912 and 1922, the period of the Balkan Wars, World War I, and the Turkish national struggle for independence, the population of Anatolia is estimated to have fallen by nearly 30 per cent, from 17.5 million to 12 million. Two-thirds of this loss

---

[11] The wave after wave of Muslim forced migrants from the Caucasus and the European Ottoman provinces in the Balkans resulted in a serious change in the composition of the population of the empire. Where once there had been significant Christian minorities, the ratio of Muslims to Christians was growing significantly. Some historians see this transformation as an element in the policy shift toward a greater Islamic policy, which Abdul Hamid II pursued at the end of the Tanzimat era (Davison 2003).

TABLE 3. *The male population of the Ottoman Empire, 1831–1906*

	Anatolia males			Rumeli males		
Year	Muslims	Non-Muslims	Totals	Muslims	Non-Muslims	Totals
1831	1,988,027	395,849	2,383,876	513,448	856,318	1,369,766
1843	3,101,980	n.a.	n.a.	873,077	n.a.	n.a.
1882	5,379,225	1,262,600	6,641,825	946,659	810,525	1,757,184
1895	6,084,419	1,221,209	7,305,628	1,237,325	1,186,615	2,423,940
1906	6,846,340	1,481,836	8,328,176	1,179,151	1,186,880	2,366,031

Source: Shaw, 1977b:117.

was due to death and one-third to further forced migration and displacement. By contrast, the loss of life in Germany and France during World War I was between 1 and 2 per cent of the population (McCarthy 1983). This high rate of loss of life in Anatolia was due not only to the actual wars being fought but also because several groups there were in conflict with each other fighting for national and personal survival. In some provinces of eastern Anatolia, more than 50 per cent of Muslims and Armenians lost their lives (McCarthy 1983; Shorter 1983).

Once the modern Turkish nation-state had been declared in 1922, further expulsions and dispossession or 'exchange of populations' would take place. Besides the 1.5 million Greeks who had fled Anatolia a few years earlier, 190,000 Orthodox Greeks were formally transferred from Anatolia to Greece by Turkey in exchange for 356,000 Muslim Turks transferred from Greece to Turkey. In the Turkish census of 1927, the composition of the population of Anatolia was shown to have changed considerably from its multi-ethnic mix in the nineteenth century. Turkish identity based on language and the notion of rootedness on Turkish/ Anatolian soil rather than religious identification as Muslims (as in the Ottoman state) was taking hold. Five years after the formal foundation of the state, the 1927 census showed that more than 85 per cent of the population considered Turkish to be their mother tongue – 11.7 million Turkish speakers out of a population of 13.3 million. The remaining population, some of whom declared Turkish as their mother tongue, also identified themselves linguistically as Greek, 120,000; Armenian, 65,000; Hebrew, 69,000; Arabic, 134,000; Kurdish, 1.1 million; Tatar, 11,000; Albanian, 22,000; and Bulgarian, 20,000.

In this new Turkish state occupying the entire Anatolian peninsula, a Turkish nationalism was gaining primacy over religious and ethnic pluralism. The process of integration and 'assimilation' of forced migrants from the former Ottoman Empire followed the course of the struggle to establish a single unified state where religion was secondary to the developing myth of the Turkish nation. The struggle of the last days of the Ottoman Empire had been to create either a unified multi-ethnic Ottoman Muslim state reduced in size from that of empire and respecting the numerous minorities within its borders or deliberately prioritizing Turkish nationalism and advancing the interests of the secularist politicians. Turkish nationalism won out and after the Albanian revolt of 1910–2, even the strongest supporters of a multi-ethnic religious Ottomanism gave up hope that the minorities could be kept within the empire and instead they joined those propounding secular Turkish nationalism (Shaw & Shaw 1977:289). A myth of origin, of Turkishness preempted and prioritized all other myths of origin. Turkish language was made compulsory. Perhaps in an effort to signify a fresh start as a modern nation, the new state turned from using Arabic script to using Roman script to write the Turkish language. Anatolia became synonymous with the Turkish modern state. The Ottoman Empire was dead and Turkey was not a 'phoenix rising from its ashes', but rather a new, modern secular state, with little to connect it to the old Ottoman entity. All its new immigrants and refugees were to become Turkish, in language, culture, and thought.

Caucasian settlement in the Balkans

The Circassians, Chechnyans, Daghestani, Abkhazi, Abaza, and other smaller groups such as the Laz, the Inguseti, and the Ossetians from the Causasus (who were expelled from their homelands as a result of military defeats between 1860 and 1914) made up the largest European or Eurasian forced migrant group to enter the Syrian provinces of the Ottoman Empire Middle East in modern times.[12] The first Circassian groups were resettled on the other side of the Black Sea in about 1860 following the Russians' defeat of Shaykh Shamil and his Chechnyan and Daghestani militias in the eastern Caucasus. Having routed this

---

[12] Three to four thousand Algerians arrived with Abdul-Qader al-Jaza'iri in the 1850s and settled in and around Damascus, Safad, and Hauran. In 1884, a group of Muslims from Bosnia and Herzegovina settled on the site of Caesarea on the coast of Palestine. A further 3,000 Cretan Muslims arrived after the civil conflict in Crete in 1896–8. A village was built for them by the Ottoman Sultan Abdul Hamid II on the coast north of Tripoli, Hamidiyah. Those who went to Damascus were settled in a specially built compound in the Muhajiriin district of Mount Kasoun above the city.

population, the Russians moved west and eliminated Circassian resistance in the mountains above the Black Sea, pushing out Circassian, Abkhazi, and Abaza peoples. By 1864, the Russians had also taken the last stronghold of the Ubikh people and driven them to the coast where they had to be evacuated by Ottoman forces and brought to safety in Ottoman lands.[13] These Circassians were 'literally stuffed into boats at Russian-controlled ports. They were given neither assistance nor supplies and at the first port of call, Trabzon, they died in great numbers of smallpox, typhus and scurvy. In the winter of 1863, twenty to fifty Circassians were dying each day in Trabzon. By the worst days of the next spring, 500 a day were dying; and 30,000 may have died at Trabzon alone. Those who landed at other ports, such as Samsun and Sinop shared a similar mortality. At the height of the immigration, 50 refugees a day were dying at Samsum' (McCarthy 1995:36). Over the next few years, hundreds of thousands of Caucasian peoples were forced from their homes and put on ships to Ottoman territory or pushed onto oxcarts to travel overland into exile. The figures are disputed, but it is generally accepted that as many as half of those who were forced from their homes in the Caucasus died on the journey or shortly thereafter.

At first, the Ottoman authorities welcomed these Caucasus Muslim peoples as potential settlers and soldiers.[14] Within fifteen years, however, nearly all of these Caucasian settlers were expelled once again. The role of Circassian soldiers and irregulars in what the European press had labelled as the 'Bulgarian Atrocities' aroused widespread condemnation of this group among European diplomats and the public at large. At the Conference of the Powers in Constantinople to settle the successful Ottoman suppression of the Bulgarian Uprising – in which Circassian soldiers and militias fighting with the Ottoman army were reported to have massacred numerous Bulgarian civilians – the Russians insisted all Circassians should be expelled. The Russians considered them too dangerous and unreliable a community to live along a sensitive border. The other European representatives agreed and formally asked the Ottoman government that 'the colonization of Circassians in European Turkey shall be absolutely forbidden and those already established in Rumelia shall be sent back as far as practicable to the

---

[13] See Allen and Muratoff (1953).

[14] The men of the Caucasus had long been associated with military prowess, perhaps in acknowledgement of their part in the Mamluk dynasties, especially in Egypt. Their women were regularly sold or taken into the households of the ruling Ottoman sultan (Shami 2000:194).

Musulman Asiatic provinces of the Ottoman Empire'[15] (Lewis 1987:96). Although the Ottoman authorities rejected this proposal, the Circassians were in fact expelled from Bulgaria and Eastern Rumelia in the following year at the close of the Russian–Ottoman War of 1877–8 when Russia defeated the Ottomans and occupied much of the region. Most of these Circassians took refuge in Thrace or Macedonia that winter, but for the Ottoman authorities, they were too many to be permitted to settle permanently. The Ottomans undertook their transportation to Anatolia and Syria from the ports of Salonika, Istanbul, and Kavalla in February 1878. A few travelled overland on ox-carts.[16]

Secondary forced migration into Anatolia and the southern Ottoman provinces

Between February and August 1878, 1,000 Circassians landed by ship at Beirut and were sent to Damascus to set up villages in the *Ghouta* (orchards) surrounding the city. Another 2,000 landed at Tripoli and headed out to Homs; 1,500 landed at Acre and were sent to Nabulus. In March of that year, 1,300 came from Salonika to Latakiyyah, and a further 13,000 arrived at Tripoli. The numbers were growing and the capacity of the provincial authorities to assist and absorb the refugees was reducing. Norman Lewis recounts the fate of the Austrian Lloyd steamer *Sphinx,* which set out from Kavalla for Latakiyyah with 3,000 Circassians but was forced by storm to divert to Famagusta in Cyprus. Forty people were washed overboard and drowned and a fire broke out on board, killing another five hundred. The numbers of refugees arriving by ship continued, with another five hundred reaching Tripoli, 1,200 at Acre in July, and 1,200 at Beirut in August (Lewis 1987:97).[17] In the course of

---

[15] See Lewis (1987:96; citing P.P. 1877). The exclusion of Circassians from eastern Rumelia was formalized by the terms of the Treaty of Berlin, which prohibited the employment of Circassian irregular troops and Circassian colonization in the province.

[16] The forced migrants travelling from Rumelia brought with them to Anatolia an advanced agricultural technology and new products such as the potato and the horse-drawn cart. The Circassians contributed to the development of animal husbandry and the production of meat and milk. The Tatars from the Crimea played a role in improving wheat production. These Tatars had been able to sell off their lands before being moved out and arrived with some accumulated capital to start their new lives. Those dispossessed in and after 1878, particularly the Circassians, had no time to dispose of their property and generally had to travel with little if any possessions (Tekeli 1994:213).

[17] Most of the details regarding the arrival of Circassian refugees were drawn from reports of British consuls or consular officials in Syria and in Cyprus (FO 78/2847 1878; FO 78/2848 1878; FO 195/1201 1878; FO 195/1202 1878). Also see Karpat (1979:19–21).

this one year, 25,000 Circassians arrived in southern Syria and between 10,000 and 15,000 came into the province of Aleppo (Karpat 1979:19).

For the most part, Ottoman government officials in the provinces were unprepared for the arrival of so many refugees over such a short period of time. Except for the Tatar immigrants, who largely arrived with money and baggage due to the more controlled manner of their dispossession, most of these waves of forced migrants had nothing but the clothes they wore and, occasionally, small arms. They all needed food, accommodation, and help in making a living. The authorities in the ports where many of these refugees first arrived made what arrangements they could to provide temporary accommodation and food. Often, small tax levies were raised in the towns and cities where their numbers were large, in order to provide them with funds. But not all these new immigrants received help. Some were reported to have resorted to robbery, banditry, and even the sale of their children. Many also became ill; in March 1878, for example, smallpox reportedly swept through the mosques and *madrasah*s of Damascus where many of these newly arrived forced migrants had taken shelter.

The problem was not one of antipathy but rather of logistics. The cities could not cope with these large surges of forced migrants and needed to move them out and into the countryside where they could be settled as farmers and become self-sufficient. One example of this logistical nightmare for the provincial authorities was the planned settlement of about 10,000 Circassians in the district of Hama. Although the government did make some help available, the inhabitants of Hama themselves donated 6,000 kilogrammes of wheat and 4,000 kilogrammes of barley for the first sowing of these new farmers. Even with these private donations, however, there was not enough assistance, and some 3,000 Circassians returned to the port of Tripoli, where they created a disturbance, demanding passage back to Istanbul. Eventually the situation improved, logistics began to work more smoothly, and the newcomers were sent to settle in districts that were near or on the frontier of settlements where there was also plenty of uncultivated land.

Some scholars have argued that the Ottoman government was actually quite cautious in its Circassian resettlement plans, having learned some hard lessons from the Balkan experience. For the Ottomans, the Circassians were potentially dangerous because of their deep commitment and loyalty to their tribal chiefs – even to the extent of disregarding the authority of the central government. Consequently the Ottoman government decided to take care to disperse the larger Circassian tribes by settling them in different areas and placing their traditional leadership elsewhere. Many community and tribal leaders were given army positions, while wealthy and notable families were allowed to settle in cities rather than the rural farming settlements. Thus divided, the Circassians were prevented from reorganizing into armed bands and attacking the indigenous populations as they had done occasionally while settled in the Balkans and Anatolia (Karpat 1979:18).

Many scholars regarded these frontier settlements of the Caucasian forced migrants as part of a specific reclamation policy of the Ottoman authorities. After centuries of neglect, the Ottomans were slowly reclaiming the southern provinces and local governance was giving way to a more centralized approach to rule (Rogan 1999). This was reflected in the development of a modern infrastructure with the construction of roads, the establishment of telegraph lines from Damascus through the length of Jordan to the Hijaz, the building of the Hijaz railway connecting the southern provinces with Damascus and Anatolia, and cadastral land surveys and land registration establishing boundaries and ownership.[18] The sponsored settlements of the new Circassian and Chechnyan immigrants along the centuries-old contested *Ma'moura* (cultivated land) and *Badia* (semi-desert grazing land) was part of the policy of taking back control of these regions. When central government was strong, the Ma'moura was pushed out into the Badia. When it was weak, the Badia was pushed into previously cultivated land by the strong nomadic pastoral tribes (Chatty 1986). These new settler communities ran in a line from Aleppo to Amman and further south to Ma'an and became the focus of contestation for control between the Bedouin pastoralists and the new farmers.

As Lewis points out, it was their location in frontier districts rather than the actual number of settlers or the amount of land they cultivated which made the Circassian settlements historically significant (Lewis 1987:100). Few Circassian settlers simply 'adopted the hoe' and got on with farming. Many had to learn to become farmers, having come from pastoral traditions. But it was their readiness and willingness to protect themselves and their families from local hostilities and marauding Bedouin which drew attention to them. The Circassians were very well fitted out for the role of

---

[18] The Hijaz Railway was begun at Damascus in 1900 and was ostensibly presented as a religious project to cut down the four-month-long pilgrimage journey to a matter of days. By 1908 it reached Madinah in the Hijaz. In its time it was recognized as a tremendous accomplishment. It was built to a very high standard at very low costs in one of the fastest such projects ever completed in the Ottoman Empire. It was built faster and for less money than any other railroad ever built (Rogan 1999:66).

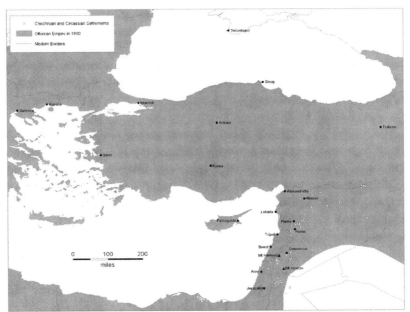

MAP 4. Circassian and Chechnyan Settlements in Southern Ottoman Provinces (adapted from N. Lewis 1987)

frontier settlers. They were able and willing to stand up to the Bedouin and the local peasantry who often held counterclaims to the land. In numerous recorded disputes, the Circassians were generally the victors, partly because they were impressive fighters, but also because the Ottoman authorities generally took their side. Again according to Lewis, the Ottoman authorities deliberately directed some Circassian settlers to areas that were particularly turbulent so that they could help subdue local feuds. The government settlements of Circassians on the Jaulan Heights in areas near the Druze settlements of Mount Hauran and Mount Hermon are one such example.[19] The Druze, a semi-autonomous, ethno-religious community originally settled in southern Lebanon and the hill areas of Aleppo, had come into conflict with the Christian Maronites of Mount Lebanon in the 1860s. The latter, with backing from the French and other European powers, established their hegemony over the mountain (formerly it was known as Jebel al-Druze). Many Druze left and

---

[19] The Druze originated from a little known Ismaili religious and philosophical movement in the tenth century under the reign of al-Hakim (996–1021) in Egypt. It is a blend of Islamic monotheism with Greek and Hindu philosophy.

established new settlements in the Hauran as well as around Mount Hermon. The area, however, was restive, and the Ottoman policy of settling Circassians in between two major Druze settlements was an effort to control the latter. Many of the Circassian men in these settler groups joined the Ottoman Army or the mounted rural gendarmes. Those who didn't were occasionally called up anyway to quell sporadic disturbances involving the Druze or local Bedouin tribes.

After this wave of migrants at the end of the 1870s, people from the Caucasus continued to arrive. For some it was a matter of finding Russian rule unacceptable, or an unwillingness to let their young men serve as conscripts in the Russian army or to pay tax in lieu. The Ottoman government also encouraged them to emigrate. The Ottoman sultan, Abdul Hamid, clearly saw these new immigrants as potential settlers and soldiers. He also took a personal interest in their affairs and, after 1887, reportedly instructed provincial government officials to do whatever they could to help expedite their settlement. For example, in 1887, he agreed to the creation of a special settlement of Caucasian forced migrants (Abaza) on his own lands, *Marj al-Sultan*, in the Ghouta surrounding Damascus.[20] This personal property, which had been used to graze his own horses, was then partially set aside and divided up among 150 forced migrant families. They received tools, seeds, and labour to build their new village, in the style to which they had been accustomed back in their old homeland.

Caucasian immigrants continued to arrive in the region. In 1882, 100 Circassian families arrived in Damascus overland via Anatolia. A number of them were immediately given positions as soldiers and the others were sent on to join their fellow Circassians in Qunaytrah on the Jaulan Heights. In 1900 another group of 150 families reached Damascus. Half of these were sent on to Qunaytrah and the rest to Zarqa' further south to work on the Hijaz railway then under construction. In 1903, 130 Tatar families arrived at Alexandretta from the Crimea, followed by another 100 Tatar families in the next year. Both groups were noted to have travelled with money and baggage and appeared to be 'peaceable and industrious'.

In 1905, a Russian ship landed at Alexandretta from Sebastapol with 364 families (1,454 individuals): Kabarday from villages in the north central Caucasus. They said they had left Russia to prevent the conscription of their men into the Russian army. They were not happy with the

[20] *Marj al-Sultan* means the 'meadow or grazing fields of the sultan'.

Russian government's forcing them to learn Russian and they feared the government might try to compel them to convert to Christianity (Lewis 1987:98). Eventually, this group settled near Aleppo and Raqqah in Syria.

From a reading of British Embassy dispatches and reports in 1905 and 1906, Lewis has summarized the numbers of Circassian families in the Syrian provinces as 1,949 families settled in Qunaytrah, on the Jaulan Heights, another 2,250 in Transjordan, and 670 families near Homs (1987:101–102). About 550 families lived in the vilayet of Beirut, with a total for both the Beirut and Damascus vilayets estimated at 25,000. However, another embassy report put these figures at more than 30,500 (FO 424/210 1906a). What is striking is that between the first great wave of deportees and involuntary migrants entering the region between the 1860s and 1890s and 1906, when these reports were made, there had been little change in population numbers. This may have been due to either a very high mortality rate among these forced migrants in the first few decades after their arrival or high departure rates – the figures of which are not available – or even perhaps the unreliability of all these figures. However, what is noticeable is the absence of population growth in most of the villages. This may have been because of low resistance to malaria, which they would have come across for the first time, as well as other endemic and epidemic diseases. This static, or at best very slow population growth might account for why the Circassians, once established in their settlements, did not try to expand the area of cultivation or occupancy after World War I.

CAUCASIAN FORCED MIGRANTS TURN SETTLERS IN THE SYRIAN PROVINCES

One of the first and largest groups of Caucasian exiles to reach the Syrian provinces in the 1860s was a group of 5,000 Chechnyans who settled at Ra's al 'Ayn on the River Khabur. These settlers arrived in one large group following the Russians' defeat and capture of Shaykh Shamil in the Caucasus in 1859. Lewis reports that this group was aware of the Ottoman Refugee Code and interpreted it to mean that they could take what land they wanted. Without any instructions from Ottoman authorities (or perhaps because no documentation has been discovered), this group chose to settle in an area of massive springs next to the River Khabur. It was not an empty or abandoned area; the local farmers and shepherds were not happy with this invasion into their midst. The nomadic pastoral sheep-raising Bedouin tribes in the area were also not consulted and this resulted in numerous disputes and violent raids and counterraids between the Chechnyan settlers and the Bedouin. The Chechnyans were very aggressive and often took the offensive, defeating even the noble camel-raising Shammar Bedouin in raid after raid. Inevitably they were feared both by the local peasantry as well as the Bedouin and came to constitute a settlement whose right to remain there was unchallenged.

As a community, however, the Chechnyans initially failed to thrive in their new settlements. Their population numbers did not appear to rise over the ensuing decades. It is most likely that the fertile sites on the Khabur River where they built their new villages were also highly malarial, resulting in high mortality rates. Smallpox, cholera, and other diseases also killed the settlers. What saved the settlements from collapse was that other Chechnyans, forced out of their homelands, arrived at Ra's Al 'Ayn in the 1870s and 1880s helping to replenish population numbers. It was reported that in 1917–8, the Chechnyan settlement was well established and settlers energetically harassed the columns of deported Armenians passing by during their march south. The same report indicated that, as a result of this interaction, Chechnyan settlers later experienced an epidemic of typhus carried by the Armenian deportees. The Chechnyans, the report continued, were 'cruelly decimated' by the disease.[21] (Lewis 1987).

Forty years after the Chechnyans settled at Ra's al 'Ayn, a Circassian group arrived at Raqqah on the Euphrates River. Forty-seven Kabarday families, part of a larger group who had arrived by ship to Alexandretta in 1905, made their way to Raqqah under very different conditions from the Chechnyans before them. The Kabarday had left Russia largely of their own accord, fleeing what they believed were government efforts to make them renounce their Muslim faith and convert to Russian Orthodox Christianity. Their resettlement along the Euphrates River was organized and planned by Ottoman provincial authorities. It was originally determined to settle the Kabarday in Raqqah, Khanasir, and Manbiju along the middle Euphrates on the Aleppo–Baghdad trade route and thus create a string of Circassian villages in the area around Raqqah from whom a gendarmerie could be recruited.[22] The Kabarday settlement at Raqqah was built just west of the Arab town. The provincial

---

[21] Lewis is quoting from Stewart (FO 195/1368 1881).
[22] A few Chechnyans from Ra's al 'Ayn were already serving as gendarmes before the Kabarday arrived.

government, along with some local contributions, was able to provide each family with land, a two-room building, a stable and yard, a pair of oxen, a plough, and five sacks of seed grain. Consular reports from Aleppo also reported that this group's leader, Talustan Anzor, came to be highly respected as a mediator and conciliator in the Raqqah district. His contribution to the community was later recognized by the provincial government with the construction of a stone built house, the first one in Raqqah (Lewis 1987:104).

Damascus district settlements

With the large influx of Circassian refugees passing through Damascus from the port of Beirut, a number of Circassian settlements are known to have been established both to the north around Homs as well as nearby in the vicinity of Damascus. One such settlement was in Dumayr, a small village just north of Damascus, but it appears to have failed as no records exist of it today. Marj al-Sultan, however, in the fertile orchards ringing the city was a well-organized and carefully planned settlement which quickly took root and thrived. In later years, as forced migrant numbers dwindled to more manageable size and as the Ottomans began to allow settlement in the cities, a number of Circassian exiles settled in the *Muhajiriin* and *Diwaniyyah* districts of the city.[23]

In 1878, 25 Circassian families, who were forced to emigrate, arrived in Marj al-Sultan. They had come from Turkey and before that they had been in Bulgaria, in the Balkans. Actually we have gone through 5 forced migrations. In 1864 it was to the Balkans (from the Caucasus). Then after the Berlin Agreement of 1878 it was to Turkey from the Balkans. Some came by land and others through Greece, Salonika and Cyprus, you know the story of the Sphinx ship, to the Syrian coast. The 25 families who settled in Marj al-Sultan came to Damascus by land – through Aleppo, Homs and so on. They were mainly Shabzugh and Abzakh tribes. At the time, Madhat Basha was the Governor of Damascus. His wife was a Circassian and he liked the Circassians. He met with those who were on their way to Al Marj al-Sultan and the Jaulan and suggested that they stay closer to Damascus in a place called Mezzeh. At that time Mezzeh was an unpopulated land devoted to cactus fields. The Circassians refused, as they were afraid that they would become assimilated if they lived so close to the city. Some went on to the

---

[23] The Diwaniyyah district of Damascus became the refuge point for the Circassians fleeing their villages and towns in the Jaulan Heights as a result of the 6 June 1967 War. Previously, Diwaniyyah had been settled mainly by Kosovar and Albanian refugees in the twentieth century.

Jaulan where the geographic nature of the place was very close to that of their homeland; heavy rain, snow, woods and mountains. Others came here to al-Marj. It was springtime. In spring this area used to be extremely beautiful with plenty of water, trees and grass. It was the private property of the sultan himself. In the spring and fall, Sultan Abdul Hamid had his 3,000 (mainly military) horses grazing in this area.

The Ottoman government gave each family two cows, two oxen, poultry, food supplies and tents. Originally they chose to establish their town along the southeastern area. But when they started digging, they discovered that this place was an old Roman cemetery and so they had to move west. They started to build their small homes, using unburned bricks [adobe] and pressed wet soil. The roofs were made of poplar trees, which were plentiful in the area. There was a very clear style. No house was to be built directly on the side of the street. They were all set back. After building the houses they set out to build the mosque in the next year, in 1879, in the Shabzugh quarter. All the houses were of one story. Only three houses were two-stories. The second story in these houses had only one room and that was used by the head of the tribe as a guest area. The reason that all the houses were built as one story was so as to provide privacy for the women of the house. (Adel 2006)

As with so many planned Circassian settlements, they were located on fault lines or frontiers of conflict. The villages in the Ghouta, the important agricultural artery for the city, had long been harassed by Bedouin, particularly the powerful Aneza tribes who sought to exact *khuwah* (tribute) from the local farmers. Khuwah payment to the Bedouin diminished what could be collected by the government in taxes. The Circassian settlers in the Ghouta quickly established their strength and unwillingness to pay tribute to the Bedouin. They did not need Bedouin protection, as they were quite able to protect themselves. In due course they entered into agreements with the Bedouin leadership to work together for the mutual benefit of both communities. Sometimes, however, these agreements broke down.

The last big clash of the Circassians in Marj al-Sultan with the Bedouin was in 1954. They were about 2,000 Bedouins. The village had only 350 people including men, women, and children. What made up for the difference in number was that most of the people in the village were well trained in using arms. Previously, the village was attacked during the Syrian Revolution [1926–1027]. (Adel 2006)

Marj al-Sultan thrived as a village and rapidly became a focal point for Circassians on their way to settlements in the south in the Jaulan and Transjordan or later for those passing through for trade and other business in Damascus, Homs, or Aleppo. For the next generation, seeking higher education in Damascus was important, but the pull to remain in Marj al-Sultan was strong. Although the second generation replaced Turkish with Arabic as the language with which to address officialdom, the Circassian language, Cherkessi, remained the language spoken at home.

Adel continued to describe the village economy and its relationship with the local Bedouin:

The life of the village depended largely on local sources and activities: farming and raising cattle and poultry. This village was known for raising buffaloes. We had many swamps because during winter, low land got filled with rainwater. That was how swamps were formed and how malaria became permanent resident as well. The animals we had included cows, buffaloes, horses and donkeys. There were no sheep at all. I remember taking the cows to graze although that job was usually done by a Bedouin who worked for us. That Bedouin could speak Cherkessi as well as I do. His family still lives in the village. His children and even his grandchildren can speak Cherkessi. They have grown up among the Cherkess and adopted Cherkessi customs and traditions.

Jaulan Heights settlements

It appears that Qunaytrah had been an abandoned settlement for much of the eighteenth and nineteenth centuries. Into that void came the Bedouin who made use of the area as important pastureland. The Al-Fadl, the Nu'am, and numerous Turcoman nomadic pastoral tribes set out to claim the area as belonging to their 'traditional tribal territory'. Rough and rocky, it was prime grazing land for sheep, though it had previously been used for agriculture.

The first Circassian settlers arrived at Qunaytrah in 1873, most probably from Sivas in Anatolia. They came with their oxcarts and animals and seem to have held back from pursuing any cultivation for about five years. Then in 1878, another 2,000 Circassians arrived from Bulgaria and the community started trying to cultivate the land. These newcomers, as well as the original settlers, were now given title to between 70–130 donums of land depending upon their family size. By this time, Qunaytrah was a village/town of 100 houses and there were about seven other villages nearby (Oliphant 1880:44). Ten years later, Qunaytrah had grown to a town of 260 buildings with a population of approximately 1,300 Circassians and a few Arab government offices and soldiers. One visitor to the Jaulan in 1885, G. Schumacher, described the Circassians he came across: 'As a consequence of the Russo-Turkish War, they wandered out of Bulgaria, and in the spring, 1878, in a starving and pitiful condition reached 'Akka ... By indomitable industry and solid perseverance they soon attained a certain degree of prosperity, built villages, cultivated fields, bred cattle, dried grass for the winter and drove the Bedawin out of their neighbourhood' (Schumacher 1888:57). He continued to describe these new settlements:

It does one's eyes good, after having seen so many devastated places, to arrive at a flourishing, evenly-constructed, clean village, whose inhabitants, with their Kaimakam (magistrate), an energetic, industrious old Turk, immigrated from the neighbourhood of the chief Turkish town, have more feeling for European systems than the citizens of many towns in this country ... Looking too at the towering hay-cocks, the swift rattling Circassian carts, the preparation of dried bricks from the fine earth of the neighbourhood, and above all the cleanliness of the streets, one asks involuntarily, 'Am I in the Jaulan?' (Schumacher 1888:208)

Another European visitor described the Circassians he came across as follows:

In many respects they are very different from the Arabs; in their industry, their settled homes, their power of initiation, their habits. They have superior agricultural instruments; they do not look upon the camel and the ass as the sole possible means of transportation; but, alone in Syria, until the recent establishment of Jewish and German colonies, employ carts ... Many speak Turkish fluently, the elder ones some Russian, most a little Arabic with a bad accent, but their ordinary tongue continues to be Circassian. The Turkish Government has permitted them to re-populate various ruined towns for a given period, without paying any taxes. Whereas the fellahin fear to attract attention by successful crops of fruit or grain, lest they be called upon to feed the Bedu and the tax gatherer, the Circassians fear no one, and at present pay no taxes. Hence, as well as from superior capacity and industry, they effect, as no fellah may venture to do, improvements of a kind which are permanent; they make walls and roads, they devise systems of irrigation, they plant hedges and trees. (Freer 1905)

The relations with the surrounding pastoral tribes were uneasy at first, particularly with the highly respected Al-Fadl, who stood to lose important pasturelands to Circassian agriculture. This tribe, with deep historical roots in Syria, had about 320 tents as well as winter villages in the area at the time of Schumacher's visit. He reported that the Al-Fadl deeply resented the Circassians. Both the Al-Fadl and the Circassians had battled each other, with the Emir Shaykh Shedadi Al-Fadl having died in one battle with Circassians (Schumacher 1888:87). Eventually, the early skirmishes and posturing for control gave way to a modus vivendi and reports in the late 1870s by Oliphant and other travellers indicated that a *majlis* (in this sense, a consultative council) run by the *Kaimakam* of Qunaytrah also included representatives of the Al-Fadl, the Na'im, the Turcoman, and the Druze to discuss matters related to the smooth functioning of the villages, as well as the use of the land for agriculture and for pasture.[24]

The Circassians on the Jaulan were drawn into much more serious and sustained conflict with the Druze than they had experienced with the Al-Fadl. As mentioned earlier, some historians claim that the Ottoman authorities purposefully selected the Jaulan as a settlement site for the Circassian forced migrants because they needed a militarily strong potential force in strategic positions between the Druze of the villages around Mount Hermon and the Jebel Druze. Jaulan was in just the right place. British Embassy reports also suggest that in 1883 the Wali of Damascus wanted to settle some Circassians in the southern Beqaa Valley [of contemporary Lebanon] in order to place a wedge between the Druze of Lebanon coming to the aid of those in Mount Hermon and the Jebel Druze in Syria. Although this planned settlement did not come about, Circassian cavalry was used by the Ottomans against the Druze causing resentment and distress for years to come (FO 195/1886 1883; FO 195/1932 1895–6; and also Schumacher 1888:57, 87).

My mother was born in Turkey in 1870 at the time of the war against the Russians. She was carried here in the saddlebags of our grandfather's horse. They came to Jaulan and settled in one of the 12 Circassian villages. Ours was the closest to Qunaytrah. Our house was the best, our villages were the best. Even the French who were familiar with the whole area admitted that ours were the best villages. All the houses had red tiles for roofs. We lived with my parents and grandparents. We had oil lamps and we used wood for heating. We had forests and we used to bring the wood from there to burn for heating. Until 1947 we had no electricity. We had an Arab school and a Circassian school, but that was closed down in 1936. Some families, mainly who supported the Circassian school, wanted to return to Circassia but others wanted to remain. We learned Arabic in school and spoke Circassian at home. When I finished school, I worked on the land for four years and then I joined the army. It was the time of the French Mandate. (Abdul-Salam 2005)

For the next fifty years these Circassian villages thrived. The Circassians prospered as farmers, army officers, and civil servants. The second and third generations had become well-educated – in Arabic and their local Circassian language – loyal citizens of the country. For many it was their third homeland, having been removed from the Caucasus then sent to the

---

[24] The Al-Fadl, one of the oldest sheep-raising Bedouin tribes in Syria with a pedigree going back centuries, was to become a refugee tribe along with the Circassians after the 6 June 1967 War. Many members of the tribe made their way to Lebanon, where they occupied the Beqaa Valley and anti-Lebanon mountains and some were finally granted citizenship rights in 1994.

Balkans before being forced out again and sent to the Jaulan where they set out new roots. In June 1967, the Circassians were again violently dispossessed of their lands, most fleeing and taking refugee in Marj al-Sultan but also in Damascus itself, accepting any shelter they could find.

Then just when we started to feel at home [in the Jaulan], we were driven out. I came [to Damascus] with my wife and children except for one who went missing in the fighting [The June 1967 War]. Three of my sons were already in Damascus. Two in the armed forces and one was studying. As I was a civil servant I was not eligible for any assistance. We stayed in an apartment of three rooms – three families in three rooms: my son who was a student in the Faculty of Mechanical Engineering, Mounir who is now a retired general and Talaat who is in America. The three of them were living in one room and the families of friends of our sons in other two rooms. So instead of living comfortably in my fine house with a garden full of flowers in Qunaytrah, here we were 3 families in a cellar. I became very frustrated and at a complete loss. I became absent- minded and started to wander about. Finally we were allowed to stay in an empty apartment of a Circassian going to America for two years. This was the chance we needed to regroup and set about becoming self-sufficient once again. (Abdul-Salam 2005)

Dispossessed migrants from the Balkans and Anatolia continued to arrive in Syria throughout the early decades of the twentieth century. One small community of Balkan refugees slowly grew on the outskirts of Damascus, settling in the orchards on the edges of the city. Here they were initially fed by the local community and then informally allowed to farm small patches of land in these orchards to grow vegetables and fruit. They had no title to the land, but over time their settlement was not challenged by the state and thus attracted other Balkan migrants. These migrants were made up mainly of Kosovar and Albanian refugees. They were fleeing the unrest during and following the Balkan Wars of 1912–3 as well as what they perceived to be a threat to their freedom of worship as Muslims in the new nation-states being created in the Balkans. As one elderly resident of this 'Arnaouti' community in the Diwaniyyah district of Damascus recalled:

My father was born in Kosovo in 1894. He came to Damascus in 1914. He knew no Arabic, only Turkish, but he was able to get a job on the Hijaz railway. He started as a labourer, then a locomotive driver and ended as an inspector of boilers. He died in 1996, without mastering Arabic. He was 102 years old when he died. My father got married only to settle down. He married without being able to speak Arabic. He married a woman from Damascus, the daughter of a pious shaykh. His wife was an Arab woman who could not speak Albanian. He built the house we are sitting in by his own hands, room by room; first one room, then another, then another. When we children were born we learned to speak

Arabic and Albanian to both our parents. When I finished my five years of schooling I, too, joined the railway and have worked there all my life. I am a Syrian, but not an Arab. I prefer to be known as Syrian 'Arnaouti' because .... [Barakat requests for the rest of the sentence to be off the record ']. The problem for me is that I was born here and grew up here and have memories here. I love Damascus. When you ask about my homeland, I cannot abandon Syria as a homeland. But there was also another homeland, that of my father's. It is not the same for the Palestinians or Armenians. Our fathers came here to have the freedom to practise their religion [Islam]. But they lost what they had had before [their homeland]. We fight to live here in dignity. (Barakat 2005)

Southern Syrian provinces

For most of the nineteenth century, Transjordan was terra incognita to Europeans and Ottomans (Rogan 1999). It had been left for nearly two centuries to local rulers to struggle to control – both Bedouin and settled farmers. Its Ottoman 'capital' was Salt – the most developed urban presence in Transjordan – a town more closely drawn to Nabulus as its trading partner than Jerusalem and Damascus. At the southernmost part of the Ottoman province of Damascus was the district of Ma'an where Syria converged with Egypt and the Hijaz. Ma'an was a creation of the pilgrimage caravan and kept alive by the trade of pilgrims coming and going to Mecca. Much of its provisions were imported from Hebron and Gaza to resell to the pilgrims.[25] For the Ottoman government, it was a significant settlement in the region as it contributed to ensuring safe passage of the annual pilgrimage caravan from Damascus to the holy cities of Mecca and Madinah. The caravan had to cross the length of Transjordan and was provisioned by a chain of fortresses at one-day march intervals. Powerful Bedouin tribes in the area were paid by the government in Damascus to protect the caravan as well as supply it with camels, and provisions.

   The first permanent settlement in the southern Syrian provinces, Transjordan, appeared in Amman in 1878. Up until that point, there was

---

[25] In the mid-nineteenth century Ma'an had a population of about two hundred households as well as a smaller village made up of twenty Syrian families lying just to the northeast. This village known as al-Shamiyyah was described by the Finnish traveller George Wallin in 1845 as being in every way, from mud-brick houses, to diet, customs, methods of cultivation, and general way of life of its inhabitants, reminiscent of Syria in the desert environment of Ma'an. What this observation suggests, and there are no Ottoman records to fill-out the picture, is that at some point – perhaps several decades earlier – a group of Syrian villagers were expelled or thrown out of their own community as a result of some internal dispute and migrated out to the peripheral lands of the southern Ottoman provinces to make a new life.

no permanent settlement in Amman, the site of the ancient Roman city of Philadelphia. Some of the ancient buildings, such as the amphitheatre, provided occasional temporary shelter for the few farmers from the Ottoman capital of Salt who regularly cultivated patches of land in the area around Amman. This largely abandoned site was important, however, to Bedouin tribes both for its pasture and its good access to water. The Bani Sakhr tribe considered this area part of its traditional *dar* [homeland].

One of the first groups of Circassians to arrive in Amman consisted of survivors of the Sphinx boat, which had lost five hundred people through drowning and fire in 1878. These were Shabsugh families who made their way to Amman via Acre and Nabulus. As earlier described by Oliphant, some of this group took shelter in the archaeological ruins of the Roman amphitheatre, until their numbers had grown sufficiently with new arrivals and they could work collectively to construct their own shelters. In the following year, a second Circassian settlement was started in Wadi al-Sir. One visitor to the area commented that this early group had:

... the listless and dispirited look of exiles who find it impossible to take root in the uninviting district to which they have been sent. Hated by Arab and Fellah, despoiled of money and possessions, and having seen many of their bravest fall or die of starvation, they seem to have no more courage left, and will probably die out by degrees or become scattered among the indigenous populations. (Condor 1892:52–53; quoted in Lewis 1987:107)

Ten years later, another visitor to Amman was to write about how much the situation had changed and how large and industrious this settler group, now of nearly 1,000, had become – attesting to the settler spirit and hard work which these Circassians exhibited. They were described by various subsequent travellers as engaged in all kinds of activities – farming, tree-cutting, trading, and transporting wheat and other farm products in their archetypical oxcarts to markets in Jerusalem. Unlike their Arab neighbours, they had little to fear in showing off their successes. Their energy and successful entrepreneurship would not attract the attention of the Ottoman tax collector, as they were exempt for a number of years. Thus, they had no concerns about making improvements to their farms, building walls, and planting trees and hedges, which normally would have exposed and made them liable to greater government taxation. Furthermore, by the end of the 1890s the Circassians of Amman had entered into alliances with the major Bedouin tribe in the area, the Bani Sakhr. Both parties agreed to support each other in case of conflict with outside parties. The Circassians were able and willing to defend themselves against any perceived injustices and regularly repulsed Bedouin incursions from other tribes (Rogan 1999).

Between 1878 and 1884, three Circassian villages were established in Wadi al-Sir, Balqa', and Jerash. Then, between 1901 and 1906, five more Circassian and Chechnyan villages were founded in Na'ur, Zarqa', Sukhnah, Rusafah, and Suwalih. These Circassians were isolated at the beginning, as the nearest Circassian colony was in Qunaytrah in the Jaulan, which had been formally settled by government order on land expropriated three decades earlier. The new settlers in Amman and its satellite villages refused to pay khuwah (protection money) to the local Bedouin. And as new settlers, they were also exempt from paying Ottoman taxes for a period of 10–15 years under the 1859 Refugee Code. For many of the local peoples, these new settlers were seen as Ottoman beneficiaries as well as agents and they inspired both fear and loathing in the early years of their settlement. The readiness with which the Circassians enlisted in the Ottoman army or local gendarmerie meant that many of these new settlers were often in uniform. In addition, they aroused further suspicion because they spoke little or no Arabic and thus were unable to communicate effectively with their local neighbours, yet were able to converse in Turkish with Ottoman officials.

Gertrude Bell, visiting the region in the early days of the twentieth century, singled out the Circassians for praise in helping the Ottomans to reassert their rule over the southern Syrian provinces. She wrote:

The axis of the Sultan's authority over the whole district is to be found in the rapid growth and unrivalled prosperity of the Circassian settlers ... they have received gifts of land and the fostering of care of a Government alive to the fact that its own interests are very closely bound up with theirs, and wherever they have settled they have made the wilderness blossom like rose. ... Rapacious, cruel, industrious and courageous, the Circassians are by nature a ruling race. They will turn the idle and ignorant Bedouin into servants or drive them eastward into the desert, and they will rule them with a rod of iron and hold them in check with relentless persistency against which they are powerless. (Bell 1902:226)

The reputation for military prowess among the Circassians of Amman was enhanced in the first decades of the twentieth century with the arrival of new forced migrants, mainly the Kabarday who had first come by sea from Sebastopol and then overland from Alexandretta. Among them was Mirza Wasfi Pasha, a charismatic leader born in the Caucasus in the 1850s. He and his family had been moved to Bulgaria as refugees after the Russian invasions of 1864–5. In 1873 Mirza joined the Ottoman army and served in the Serbian War of 1876. But he gained his fame during the Russian–Ottoman

War of 1877–8 when he took part in the Siege of Plevna in Bulgaria. After the expulsion of the Circassians from the Balkans, Mirza was assigned to Damascus in the 1880s and also commanded the military police in Beirut, Mecca, and Yemen. He brought his family to Amman sometime early in the 1900s. Once in Amman he was quickly acknowledged as the leader of the Circassians. In 1905 he established a voluntary Circassian armed unit, which had semi-official status among the Ottoman administration. In the following few years, his militia served not only locally to maintain security against local Bedouin but was also deployed against the Druze in the Jaulan and in Karak during the revolt of 1909–10. During World War I, this unit served in the Ottoman Army and protected the Hijaz railway. With the defeat of the Ottomans by the Allied forces, Mirza Pasha and the Circassian units threw their support behind the Arab supporters of Emir Faysal in Damascus. Learning of Emir Faysal's defeat by French forces at Maysaloun in Syria, the Circassians then turned to Faysal's brother, Emir Abdullah, in an effort to create an Arab kingdom in the former Arab provinces of the Ottoman Empire. The Circassians and Chechnyans, however, were not organized as a cohesive political group. Rather, as individuals, they played important roles, particularly as civil servants, administrators, and soldiers in consolidating the nascent Transjordanian state. They have long been well represented in the officer corps of the nation, from the founding of the Jordanian Arab Legion and the Transjordan Frontier Force (Vatikiotis 1967).

Zarqa and other Chechnyan settlements

The first Chechnyan settlement in the southern provinces of Syria was established in Zarqa in 1902. At the same time, more Circassian settlers also came to the town to work on the construction of the Hijaz railway. A few years later, a second wave of Chechnyan settlers arrived in Zarqa from Anatolia via Syria. They went on to found a number of villages [Suuwaylih and Sukhnah] as well as to live in some of the existing Chechnyan and Circassian settlements.

In 1902 my grandfather made the decision to come here. There was a wave of Muslim migration from the Northern Caucuses after the end of the Shamil–Russian Tsar Wars (Russo Circassian wars) which ended in 1859. He was exiled to Russia at first but then he demanded to be allowed to go to Mecca, which he did and he died there. Further migrations started around 1875, I would say. That is when the Circassians and the Chechnyans began coming. They crossed the mountains in carts driven by cows and mules. Some took shelter in Turkey [Anatolia], but some were not happy and asked Abdul Hamid (the Ottoman

Sultan) if they could migrate to Bilad al-Sham and thus get closer to Mecca. So the Circassians sent some groups of people to check out the land, and the group that my grandfather belonged to came to Jordan. At that time Jordan was green, there were rivers running and they selected Zarqa to settle in, then the rest of the families came, and as time passed they had a religious leader, not a political leader and they abided by whatever this religious leader said and formed a small community in Zarqa. ... At the beginning they had some conflicts with Bedouins, as they didn't understand them. But what they tried to do from the beginning was to keep their national identity and their customs, and they made sure that the children spoke the native language – the Chechnyan language. Even now, we speak our native language in my home. All six of my children, who were brought up in the USA use the Chechnyan language. So we keep our traditions and we watch how older people behave. My father taught me and I taught my children. I would say that we kept 90% of our customs. Then we got involved with the Jordanian Royal Family as they have great trust in Chechnyans and Circassians; we joined the Army as we were known for being good fighters. We still wear our national dress in the Royal Court. (Sheshani 2006)

ETHNIC IDENTITY AND NATIONAL LOYALTY

The early period of the Circassian and Chechnyan migrations and settlement in the Syrian provinces was met with some apprehension, especially by the non-Muslim [Christian] inhabitants of the region. They feared that these newcomers, dispossessed and uprooted from their native homes by Christian governments (Russia, Bulgaria, and Greece), might turn around and become violent to the local Christian Arabs. This fear was fanned by a number of exaggerated rumours which preceded the arrival of the Circassians. They were said to have been unruly while living in the Balkans, attacking Bulgarian Christians and abducting women as well as resorting to robbery (Karpat 1979:23). These wildly exaggerated reports were investigated by the British Vice-Consul. In a report by the British Ambassador in Istanbul to the Marquis of Salisbury, the British Foreign Secretary, in 1878, an explanation was given for the variety of lawless actions perpetrated by the Circassians, which went back to the enormous hardships their forced eviction had inflicted on them as they were made to travel from one part of the Ottoman Empire to another in conditions of dire poverty, near starvation, and ill health. In a sympathetic and frank description, he continued to explain that the Circassians, accustomed to the mountain climate of the Caucasus, were now being forced to live in the warm and humid climate of the Mediterranean and were thus falling sick to every epidemic and illness. The breakdown of their social order as a result of these forced migrations was bringing many to the brink of starvation. In order to survive, the Ambassador argued, some were forced to steal; others had to settle in rural areas where they were viewed as interlopers supported by the state. Surrounded by unfriendly neighbours such as the Bedouin, Kurds, and Turcoman, who all resented the Circassian usurpation of their own grazing lands, they had to establish their prowess and gain respect by force of personality and physical strength (FO 424/70 1878; Karpat 1979).

Thirty years later, British consular reports (1906) suggested that the Circassians had acclimatised and gained the respect of their neighbours by sheer will and hard work, refusing to be browbeaten into paying khuwah (tribute) to the Bedouin. The reports of these Consular officials regarded the Circassian migrants as having successfully acculturated as peasants who were 'employed in agricultural work on *miri* or Crown land … In other parts of Syria there are large and flourishing [Circassian] communities, a few being scattered a considerable way south along the line of the Hedjaz Railway. In many of these districts the Circassians have transformed barren tracts into well-cultivated and prosperous lands' (FO 424/210 1906b).

By the early decades of the twentieth century, the Circassian and Chechnyan communities were well established in Anatolia and the Syrian provinces of the Ottoman Empire. There were clusters of Circassian villages along the Euphrates, but mainly they were found along a frontier line between the 'desert and the sown' near Homs, Damascus, Jaulan, Jerash, Zarqa and Amman. With the defeat of the Axis powers in World War I, these settlers found themselves no longer Ottoman subjects. They threw their weight behind the newly created states in which they were settled – Turkey, Syria, and Jordan. In the following years, their image changed from that of pioneer settlers, both feared and admired for their energy and vigour, to respected civil servants, army and office workers and – particularly in Amman – land owners. The 1967 June War turned the Circassians who had been settled in the Jaulan into refugees (*nazihiin* or internally displaced) again. Nearly 25,000 Circassians were driven out when Israel occupied the Jaulan. Most fled to Damascus where they were given assistance from the Syrian and Jordanian Circassian Welfare Societies as well as government and international agencies. Some received assistance from the Tolstoy Society and from relatives who had previously immigrated to the United States. Most of them however settled in Damascus and, after some initial difficulty, started to rebuild their lives for a second or third time.

In Jordan, the Circassians' and Chechnyans' transformation from refugee to settler to respected citizen was complete. Their villages became towns and their former farmlands often were absorbed into the suburbs of Amman, Zarqa, Wadi al-Sir, and Jerash. For significant numbers of Circassians and Chechnyans, their lands became a passport into the wealthy land-owning elite of the capital. Although many of the young in these communities, both in Jordan and in Syria, had left their villages in recent decades for the cities in pursuit of higher education and also for greater work opportunities, a return movement to the villages (now often suburbs) is emerging among those who have done well. In the more prosperous Circassian settlements, modern houses are being built as weekend retreats and summer homes by those who have made good in the cities or in the diaspora in the USA and elsewhere. After World War II, a small movement of Circassians entered Jordan from the Soviet Union. Many of these, however, continued their migration to the United States where they settled around Paterson, New Jersey. In recent decades, the Circassians in Paterson became the diasporic core with the organization of a World Circassian Congress and reunions often emanating from New Jersey but held somewhere in Turkey or in the Caucasus (Weightman 1970:92).

As a group, the Circassians and Chechnyans in Jordan and Syria have remained loyal and firm supporters of their new states. The ties between the Hashemite monarch and the Circassians are especially strong with continued high recruitment into the Royal Guard of the Royal Household coming from the broad Circassian community. As a minority – even some would say a dominant minority – they are not politically active. However, that is not the same as saying they are politically unaware or indifferent. Jordanians of Circassian and Chechnyan origin are active in civil society, in education, and in some businesses as are Syrians and Turks with roots in the Transcaucus region. In each of these countries, Circassians have become largely a middle-class urban community with a strong presence in the civil services and national military establishments.

For many Circassians, the safety net and focus of social and cultural life revolves around the Circassian Charitable Associations that were formally organised in Amman in 1932 and in Damascus in 1948. Much of their social life centres around these organizations: promotion of education, Circassian language teaching, newspapers and magazines, public libraries, sports clubs, and even the setting out of guidelines for the appropriate '*mahr*' (brideprice) to be contracted on marriage.[26] For these proud people, the associations were set up and designed to ensure that no Circassian or Chechnyan would ever have to ask the state for welfare or a handout if they fell on hard times. In recent years these associations have become an important focus for the transmission of Circassian languages through the numerous courses they offer.[27] They have also become an organisational point for the numerous visits to Caucasia that have taken place with increasing regularity since the fall of the Soviet Union.

We have three ways of learning Cherkessi [Circassian language]. The first is to use it at home. We do that and it is effective. Whenever the children need something they have to use Cherkessi to ask for it or they don't get it. The Cherkessi Society, which has seven branches in Syria, is the second place where language is taught. The Cherkessi Society offers free Cherkessi language courses and Cherkessi language is also taught in the Society's kindergarten along with the official Arabic curriculum. To tell the truth, the Cherkess feel comfortable in Syria. From day one, the Cherkess have enjoyed many rights. We have the right to publish a newspaper and to establish Cherkessi schools. Marj al-Sultan Rural Club was the first club to be established in the Syrian rural area and so was the public library of Marj al-Sultan, which was established in 1951. Until 1956, Cherkessi language here was only a spoken one. But since then, the Russian alphabet was introduced in Syria. Actually, the Cherkessi language was first written in Greek alphabet then in the Arabic alphabet after Islam, then with the Russian revolution the Latin alphabet was adopted. In 1936 Stalin imposed the Russian alphabet and since then, we read and write Cherkessi using the Russian alphabet. However, Turkey, where 5 million Cherkessi live, rejects the Russian alphabet. They find the Latin alphabet more convenient. The third way of learning Cherkessi is by computer and TV. Now cartoon movies are available on CDs in Cherkessi and there is a Cherkessi TV channel being launched in Turkey which is to run for 24 hours a day. This is being taken by Turkey to improve its efforts to gain approval to join the EU. The Turkish government is demonstrating its good intentions towards minorities. (Adel 2006)

Not only is language acquisition promoted, but general higher education is also widely supported by the Circassian charitable societies. Circassian

---

[26] According to Weightman, there was a large posted document at the headquarters of the Circassian Charitable Association in Amman drawn up in 1953, which declared that the dowry for a Circassian girl would be reduced from 300 Jordanian dinars to 150 dinars. The heads of the prominent Circassian families had all signed this important document governing intercommunal social life (1970:95).

[27] In Syria today, there are about 135,000 people of Circassian origin. About 70 per cent of them speak Circassian languages. Of the remainder, perhaps 50 per cent understand, but cannot speak, and a small minority (25 per cent) can neither speak nor understand the language; generally the young are too busy or too preoccupied to start learning this language (Abdul-Salam 2005).

youth are encouraged to enter university and pursue professional degrees. Although military careers still represent important options for the Circassians in Jordan, they are not as important in Syria, where a wide range of professions are taken up by Syrians of Circassian origin. Higher education, as in many refugee and settler societies, is highly valued and the Syrian Circassian Society, with support from the Circassian republics in the Caucasus, provides 10–15 scholarships each year to students willing to pursue higher education abroad.[28]

For the first time in nearly 130 years, the imagined homeland has become a real space to Circassians in diaspora. With the fall of the Soviet Union, large numbers of Circassians from Turkey, Syria, and Jordan as well as the United States have begun to make trips, especially in the summertime, to find long-lost relatives and make real their long imagined villages.[29] Often these visits to the homeland community have generated a shock of nonrecognition of the 'self' in others. The self, which is often conceptualized abstractly in terms of cultural belonging, is also perceived as having particular physical characteristics. As Shami relates of these encounters, the Circassians visiting from Turkey, Syria, and Jordan were surprised to find that their countrymen and -women in the homeland left behind in the nineteenth century were generally shorter and darker than they had imagined. In the context of the Middle East, Circassians were proud of the general perception of them as being a people who are fair and tall in stature. This disjunction as explained by some of the host Circassians was that it was the nobility [hence the taller and more fair] that had fled; whereas the poor and the slaves had largely remained in Caucasia. Although there is no historical evidence to support such a version of the emigration, it is now repeated enough to have acquired a finish of historical respectability (Shami 1995:89).

The Circassian charitable associations in Turkey, Syria, and Jordan have been at the centre of these voyages of discovery, often organizing the actual travel programmes. In addition, a World Circassian Association has been established which has held a series of meetings and conferences attended by delegates from Circassian communities all over the world. It has also been reported that at least 200 families from Syria and Turkey

---

[28] The modern Circassian 'republics' of the northern Caucasus include the Russian Adygie Autonomous Republic, Cherkess-Karachav, and Kabardino Balkar as well as Abkhazia and South Ossetia.

[29] Both Syria and Jordan, however, have had a series of exchanges of students as well as 'official visits' between representatives of the Soviet republics, folklore groups, and leaders of the diaspora Circassian charitable organization since the early 1980s.

have immigrated back and settled in Kabardino-Balkar and in Adygie (Shami 1995), seeking to come closer to their identity as Circassians. However, families who have migrated back have tended to socialize with other Circassians who came from the same country. Thus the Circassians who returned from Syria have come to be known as Syrians, those from Jordan, as Jordanians. As Emine, one of Shami's informants, put it, 'We left Turkey so as not to become Turks, only to become Turks here' (Shami 1995:91). This phenomenon suggests that some transformation of culture has taken place 'in exile'; perhaps an element of assimilation or, as Voutira reported with reference to the Pontic Greeks in Chapter One, a hybridization of sorts, with the exiled community taking on some elements of its immediate surrounding while propounding a purity and intactness of its culture.

This sudden and open access to the long imagined homeland, putting a place back into space, has resulted in some penetrating reflections on the nature of identity and being. As Shami discusses in her paper, concepts of ethnic identity are being reviewed and reconsidered. Turkey and Jordan present two extremes: one a nationalist model and the other a tribal one. In Turkey where a powerful nationalist ideology based on Turkish ethnicity prevails, Circassians and other ethnic groups have one clear option, and that is assimilation into a Turkish identity. Some Circassians in Turkey have done that, only retaining a vague notion of their Circassian culture, language, and origins. Others who made the decision to hold on to their 'Circassianness', have formed associations that strive to establish a social revolution in Turkey recognising them as Circassian Turks. Still other Circassians, the dönüşçü, advocate a return to the Caucasus. In Jordan, on the other hand, a completely different concept of ethnic politics has emerged. Tribalism has a strong resonance as one of the major political idioms of the country. As a result, the Caucasian communities in Jordan decided to form a Circassian-Chechnyan Tribal Council in 1980 to be able to compete with the other major political players in the country. The men who formed the council represented the fairly prominent Circassian and Chechnyan leaders in the country. By the mid-1990s, all the major Jordanian 'tribes' had formed themselves into tribal associations. Thus between Turkey and Jordan are two extreme forms of presenting ethnicity – one calls for integration without assimilation while the other largely rejects assimilation as well but calls for a return to the homeland. These two competing ways of interpreting ethnic identity are present in Syria where both return as well as 'non-tribally' conceptualized integration are evident.

Identity and ethnic affiliation, however, is self-defined and remains a fluid notion. A Circassian one moment may perceive himself as Jordanian, Palestinian, Syrian, or Turkish, for that matter. The context, both social and political, makes matters of identity complex, fragmentary, and illusionary. Mahmoud Sharkas, for example, told me of his birth in Haifa.[30] Unlike most Circassians in Palestine, his grandfather had arrived as a cavalry officer in the Ottoman army and his son, Ahmad's father, had been born at a time when he was posted in Jaffa. Mahmoud himself was born in Haifa – his mother was a Palestinian Arab. In 1948 he was evacuated out of Haifa by boat along with his mother and siblings and landed at Sur in Lebanon. From there they were moved with other refugees, mainly Palestinian, to Tripoli, Lebanon, where they remained for five years. Then in 1952 or 1953, Mahmoud's father left for Saudi Arabia to work with the Aramco oil company. The following year, Mahmoud wrote to his father pleading with him to take them back to Palestine. The father returned, took his family to Syria where they got Palestinian passports, and then on to Jordan. Once in Amman, Mahmoud was sent to school in Wadi al-Sir, where he found himself in a government school surrounded by Circassians for the first time in his life. He was fifteen years old and was just beginning to recognize himself as Circassian. He persuaded his father to move into a Circassian community where they could all belong to the local Circassian Charitable Association. Having completed his university education in Alexandria Egypt, he then went on to take a doctorate at Harvard University in the United States. Returning to Amman, he continued his association with the Circassian Charitable Association and today is a regular attendee of the association and club.

Only as an adult did Mahmoud develop a full sense of his identity as a Circassian. He began to research and dig out archival material on Circassians in Jordan. He also began to trace his father's roots back to the Caucasus. His identity today is firmly Circassian, as reflected in his family name, Sharkas, which simply indicates that he and his family were identifiable as being the 'other', different from the rest of the community in Haifa and hence were given the name of 'the Circassian' to differentiate them from the rest of the settlement. Jordanian, Palestinian, and Circassian identities are all associated with Mahmoud. None were mutually exclusionary or exclusive. It has been his choice to prioritize one and sublimate

[30] There are about 3,000 Circassians in Israel today, mainly in the villages of Rehania and Kfar Kama, both founded in the 1870s (Haron et al. 2004).

another, as a response to political and social contexts that have changed dramatically throughout his life.

CONCLUSION

The European Caucasian Muslims, mainly Circassians, Chechnyans, Daghestanis, Osssetians, Abkhazis, and Ubykhs as well as Albanians and Kosovars, arrived in the Middle East towards the end of the nineteenth century as forced migrants and refugees. Sometimes they were twice displaced over the space of a few decades. Although their dispossession and migration was, in the main, anticipated and welcomed by the Ottoman state – as an outcome of treaties of peace with the Ottoman archenemy, Russia – their actual arrival in the Syrian provinces generally overwhelmed the awaiting officialdom. The early years of these settler migrants were tenuous, as Lewis, McCarthy, and Karpat have so carefully enumerated. Many of the original settlements in Syria, Jordan, and Palestine failed to thrive. Some died out entirely or were abandoned before replenishment arrived with the next wave of dispossession and forced migration at the end of the nineteenth century and early twentieth century.

Many of these forced migrants had to adapt to a different physical environment as well as transform their livelihood. Most of the original settlers came from mountainous terrain and were expected to adapt to carving out livelihoods on the largely flat open ground on the frontiers of the semi-arid steppe. They were expected to farm the land, eventually providing revenue for the state once their period of 'exemption' from tax-farming had lapsed. They were also expected to pacify the region of their settlement, establishing their superiority over quarrelling neighbours and refusing the Bedouin efforts to coerce them into paying a form of protection money. These settlers could and did protect themselves from marauding tribes as well as the hostility of their immediate neighbours. Going one step further, they often entered into alliances with Bedouin such as the Al-Fadl in Jaulan and the Bani Sakhr near Amman, bringing stability to a wide area of agriculture.

For many Circassians, the formalization of their land ownership under Ottoman rule as well as the employment opportunities which the Hijaz Railway Project opened up, meant that significant economic inequalities – and thus class distinctions – would emerge. Those who were literate in Arabic and Turkish were able to gain employment with the Ottoman bureaucracy; those whose language skills were less sophisticated often found work on the railway. For most, the prevailing economic conditions went far in shaping their relations with their neighbours, largely indigenous Arabs and Bedouin, but also other settler groups such as Druze, Kurds, and occasionally Armenians.

Within the Circassian community, concepts of family, group solidarity, and leadership were shaped by the cultural ideals of the old homeland and influenced the new social order that the Circassians set out to create.[31] Most of their settlements were organized with neighbourhood leaders, each with a guest-house where men of the community would gather to discuss settlement matters, mediate disputes, or plan defences. They were also places where the elders could reminisce about the Caucasus, and where the younger generation might actively consider visiting or returning to one day. In many of these settlements, the distinctive two-wheeled carts of the Circassians could be seen taking their own produce to market towns, occasionally also carrying barley cultivated by the Bedouin (Hacker 1960). The description of Amman in the early decades of the twentieth century probably reflects the look of the other major Circassian settlements in Qunaytrah as well as Marj al-Sultan: 'a small, self-contained, largely self-sufficient community. It was a sizable village of a few thousand inhabitants – middlemen, trading agricultural products for simple manufactured articles, for cloth, tea, sugar, kerosene and household utensils brought from Damascus and Jerusalem' (Hacker 1960:20).

During the Allied attack on the Ottoman Empire in World War I, most of these new settlers fought with the Ottoman army to repel the Allied invasions. However, once the war had been lost, most Circassian soldiers put their Ottoman uniforms aside and threw their weight behind the new Arab central governments under mandate to the League of Nations. The imposition, then, of the French and British mandates drew these Circassian settlers into the Arab ideological fold. The commonality of political cause – fighting for independence as Jordanians or Syrians rather than as Ottoman subjects – was to be a significant step in their integration into the new 'mandated' states which had come into being after the Treaty of Versailles, following the Paris Peace Conference in 1919. Although they suffered the deprivations and famines of the rest of the population, they did not join the insurgency, which became the 'Great Syrian Revolt' of 1926. In keeping with the policy of divide and rule, the French succeeded in raising some irregular troops from among the Circassians along with other recent

---

[31] Few detailed ethnographies of Circassian communities exist in English. One excellent such study is Seteney Shami's Ph.D. dissertation, *Ethnicity and Leadership: the Circassians in Jordan* (1982).

refugees, such as the Armenians (Provence 2005:130–131). However, the general policy of inciting sectarian conflict to defeat the greater Arab Revolt did not succeed. Although Circassians, especially in the Jaulan and in the Hauran in Syria, continued to be in conflict with their Druze neighbours, their engagement with the French mandate authority was as salaried soldiers rather than as anti-nationalist supporters.

The Circassians, in general, were determined to succeed in their new homelands and many of those whom I interviewed in 2005 and 2006 talked about the decades of hard work, making their communities successful, whether in Marj al-Sultan, Jaulan, or Amman. Although belonging to different tribes and elaborating slight differences in custom and sometimes 'invented' traditions, these Muslim Europeans were decidedly progressive in the emphasis they placed on educating their youth, and on maintaining their languages. Marriage, with its elaborate ritual of elopement, was kept very much to Circassian and other Caucasian peoples, although close cousin marriage, as preferred by the Arabs, was not acceptable.

Towards the end of the British and French mandates and as the Great Depression loosened its grip on the Middle East, these Circassian settlements began to thrive. They were no longer implanted forced migrant groups in an Arab landscape, but a community integrated into the local, sometimes heterogeneous population as well as into the wider government. The focus of social life for many Circassians continued to be their charitable associations and sports clubs. Their plethora of newspapers and libraries were unique among exile communities, considering how large the Circassian rural farming communities continued to be. In time, more of the young migrated to the cities and entered into government service, education, and other professions. Their numerous charitable societies were, and still remain, active associations looking after the elderly, the infirm, and the young. The special character of the small Circassian town of Amman was rapidly and largely overwhelmed by the Arab population growth of merchant families from Damascus and Nabulus, of newly settled Bedouin, farmers from Salt and Karak as well as Palestinian refugees after 1948 and 1967. The Circassian settlements of Qunaytrah and the Jaulan were also emptied after the Israeli occupation of 1967, their inhabitants dispersed to other places with sizeable Circassian communities.

For all the strength of Circassian social customs and traditions, the unity of these communities remains very much at an ideational level with an emphasis on the importance of community solidarity, good citizenship, and political awareness. Political leadership, however, is limited to the community level. It is not expressed in any effort to form or sustain political parties. Even the remembered and partially imagined homeland is not a source of political capital. Many Circassians today do visit their places of origin. Some have entertained notions of remaining in Caucasia and others have seen their children marry and put down new roots there. But for the most part, the Circassians, as refugee and settler groups, have been absorbed into the states they found themselves in after decades of turmoil and dispossession. Today, Circassians form sizeable communities in Turkey, Syria, Jordan, and Palestine. The figures are impressionistic, as few national census statistics separate out the Circassians as an ethnicity. Shami gives the following figures: one million in Turkey, 50,000 in Syria, 30,000 in Jordan, and 2000 in Palestine[32] (1995). In the Russian federation, there are three republics (previously autonomous regions of Kabardino-Balkar, Cherkess-Karachav, and Adygie) with significant Circassian populations. The estimated population size for the Caucasus is about 500,000 (Shami 1995).

After the 6 June War of 1967, some Circassian families from the Jaulan set out to recover their lost homelands and travelled to the Soviet Union in search of relatives and roots. With the collapse of the Soviet Union, many Circassian families in Syria and Jordan went on voyages of discovery to what they believed were their original homelands. Some remained there. Others found it not so easy to stay or to return, and entered into cycles of movement between the old and the new homelands. The relative freedom of movement – depending on economic ability – made the homeland both more real and more imagined at the same time. Those who I was able to interview in 2005 and 2006 had visited once if not more often. Some had bought land and built homes with the idea of remaining, only to find after a few months that, as beautiful as the Caucasus landscape was, they remained deracinated. Their social ties and networks were rooted in their Circassian communities in the Middle East and no longer in the Caucasus region. They were integrated into these new nations, and their identity remained Circassian.

I went to visit the Caucasus twice. I met with about 40 relatives all from the Kaghados. They offered me land and help to settle there with my children. But the idea did not appeal to me so much. Life there was different from our life here. A person who was born in Syria has become used to a certain style of life and would find it difficult to take such a step. Nothing can compare to Caucasus. It is more beautiful than Switzerland. It has magnificent mountains, woods and valleys. The

---

[32] Shami's estimates are far more conservative than those of the Syrian Circassian community leaders' claim that there are around 135,000 Circassians in Syria (Abdul-Salam 2005).

soil is so fertile. If a branch fell to the ground, it would grow into a tree. I am not exaggerating. They would have easily given me a house and helped us settle, but my wife would not consider the idea. Her family and friends are here. However she likes to go for visits. There are a number of good package tours and some of the Circassians who came here married Circassian girls from Syria. In addition a number of Syrian Circassian students who went on scholarship got married to girls from there. Some stayed there and others brought their wives back here. (Qahtan 2006)

In 2000, Seteney Shami published an unusual article comparing the journey of a Turkish Circassian woman back to her homeland in the 1990s with that of a Circassian slave woman being taken from Istanbul by a slave dealer who had purchased her for onward auction in Cairo in the 1850s (Shami 2000). The former, Shengul, was being sent by her family to establish new roots in the old homeland. She was going back, returning, to recover her identity as a Circassian and also as a hostage to her Turkish Circassian family's desire to have a foothold in Caucasia, a safeguard for the future in case things did not turn out well in Turkey. The latter, Shemsigal, was being torn from her roots, her identity erased by the probable poverty of her family which had led to her being sold as a slave. For both women the voyages were by sea, dark, polluting, wet, and filled with danger, hunger, and misery. The contemporary Shengul, a single woman, was for a variety of reasons not able to marry into the group, and yet not allowed to marry out of it. Thus, at 37 years of age, she was free to travel. The slave girl, Shemsigal, perhaps sold off to provide the rest of her family with food or to pay off debts, also was freed to travel by the severing of her bonds to her family. Both were cut off from the customs and traditions with which they had grown up. Shengul, in her journey to her new/old homeland in the Caucasus, was looking to make a new life for herself. Shemsigal had no such choices. She would probably lose all ties to her past and any offspring she might have as a slave would most likely have no link with her Circassian identity. Shengul, on the other hand, looking to strengthen her Circassianness, found that being back in Caucasia left her with feelings of real ambiguity. She had come to find work, education, and some independence, but she had also come to reaffirm her identity as a Circassian. Instead, she found life among her 'homeland' Circassians alien. It was as though in the diaspora, Circassians had incorporated practices of formality, decorum, and authoritarianism between generations and age groups, which were no longer, if ever, practised in the 'homeland'. Their adherence to Islam was also more rigid and encompassing than anything she had come across in the heartland of her ethnic identity. While the

Circassian settler society had held on to and elaborated certain traditions and customs in their exile, those at home had changed, evolved, and developed, making the return of some Circassians searching for their roots traumatic as well as transformative. The homeland was imagined and imperfectly remembered. In much of Circassian oral history there are narratives of sea crossings and dispersal, but very little about the costs of physical and emotional resettlement. This is generally left unspoken. Yet Shami's juxtaposition of these two tales of Circassian departure and return highlight the nature of memory and ethnic identity as well as the nature of historical remembering and nostalgia (Shami 2000:202).

Nostalgia is the desire or longing with burning pain to journey [to the homeland]. It also evokes the sensory dimension of memory and exile and estrangement; it mixes bodily and emotional pain and ties painful experiences of spiritual and somatic exile to the notion of maturation and ripening. Nostalgia, in the American sense, freezes the past in such a manner as to preclude it from any capacity for social transformation in the present, preventing the present from establishing a dynamic perceptual relationship to its history. (Seremetakis 1994:4; quoted in Shami 2000:202)

I asked Abdul-Salam, who was born in the Jaulan in 1916 and whose grandparents had travelled to Syria from Abkhazia via Anatolia, whether he would return to the Jaulan or to his forefathers' homelands in Abkhazia had he the opportunity. His children and grandchildren, listening to his interview with me all replied '*Abkhazia, of course*'. Abdul-Salam hesitated before answering:

I would not mind going back to Abkhazia if it were to become independent. But no one recognizes the Abkhazi Republic. If the Jaulan were returned to Syria, I would go back. I would, for sure, go back leaving everything behind. If I could go back to either, I think I wouldn't have as many people who know me in Abkhazia as in Jaulan. (One son interrupts: If you go back to Abkhazia, it would be better for you!). I am old now. It is no good for me anymore. If I were young, I would go on foot [to Abkhazia]. What would I do there now at 90 years of age. (Abdul-Salam 2005)

For Abdul-Salam, his remembered Circassian homeland in the Jaulan beckons more attractively than his imagined homeland in the Caucasus. Of course, age is a factor in his preference. But the enthusiasm of youth to return and make the arduous journey of discovery of kin and imagined ancestors is offset by the wisdom of age which recognizes the need for kinship ties and social networks. For Abdul-Salam, his 'homeland' is where his family and friends are, rather than in the virtual place in spaces left long ago.

Self-identification of individual Circassians remains firmly based on ethnic qualities, language, culture, and customs. For many, these markers sat comfortably with those of national identity. Being Circassian and being Jordanian or Syrian were not contradictory. The homeland was a place that no longer existed. And the recent opportunity to return to the space of the original homeland, though enthusiastically visited, was not for the majority a reality that sat easily with their imagined pasts. Integrating but not assimilating – as seemed to be demanded in Turkey – was one of a number of solutions to the complex responses of being the other in a larger heterogeneous society also made up of numerous others.

4

The Armenians and Other Christians: Expulsions and Massacres

My native family name is Vosgueritchian. It means goldsmith, because my grandfather had been a goldsmith in Severeg, which is in Western Armenia. My grandfather had been part of a large family. He had four sisters and a brother, but they are all gone, he was the only survivor. He reached Egypt after a very long journey. He came by himself. He found work and he built himself up. He had lost his entire family when he was very young. He was in an orphanage. One day when they needed to decide his age, they lined him up with other boys and put the back of the spoon in his mouth and a doctor passed around looking at the teeth of the boys and say, he is nine years old, for example. This is how they decided his age and said he must have been born in 1905. He left Severeg in 1915 with his whole family. There had been many disturbances and one night the doorbell rang at the house and there were wagons. The whole family went but he and his brother was taken in by a Turkish family and saved on that occasion. Later, he and his brother had to join the marches and his brother died on the road. He arrived in Aleppo alone and was taken into an orphanage. He remained there a few years and then in 1918 he left the orphanage to go back and volunteer to be a soldier [for Turkish independence]. By 1923 he was in Constantinople [Istanbul] with four friends who had also fought with him. The War [Greco-Turkish War of 1919–22] was over. They were all still only 17 or 18. They heard about an orphanage in Corfu so they went there and from there they decided to come here to Cairo. So they hid themselves on a ship and landed at Alexandria. In those days the Armenian Church used to send people down to the port everyday to see if there were orphans or refugees coming and they would protect them and take them under their supervision. The Church then arranged for them to get papers and passports and regularized their situation. After so many months of moving around from one place to another all around the Mediterranean, they were happy that they were now documented and had legal papers.

My grandfather had not had a chance to go to school. But he was very talented. He could work anything from iron or metal. He became an ironsmith because he was so clever with his hands. He took many jobs and built himself up until he had his own factory in 1940 with workshops in Alexandria and branches in Cairo. He was an active member of the Armenian community and he married an Armenian from Sebastopol. They lived in Alexandria and brought up their family there but they also kept up with their friends in Cairo. The Armenian Church in both Alexandria and Cairo was very strong. It had schools, sports clubs and other cultural activities. We children were always taking part. I grew up speaking Armenian. I went to the Armenian primary school but then I went to the American College. We don't have this feeling of being different. We are Egyptians, I mean we are Armenians by birth, so we speak our language, we cook our food, we dance our dances, we have our customs ... you know for Christmas. The Armenian community around the world is very well organized. Everywhere it has a Church, a school, a sporting club, a cultural club. These things keep Armenians together wherever they are. Here in Cairo, we are comfortable. We have been to visit Armenia, we feel we are a part of it, we are happy when we are there, but when we come back to Cairo we know we belong here.

Sonia (2006), Cairo

Of all the formally recognized minority communities or millets of the late Ottoman Empire, after the Greek Orthodox the Armenians held perhaps the most prestigious place in its multilayered and plural urban society. As the empire began to recede and the Greek Orthodox community largely withdrew to its newly created nation-state of Greece (1929), some Armenians became caught up with the nationalist fervour which was

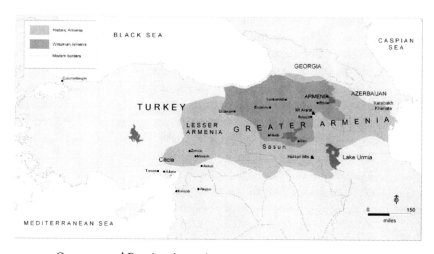

MAP 5. Ottoman and Russian Armenia

sweeping Europe and impacting on the fringe European provinces of the Ottoman Empire. With growing success, majority nations were being imposed upon state spaces in the European regions of the Ottoman Empire, and one after another the Bulgarians, Serbians, and Romanians were recognized as states and nations: nation-states. The Armenians, on the other hand, were widely dispersed, perhaps as a result of centuries of successful trading and business throughout the Ottoman Empire. Nevertheless, at the end of the nineteenth century and the early decades of the twentieth century, they made a concerted effort to garner international support for a state of their own. Their bid for secession from the Ottoman Empire largely collapsed because their heartland was an integral part of the Anatolian plain and, perhaps, because European encouragement and support did not match its earlier commitment to nation building in the Balkans.

There are many theories related to the tragic conclusions of the 'Armenian question' and they tend to fall on two sides of a seemingly impermeable divide: an Armenian position and an Ottoman/Turkish position. Historians and other scholars generally fall into one camp or another.[1] However, the facts are fairly robust. In an era when people were being dispossessed and expelled from their homelands in the millions (see chapters 2 and 3), the Armenians, too, were dispossessed, massacred, and forced out of their lands on death marches (Karpat 1985). Here again, opinion is divided as to what provoked or explained the mass destruction of the Armenians in the period between the outbreak of World War I and the founding of the Turkish Republic in 1923.

In those nine years, more than 'a million Armenians were killed in mass shootings, massacres, deportations, and induced starvation' (Melson 1996:142). This mass destruction was called the first domestic genocide of the twentieth century and has been the subject of immense scrutiny. A number of theories abound to explain why it happened. One theory traces its origins to the provocative behaviour of the Armenians themselves – or, at least, to their nationalist and revolutionary parties. Another theory blames the perpetrators – the 'Young Turks' with their secular Pan-Turkish ideology, who came to power after the overthrow of Sultan Abdul Hamid in 1908 – as the primary cause. Although the Young Turks contributed significantly to the creation of the modern Turkish state, they were also responsible for the Armenian deportations, which

---

[1] See, for example, the contrasting positions of Shaw & Shaw (1977), Davison (1954), Walker (1997), Hovannisian (1997a), McCarthy (2001), and Dadrian (1997).

became genocide by any definition of the term.[2] Whether through their failed revolutionary aspirations or their population concentrations in what was increasingly becoming the heartland of the Ottoman Empire, the Armenians paid dearly for their late expression of nationalism and their reliance on unstable international alliances.

Sharp controversy remains today concerning the motives of those involved as well as the extent of the death and destruction. This chapter focuses on the Armenians who survived and went on to find new homes and communities. Yet to build a picture of those who escaped death, we need to have a general sense of numbers. Any extensive massacre or genocide will lead to controversy over the number of victims. Those who deny tend to minimize numbers; those who affirm tend to overestimate the casualties. The Armenian genocide is no exception. It may be useful to briefly look at the figures that Arnold Toynbee used to gauge the extent of the destruction. Toynbee estimated a pre-deportation figure of 1.6 million (an average of the Armenian patriarchate figures and those of the Ottoman census). He estimated that some 600,000 Armenians escaped deportation. Among these were 182,000 who fled as refugees into the Russian Caucasus and 4,200 who fled into Egypt, leaving some 400,000 Armenians in the Ottoman heartland throughout this period. He points out that the Armenian populations of Smyrna and Constantinople were not deported; nor were Armenian Catholics, Protestants, and converts to Islam. Of the one million who were deported, an estimated 500,000 (later revised to 600,000) Armenians died.[3]

The half million or so Armenians who survived were dispersed throughout the southern provinces of the Ottoman Empire. Many of the parentless children were taken in and brought up in Armenian Church-sponsored orphanages or adopted through the offices of various humanitarian agencies such as Near Eastern Relief and given new lives in Europe and the United States. The extensive, widespread Armenian trade and commercial

---

[2] Melson's work on genocide and revolution compares the Holocaust during World War II and the Armenian deportations and massacres during World War I. Making the association between revolution and genocide, he uses the UN definition of genocide to guide his work. This widely accepted definition formulated in 1948 takes genocide to mean actions 'committed with intent to destroy in whole or in part a national, ethnic, racial or religious group as such'. Although he finds this definition both too narrow and too broad, it clearly places the Armenian massacres in the category of genocide; either genocide-in-part or genocide-in-whole (Melson 1996:23).

[3] Arnold Toynbee had been sent out to the Ottoman Empire to set up an independent inquiry as to the Armenian massacres. His work is part of the Bryce Report (1916). Toynbee's analysis stops with the spring of 1916. It does not take into account what happened after 1916.

links provided respite and succour to refugees in their darkest hours. In the intervening decades, the Armenians have emerged as successful communities in diaspora as well as throughout the Middle East. In Lebanon, Syria, Jordan, and Egypt, they are today successful minorities well integrated into the political (especially in Lebanon) and social life of the nation-states that were once the Arab provinces of the Ottoman Empire.

HISTORICAL BACKGROUND

Armenia lies in the highlands surrounding the Biblical mountains of Ararat, upon which Noah's ark was said to have come to rest after the flood. Throughout history, that area of eastern Anatolia and southern Caucasia known as Armenia has enjoyed periods of independence as well as subjugation. In A.D. 301, Armenia adopted Christianity as its official state religion, ten years before the Roman Empire granted Christianity official toleration under Galerius and thirty-six years before Constantine was baptised. After the year 636, with the Arab conquests of Sassanid Persia, Armenia emerged as an autonomous principality within the Islamic Empire (Hovannisian 1997a:vii–xi). After several centuries of tug-of-war between the Byzantine and the Islamic Empire, a kingdom of Armenia emerged in Cilicia for nearly two hundred years. By the 1500s, Armenia was divided up between the Ottoman Empire and Safavid Persia. The Russian Empire later incorporated eastern Armenia (Erivan and Karabakh Khanates) in 1813 and 1828 (Kouymjian 1997; Shaw & Shaw 1977; Walker 1980).

From the beginning of the eleventh century until World War I, the Muslims gradually replaced the Orthodox and Apostolic (Gregorian) Christian population in Anatolia. Over the years, conversion to Islam took place and cemented the Muslim predominance of Ottoman rule. In the final century of Ottoman rule, a large inpouring of Muslim refugees from Transcaucasia and the Russian border zones took place. But throughout this long period, no major Christian religious group can be said to have disappeared. Greek Orthodox, Gregorian or Apostolic Christians, and Nestorians or Assyrians remained important minorities.[4] Until the beginning of the twentieth century, Anatolia was a mix of Muslim and non-Muslim communities. The Greeks of Anatolia were found in the seacoast

---

[4] Some of the 'unclassified' Christians of the Ottoman Empire were assumed to belong to the Armenian millet. The Nestorians or Assyrians, for example, voluntarily joined the Armenian millet in 1783 (Barsoumian 1997:184).

provinces of the north and west. The Jews were in western Anatolian cities. Armenians were in eastern Anatolia, and, in addition, had spread into central and western Anatolia. In the east, smaller groups of Christian splinter groups, especially Syrians (Catholics and Orthodox), Assyro-Chaldeans, and Nestorians of the Assyrian Church of the East remained in largely agrarian village pockets in their traditional homelands in Anatolia and the Euphrates valley as well as Persia (Baum & Winkler 2003).

Armenians in the late Ottoman period

Between 1768 and 1878 the Ottoman Empire fought six wars with Imperial Russia, losing all but the Crimean War. And with each loss, it surrendered more territory, largely in the Balkans and in southern Transcaucasia. The latter remained a contested area for a further fifty years and left the Armenian population straddling both the Russian and Ottoman empires. Its male adults served in both the Russian and Ottoman armies. The Armenian heartland received millions of Muslims that Russia either expelled or drove into the Ottoman Empire and witnessed hundreds of thousands of Armenian Christians fleeing into the Russian-held Armenian lands (McCarthy 2001:7).

Yet between 1878 and 1911, Ottoman Anatolia experienced what was perhaps the most prosperous period of its history. The great wars with empires were largely over; the Tanzimat centralizing reforms had left the new sultan Abdul Hamid II with more control over his empire than any other ruler since the sixteenth century. The worst of the epidemics which periodically struck the region – bubonic plague, cholera, and typhus – were over, as was most of the forced movement of displaced people into and throughout the empire. Anatolia's population was said to have grown by 50 per cent during this period (McCarthy 1983:2) with high fertility of the population along with reduced deaths through warfare, famine, and disease. Although the Ottoman Empire was renowned for its census figures, the Armenian figures were heavily contested. Europeans provided population figures that were often based on journalistic accounts or reports from one or another missionary outpost. Historians and politicians have used various estimates of Armenian populations to support political and moral arguments. Each side in the burgeoning 'Armenian question' presented figures that best suited its point of view. Official Ottoman statistics in Asia Minor prior to 1878 were too few and too general to be of much use (Karpat 1985:51). However, after the Berlin Congress of 1878 came a flood of information as both Russia and England expressed interest in eastern

Anatolia. British statisticians began to study Ottoman census figures as well as those of the Armenian patriarchate and make estimates of their own.[5] Perhaps the most important and detailed figures were presented by the Armenian patriarchate immediately after World War I at the Versailles Peace Conference. The figures were intended to convince the delegates and world opinion that before World War I Armenians outnumbered Turks in the Armenian areas of eastern Anatolia and that in 1919 a large enough population of Armenians remained to create a viable stable Armenian state (McCarthy 1983:47).[6] British statisticians later recognized the patriarchate's numbers as an exaggeration of Armenian figures and an underreporting of Muslims. The patriarchate claimed a total of 2.6 million Armenians in the Ottoman Empire in 1913. The Ottoman census of 1893 showed about one million Armenians living in Ottoman lands. Statistics for later years indicated that the Armenian population grew considerably; by 1914 their number had reached 1.1 million despite the fact that a sizeable number had migrated to Russia as a result of the loss of further territory both to Russia on the eastern front and to Europe in the north in the period from 1897 and 1913. Whatever the actual total figures, an Armenian population in the ten contested Ottoman governorates or *vilayets* of Anatolia were somewhere in the region of one million. The Muslim population in the same ten vilayets were, by conservative estimates, more than five million (Karpat 1985:55).

A protected minority

During the late Ottoman period, the Armenians had been granted considerable autonomy within their own 'millet' and lived in relative harmony

---

[5] This is most prominently recognition of the role of Major Henry Trotter, military attaché and statistician under British ambassador George Goschen in the 1880s. Referred to in Karpat (1985:52).

[6] The estimates from the patriarchate statistics of the six vilayets of Anatolia put the total Armenian population at just over 1 million. This was based on records (avowedly) of baptisms and deaths kept by ecclesiastical officials. The same records show a serious undercount of Muslims in the same vilayets. Whether conscious or unconscious, such an undercount met the political aims of those who desired Armenian independence (McCarthy 1983:48–51). European estimates of the population of the Ottoman Armenian communities were numerous and often at variance with each other. Some were based on Ottoman population registers, others from reports of European consuls or personal estimates, and some from members of the Armenian millets. Their totals ranged from 726,000 to 1.4 million. Ottoman census figures for Armenians in eastern Anatolia are much in line with those of the Armenian patriarchate, while those for western Anatolia suggest an Ottoman undercount (McCarthy 1983:51).

with other groups in the empire. As Davidson eloquently argued, in the nineteenth-century Ottoman Empire, religion 'provided a man's label, both his own conceptual scheme and in the eyes of his neighbour and his governors. He was a Muslim, Greek Orthodox, Gregorian Armenian, a Jew, Catholic or Protestant before he was a Turk or Arab or Greek or Bulgar, in the national sense and also before he felt himself an Ottoman citizen' (Davison 1954:844). Although the empire was governed by Muslims and was based on Islamic law, the several Christian communities and the Jewish community enjoyed partial autonomy. The semiautonomy of the Christian millets did not mean complete equality nor did it lead to any systematic persecution of Christians by Muslims or by the Ottoman government. Christian groups in the empire, however, maintained and exploited their close and often intimate association with European state representatives. After 1800, these Christian minorities gradually absorbed Western ideas of liberty and nationality and increasingly complained frequently and loudly about their lack of equality. The first response of Sultan Mahmud II (1808–39) was crucial in that he made it clear that in his view all his subjects, of whatever creed, were equal (Temperley 1936:40–41). The significant era of reform came in the Tanzimat period of 1838 to 1876, when the empire made serious efforts at Westernization and proclaimed the doctrine of equality of Christians and Muslims in several edicts of reform (see Chapter Two). With a total population of 35 million in the mid-nineteenth century, of which about 14 million were non-Muslims, the overwhelming majority of non-Muslims were Christians with perhaps only 150,000 being Jews. The Greek Orthodox population was the largest Christian minority, followed closely by the Gregorian Armenian. Towards the end of the Tanzimat period, it was becoming clear that some of the opposition to the doctrine of equal citizenship emerged from the Christian millets themselves (Davison 1954). The ecclesiastic hierarchies that ruled the Christian millets were opposed to Tanzimat efforts at equality, seeing them as potentially undermining their own power over their minority community. Furthermore, the Tanzimat leadership failed to understand the driving force of the nationalistic spirit growing ever stronger among Greeks, Serbs, and Romanians of the empire and 'beginning to infect the Bulgars and Armenians' (Davison 2003:68).

The Armenian ethno-religious minority of the Ottoman Empire was tightly managed and controlled by its Gregorian Church and had its own patriarchate and millet. However, the Greek Orthodox Church and its patriarchate, which represented a larger minority group, considered it heretical. When the kingdom of Greece was created in 1832, a number of Ottoman Orthodox Christians left the empire to join the new nation-state, leaving behind many important government posts that were taken up by Armenians (as noted in Chapter Two). Hence, from the second quarter of the nineteenth century, the Armenian millet acquired greater importance and influence, politically and economically, especially after the secession and independence of Greece. The Armenians were then considered the most reliable element in the Empire and were called *Millet-i-Sakika* or The Loyal Millet (Barsoumian 1997:184). By 1850, Armenian influence was such that they were granted a Protestant and Catholic millet in addition to their Gregorian or Apostolic Church millet.[7]

Another Christian minority – the Assyrians – was granted its own millet. Several years before, the Assyrians had shared much the same area and homeland as the Armenians and were administered by the Ottomans as a subsection of the Armenian millet. The Assyrians largely inhabited the Hakkiari Mountains between Lake Van in Anatolia and Lake Urmia in Persia. This area, which was also home to many Armenians and Kurds, was largely known as Kurdistan. In their rugged mountain villages, these Christians followed the Assyrian Ancient Church of the East, also called the Nestorian Church.[8] The Assyrians spoke a dialect related to Syriac – Aramaic. Both their language and religion separated them from the dominant local Muslim population of Kurds, Turks, Arabs, and Persians. Their patriarch held the community together tightly, dealing with their internal religious and social affairs as well as with their relations with the adjacent Kurdish community and the Ottoman state. Like their closest Christian neighbours, the Armenians,

---

[7] During the late Ottoman period, Armenians belonged to three millets. The original millet was organized by the Gregorian or Apostolic Church. By 1850, however, the Ottoman sultan granted the Armenian community two further millets: a Protestant and a Catholic. These new millets were an outcome of the significant European and American missionary activity during this time by mainly Presbyterian and Congregationalist missionary groups. The American Board of Commissioners for Foreign Missions sent its first missionaries to the Middle East in 1819. After finding no success with Muslims and Jews and little success with Orthodox Christians, they turned their attention to Armenians, who were more willing to accept Protestantism despite strong opposition from the Armenian Gregorian Church. Missionaries from the American Board of Congregationalists grew from 12 in 1819 to 209 in 1913. In that same year, American missions were educating 26,000 students in 450 schools, mainly Armenians from Anatolia (McCarthy 2001:69).

[8] The Nestorian Church originated from the Nestorian controversy about the nature of Christ. The fourth-century bishop of Constantinople, Nestorius, regarded Christ as having a dual nature, one human and one divine. Nestorius was condemned by the Council of Ephesus in 431. Those who refused to acknowledge his condemnation are referred to as Nestorians. See also Nisan (1991) and Arberry (1969).

the Assyrians were persecuted and became victims of massacres at the outbreak of World War I.

Constantinople, in many ways an Ottoman microcosm, was throughout most of the 1800s a city half Muslim and half non-Muslim.[9] The old city, as in earlier centuries, had nearly 400 mosques, more than 100 churches, hundreds of libraries, *madrasahs* (schools), and more than 300 *sufi tekkiyyes* (mystic religious orders). The Greek, Armenian, and Jewish millets had each developed their own class structure. Their upper strata, composed of high clergy and the merchant elites, resided in Istanbul and the landed gentry in the countryside. They were, nevertheless, bound by a profound allegiance to the Sultan and the system he represented. Those of the lower strata in these millets – the new merchants and craftsmen – accepted the general principles of European commerce, which was gaining a strong foothold in Constantinople and conformed to its business practices. In 1826, an incomplete population survey – which probably counted only male household heads inhabiting the city itself – indicated 45,000 Muslims, 30,000 Armenians, and 20,000 Greeks. Over the next few decades this large Armenian minority was to become even more prominent in terms of its contribution to the new social class developing as the old bureaucratic order was replaced by a European-oriented one. The emigration and decline of the Greeks after 1821 helped other ethnic groups rise to power, none more so than the Armenians.

By the 1870s the reform movement of the earlier decades and its push for Westernization had come to an end. The millet system, which had been so beneficial to the economic and political growth of non-Muslim communities, was dramatically reformed. With the accession of Abdul Hamid II came significant and disturbing changes. He suspended the Ottoman constitution, which Midhat Pasha had worked so hard to create, as well as the Ottoman Parliament in 1876. His increasingly authoritarian and conservative rule cast a shadow over the Ottoman Empire, and the liberal spirit of the Tanzimat reform era ended. While nationalist movements in

[9] By 1885 the Muslim population had risen to over 54 per cent and in 1900, it reached approximately 70 per cent. Thus by the end of the nineteenth century Constantinople had become once more Islamic and Turkish in character, just as it had been from the fifteenth century through to the early nineteenth century. The Ottoman state throughout the nineteenth century had promoted the expansion of minority rights and commerce through both the Tanzimat reforms and European pressure to maintain various Capitulations. As such the non-Muslim populations grew and benefited more than its Muslim populations and this reality was seen in the faster growth of its non-Muslim (Christian and Jewish) communities (Karpat 1985:886–887).

the European parts of the empire gained ground, Abdul Hamid heavily repressed similar political movements in Anatolia, which he believed were threatening separatism; foremost among these movements were the Armenian nationalist and, later, separatist movements.

Armenian nationalism was slow to start in the nineteenth-century Ottoman state. Perhaps this was due to the Armenians' close attachment to their church and the patriarch's position as head of the Armenian Gregorian millet system, which gave him a basic constitutional place in the Ottoman system. Nevertheless, local Armenian support for imperial Russian expansion into Transcaucasia and the eastern frontier of the Ottoman Empire eventually did shape much of the Armenian nationalist movement. Between 1800 and 1877 Russia expanded into Transcaucasia. It annexed Georgia (1800), took over areas that are today Azerbaijan and the Armenian republic (1829), and twice attacked Anatolia (1855 and 1877). In each of these invasions, Armenian militias, perhaps influenced by nationalist ambitions, aided the Russians in the hope that Christian Russia would help them create their own independent Armenian homeland. Yet the peace conferences at the end of these campaigns compelled Russia to retreat from some of their gains in Anatolia. In these withdrawals, tens of thousands of Armenians who had fought with them also fled (McCarthy 2001:66–70). During this period, the forced displacement of peoples – largely Muslims – was taking place in areas that held substantial Armenian minorities. These forced migrations created tensions, hatreds, and fears made all the worse by the arrival of more than 1.2 million Circassian and Abkhazian Muslims expelled by Russia from the western Caucasus (McCarthy 2001:68).

Throughout the 1860s and 1870s, Armenian nationalist groups expanded their activity, making numerous unsuccessful attempts to gain Russian support for their nationalist struggle, especially in Van and Zeytun. The outcome of the treaties of Berlin and San Stefano at the end of the Russian–Ottoman War of 1877–8 did not accommodate the Armenian nationalist movement – much to the disappointment of its leadership.[10] Thereafter and until World War I, Armenian nationalist groups in the Ottoman Empire and abroad set about creating a revolution that would engage the attention of Europeans. With offices in London,

---

[10] The European Signatories of the Treaty of Berlin in 1878 did express concern about the 'Armenian question' in Anatolia and the issue of equality before the law for non-Muslim subjects of Ottoman Empire, but this concern was not backed up by action (Dadrian 1997:49).

Paris, and other European capitals, Armenians began to garner support in the international media.[11] As noted in Chapter Two, three political parties were founded: by Armenian émigrés in Europe (Hunchaks), young Armenians in Van (Armenakan), and Armenian students in Russia (Dashnaks).[12] Emboldened by how Bulgaria had been created as a nation-state in 1878, these Armenian students and revolutionaries aspired to do the same for Armenia.[13] From a strictly chronological point of view, however, the Armenian question formally arose as an internal problem between the Armenian community and the fully armed Kurdish tribes who lived nearby (Dadrian 1997). At one of the first sessions of the Ottoman Parliament in 1877, the matter of defending the unarmed Armenian population in the eastern provinces from the depredation of Kurdish tribes was raised. It was a matter of seeking some measure of redress against cumulative wrongs as well as a quest for administrative remedies against inequalities and persecution. Only later, when hope of legislative redress with the Ottoman government appeared impossible, did the idea of separatism or independence become widespread among Armenians as a way to gain the sympathy of the European Powers,[14]

[11] See Hovannisian (1997b) for more details.
[12] The Armenakan party was founded in Van in 1885. Its revolutionary programme stressed the need for nationalist organization and arming its adherents. The second group, the Hunchakian Revolutionary party (Hunchaks) was founded in Geneva in 1887 by students and émigrés and then exported to Anatolia. The founders were Russian Armenians. None had lived in the Ottoman Empire. Their programme called for the assassination of Ottoman Turks and Armenians who stood against the nationalist cause. From Europe, Hunchak organizers were sent first to Istanbul and then to the cities in the east. Their main recruits were young educated Armenians. The third revolutionary party was the Dashnaktsuthian (Dashnaks), founded in 1890 in Tiflis, Russia. Moscow, St Petersburg, and cities in the Transcaucasia where Armenian students became the centres of the party. Its programme was dedicated to the importation of arms and men into the Ottoman Empire and to the use of terror and the looting and destruction of Ottoman government installations (Nalbandian 1963).
[13] The Bulgarian model was one where a small group of Bulgarian revolutionaries had killed a large number of local Muslims in the hope that a massive retaliation by Muslims would then bring support from Russia to force out all Muslim Bulgarians. That was the exact model which resulted in the creation of the nation-state of Bulgaria. Unfortunately for the Armenians, there was no place in Anatolia where such a model could work, as there was no single large area in the Ottoman Empire where the Armenians were in a clear majority (Shaw & Shaw 1977:202).
[14] At a meeting between the Armenian Patriarch Nercess and the British Ambassador Sir H. Elliot to determine the agenda regarding Armenian wishes to be presented to the Constantinople Conference of December 1876 to January 1877 to try to avert a Russian–Ottoman War, the Armenian patriarch was quoted as having said: 'If in order to secure the sympathy of the European Powers it was necessary to rise in insurrection, there would be no difficulty in getting such a movement' (Dadrian 1997:47).

Armenian nationalist agenda: Terrorism and vilification in Anatolia

Having recognized the weakness of their position vis-à-vis Europe and Russia, the Armenian nationalists set out to put their struggle on the European political map. This was to be a campaign of terror, which would result in greater repression and then an outpouring of European sympathy – as had been the case in the Bulgarian Terrors a decade earlier. In that case, Russia had intervened, causing mass expulsion and death among Bulgarian Muslims and creating a new Bulgarian state. For the Armenian nationalists, their plan would inevitably cause some loss of Armenian life, but the risks were considered well worth the effort. Cyrus Hamlin, the American missionary educator, made a record of this plan after a meeting with an Armenian Hunchak leader:

One of the revolutionaries told Dr. Hamlin, the founder of Robert College, that the Hentchak (Hunchak) bands would 'watch their opportunity to kill Turks and Koords, set fire to their villages, and then make their escape into the mountains. The enraged Moslems would then rise, and fall upon defenceless Armenians and slaughter them with such barbarity that Russia will enter in the name of humanity and Christian civilization and take possession'. When the horrified missionary denounced the scheme as atrocious and infernal beyond anything known, he received this reply: 'it appears so to you, no doubt; but we Armenians have determined to be free. Europe listened to the Bulgarian horrors and made them free. She will listen to our cry when it goes up in the shrieks and blood of millions of women and children ... We are desperate. We shall do it. (Langer 1960:157–158; quoted in McCarthy 2001:70–71)

It is rare that history repeats itself exactly; the differences between Bulgaria and the region of eastern Anatolia were that although it contained many Armenians, they were never an absolute majority, making the Armenian nationalist drive to put the plight of the Armenians on the European mental map quite difficult. At first, some of these strategies seemed to work. According to McCarthy, the initial attacks took place in the Sasun region against Kurdish traditional leaders who had coerced Armenian villagers to pay tribute to them (2001). Hovannisian provides a more detailed description of the events leading up to the first major massacre and test of Armenian revolutionary armed resistance in Sasun in 1894 (1997b:219–220). The year before, Armenians in the area had complained of the demands made by Kurdish notables who insisted on tribute payment in return for protection or, more accurately, refraining from raids by Kurdish tribes on these Armenian villages. This rural and remote area – as was also the case in the southern Syrian provinces – had the double jeopardy of having to pay off the pastoral tribes with tribute as well as the

Ottoman tax collector. The poverty of the region drove the inhabitants to be receptive to the Armenian nationalist agenda preached by the Hunchakist agitators. In the summer of 1893, numerous Armenian villages took up arms to defend themselves against Kurdish raids. The following summer, both nomadic Kurdish tribes and government tax collectors arrived to collect their payments. The armed Armenians resisted both. Kurdish chiefs and Ottoman tax officials complained to the regional governor, who responded by sending a military unit to the area to assist both groups of collectors. After a month's resistance against the Ottoman forces, the Armenians agreed to lay down their arms in return for an amnesty. Instead, they were subjected to looting and burning, torture, murder, and rape. As many as 3,000 Sasunites died in that massacre (Walker 1980:136–142).[15]

Word of the Sasun massacre quickly spread. The British consuls at Erzurum and Van relayed the details to the British ambassador in Constantinople. Missionaries and correspondents broadcast the information to Europe and a general outcry was registered; British, French, and Russian ambassadors proposed a joint commission of inquiry. This was rejected by the Ottoman state, but a compromise allowed European observers to accompany a governmental commission of inquiry, which was held in early 1895. The outcome was predictable. The Ottoman commission found that the Armenians had engaged in 'seditious' action and this required pacification by armed force. The Europeans disagreed and noted instead that the 'absolute ruin of the district can never be regarded as a measure proportionate to the punishment even of a revolt' (Great Britain 1895). Both sides had their extreme positions and the Sasun Commission findings inevitably were found to be inadequate by the Europeans who reluctantly returned to the Armenian question they thought they had left behind after the 1878 treaties of Berlin and San Stefano at the end of the Russian–Ottoman War.

After lengthy diplomatic exchanges, the British, French, and Russian ambassadors sent a memorandum to Sultan Abdul Hamid reminding him of his obligations to the Armenians under article 61 of the Treaty of Berlin

---

[15] Ottoman historians describe the events leading up to the Sasun massacres with a different orientation. They see the Sasunite attacks on the Ottoman tax collectors in 1894 as most significant. The Ottoman government is then credited with sending its army to pursue the Armenian guerrilla bands who were attacking Muslim inhabitants of villages along the withdrawal path. The Ottoman forces along with the Kurdish 'Hamidiyyah' semi-regular forces then slaughtered the Armenian guerrillas as well as all the Armenian villagers who had sheltered them or resisted the Ottoman army (McCarthy 2001).

and recommending to him, as counselled by article 61 that he consolidate the Armenian provinces of the empire, nominate governors for these provinces, grant Armenian political prisoners amnesty, allow émigrés to return, provide reparations to the victims of Sasun and other affected districts, and appoint a high commissioner to execute these reform provisions. Furthermore, this memorandum sought to have the nomadic Kurds controlled and be permitted to migrate only under governmental surveillance and to be encouraged to adopt a sedentary way of life. Finally, the Kurdish 'Hamidiyyah' corps was to be disarmed and left without uniform in peace time and only be attached to regular army units when activated in the future (Great Britain 1896). Inevitably the Sublime Porte tried to seriously dilute these recommendations, which the sultan most likely regarded as dangerous precedence for the empire's sovereignty. In London, Lord Salisbury assured the Ottoman ambassador that Queen Victoria's government did not seek autonomy or special privileges for the Armenians, but simply justice and equitable treatment (Hovannisian 1997b).

While these negotiations were taking place, Armenian nationalists, especially the Hunchakists, organized a number of marches and demonstrations. Given the climate of fear and ethnic distrust, these turned violent and spread. Muslim youth began to appear with clubs to beat to death any Armenians they found. The killings went on for weeks and marked the beginning – if the Sasun massacre is not considered the crucial spark – of what is known as the massacres of 1895–6. The Hunchak party led another rebellion in Zeytun, which spread to the region of Marash as well. The Armenian leader of the rebellion claimed 20,000 Muslims had been killed by his rebels. The Ottoman army defeated these rebels, killing uncounted numbers of Armenian rebels and civilians. In 1896 an Armenakan-led revolt in Van resulted in the death of at least 1,700 Armenians and 400 Muslims. These attacks, counterattacks, and massacres continued and spread further east. Finally, an attempted assassination of Sultan Abdul Hamid II and an Armenian attack on the Ottoman Bank of Istanbul killed twenty police guards. The exact numbers of deaths during these two years are not known. One estimate compiled from largely German sources puts the figure in excess of 88,000 (Lepsius 1897:330–331). Seeing the writing on the wall, many middle-class and urban Armenians made the decision to leave Constantinople and Anatolia. Some immigrated to more distant parts of the Ottoman Empire where the Armenian Church was established, such as Lebanon, Syria, Palestine, and Egypt. The first wave of Armenian forced migrants moved under

relatively comfortable conditions, selling homes and property and resettling in areas where Armenians already had thriving communities. A first
wave arrived in Alexandria, Egypt in the late 1890s and joined an already
well-established Armenian community. The newcomers were small in
number and had capital to invest in local industry, mainly textiles and
gold. These Armenian settlers joined the middle classes and brought added
life to community associations such as social clubs, sports clubs, schools,
newspapers, and journals. The Armenian political parties, the Hunchaks
and Dashnaks, also were revitalized by this wave of immigration from
Anatolia.[16] The Armenian church in Egypt was tied to the Orthodox
patriarchate in Jerusalem in 1916 (ACSHSS 2003; APJSO 1997).[17]

By the end of the nineteenth century, the Armenian nationalist revolutionary plan had achieved only partial success. The educated, elite
Armenians constituted a sizeable minority in Constantinople and actively
engaged in debates regarding constitutional rights. The rural Muslim
population in Anatolia, however, was inflamed. The Ottoman army subdued Armenian rebels and civilians in a heavy-handed and inexcusable
manner, but unlike the case in Bulgaria, there was no European intervention. Both British and Russian representatives in Istanbul had protested the
Muslim massacres of Armenians. The British considered a plan to sail into
the Dardanelles and depose the sultan and to accede to Armenian demands
for their own nation. But Russia did not wish to see the Ottomans replaced
with British, French, Austrian, or international control. In the end, no
European power was ready to go to war with the Ottoman Empire or
each other in the 1890s. Russia was still seen as a potential danger to the
European balance of power. It was only a decade later that growing
German power would push Britain to look at Russia as an ally. For the
Armenian nationalists, they had made the mistake of believing European
rhetoric. Although public opinion in Europe was concerned about the
Armenians, their own governments were far more interested in the balance
of power between Russia, Great Britain, France, Austria, and Germany
(McCarthy 2001:72–73).

After 1896, Armenian nationalists were deeply disillusioned by Europe.
For some, the socialist ideology of the Hunchaks was felt to be the reason

---

[16] The first wave of Armenian immigrants to Egypt came in the ninth century. Another wave
came with the arrival of the Seljuk Turks in Asia Minor in the eleventh century (Habib
2002:38; Mr. Baladyan 2005).

[17] In 1916, the four centres of authority in the Armenian Church (the Sees of Sis, Aghtamar,
Constantinople, and Jerusalem) were amalgamated into a new post of 'Catholicos-
Patriarch' in Jerusalem (ACSHSS 2003; APJSO 1997).

for this failure. The party duly split, with some members concentrating on the nationalist objective of emancipating Western Armenia and others continuing in their international socialist vein (Hovannisian 1997b). Over the next decade, Armenian revolutionary activity was carried out by small bands of guerrillas who roamed the Armenian mountains and continued to attack Muslim villages, government officials, and Kurdish tribal elements. But these activities could not reverse the economic decline and impoverishment of the Armenian and Muslim peasantry and the continued emigration of Armenians from their historic homeland to the southern provinces of the Ottoman Empire – northern Syria, Jerusalem, and Egypt were the preferred destinations (Hovannisian 1997a: 226–7; McCarthy et al. 2006; Salt 2003: 3).

In 1905 another attempt to assassinate Sultan Abdul Hamid II was commissioned by the Dashnak party. In this resolve they were not alone, as the sultan had degenerated into a universally feared and reviled figure among émigrés, reformers, and revolutionaries of all the Ottoman nationalities.[18] Although the assassination attempt failed, the plot's organizer, Kristapor Mikayelian, was killed accidentally by the explosives intended for the sultan. Abdul Hamid escaped the assassination attempt because he had altered his normal Friday routine slightly, and the diversion was enough to shield him from the massive explosion which destroyed his waiting carriage and attending police officers (Hovannisian 1997b:227).

Among the groups who regarded the sultan as the major cause of the decline and decay of the Ottoman Empire were a group of young modernists called the Young Turks. They believed that efficient, just government was possible and that such reform would end the disintegration of the Ottoman Empire. Although they were reformers, they did not believe in regional autonomy as the solution to the empire's problems. Thus, they were not sympathetic to the Armenian nationalists' demands for self-rule or

---

[18] In 1899, one of the nephews of Abdul Hamid fled to Europe along with other members of the royal family opposed to the sultan's despotism. In 1902, Prince Sabaheddin held a Congress of Ottoman Liberals in his Paris residence. Forty-seven delegates attended, representing Turkish, Arab, Greek, Kurdish, Armenian, Albanian, Circassian, and Jewish groups in an entente against the sultan. The resolutions called for equal rights for all Ottoman citizens, local self-administration, measures to defend the territorial integrity of the empire, and restoration of the constitution suspended since 1877. Hovannisian notes that even at this early stage, Armenian nationalists opposed some of the Young Turks who were strongly opposed to any talk of separatism. Ahmed Riza, one of the leading Young Turks, was to take the position that 'Autonomy is treason: it means separation!' (Hovannisian 1997b:229).

European intervention. Rather, they believed the answer to a reawakened and healthy empire was through the establishment of a properly functioning central government. In 1907 the Ottoman reformers abroad as well as a circle of army officers headquartered in Salonika brought their membership together and formed a formal society, the Committee of Union and Progress (CUP). At a second Congress of Ottoman Liberals in Paris, this body – which included the Armenian Dashnaks – pledged to overthrow Sultan Abdul Hamid and to introduce representative government. In July 1908, Sultan Abdul Hamid gave in to the demands of his insubordinate officers and abdicated. For a moment, optimism for an Ottoman Christian and Muslim brotherhood and equal citizenship seemed possible. However, the upheavals of that year were seized upon by European states to complete the dismemberment of the Ottoman Empire's European holdings: Austria-Hungary annexed Bosnia and Herzegovina; Bulgaria asserted its full independence; and Crete declared its union with Greece. As an immediate response, Sultan Abdul Hamid's supporters launched a countercoup in an attempt to return him to power. The Sultan was then finally deposed and exiled to Salonika. For the Armenian nationalists, however, this counter-coup and the reaction to it outside of Constantinople and in particular in the region of Cilicia were ominous.

Armenians had lived in Cilicia for millennia. Between the eleventh and fourteenth centuries there had been an Armenian kingdom in Cilicia, but the region was an ethnic and confessional mixture. Armenians had played a major role in commerce, in crafts, and in the new developing industry and were taking advantage of the education opportunities provided by American and European mission schools in Adana, Tarsus, Aintab, Marash, and elsewhere. After the 1908 Young Turk Revolution, many Armenians felt the time had come for them to insist on their rights as Ottoman citizens and to enjoy freedom of speech. There are many versions of the origins of the massacre at Adana in the following year, but most accounts lay some blame on the Armenian prelate of Adana, Bishop Mushegh. Mushegh promulgated the Armenian nationalist rhetoric, proclaiming that the centuries of Armenian servitude had passed and now was the time for Armenians to defend themselves, their families, and their communities. For Muslims, this new era of constitutionality appeared threatening to their traditional relationship with Armenians. At the same time, the countercoup was taking place in Constantinople to restore Abdul Hamid to the throne. Traditionalists and Conservatives attacked the Armenians of Adana, and the violence soon spread to the outlying villages. When Ottoman authorities finally intervened two days later, more than

2,000 Armenians were dead. After an uneasy ten-day truce, violence broke out again, this time spreading throughout Cilicia all the way to Marash in the northeast and Kessab in the south. One eyewitness, American missionary Reverend Herbert Adams Gibbons of Hartford, Connecticut, described the scene during the April massacres:

Adana is in a pitiable condition. The town has been pillaged and destroyed... It is impossible to estimate the number killed. The corpses lie scattered through the streets. Friday, when I went out, I had to pick my way between the dead to avoid stepping on them. Saturday morning I counted a dozen cartloads of Armenian bodies in one-half hour being carried to the river and thrown into the water. In the Turkish cemeteries, graves are being dug wholesale (as reported in the *New York Times* 1909)

An Ottoman Parliamentary Commission of Investigation reported that there had been 21,000 victims, of which 19,479 were Armenian, 850 Syrian, 422 Chaldean, and 250 Greek (as quoted in Hovannisian 1997b:231; Papikian 1919). This was perhaps the first massacre of the Young Turk era and several Ottoman officials as well as Armenians were hanged in Adana for provoking the violence. Once the Young Turks regained control of Constantinople, they claimed the massacres were the work of reactionaries and conducted a public memorial service for both Turkish and Armenian citizens of the empire. Furthermore, and perhaps because of this public sympathy for the massacred in Cilicia, the Dashnak Armenian party remained loyal to its entente with the Young Turks. In the Dashnak's Fifth General Congress of 1909, the party pledged continued support of the government and rejected any move towards separation. By September of that year, the Dashnaks entered into a protocol of agreement with the CUP to implement the constitution fully and to extend its guarantees to the rest of the Ottoman provinces so as to avoid any repeat of the Adana massacres. In particular, the agreement called for efforts to counteract harmful rumours that the Armenians were aspiring to secession and independence.

Over the next four years, between 1908 and 1912, the Dashnak party remained loyal to the constitutional regime. The party cut back on the activities of its guerrilla forces and campaigned actively for parliamentary elections. It was, however, actively criticized by the Hunchaks and other Armenian political groups for continuing to collaborate with the CUP. Nevertheless, despite this growing unease among some Armenian nationalists, when in 1912 the combined armies of Greece, Bulgaria, Serbia, and Montenegro invaded the last of the remaining Ottoman possessions of

Macedonia and Thrace, the Armenian nationalists generally exhorted their followers to fight to defend the Ottoman state.[19]

The victory of these combined armies, their occupation of Macedonia and much of Thrace, and their demand for further territorial concessions weakened the moderate Ottoman cabinet. In 1913, a coup lead by Enver Bey culminated in the ascendancy of an ultranationalist – Turkish, not Ottoman – cabinet. From that time on until the end of World War I, the politics of the Ottoman Empire, formulated around a small group of Turkish nationalists, were to undermine and then destroy Armenian hopes for self-determination without separation.

Armenian nationalists and their political societies did enjoy a period of semilegal status between 1908 and 1915. They maintained newspapers and party clubs, and also vied for parliamentary seats allotted to the Armenians. Yet these privileges in the urban centres – and particularly in Constantinople – did little to improve the miserable conditions of the rural peasantry in general, Armenian and Muslim alike. Fighting between Armenian and Muslim militias could not be addressed from the capital; widespread anarchy in the rural countryside was reported by European consuls and American missionaries. And Europe generally expressed concern, urging intervention into Ottoman affairs. By 1912 Czar Nicholas, who had been silent for fifteen years, proclaimed his concern for the 'wretched Armenians' of the Ottoman Empire. In part, this was an expression of concern regarding the growth of German influence – the Caucasus could very well become Kaiser Wilhelm's outposts, were he so interested. Simply blocking German expansion into western Armenia was cause enough for Russian agitation. Uplifted by such international concern, Armenian patriarchal circles began to prepare statistics to demonstrate that despite decades

---

[19] Although the Young Turks had originally welcomed other nationalities of the empire to join them as equals, this position did not last. The Young Turks had three options before them for the future of the state: Ottomanism, Islamism, or Turkism. Ottomanism was the position supported by the exiled nephew of the sultan, Prince Sabaheddin, and meant the strengthening of the institutions of the existing empire and making them available for all its citizens. This meant the modernization of the multiethnic and plural state as suggested in the Constitution of 1877. Islamism in this era meant the deepening of relations with all Muslim peoples within the empire and throughout the world. And finally there was Turkism or Turkish nationalism based on the idea of a Turkish race, the ruling elite of the empire which had a vast network of kinship with other Turkic people stretching from the Balkans to Siberia. The latter was nonreligious in conception and thus particularly attractive to the inside core of the largely atheist and positivist Young Turks. This position also represented a dramatic break with Ottomanism and Islamism, which both accepted the 'privileged' minority status of Christians and other 'People of the Book' in Islam (Walker 1997:242).

of massacres, persecutions, and emigration, the Armenians still formed a plurality in their historical homelands. These patriarchal statistical records showed that in 1912 there were one million Armenians in the six main provinces referred to as Turkish Armenia, with another 400,000 in Cilicia, and 530,000 in Western Anatolia and European Turkey. Thus, in the core six provinces, Armenians formed 38.9 per cent of the population, with Turks 25.4 per cent and Kurds, 16.3 percent (Armenian Delegation 1919:44–46; quoted in Hovannisian 1997b:235). The czar and representatives of six European nations then used these statistics to hammer out a compromise settlement which, although not fulfilling all Armenian expectations, did represent the most viable reform proposed since the internationalization of the Armenian question in 1878. Ominously, only the Ottoman Grand Vizier and Foreign Minister signed the agreement along with the Russian Chargé d'Affaires.[20] Most of the CUP leadership was opposed to the foreign pressure, which they felt undermined their entire government. For the Armenians, it seemed that their struggle for civil rights and regional autonomy might now come about. However, events in Eastern Anatolia and the pragmatic platform of the core CUP group were to move in another direction and, in a matter of months, sweep most Armenians in western Anatolia and Cilicia out of their historic homelands through deportation and massacre on a massive scale.

Wars in the East and the Armenian massacres

The struggle for Armenia was a complicated, obscure affair with events and chronologies interpreted from extreme positions. Hovannisian and Walker take very much a 'victimization' approach to this period in history, while McCarthy and Shaw take an Ottoman or Turkish perspective.[21] For

---

[20] This compromise document included: the unification of the six Armenian *vilayets* into a single province; the appointment of a Christian governor for the province; the formation of a mixed Muslim–Christian gendarmerie commanded by European officers; the dissolution of the Kurdish Hamidiyyah Cavalry; publication of official decrees in Turkish, Kurdish, and Armenian with the right to use those languages in legal proceedings; permission for each nationality to establish and administer private schools; establishment of a commission to establish the extent of Armenian losses caused by usurpation and supervised restitution; exclusion of Muslim refugees (mainly from Russia) from the new Armenian province; and an obligation of the European powers to ensure enactment of the programme (Hovannisian 1967:30–33; Mandelstam 1917:218–222).

[21] There is a vast literature on the Armenian massacres or genocide. An excellent starting point is Toynbee (1916). There is also Morgenthau (1918). Of the recent literature there is Hovannisian (1967) and his edited collection (1987); also Walker (1980). The Ottoman

the former, the Armenians had not behaved in any manner so as to warrant the fury of mass slaughter, death marches, and summary executions that have been recorded for the period of April to August 1915. For the latter, the Armenians, especially those who fought alongside the Russian invaders into eastern Anatolia, had become 'provocateurs', a 'fifth column', and threatened to undermine the Ottoman war against the invading Russians. At the same time nearly a million Muslim refugees from the Russian front were streaming into the Ottoman state and needed to be settled. What is clear is that in the first years of World War I, a partial, if not full, genocide was taking place.[22] Whatever the numbers of Muslim refugees who had died in their flight from Russian borderlands and Transcaucasia, an equal if not greater number died in the determined Ottoman drive to cleanse eastern and central Anatolia of its Armenian population (Melson 1996:141–148). However, the scale of the horrors of the Armenian 'forced marches', as reported in Western media, followed a few decades on by the Jewish Holocaust in Europe, has meant that discussions of this Armenian tragedy in history are generally polemical or enshrouded with deep emotional and personal pain.

In Turkey … in 1915 … the deportations were deliberately conducted with a brutality that was calculated to take the maximum toll of lives en route. This was the CUP's crime; and my study of it left an impression on my mind that was not effaced by the still more cold-blooded genocide, on a far larger scale that was committed during the Second World War by the Nazis. Arnold Toynbee (1967:241–242)

Just before the outbreak of war in Europe, on 2 August 1914, the Ottoman Empire signed a secret pact with Germany undertaking to go to war if Russia attacked Austria or Hungary. This was not a unanimous decision, as members of the Ottoman inner circle still preferred to remain neutral. However, it was felt that should Russia win its war, their neutrality would leave them vulnerable to even more loss of territory, as had been the case in the preceding decades (Öncü 2003:85–88). On 30 October 1914 the Ottoman government entered World War I on the side of Germany. In essence, two wars were to be fought: one along its northern and far western

and Turkish perspective is represented by McCarthy (1995; 2001). Melson (1996) attempts to step back and take a wider perspective in the context of all the genocides of the twentieth century. Surprisingly, although he discusses the ethnic cleansing and partial as well as full genocides of our contemporary era – including the Tutsi, Cambodian and Bosnian cases – he never once makes the association of the ethnic cleansing of Palestine in 1948 as being of the same order as his subject matter.

[22] Armenians living outside of eastern Anatolia, in Constantinople and other major cities in western Anatolia, were not subject to these expulsions and massacres to the same extent, as becomes clear in some of the narrative histories cited in this chapter.

frontiers against Europe and the other against Russian armies encompassing an intercommunal war between Armenians and Muslims of eastern Anatolia and the southern Caucasus (McCarthy 1995:179). In its proclamation of war, the Ottoman government spoke of seeking a natural frontier, including uniting 'all branches of our race'. In this context, the Young Turks, who would have issued these aims, were clearly expressing their vision of the empire as Turkish rather than Ottoman (Toynbee 1916:28–29). By contrast, most Armenians still maintained their loyalty to the multiethnic, plural ideals of Ottomanism. Many enlisted into the army. A unit of 8,000 Armenian soldiers fought in the Ottoman Army at Sarikamish, Caucasia. However, the leader of the Dashnak party fled to Tiflis at this time to assist in the formation of Armenian volunteer partisan units to operate with Russian forces against the Ottomans along the Eastern front (Walker 1997). Between 1914 and 1920 the wars on the Eastern front of the Ottoman Empire were perhaps the worst in human history (quoted in McCarthy 1995:179; Singer & Small 1972). Ottoman weakness, Russian imperial designs, European meddling, and Armenian revolutionary nationalism all combined to bring about widespread devastation, pillage, suffering, and death. The cities of Van, Bitlis, Bayazit, and Erzincan were left in rubble and thousands of villages destroyed (McCarthy 1995:236; Niles & Sutherland 1919:216–222). Millions of Armenians and Muslims died. The Armenians came out of these struggles with a state incorporated into the Soviet Republic, and the Young Turks were left with a country in ruin.

In the lead up to the 1915 deportation of Armenians, it is useful to describe one of the military battlefronts between Ottoman and Russian forces over territory the Armenians considered their own. The events largely preceded the expulsion and massacres of Armenians, but even so, some historians refuse to link the events or to see one as leading up to the other (Walker 1997).[23] In November 1914, Russian forces moved south

---

[23] Other historians saw the Armenians as a deadly threat to the Ottoman state. Referring to the rise of Armenian nationalism near the end of the nineteenth century, Bernard Lewis wrote: *For the Turks, the Armenian movement was the deadliest of all threats. From the conquered lands of the Serbs, Bulgars, Albanians, and Greeks, they could however reluctantly, withdraw, abandoning distant provinces and bringing the Imperial frontier nearer home. But the Armenians, stretching across Turkey-in-Asia from the Caucasian frontier to the Mediterranean coast, lay in the very heart of the Turkish homeland – and to renounce the lands would have meant not the truncation, but the dissolution of the Turkish state. Turkish and Armenian villages inextricably mixed, had for centuries lived in neighbourly association. Now a desperate struggle between them began – a struggle between two nations for the possession of a single homeland that ended with the terrible holocaust of 1915 when a million and a half Armenians perished.* (Lewis 1961:356)

into Ottoman territory. The following month, Enver Pasha attacked the Caucasus and was pushed back from Sarikamish, losing three-quarters of his men and laying open the way into Anatolia. The following spring, Russians advanced south. Armenian revolutionary forces seized the Ottoman city of Van on 13 and 14 April 1915 and held it for nearly four months. However in August 1915, Ottoman troops drove the Russians and their Armenian collaborators out of Van (McCarthy 1995:183).[24]

The defeat of the Ottoman army in the Caucasus in January 1915 marked a turning point for Armenians in the empire. Although Enver Pasha publicly thanked Armenians for their conduct during the Sarikamish campaign in a letter to the Armenian Bishop of Konia (Lepsius 1897), the end of that month saw violent measures initiated against Ottoman Armenians. Many of those who had enlisted in the army were forced to give up their arms and were consigned to manual labour.[25] Armenians who had not enlisted also were directed to surrender their arms. In a number of towns, Armenian men were jailed until sufficient arms were delivered to the Ottoman authorities. These arms searches became, according to Walker, a pretext for a general persecution of Armenians (1997:246). Once the disarmament programme had been underway for some time, a systematic programme of deportation was initiated. Between April and August 1915 Armenians from most of the major centres of central and eastern Anatolia were ordered to leave their homes and forced to march – to almost certain death – towards the Syrian

---

[24] A good example of the complexity and deeply polemical positions of many Ottoman and Armenian historians is illustrated by the opposite view of Walker in this regard. Walker maintains that the disturbances in Van in April 1915 cannot be regarded as an Armenian uprising. To him, the examination of events and a close inspection of chronology reveal that the Armenians did no more than protect themselves against the brutality of the Ottoman government. In no matter, he states, were the actions of the Armenians coordinated with the movements of the Russian army and thus the Armenians cannot be considered the provocateurs of the death marches. Nevertheless, he maintains that the Ottoman government took the Armenian defence of Van as a pretext for extreme measures. On 23 and 24 April, the Ottomans arrested 235 community leaders, writers, and educators in Constantinople, holding them at the central police station for three days before exiling them to villages in central Anatolia. A second wave of arrests, including Armenian parliamentary deputies Vartkes and Krikor Zohrab, brought the figures to 600 with important Armenian public figures sent off to Diyarbekir. Walker sees these arrests and killings as central to the government's plans for the brutal destruction of the Armenian leadership and a wider campaign against all Armenians. He notes that Shaw and Shaw (1977), leading Ottoman historians, make no mention of these events in their major writings (Walker 1997:250–252).

[25] According to Walker, the Armenians in the Ottoman armies numbered as many as 100,000 (1997:246).

Desert and then Mosul. Very few ever reached Mosul itself. The operations began in the heartlands of the Armenian–Ottoman intercommunal war: in Zeytun on 8 April and in Van two weeks later. This spread to Cilicia and other major urban cities of Ottoman Anatolia. According to Walker, the pattern was the same: first the fit Armenian men from a town or village would be summoned to the government building. They would be held for a few days in jail, then marched out of town and, typically, shot. Shortly afterwards, women, children, and old men would be summoned in the same way. They were not jailed, but told that they had to leave in a few days to new homes. They were then driven out by gendarmes along designated routes. Many collapsed and died along the way. Sometimes they were attacked by other gendarmes, marauders, or Kurdish irregulars. Muslim villagers were instructed not to harbour any Armenians on pain of death. Those who could not continue the journey were shot. They were largely driven south-westward in the direction of Aleppo. This city became the main staging post for the deportees; from there they were sent east along the Euphrates River to Deir-ez-Zor, which became a vast concentration camp. Occasionally, eyewitness accounts as well as records kept by the British Army towards the end of the war indicated that local residents took pity on these desperate people and arranged marriages for young Armenian women as well as fostering arrangements for young men and children.[26]

In the weeks and months that followed, Armenians from the towns and villages of western Anatolia and Cilicia were attacked or driven out of their homes. The German consul von Scheubner-Richter, who observed some of this depredation, wrote to his ambassador on 2 June 1915:

> The discussion which I have had with the commander in chief on the subject of the expulsion of the Armenians has yielded nothing positive. The Armenian inhabitants of all the plains – doubtless to those of the plain of Erzurum – will be deported to Deir-ez-Zor. Such a transfer of population is tantamount to a massacre, since, in the absence of any means of transport, hardly half of them will arrive alive at their destination, and it is possible that this operation will cause the ruin of not only the Armenians, but of the whole country. One cannot justify these measures by military

---

[26] A number of the eyewitness accounts held in the Zoryan Institute in Toronto recount how some survivors were adopted by Bedouin families and spent several years in the Syrian Jezirah herding sheep until British forces took over the region and demanded the release of these boys. Interviews with residents in Aleppo in 2005 also reveal that an underground network organized by a Muslim physician who had daily contact with Armenian refugees and was operating to identify young adolescent Armenian girls and arrange for them to be moved out of the internment camps and married off to local Muslim men in order to save them from rape and death. (Zoryan Institute)

considerations, since it is not a question of revolt among the Armenians of the region, and the people who are being deported are old men, women and children. The Armenians who have been converted to Islam have not been expelled. (Lepsius 1897:80)

By the end of August 1915 a large proportion of the Armenian population of central and eastern Anatolia had been driven out of their lands, pillaged, raped, starved, and murdered. The Armenian leadership in Constantinople had been destroyed, Cilicia was in ruins and the mainly Armenian cities of Van, Bitlis, Mush, and Sasun largely emptied of Armenians and replaced with the 750,000 or more Muslim refugees fleeing the fighting in Transcaucasia (Lepsius 1897:495). Some Ottomans had opposed these violent polices of the CUP, both at the official and the popular level. In several localities, decrees had been issued making it illegal for Muslims (Turks or Kurds) to harbour or shelter Armenians. However, many local families violated these orders and after the war ended, thousands of Armenian children reemerged in Anatolia, kept alive in Muslim households during the conflict (see Hovannisian 1992).

Between 1914 and 1918 the Ottoman Empire was largely redrawn. Ottomanism had died with the entry of the state into World War I. Pan-Arabism had also been destroyed with the breaking away of the Arab provinces of Syria, Palestine, and Mesopotamia to British and French overtures. What emerged in its place was a Turkish nation and state. The Armenians of the Ottoman Empire had been largely eliminated in the Young Turks' bid to create a pan-Turkic state extending from Constantinople to the Caspian Sea. Armenian nationalism suffered a further defeat with the separation of Transcaucasia from Russia and then its fragmentation into the republics of Georgia, Azerbaijan, and Armenia.

On 30 October 1918 the Ottoman Empire signed the Armistice of Mudros with the Allied powers. It was agreed that the Ottomans would be disarmed and the Allies would make only minimal changes to the Ottoman state and unoccupied lands until a final decision had been agreed by treaty. In the east, Ottoman forces had retaken all the land that had been lost in the 1877–8 war. They had even marched across Transcaucasia to Baku to aid the Azerbaijan Turks fighting Armenian nationalists. Yet once the Armistice of Mudros was signed, the Ottoman army retreated to approximately its 1914 border to await developments and a final peace treaty.

In the two years before the 10 August 1920 Treaty of Sèvres was signed, much was to change. The Russian Revolution saw imperial Russia give way to a soviet state with a determined ambition to hold on to all the territory that had been part of the Russian Empire. The Russian army in eastern Anatolia had melted away in the previous year, leaving behind only the Armenian troops. For a short period these troops belonged to the Transcaucasian Federation of Georgia, Armenia, and Azerbaijan. Georgia and Azerbaijan were rapidly absorbed into the new Soviet state, leaving only Armenia as an independent republic. In Anatolia itself, the defeated Ottoman troops at first reluctantly and then with greater enthusiasm repelled the provocative Greek, French, and also Italian land grab and thus, under the leadership of Kemal Ataturk, carved out a rump Anatolian state (Hovannisian 1987; McCarthy 2001).

From mid-1918 to the end of 1920, Armenians made significant efforts to build a viable, democratic state in the Transcaucasian territory under their control. The Republic of Armenia, which they shaped, was dependent on Allied and European support. Three Armenian delegations – from the new republic, from the Populist Party as well as the Dashnaks – attended the January 1919 Paris Peace Conference and made sure that Armenian goals of a Greater Armenia including Cilicia and a Mediterranean outlet remained on the agenda (Hovannisian 1987:319–321). Their public relations success can be found in one of the first acts of the peace conference, which declared that 'because of the historical misgovernment of the Turks of subject peoples and the terrible massacres of Armenians and others in recent years, the Allied and Associated Powers are agreed that Armenia, Syria, Mesopotamia, Palestine and Arabia must be completely severed from the Turkish Empire'. These states were all to be provisionally recognized as independent nations subject to the 'administrative assistance' of a mandatory power. Palestine and Mesopotamia were awarded to Great Britain and Syria to France. But no nation among the Allies or associated powers was prepared to accept the mandate for Armenia. The Allies tried to persuade the United States to do so, but as it had never formally declared war on the Ottoman Empire, it refused to take any part in this particular mandatory exercise or any other as recommended over Syria in the King Crane Commission (quoted in Hovannisian 1997c:320; United States 1943:785–786, 795–796).

Throughout 1919 and 1920 the Allied powers remained publicly committed to the establishment of a united Armenian state combining the former imperial Russian Armenia and the former Ottoman Armenian provinces with an outlet on the Black Sea. However, the Armenian nationalists wanted more and continued to negotiate for a greater Armenia to include Cilicia and access to the Mediterranean. The Allies continued to hope that the United States would accept a League of Nations mandate over this projected Armenia. But, although the Allies advocated a free Armenia, none was prepared to commit troops to make that goal a reality. During this same period, the Turkish nationalist movement took shape with the aim of preserving the territorial integrity of Anatolia and rejecting the neocolonialist League of Nations mandatory schema. By the end of 1919, Mustafa Kemal [Kemal Ataturk] had won over much of the remaining Ottoman army and created a new government seat in Ankara. By 1920 it was obvious that the Allied powers had to redefine their obligations towards Armenians in the light of the growing successes of the nationalist Turkish struggle (Walker 1997:304). By May of 1920, Armenians in the Republic of Armenia were increasingly faced with the choice of standing up to a new Turkish invasion or succumbing to Soviet pressure and joining Soviet Russia. On 10 August 1920 the Treaty of Sèvres was signed but never enforced because of the armed refusal of Mustafa Kemal and his nationalist Turks to accept it. Nevertheless, it is of value to reflect in greater detail on the conditions (also see Chapter Two) as they go some distance in explaining how Mustafa Kemal was able to so quickly bring together an opposition force to counter this European imperialist platform. The Treaty of Sèvres demanded:

- Izmir and the surrounding region be put under Greek administration with a plebiscite to be held after five years to decide if the region should be annexed permanently to Greece.
- The Ottoman Empire was to accept President Wilson's decision as to the border between it and an Armenia with access to the sea.
- Syria and Iraq were provisionally recognized as independent states subject to mandatory assistance by Britain and France.
- The Balfour Declaration, creating a Jewish Home in Palestine, was written into the treaty.
- The Sharif of Mecca was given a free and independent state in the Hijaz and northwestern Arabia only.
- Italy was recognized as having a special interest in southern Anatolia (the Antalya and Konya regions).
- The French were recognized as having a special interest in Cilicia (Adana, Antep, Urfa and Mardin regions).
- The Ottoman land forces were to be reduced to 50,000 men, most of whom would be gendarmes. There would be no regular army.
- The Capitulations were to be restored. An allied commission would oversee the state budget, taxes, loans, and in effect control Ottoman finances.

What territory remained to the Ottomans was – as foreseen in the Sykes-Picot Agreement of 1916 – just northwest and north central Anatolia, a region which excluded more of the Turkish population than it included. Greece, which had not fought against the Ottomans in the war, was given Izmir and its surrounding territory, which had been 75 percent Turkish before the war. An Armenian Republic was left without defined borders. Italy and France were to share southern Anatolia. It is little wonder that, although the government of Ferit Pasha signed the Treaty of Sèvres, it was rejected by Mustafa Kemal and his nationalist followers. Even as it was signed, the Treaty of Sèvres was dead. Ferit Pasha's government was bleeding, and resistance to the Allied plans to dismember Anatolia grew daily (McCarthy 2001:130–131).

In October 1920, two months after the Treaty of Sèvres was signed, and reportedly moved to action by reports of massacres of Muslims in Armenia, the Turkish National Assembly in Ankara allowed one of the important veterans of the Ottoman war in the east, Karabekir, to take his forces and attack Armenia (McCarthy 2001:144).[27] This was swiftly accomplished and by the end of the month he held Kars and the 1877 Ottoman–Russian border was reestablished. The Armenian republic sued for peace and in December 1920, the Treaty of Alexandropol was signed. Armenians accepted the new borders and gave up their claim to eastern Anatolia. The crippled Armenian government then had no choice but to save what little territory remained to it by opting for Soviet rule and seeking the protection of the new Soviet state and its Red Army (Hovannisian 1983:277–292). Another wave of Armenian refugees left their homeland, some refusing to live under Turkish rule and others preferring not to live under a socialist state. These refugees found shelter in the new mandated states of the Arab world – Syria, Lebanon, Palestine, Transjordan, and Egypt. Others made their way to Europe and North America. Nearly 600,000 or more Armenians of Anatolia had been lost in World War I and the Turkish War of Independence – leaving less than 400,000 Armenians in Anatolia or 40 per cent of their total pre-war figures. Of those that were expelled, some had been forced out in organized death marches, others had fled, many had been murdered, and others died of starvation and disease. Some survived the forced marches and were

---

[27] Hovannisian gives another justification for this attack on Armenia. It was derived from Mustafa Kemal's recognition of the menace which an expanded Armenia – as determined by the Treaty of Sèvres – had on his efforts to create a Turkish republic. He needed to establish a border with Armenia which did not eat into eastern Anatolia. Thus the armies loyal to Mustafa Kemal breached the frontier with Armenia in October 1920 and forced the Armenian government to repudiate the terms of the Treaty of Sèvres, renouncing all claims to Turkish Armenia (Hovannisian 1987:36).

pulled in and given a helping hand by Armenian and other communities in the Middle East. Others carried on, leaving the region and emigrating to Europe, Canada, and the United States.

SURVIVING THE DEPORTATION AND THE DEATH MARCHES

Missionary activity in the Ottoman Empire dated back to the 1830s and was largely American. These Protestant missions had quickly discovered that conversion from Islam was going to be unlikely, so they turned their attention to Armenian Christians whom they were able to convert to more evangelical denominations (Grabill 1971:27). They had great success among these 'natives to the soil' and by the time of the Armenian massacres of 1915 there were more than 551 elementary and high schools, eight colleges, and countless dispensaries serving Armenians and some Greeks in Anatolia (Richter 1910:72). Humanitarian relief for the Armenians was largely an American effort growing out of the American Protestant missionary presence in the Ottoman Empire. This relief first reached the Armenians through private agencies, but in 1915 an influential group of missionaries, philanthropists, industrialists, and educators founded the Armenian Relief Committee. Even after the Ottoman Empire severed relations with the USA in 1917, American missionaries remained in their posts and tried to protect the Armenians. In 1918, with the Armistice of Mudros, the American public was able to renew and intensify its relief operations. The Armenian Relief Committee became known as the American Committee for Relief in the Near East (ACRNE) and raised US$20 million in private donations in 1919. Early in that year a field mission to Anatolia and Caucasia returned to the USA with reports of appalling conditions. By March 1919 the first ACRNE medical teams reached Armenia and took charge of eleven hospitals and ninety orphanages with 13,000 children. Another 30,000 orphans were eventually taken in by ACRNE. The President of ACRNE declared:

The hope of the future of the Armenian nation is wrapped up in large measure with the orphan and women problem which we are attempting to solve .... The children who survived the terrible ordeal of the past five years have matured prematurely and reveal unexpected recuperative capacity. Thousands of the weaker children have perished; we deal with the survivors. (Barton 1930:119)[28]

---

[28] This is quoted in Hovannisian (1997c:312). The origins of another international humanitarian aid agency, Save the Children Fund, also emerge from this tragedy. Its cofounders, Eglantyne Jebb and her sister, Dorothy Buxton, had travelled to the Balkans just before World War I and witnessed the terrible suffering of children.

By the summer of 1919, ACRNE was incorporated as the Near East Relief and had sent more than 30,000 metric tons of food and clothing to be distributed to the destitute in Constantinople and the western provinces of Anatolia.[29] This represented more than half the relief supplies being distributed at that time. Earlier, in February 1919, the American Congress created the American Relief Administration to administer a US$100 million appropriation to assist non-enemy countries as well as 'Armenians, Syrians, Greeks and other Christian and Jewish populations of Asia Minor, now or formerly subjects of Turkey'. Herbert Hoover, a future president of the United States, was appointed head of the American Relief Administration (Hovannisian 1997c:312). Another 50,000 metric tons of flour, grain, condensed milk, and other foodstuffs was sent to Armenia in a series of boat shipments to the port of Batum on the Black Sea.

Many orphans or separated children survived solely because of the efforts of Near East Relief and the Armenian Church. One survivor relates his dependence on the Church both at the beginning of his life and towards its end.

I was born in 1915 in Adabazar, Turkey. I don't remember very much before I was about 3–4 years old. My first memory was in Constantinople in the Canadian Hospital. My left leg was infected. I remember I was taken out into the sunshine for my leg to heal. Then, a few months later I remember I was with my two brothers and we were in an Armenian Church orphanage with an American lady called Miss Kuchmen. Then we were all sent to Switzerland to another Armenian orphanage. We were sent by sea and landed in Marseille. I think I was about 9 years old then. I remained in Switzerland for almost 11 years. It was near Lausanne and we were in a primary school run by the Armenian Church. Then I went to secondary school in Geneva. The Church supported me and I entered the Ecole Superior de Commérce de Genève for a three year course, but after two years I became ill and could not finish. I was in hospital for a few months. My mother, an older brother and two sisters were in Egypt and used to write to me and send me photographs. After my two other brothers left Switzerland to join them in Egypt I was alone in Switzerland. Finally I decided to join my family in Egypt. I took the boat to Alexandria and then the train to Cairo. After 20 years, I saw my mother, my oldest brother and my sisters for the first time. It was a pity that, although she was my mother, I didn't feel the feeling of a mother and a child, after all these years. I was already 20 years old. I was grown-up. I regretted the decision to come to Egypt. I

---

[29] World War I saw the greatest humanitarian crusade in American history unfold. Near East Relief was the sole agency incorporated by Congress to aid refugees 'in biblical Lands'. Americans contributed to Armenian relief by building refugee camps and hospitals and by distributing food and clothing to hundreds of thousands of the destitute and orphaned. Most first-generation Armenian Americans owe their survival to the Near East Relief (Mirak 1997:405).

lived with my mother and my brothers until they all died. By the 1980s I was all alone again. For twelve years I lived by myself. In 1992, I had to leave my apartment and so I went to an asylum for old people belonging to the Coptic Church. I stayed there a year and then I was moved to the Sister Teresa Asylum. I stayed there for three months until I was able to come here. My sisters, who got married and went to the US, they have looked after me. Their husbands arranged my transfer here to this place which is run by the Armenian Church. Here I am comfortable, I have my own room and I can speak Armenian to everyone. But I have no friends and I have no nationality. In 1948 I applied for Egyptian nationality but it was not given to me. Now, I only have a travel document. I have to renew it every five years. But I have never travelled. I have no wish to travel anymore. I read articles about Armenia and I like Armenia, but I don't wish to go there. I am a patriot, and I like my homeland, but when I think about the situation in Armenia, I don't want to be there. (Hampartsoum 2006, Cairo)

Beginning in the early 1980s, oral history projects sprang up to record the memories of the survivors of the Armenian forced marches and massacres of 1915. One project undertaken in California by Miller and Miller (1987) set out to understand the survivors' response to this genocide (also see Miller & Miller 1982). Recognizing that revenge and 'terrorism' was a commonly reported response by the Armenian community to the 1915 genocide, they sought to understand the wider and perhaps less uniform reactions. Their research was based on 92 in-depth interviews with survivors of the genocide living in California. While revenge did constitute one response of the survivors, they found five equally distinct responses: repression, rationalization, resignation, reconciliation, and rage. A similar project begun in 1977 by the Armenian Assembly in America set out to record the oral histories of 400 survivors. The Zoryan Research Institute in Cambridge, Massachusetts and Toronto, Canada also collected nearly 3,000 oral histories on videotape in English, French, and Armenian. Two of these narratives are summarized below:

Rebecca was born in 1899 in Kayseri. She was one of five children of a Protestant Armenian family of landowners. Her grandparents were still on their farm, a two and a half hour carriage drive away. All her summers were spent with her grandparents on their farm. The town was divided. The upper part of town had the homes of missionaries. The lower part of town was Greek and Armenian. She was the first generation to go to school (at the American Missionary School). In 1915 she was in the 10th grade when she remembers the Turkish officers coming to the school. The missionaries hid her among the Greek students. All the other Armenian students were taken away and put into a German orphanage one hour's walk away. She knew that her father had made it to America, but she didn't know where to her mother had been exiled. She had returned one day from her boarding school to help her mother pack up her belongings on a donkey and set out for Aleppo. Later she discovered that her mother had walked all the away to Aleppo but she lost trace of her after that. She went into hiding for eight days, moving at the instruction of the missionaries with other Armenian children among the empty houses abandoned by the rich Armenians in the town. Ten Armenian doctors were hung in the town square at this time. She was reunited with her two sisters and two brothers and together they made their way to Constantinople where she was taken in by a Turkish doctor and his Greek wife and entered into a nursing course. Two years later, in 1917 she graduated with a nursing degree and worked with the Turkish doctor in a local hospital. In 1918 she was able to locate her sisters and brothers by the help of the Red Cross/Red Crescent. She also located her father in America who sent a check for $800 to pay for the passage of all five siblings to the US. On December 31st, 1918 she landed at Ellis Island. She got a job with Near East Relief and her sisters and brothers dispersed to find work. Today [1988] she has one brother in France, another one in Long Beach and a sister in New York and another in Long Beach, California. (Zoryan Institute oral testimony recorded in San Francisco 1988)

Maryam Davis was born in 1909 in Terjan Erzurum. Her grandfather was a priest and they lived in a large house with many animals. Her father was an Armenian nationalist who fought for Armenian independence. One day in 1915, the Turks came and burned down the village. Her father escaped, but her uncle was hung in the town square. There were only Armenians in her village until the day the Turks came to tear down the village. All the women and children and old people had to pile their belongings in carts and move out. They were taken to Egin where both her mother and her brother died. When her mother's body was thrown into the river by the Turks, Maryam rushed into the water and tried to pull the body back to the shore. Finally she was saved from drowning by a Turkish holy man on a donkey who saw her and pulled her out of the river. She then realized she was an orphan and a street child. She slept on the street against the chimney of a bakery because it was warm at night. She was looked after by a Turkish man who was a local peddler. Every once in a while there would be a round-up of Armenian orphans by the Turks who would march them all off to the Syrian Desert. Then in 1919, the Near East Relief arrived and opened an orphanage in the town. Betty Murdock was one of the relief workers and slowly orphans agreed to enter and to be looked after by her and her staff. It took Maryam two months before she agreed to join. Eventually there were several hundred orphans being looked after at the orphanage. In 1920, she was sent to the Presbyterian Mission School. Later that year, Betty Murdock proposed to adopt and bring her to the US. Maryam agreed and was officially adopted at the age of 14 and brought to the US. Her years as a street child made it difficult to adjust to the 'controlled' living in the US and eventually Maryam found her way to Greenwich Village in New York where she became part of the bohemian scene for many years. (Zoryan Institute oral testimony recorded in Cambridge, Massachusetts 1983)

What both these interviews reveal is the extraordinary importance of the religious organizations in supporting and keeping the Armenian death-march survivors alive. Near Eastern Relief and many other humanitarian agencies as well as the Armenian Church worked tirelessly to find and support these refugees. Because of the nature of the deportations and forced marches, very few of the elderly survived. Humanitarian aid was directed at the youth. Orphanages for Armenian children were opened throughout the region, in Aleppo, Beirut, Damascus, Cairo, and Alexandria; most of them were sponsored by the Armenian Apostolic, as well as the Catholic Church and Protestant denominations. Interviews in 2005 and 2006 in Beirut, Damascus, Aleppo, Amman, and Cairo revealed the importance of both recovering contact with kin and coming under the wing of the Armenian Church for immediate survival and later in support of the coalescing and greatly expanded community.

The Armenian community in Egypt was particularly well established. The migration of Armenians to Egypt dated back to antiquity but had a substantial growth in the Byzantine era, followed by a flowering culturally, commercially, and religiously in the Fatimid period between the tenth and twelfth centuries. Another increase in migration numbers occurred during the Seljuks' westward expansion in the eleventh century. At the beginning of the fourteenth century, a schism occurred in the Armenian Church which resulted in the Armenians of Egypt coming under the jurisdiction of the Armenian Orthodox patriarchate of Jerusalem (Habib 2002:46). Over the next few centuries, new waves of Armenians arrived, escaping various devastations and plunder in Ottoman Armenia.

Many Armenians in Egypt established themselves as jewellers, merchants, tailors, furriers, ironsmiths, coffee shop owners, and grocers. The literate were employed as bankers (*sarrafs*), and their prosperity rose and fell with the fortunes of the Egyptian economy and sovereignty. By the nineteenth century the Armenians were well integrated into the society ruled by Muhammed Ali. The elite spoke Turkish or French while the lower classes spoke Arabic. A small charitable institution and a parochial school were the only establishments run by the Armenian Church in Egypt at this time. Habib claims that during the first half of the nineteenth century Armenians in Egypt had no interest in forming a structured community. It was only with the first wave of Armenian refugees arriving in 1894 and 1896 that a political awareness and activity around the Church emerged. The newcomers were from a different background and unable to speak Arabic; hence, they tended to congregate around fellow Armenians of Egypt, making little attempt to integrate into a wider social, economic, or political circle. Numbering about 10,000 at the end of the nineteenth century, the Armenian community grew to about 40,000 by the early 1920s.

As a whole, Armenians in Egypt are regarded as a religious minority and are acknowledged as so by the government of Egypt (Article 38 of the

Constitution of Egypt). The Archbishop of the Armenian Orthodox Church is the religious head of the community. The Church is empowered by the Egyptian Constitution as a judicial body with full authority over Armenian community property, as well as the administration of educational and cultural institutions. This autonomy, which is reflected in matters of religion, personal status, schools, property, and community life, is a residual of the millet system of the Ottoman Empire.

The Armenian Church has been the focus of communal life both for incoming refugees as well as the established residents. With the rapid rise in numbers by the 1920s, new church schools and social clubs were established through fundraising efforts and individual donations. In the 1950s, the Armenians were a successful ethno-religious minority in the country. Surprisingly, they were not compelled to emigrate as the Jews, Italians, and Greeks were after the 1951 coup by Jamal Abdul-Nassir. However, the economic reforms and nationalisation efforts after 1961 cut deeply into the prosperity of the community.[30] Many Armenians emigrated during this period. Currently there are about 5,000 Armenians in Egypt concentrated in Heliopolis, Cairo, and Alexandria (Habib 2002:48). They are predominantly middle-class professionals and entrepreneurs. Politically they remain neutral, choosing not to take sides in any sectarian conflicts. One Armenian informant explained this to me as 'Armenians are loyal to the government in power'. It is a position of neutrality which is also followed by Armenian communities in other countries of the Middle East, particularly Lebanon (see Migliorino 2007). When interacting with non-Armenian actors, Armenians in Egypt mix with Muslims. Many Armenians see the Christian Copts as a threat. Or put another way, they consider that a coalition of two Christian groups could appear as a threat to the dominant Muslim population. Whereas the Copts are indigenous Egyptian populations, the Armenians are very aware that they are immigrants to Egypt, 'temporary residents' who wish to protect their economic, religious, and cultural institutions by maintaining good relations with the dominant Muslim population. Some of these Armenians are the survivors of the Armenian deportations of 1915.

---

[30] After 1961 when Syria withdrew from the United Arab Republic expropriation of large businesses and factories which many Armenians owned, and banks in which many Armenians had administrative positions, took place. Many Armenians were left with little choice but to emigrate. The tightening of private initiative and growth of regulations precipitated a large-scale emigration to Canada, the United States, and Australia (El-Hamamsy 1975:24).

I was born in 1911 in Yozgam, a town in Caesarea in Anatolia. My mother had four boys. The oldest was 18 at the time of the massacres. My father and my oldest brother were arrested. The other two were 12 and 14. My mother used to hide us under the stairs for days to keep us from being taken. One day we saw groups of people, each tied four by four with a chain and my father was one of them. I remember I asked where he was going and she told me to a place named Deir-ez-Zor. From that day on my mother took us from one place to another, always avoiding the soldiers. When things calmed down my mother let me go back to school. And my brothers started to work in a tailor shop. In 1920 during the Greek–Turkish War our home was fired on, so we escaped to the Greek Church. After several years, my mother took us to Constantinople. My eldest brother went to Aleppo to work in a car maintenance shop. It was 1922. I went to primary school in Constantinople. We stayed there until 1927. Then in 1928 we decided to come here to Egypt. We arrived by boat to Alexandria. Someone from the Armenian Patriarchate met us and assisted us in finding a place to stay. Then we moved to Cairo and rented rooms in Heliopolis on Zagazig Street. In Cairo I studied two more years at the French Jesuit School. During this time my two other brothers joined us; one who had been left behind in Constantinople and the one who had been in Aleppo. The three of us, we built a bakery and I worked there for 25–30 years. Then I left the shop to my brothers and I bought another one where I was selling coffee and different drinks. I worked there for 30 years. I married an Armenian girl whose family was in Cairo. I was 30 at the time. I moved out of our family apartment shared with my three brothers and my mother and rented space above the bakery shop for my wife and two sons. I used to speak Armenian with my sons and my wife, but Turkish with my mother. I sent my sons to the Armenian school until secondary school. Then they went to the American University in Cairo. I have many friends in Cairo, but they are all Armenian. I have never had any foreign friends. I still have a Turkish passport. I visited Turkey twice once in the 1930s and once in the 1960s. I also have an Armenian passport. I have been to visit Armenia twice during the Communist era, once in the 1970s and once in the 1980s. But I feel Egyptian. Here I ate Egyptian bread and it was in Egypt that I made my money. I have lived most of my life here in Egypt, so it is Egypt where I belong. (Hrant 2006, Cairo)

In Egypt as elsewhere in the Middle East, the Church, family, and preexisting community emerge as important themes in the survival, resilience, and accomplishment of these forced migrants. Identity as Armenian is also important, but it is highly contextualized, its expression taking various forms. For some, speaking Armenian was an important marker of identity, and for others, not. In some cases, the survivors were Turkish speakers, as was Hrant's mother above and so the household had to use both Turkish and Armenian. In some parts of the Middle East, such as Palestine, being a refugee was as important as being Armenian in terms of accessing crucial initial assistance.

Many Armenian refugees moved from place to place to place within former 'Greater Syria'. Each move brought with it greater opportunity for the family and tighter linkages with other Armenian relatives and contacts. Gulizar's narrative of her family's journey from Dourt Yull, Anatolia to Aleppo, Iskenderun, Damascus, Jerash, Amman, Jerusalem, Karak, and finally Amman is a case in point.

My family used to live in a town called Dourt Yull. All the Armenians living there were given notice to leave their homelands. They were moved out on the same night that my mother gave birth to a baby girl. My father had a horse – he was a merchant – so he put my mother on it with the baby in her arms. It was a long journey and they suffered very much on the way. My baby sister died, like many other children on that journey. Their first stop was Aleppo. My mother told me that most of the Armenian women didn't have their periods for many years at that time, so when my mother became pregnant again with me, my father couldn't believe it at first. When I was born, he gave me these earrings which I have been wearing since I was one week old. I never took them out of my ears as they were a souvenir from my father. I was baptized in Aleppo. Then my parents moved to Iskenderun and from there to Damascus where they stayed with other Armenians at the Armenian convent in Bab Sharqi [Her father died in Damascus and her mother remarried

MAP 6. Itinerary of One Family's Forced Migration from Armenia

shortly thereafter]. Then it happened that my aunt's husband heard from friends that farmers in Jerash needed workers for their fields. My stepfather went to Jerash to work and my mother took me and my brother to live in Jerash. My family rented a room from the Circassians and my stepfather worked in a village called Sakhra. Then my aunt and her husband moved to Amman and my family followed. I was almost five years old and I remember our trip to Amman as I rode on a camel the whole way. In Amman we rented a house in Wadi Sir, near the Circassians. I was sent to the Rosary School and I learned Arabic and English. But at home we used to speak Armenian and Turkish – both my parents spoke Turkish because in the town they came from it was forbidden for Armenians to speak their language. My mother didn't speak any Arabic at all.

I did well in school and was given a place at a boarding school in Jerusalem in 1928. But I missed my family very much. In 1929 my family decided to move to Jerusalem. During this time the war erupted between the Arabs and the Jews so my parents took shelter and stayed with an Armenian family at the Armenian convent until they could rent a house in Jerusalem. In 1932 I got engaged. I was fourteen years old. It happened that my husband had friends in Jerusalem who told him about me so he came and proposed. He was an orphan from the town of Dourt Yull as well. He was born in 1909. When the Turks forced the Armenians out of their homeland, all the orphans were moved out of Dourt Yull by land and then by sea to Lebanon. Some went into orphanages there; others were sent to Cyprus and to France, and some to Jerusalem. My husband was among those who ended up at the Armenian Convent Orphanage in Jerusalem. When orphans reached the age of 16 they were told to leave the Convent and start working. My husband was a shoemaker and he started looking for work. He was on his way to Haifa to find work and at the train station he met an Armenian man who had a business in Karak who was looking for an assistant. This man was also from Dourt Yull. So my husband went to Karak with him. In Karak, there was a Jewish man working with my husband who owned a hotel. This man liked my husband and so in 1929 when the war erupted between the Arabs and the Jews, the Jewish man wanted to sell his hotel and take his family to Tel Aviv. He asked my husband to buy the hotel from him, but my husband had only three Dinars. Yet the man agreed and sold him the hotel. After a while my husband got sick so I asked him to buy me a sewing machine as I knew how to sew and had a certificate from Jerusalem. I started making dresses for the women in Karak and also giving lessons in sewing and embroidery. I had more than 30 students. I was able to send my son and my daughter to Jerusalem for school.

In 1948 when the Jews got their independence, my brother, who was a mathematics teacher at a big school in Jerusalem, had to leave and he came to stay with us in Karak. Then a year later he moved to Amman. I wanted to come to Amman for my children's sake. So in 1951 I took my children alone and went to Amman. My husband stayed in Karak. I then sent my boys to the Bishops School and my daughters to the Ahliyeh School for Girls (CMS Protestant Mission School). Now at home we began to speak Armenian, Turkish and Arabic. I insisted that my children learn Arabic since we are living in an Arab country. (Gulizar 2006, Amman)

In Lebanon and Syria where preexisting and well-established Armenian minority communities were widespread throughout the region, the new immigrants and survivors were quickly taken in and helped back on their feet. In nearly all these cases, it was the Armenian Church which provided the first line of relief. These refugees may have spoken Armenian at home, but had to quickly learn Arabic in order to survive. Their social integration within the Armenian community was quick; wider economic integration through the established trades was slower and required new language acquisition. Politics within the Armenian community was also widespread – as the nationalist agendas of the main Armenian political parties continued to operate among the Armenians in relation to the new homeland which was partially imagined and did not sit in the physical space which many preferred. But political involvement at a national level was one of studied neutrality as in Lebanon and in Syria, or full support for the party in power as in Egypt.

The Armenian community in Greater Syria (Palestine, Lebanon, and Syria) was, like the Egyptian community, of long standing.[31] The Armenian patriarchate in Jerusalem was the focal point for Armenians in Egypt and Palestine while in Lebanon and Syria (as well as Cyprus, Greece, and Iran) it was the patriarchate (Catholicosate) of Cilicia based in Antelias, Lebanon.[32] The Armenians surviving or fleeing the forced marches managed in numerous ways to find family and or to seek out and access Church support. In either case, the strength of the kin ties and the Church allegiance was striking. Many refugees moved between Syria and Lebanon – both were French-mandated states of the League of Nations between 1920 and 1943. In Lebanon, where the French were creating a new nation by adding tracts of 'historical' Syria – Tripoli and the Beqaa Valley – to Mount Lebanon, 'Armenianness' in a sectarian nation became an important feature of the political landscape. In Syria, by contrast, pan-Arabism continued to remain an important feature of the new social order, perhaps reflecting the ruminants of the old Ottoman multiethnic cosmology. There, multiculturalism and ethnic pluralism were

---

[31] According to British intelligence, some 3,000 Armenians were deported to Tafila in Transjordan from Cilicia and eastern Anatolia. Thousands more entered as survivors of the death marches across northern Syria. By 1918, fewer than 1,000 remained in Tafila, the rest being resettled into the towns of Transjordan and Palestine (Rogan 1999:231).

[32] The Armenian Apostolic Church is based in Etchmiadzin, Armenia. There is in addition a patriarchate of Jerusalem, which has perhaps 10,000 followers in Jerusalem and the Holy Lands, Israel, Jordan, and Egypt; and the Catholicosate of Cilicia based in Antelias, Lebanon with followers in Lebanon, Cyprus, Syria, Greece, and Iran with perhaps 800,000 followers. The latter is in some conflict with the patriarchate in Etchmiadzin, Armenia and both compete over followers in the diaspora, particularly in the United States.

accepted parts of the social landscape but not an integral part of the political scene.[33]

I was born in Beirut. My parents were from Zeytun in Armenia. My father had his secondary education in Marash and then he was sent to the Sultaniyyah School in Aleppo where he took his Baccalaureate. He graduated in 1912. It was a very prestigious school and he immediately entered the Ottoman government. He was taken into the railway administration. So he escaped deportations or massacres because he was working. He was sent to a small station in the Bekaa Valley of Lebanon at Rayyak. After the War my father went to Cilicia with the French. When they suddenly left, my father went to Constantinople and from there travelled to Europe and then back to Lebanon to find his family. In Lebanon he got a job with Radio Orient because he knew French and also he could do Morse code. In Beirut he met his future wife. She had been from a well-to-do family. They had sent her away to a boarding school in Constantinople between 1914–1916 so as to avoid the deportations. Afterwards she came to Beirut to join her family. After he married her my father studied engineering at the Jesuit Faculty of Engineering.

When the French left the Sanjak [of Alexandretta] in 1939, there were many Armenians who did not want to remain and be ruled by the Turks so they left for Aleppo and for Lebanon. Many were very poor so the French built two villages for them. One was at Anjar and the other was near Sur in Lebanon. My father was the engineer responsible for these constructions. He was also responsible for many irrigation projects, in Aleppo, in Syria in Lebanon. He used to travel a lot. So I stayed in Beirut with my grandparents. I went to the Lycée Française. There was an Armenian school, but it was too far away and, anyway, my father wanted me to learn French. I used to hear my grandparents cursing the British and the French for what was happening in Aleppo and Cilicia and Iskenderun. But we were told we had to learn French and English in school. We always spoke Armenian at home but we went to French school.

I studied civil engineering at the same school as my father in Beirut. But I had problems with the school. They approached me for school elections, but I was not a Lebanese Armenian, I was Syrian. It was a problem. So I left and went to Aleppo and studied engineering there. Then I travelled around Europe. I lived in Austria, in Sweden, in Finland, and France. Now I am here in Damascus. I am a newcomer to Damascus. We are maybe 6,000 Armenians in Damascus. We were once much

---

[33] Migliorino makes the important point in his book *(Re)constructing Armenia in Lebanon and Syria* (2007) that the French administration of the two states between 1920 and 1943 encouraged the Armenian community to develop and create a space for itself in both the social and political universe of each state. In Lebanon, the Armenian community was politically drafted into the sectarian political structure, providing it with a formal role in government. In Syria, however, other than a sole representative of the community in Parliament, it was encouraged to restrict its politics to its own internal affairs and those of the Armenian diaspora. Despite serious restrictions in the 1950s and 1960s, Armenian cultural identity and expression has flourished in Syria, leading Migliorino to use the term '*Kulna Suriyyin*' (We are all Syrians) to describe the accommodation of Armenian ethnicity with citizenship in the state (2006).

bigger, but in the 1960s, during the economic reforms, many large business were affected. Armenians are special merchants, many left, but still we have a large presence. The Church is very strong. We have a very coherent community. We have the Apostolic and Catholic Church. We have two choirs; we have social clubs and dance troupes. We have three schools one connected with the Armenian Church, one with the Armenian General Benevolent Union and one with the Dashnak party. We have a very coherent community here. I can say I am a loyal Syrian citizen – this has a priority for me – but at the same time I am an Armenian. I am integrated but not assimilated. Maybe I am in the minority. I have very good relations with Armenia. But I am not ashamed to say that I was born here and I owe everything to here. I do not see any contradiction between my loyalty and my duty. I went to a Syrian University. I never felt discrimination (unlike in Lebanon, where you are Christian, or you are Muslim or something).

I am convinced that Armenia is an Oriental country. All these attempts to integrate Armenia into the West are silly. So I consider that Armenian–Arab relations are extremely important. Forty years ago, when I first started to think about this I wondered how to assist Armenia and be a good Syrian. We were being massacred and the Syrians saved us. How can you forget? So the thing I decided I could do was to enrich the Armenian libraries with books from the Orient. I was a student and I began in 1947 to send books to the Armenian Academy of Science. I have sent some 25,000 books: orientalistic, not novel, but academic, encyclopaedias. I wanted them to train Arabists. Our future is with these people. I have sent many manuscripts. So I am a very Syrian patriot, but I am also an Armenian Arab nationalist. (Varukan 2005, Damascus)

The Armenians of Syria, numbering perhaps 90,000 today are a Christian and non-Arab population in a prevailing Arab and officially secular state; the majority of the people in the country, however, are actively religious Muslims and Christians belonging to a number of sects and denominations. Armenians in Syria speak a non-Semitic language and have their own alphabet. They run a number of communal institutions including schools, cultural clubs, welfare associations, and social and recreational organizations as well as their own newspapers and journals. They are linked with the Armenian diaspora worldwide and with the Republic of Armenia. They are integrated without being assimilated. They have, as Migliorino states, found a way of expressing their 'cultural diversity within contemporary Syrian society, one that has seemingly found and cultivated a "diverse" way of being Syrian' (2006:99).

By the end of World War I the largest number of Armenian survivors in the Middle East found themselves in Syria; by the mid-1920s they were spread widely throughout the country in the north in the region of Aleppo, the Euphrates region, and the *Jazirah*, in the major cities of Homs, Hama, and Damascus as well as Dara'a in the south (Hovannisian 1967). The existing Armenian Apostolic Church formed the central pivot around which the refugees constructed their lives. A system of institutions revolving around the Church grew rapidly and included schools, charities, and cultural associations, all which catered to the material and spiritual needs of the community (Migliorino 2006:100). A cultural identity which drew heavily from the past, but which also integrated the trauma of the recent genocide, developed and was encouraged both by the Armenian Apostolic Church and its nationalist political party leadership. The French administration of Syria also encouraged and created opportunities for the Armenians to develop their social and communal strategies with some autonomy. The religious authority of the Armenian Apostolic Church was not undermined by the French; it was purposively respected as a continuation of certain aspects of the Ottoman millet administration (Thompson 2000).

Many of the Armenian refugees who arrived in Syria after the 1915 deportations had family to help them. However, many did not and had to turn solely to the Armenian Apostolic Church for life support. With the backing and encouragement of the French administration, the Church was able to draw on traditional relations between it and its flock in Ottoman times and construct new ways of reaching out and looking after the welfare of this large new group of needy refugees. An internal system of housing provision, food distribution, welfare, and education and job creation grew up around the Church. Just being Armenian was enough to get a start. The religious policy of the French Mandate [in both Syria and Lebanon], which maintained a system of legally-established freedoms in the area of religious affairs, personal status law together with the political support which was accorded to the Armenians was crucial in the tremendous expansion of the Armenian churches in Syria (Migliorino 2006:101).

I was born in Damascus in 1934, in a very poor place, in a small house in the area near Bab Sharqi, near the Church of Ananais. We were very privileged to have this space as there were others in much worse conditions than us. Before me, they had been living in Lebanon. We were five girls and three boys. My father came from Turkey, from Cilicia. There had been problems there for more than 60 years. My mother and father came to Damascus in the second Armenian migration, not the first one in 1915, but rather in the one of 1921. They came in February 1921. They were thrown out of Cilicia and then went to Aleppo for a little while. At that time all the family members were alive. None of our family members died on the road from Cilicia to Syria. My father was educated but he had no profession. But he was lucky. He was born in Marash in 1908. He was 12 or 13 when he came here. At first he worked in the Church as doorman, carrying goods, and cleaning, simple things. But he liked learning. He taught himself Spanish, Italian and French. Then he worked with the Franciscans. When he was about 20 he wanted to migrate to Argentina. But his parents wouldn't let him go. The grandparents wanted the family to stay together. They were afraid of war. So they didn't let him go. And they made him marry early. I was the first-born, just a year or two after the marriage.

My grandfather had been a soldier in the Turkish Army. The family used to live in the military sector of Marash. They were exempted from deportation. They were privileged – very few Armenians were – but they were. At that time all of Syria and Palestine were under the Ottomans. My grandfather had been stationed in Baalbeck (Lebanon) and had fought against the French. When my father decided to leave Marash in 1921, there had been about 4,000 Armenians who were killed. He took the family to Aleppo and then on to Rayyak (the end of the train line from Aleppo to Lebanon). From Rayyak, they came to Damascus. They came here with nothing. The men could find no work. But there were some charitable associations here to help the Armenians. There were also Armenians from a long time ago who had settled centuries ago but who didn't speak Armenian, they only spoke Arabic, but they helped. The good thing was that many Syrians knew some Turkish, so they had a language they could communicate with. But for the most part there was no language in common.

In the beginning it was very hard. For us, our family was 10 people: my grandfather and grandmother, my mother and father, and uncles and aunts. All of them were given a space under a tree and a blanket to make a tent. Then some help came from the Armenian Church here in Bab Sharqi. My grandfather was privileged. He was given some space at the cemetery of the Armenians near a mausoleum where they covered themselves in the cold of February and slept. In the daytime, the landowners of the Ghouta used to come to find day labourers for their fields. He wanted work and he would go round and round to try to be picked for the agricultural work. Eventually some relatives came from Aleppo with more resources and they worked together and established a 'camp'. This became the Armenian 'camp' near Bab Musalla. After a time, my grandfather moved us to a very small house with two rooms. We had a small space where we worked and made small goods for selling in the souq near the Umayyad Mosque. My grandmother used to cook in a big pot for the whole family. She used to cook one dish and give it out to everyone. We didn't even have a table, just a cloth on the ground. It was very primitive at the beginning. It is hard to imagine how we managed then. But I always tell my children that if we had to return to that time, I could live like that; but they couldn't [he laughs]. We had terrible times, but we have come out of it. And we are going to remain an Armenian community. If we had stayed in Turkey, maybe we would never have had what we now have. (Sarkis 2005, Damascus)

CONCLUSION

Armenians have been widely dispersed throughout the Middle East for centuries. The well-to-do and middle classes have served as merchants and traders in the Ottoman Empire and in the British- and French-mandated states in the inter-war years as well as in the contemporary independent states of the region. Surviving the waves of expulsion, massacres, and forced deportations at the end of the nineteenth and beginning of the twentieth century and reconstructing their society in new places has meant reliance on the Armenian Apostolic Church as well as the Catholic and Protestant missionary relief agencies. It has also meant a sustained effort on the part of these uprooted Armenians to accommodate the political administrations and social contexts of their new 'homelands'.

With the first outbreak of violence against the Armenians in the late nineteenth century, many made their way to the United States. An estimated 3,000 Armenians arrived there in 1890 reaching 5,000 in 1894 (quoted in Chorbajian 1982:71; Collier 1978:370). After 1894, in the aftermath of the Adana massacres, an estimated 50,000 Armenians came to the United States and by 1899, the total of Armenians had reached 70,000. Furthermore, there was heavy emigration to the United States from 1915 to the early 1920s. Despite restrictive immigration laws in the United States at that time, nearly 30,000 Armenians went to the country in the 1930s. In the years after World War II a steady influx of Armenians who had fled the 1915 genocide arrived from 'asylum countries' like Palestine, Israel, Egypt, Iraq, Iran, India, Cyprus, Syria, Lebanon, and France. This last group was far better educated and more affluent than the first wave. Today, the Armenian population in the United States is the largest outside of the Republic of Armenia, numbering more than 500,000 (quoted in Chorbajian 1982:71; Collier 1978:370).

Substantial communities of Armenians are found in Massachusetts, Connecticut, and Rhode Island as well as in New York, New Jersey, and Pennsylvania. Very large Armenian communities exist in California, in Los

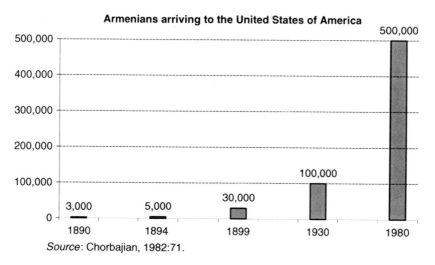

CHART 2. Armenian Immigrants to the United States

Angeles and the Fresno area. These groups are all organized around the Armenian Churches, which has more than one hundred churches in the United States. Ninety per cent of them are Apostolic or Orthodox Churches and the other 10 per cent are Protestant or Catholic. These communities have strong cultural centres, elementary and secondary schools, athletic programmes, and summer camps as well as literary and historical publications and newspapers.[34] The Armenian communities in the Middle East are also organized in a similar fashion, around the Church from which social clubs, sports groups, schools, benevolent societies, nursing homes, and language and dance classes are organized.

Armenians throughout history have determinedly located relatives and created ties with other Armenians where, before their deportations, there might have been none. It has also meant that Armenians have relied heavily on their kin networks. In nearly all the oral narratives recorded during the 1980s as well as my own interviews, it is striking the lengths that individuals went to in order to locate their families. Once together, they worked extraordinarily closely to support each other to gain a foothold on the economic ladder and to reestablish their social world.

Armenian identity was as much a matter of 'myth' of kinship as of origin and ties to the homeland. The fact that the physical place has moved to a new locality from Cilicia to the south Caucasian territory of the former Soviet Armenia is insignificant for most. The majority of Armenians interviewed had visited this new Armenian republic. Few had chosen to stay for more than a few months. Among the wealthy there had been some exploratory effort to gauge business ventures but few had decided to invest in Armenia. Yet, by and large, Armenians expressed dual identities: nationalists of their adopted country as well as their Armenianness and ties back to the 'homeland' which has taken shape in the south Caucasus. The place, the homeland, is the same, but the space it takes up has shifted.

The language is also an important marker of identity. Where once French and Turkish were marks of upper-class status and Armenian suggested more working-class background, the deportations became a leveller and Armenian became the language of the home and in the community. The first generation had to work to learn Armenian even though French and then English became the language of the elite outside of their homes. The second and third generations have also made great efforts to promote Armenian as the language of the home. Many of the survivors

---

[34] A special issue of *Ararat* is devoted to the Armenian American community. See 'Armenians in America: Special Issue' (1977).

facing interethnic marriage among their children and grandchildren insist that Armenian be the language spoken to the youngest generation. With other markers of separation among ethnic groups disappearing, language increases as a marker of identity among Armenians throughout the Arab Middle East. The Armenian Apostolic Church (as well as Armenian Catholic and Protestant congregations) and their associated social clubs provide classes for the youngest generation and so perpetuate significant elements of the differentiation which allows the Armenians to integrate in their new homelands without assimilating.

5

Palestinian Dispossession and Exodus

There was a war between the Palestinians, the Jews and the British. The events started in the 1920s, in Jerusalem, in Nabulus and Jaffa. We – the children – stayed in Jerusalem because my father was sentenced to death by the British. First he was imprisoned in Sarafand. He was working with Al Haj Amin Al Husseini and the Arab High Committee. They worked against the Jews and against the establishment of a Jewish State. They were imprisoned, arrested and deported several times [by the British]. Then they were not allowed to stay in Jerusalem or anywhere in Palestine anymore. My father and Al Haj Amin Al Husseini escaped arrest and went to Damascus in 1935. We remained in Jerusalem, my brother, my mother, my sister, my aunt and my grandmother. Then, in 1937, my father made the decision to stay in Damascus. He was in the Resistance. When he sent for us to come to Damascus we were very sad to leave Jerusalem. We packed and got big trucks to move our things to Damascus. My uncle's family was with us. They also packed and moved to Amman. I was 12 years old at the time.

Salma (2005), Damascus

The events that Salma refers to as starting in 1920 began with the British mandate over Palestine in that year and the large increase of Jewish immigration to the area. The future of this League of Nations mandatory state had been largely determined by the Sykes-Picot Agreement of 1916 and the Balfour Declaration of 1917 and included the former Ottoman provinces of Beirut, Jerusalem, and Hijaz. It had been Ottoman policy to refer to its provinces by key cities and their hinterland. Thus, for example, the province of Beirut extended from Jaffa north to Jericho and the Jordan River and included the districts of Acre, Beirut, and Nabulus. The borders of Palestine were never clearly demarcated, even during the late Ottoman period. The 'land of Palestine' was regarded by the Ottomans as a general region and not a specific administrative unit with clearly defined borders. Among the educated elite of the time, *Filistin* (Palestine) was a common concept referring to the whole of Palestine or sometimes the district of Jerusalem in the general area of *Bilad al-Sham* (Greater Syria) which encompassed the modern states of Syria, Lebanon, Jordan, and Palestine/ Israel.

The area awarded to Great Britain as its Mandate of Palestine was originally about 45,000 square miles (118,000 square kilometres). In 1921, Britain took the area east of the Jordan River – nearly 80 per cent of the original mandated territory – and created a 'sub-mandate' of Transjordan as a new protectorate. Two years later, in 1923, the British and French exchanged strips of land in the Jaulan Heights along the northern border of the British mandate to smooth out the line separating British and French mandates. After these various adjustments west of the river Jordan and extending south to the Negev, the 'Palestine' of the British mandate of Palestine was reduced to about 10,000 square miles (26,000 square kilometres). It was in this area that the British permitted Jewish settlement along the terms laid out in the Balfour Declaration. However, the British closed the rest of mandated Palestine, Transjordan, and the southern part of the Mandate – the desert of the Negev – to Jewish settlement.

When Palestine's first High Commissioner Sir Herbert Samuel was asked to write an introduction to *The History of Palestine* (1922), he decided to describe this country as characterized by such a diversity of religion, or civilizations, or climate and physical characteristics that one could pick the century one preferred to visit. He pointed out that the traveller

... may find among the Beduin of Beersheba precisely the conditions that prevailed in the time of Abraham; at Bethlehem he may see the women's costumes, and, in some respects the mode of living of the period of the Crusades; the Arab villages are, for the most part, still under mediaeval conditions; the towns present many of the problems of the early nineteenth century, while the new arrivals from Eastern and Central Europe, and from America, bring with them the activities of the twentieth century and sometimes, perhaps, the ideas of the twenty-first (Luke & Keith-Roach 1930).

The coeditor of this handbook, Edward Keith-Roach, was also a writer for *National Geographic* magazine and in 1934 he published a piece on 'Changing Palestine' in which he declares that 'the last decades have shown greater changes in Palestine than have occurred since the beginning of the Christian Era' (Keith-Roach 1934). Such a perception of Palestine was a commonly held view in Europe and the United States. The widely

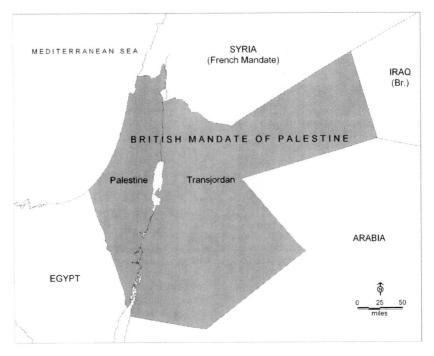

MAP 7. British Mandate of Palestine

accepted opinion was that the 'Holy Lands' were backward, even primitive, and had hardly changed since the time of King David and Jesus Christ. This viewing lens was a carefully constructed vision to suit particular purposes. For many, it underpinned the argument that only active Western involvement would be able to modernize and bring progress to the Holy Land. For European Judaism, it offered an intellectual justification for Jewish settlement in Palestine. As van Oord makes clear, the lens through which the Holy Land was viewed in the late nineteenth and twentieth centuries was not the result of objective description but rather was a carefully constructed narrative to suit the purposes of the narrators, be they politicians, travel writers, or religious scholars. They all set out to describe the land and people of Palestine in terms of historicized difference (van Oord 2008).

WHO ARE THE PEOPLE OF PALESTINE?

It is generally accepted that the indigenous people of Palestine are extremely heterogeneous in origin. They include the descendants of the Philistines, Canaanites, and Hebrews; Arabs from the conquests of the seventh century; the European Crusaders of the eleventh and twelfth centuries; and offspring of Muslim and Christian pilgrims. As the Holy Land to the three Abrahamaic religions, it has long supported Muslim, Christian, and Jewish settlement of varying size. However, with the exception of a brief period in the eleventh and twelve centuries, when the European Crusaders ruled the region, the Arabs in Palestine have maintained an uninterrupted presence as the majority population until the mid-twentieth century.

It is generally held that the Ottoman conquest of Syria in the early sixteenth century brought security and stability to the region after several centuries of disorder during Mamluk rule. This first century of Ottoman control also opened Palestine up to interregional trade, stimulating economic and population growth (Hütteroth & Abdelfattah 1977; Lewis 1954:469–501). In the late eighteenth and early nineteenth centuries, however, some historians claim the region suffered a decline. One conventional interpretation of the cause of this decline and depopulation was the misrule and tyranny of the local Ottoman governor of Acre, Ahmad al-Jazzar. Cotton production, which had thrived in the eighteenth century, went down and Palestine's economy became depressed. This decline led some peasants to revert to a form of seminomadic pastoralism combined with agriculture, which allowed them to pay what protection money was required to the Bedouin pastoralists from the Syrian and Arabian steppe land or *Badia* while managing to avoid the Ottoman tax farmers (also see Lancaster & Lancaster 1995). Encouraged by the lack of Ottoman authority or presence in the area, these Bedouin tribes moved deeper into agricultural areas and demanded protection money [tribute or khuwah] from the settled farmers. Some farmers gave into these demands, but others packed up their own moveable property and left. During this period of population stagnation or decline, Jerusalem and Hebron were said to lie on the 'frontier of Arabia, where rebellious Bedouins disturb the peace' (Johns 1994:26). The traditional view of this decline was that a vacuum was created which the Bedouin nomadic pastoral tribes from the Badia were filling, thus putting an end to agriculture. However, Johns argues that the absence of permanent Ottoman authority in the region did not necessarily create a vacuum but rather permitted a succession of local urban notables and settled tribal (*hamula*) elites to gain the upper hand and operate in a manner resembling the pre-Crusader Syrian city-states (1994:28).

Doumani challenges this standard view of the destructive activities of the Bedouin pastoralists throughout the period of early nineteenth-century Ottoman Palestine. He writes that such a black-and-white view of the classic opposition between the nomadic and the settled ignores the multitude of economic, political, and cultural connections that linked the Bedouin with the settled regions: 'the Bani Sakhr and Huwaytat tribes, for example, have for generations sent thousands of camel loads annually to Nablus, supplying the city's merchants and soap manufacturers with *qilli*, a raw material crucial to the city's soap industry. They also provided raw wool, *samn* (clarified butter), horses, camels and other primary products in return for iron, textiles and other manufactures' (Doumani 1992). This revisionist perspective, nevertheless, does not rule out the control the Bedouin held in these areas during various centuries and their demands for protection money or tribute as well as political and social networks and even kin ties between some Bedouin and local notables.[1]

Palestinian peasants generally clung to their land and their villages in the central hills of Palestine. During periods of heightened security, whether organized by Bedouin or by Ottoman central authority, they tended to return to the low-lying plains to re-start agricultural activity or re-build their villages. Thus, population density in these open plains continuously fluctuated throughout the centuries. While the plains were accessible to the military authority of the Ottomans and vulnerable to the periodic efforts of the Bedouin to collect protection money or tribute, the central hills of Palestine provided natural barriers. This hill country allowed Palestinian farmers, town dwellers, and local notable ruling families a measure of political and economic autonomy not unlike that which occurred in Mount Lebanon and also the Alawite hills of northwest Syria (Farsoun & Zacharia 1997). Palestinians raised cotton in the western plains, but most of the terraced hills of central Palestine were planted with olive trees. Wheat, corn, barley, and sesame were grown in the valleys and nearby plains. Olive oil, soap, textiles, grain, and sesame seeds were important export commodities for the regional market.

Whether due to Bedouin tribal depredations, contestation among local notables and elites, or regional economic factors like the decline in the

---

[1] Farsoun and Zacharia maintain that for much of the Ottoman period the kinship-based *hamula* social organization of Palestinian peasantry protected the individual and kin from both external attack and internal feuds. Groups of villages were organized into sub-districts called *nahiya*s, each under the control of a shaykh who typically belonged to the strongest family of the most powerful hamula in the area. As often, these nahiya shaykhs were of recent Bedouin origin. Nonetheless, the staying power of these hamulas and the leading families within them is remarkable. For example, the leading families of eighteenth- and nineteenth-century Nabulus – the Jayyusi, Jarrar, Qasim Rayyan, Tuqan, 'Abdul-Hadi, and Al-Masri – continue to dominate today (Farsoun & Zacharia 1997).

cotton economy, it is clear that the region suffered a general decline in agriculture over the centuries, which was not reversed until late in the eighteenth century. In the general area of Palestine, the southern Bilad al-Sham, this period saw a patrilineal, clan-based peasantry, particularly in the hill country, resistant to externally imposed authority and surviving by farming small plots of land. The peasantry was armed and the Ottoman authorities did not have a direct military presence in or control over the hill region. The Ottomans relied on local notables, who were often rural shaykhs, for control, administration, and taxation until the reform and centralization movement of the mid-nineteenth century. Until then, the rural political economy of the hilly regions of Palestine was intimately tied to the larger economic system of trade, exchange, or barter with the nearby city or commercial centre. The cities were centres of small-scale manufacture, crafts and artisan work, administrative offices, and religious and juridical activity. Thus in this part of Bilad al-Sham, Bedouin pastoralists, peasant farmers and urban craftsmen, intellectuals and religious scholars were interlinked in a complex political economy. The social organization and particular economic flourishing in towns and villages of Palestine both in the hills and along the coast during the late eighteenth and early nineteenth centuries have become a topic of interest and concern among a school of contemporary historians (Doumani 1992; Issawi 1966a; Owen 1981a; Scholch 1982); their work has helped to undermine the predominantly European narrative of a Palestine as a backwater, in decline and barely out of the 'primitive' stage of civilization or the Biblical era.

By the mid-nineteenth century, European interest in Palestine was growing; the land was being discovered, but as Doumani suggests, it was a discovery of the physical space without the recognition that people were living there (Doumani 1992). In the minds of many Europeans, Palestine was 'empty' before the arrival of the first significant wave of European Jewish settlers in 1881–94. The 'emptiness' here meant the absence of 'civilized' people. It was a narrative and a positioning which suited European colonial mindsets. Thus the native population of indigenous Palestine was no more recognized than the American Indians were in the 'virgin' frontiers of the American West. The Zionist slogan 'a land without people for a people without land' could be viewed, therefore, as no more than the manifestation of European intellectual racism and imperial ambitions.

Both European and Israeli historians have studied this late period of the Ottoman Empire and seen what they wanted. For many European researchers, there was an unwillingness to address the question of the native population other than to document an unchanging traditional society before its anticipated extinction due to contact with the West. For others, there was the recognition that a thriving Palestinian subsistence and commercial economy was gradually pushed into increasing commercialization which undermined its subsistence base and turned it into a region dependent upon European trade. Both Owen and Issawi stress the relative importance of the European over the regional trade sector, while Doumani disputes these conclusions and argues for greater acknowledgement of the indigenous regional dynamics of agricultural specialization in Palestine (Doumani 1992; Issawi 1966a; Owen 1981a). Whatever the interpretation, it is clear that by the middle of the nineteenth century the Ottoman state was interested in promoting settled agriculture, improving trade, and taxation of the Palestinian coast and the central hill districts of Galilee, Nabulus, Jerusalem, and Hebron. Across the River Jordan the Ottoman state worked to reestablish its own political authority over the local urban elite, and then turned to Europe for expertise to modernize and bring 'progress' to its southern provinces.

Until the middle of the nineteenth century, Ottoman authorities in Istanbul [Constantinople] regarded the southern Syrian provinces as very much a frontier zone; it extended from the Hauran to the Hijaz and was crossed once a year by the pilgrimage caravan from Damascus to Mecca. It was perceived as a region in which – as with Anatolia in general – the population was decreasing and tax income to the coffers of the Sultan was limited (Karpat 1974). Over the next few decades the Ottoman authority sought quick solutions to reverse the decline in tax income as well as to be able to invest substantially in its development (Rogan & Tell 1994). These solutions included: effective single-source tax collection to replace what was, in effect, efforts of double taxation by both the Bedouin as well as the official Ottoman government tax collectors. There was strong opposition to this effort both among the farmers and the Bedouin tribes.[2] Eventually

---

[2] In May 1867, much of the district just south of Ajlun was a fertile plain with only a single settlement. The absence of the state and tribal incursion had reduced permanent settlement to the single village of al-Salt. Its location provided its farmers with security to negotiate access to farmlands with the surrounding tribes. Security of cultivation was ensured by giving a share of the harvest, as tribute, to the tribes (*khuwah*). This protection payment was in a way a form of taxation. The Ottoman sent an armed unit of soldiers to overturn this relationship and force the Bedouin tribes to submit to Ottoman rule. At first, both the residents of al-Salt and the Bedouin resisted the Ottoman force. Eventually the villagers submitted to the Ottomans without a fight. The Bedouin were engaged in battle several months later, resulting ultimately with defeat and the arrest of the tribal leader and his incarceration in Nabulus in October 1867 (Rogan & Tell 1994).

the Ottomans established administrative and military units at a number of points: al-Salt, Karak, and finally at Ma'an. Once these security measures were in effect, the Ottoman government turned its attention to resettling the areas radiating out from these administrative and security posts. With effective resettlement, the Ottoman state could expect proceeds from tax collection of agricultural produce to render the district self-supporting and certainly go some way to covering the costs of mounting the annual pilgrimage to Mecca (see Barbir 1980:122–125).

The first wave of settlement, once Ottoman administration and security had been secured in these areas, was by local farmers encouraged to move out from older settlements to establish new villages.[3] The next wave of settlement, which lasted for the last quarter of the nineteenth century (from about 1878 to 1906), was largely of Muslim refugees from the European Ottoman lands lost to Russia. These were Circassian, Chechnyan, and Turcoman refugees generally grateful to the Ottoman state for providing them with new lands upon which to rebuild their shattered lives. The third wave of settlement was largely by Bedouin fearful of losing all claims to their traditional grazing lands. Many of the tribal leaders encouraged their tribesmen to adopt a settled existence and sharecrop in plantation villages often actually worked by Palestinian and Egyptian peasants (Rogan & Tell 1994:47).

During this period, the Ottoman government sought advice from numerous international agricultural experts. These specialists encouraged the Ottoman state to find and train adequate manpower to cultivate land. As the demand for agricultural commodities began to increase, mostly from abroad, the government decided to set in train a raft of measures to increase rural production. Furthermore, as Karpat points out, the 1856 Treaty of Paris was an important psychological turning point in Ottoman relations vis-à-vis Europe. The Ottomans regarded this treaty as drawing the Ottoman Empire into the comity of European nations, recognizing it as an equal to the European states despite its different religion and its numerous wars in the past (Karpat 1974:59).[4] The Ottoman Empire now looked to Europe to rejuvenate and modernize what it had come to regard as its agricultural backwater; some historians regarded this move as the death

[3] Rogan identifies numerous Christian families from Salt who established themselves in this manner in new villages such as al-Rumaymim between 1870 and 1879 and al-Fuhays between 1869 and 1875 (Rogan & Tell 1994).
[4] The recognition was informal. To the Ottoman leadership, the Treaty of Paris of 1856 marked a turning point in diplomacy, the courteous recognition that the nations of Europe accorded to the laws of the Ottoman state.

blow to a thriving largely Palestinian subsistent mode of existence into a market economy and finally, before its complete destruction, into dependent capitalist underdevelopment. No less significant for this destructive turn was the 'peaceful crusade' of religiously inspired European immigration, investment, and institutional development (Farsoun & Zacharia 1997).

THE END OF EMPIRES AT THE BEGINNING OF THE TWENTIETH CENTURY

Palestine was an integral part of the Ottoman Empire for more than four centuries. Its fortunes, like that of the empire itself, waxed and waned as central political power and economic strength also rose and fell, re-formed, and rose again over the centuries. The empire had survived periods of decline in the past and instituted successful reform. Only towards the end of the nineteenth century were these reforms doomed as Europe began to seriously consider the potential for trade and raw material, which the Arab provinces of the Ottoman Empire represented. As the empire began to crumble prior to the end of World War I, European powers started to vie for control of the Arab Ottoman provinces. In 1915, Great Britain was eager to secure Arab support in dividing up the Ottoman Empire and also in opening a southern front in its war against the Axis powers. Responding to British overtures, the Sharif of Mecca, al-Emir Hussein, issued a call to the Arab people to revolt against Ottoman rule and to fight on the side of France and Britain.[5] Yet, however strong the Arab people's aspirations may have been for single state 'nationhood', France and England had other plans and were simultaneously engaged in secret negotiations with regard to the Arab Ottoman provinces.[6]

---

[5] Eight months earlier, Great Britain had reported to be 'prepared to recognize and uphold the independence of the Arabs in all regions (with some noted modifications) lying in the frontiers proposed by the Sharif of Mecca' (Antonius 1938).

[6] Zogby regards this move as a reflection of the need of Great Britain to maintain access to ever-increasing raw materials to fuel its industrial growth. It needed to protect these sources and markets from its rivals and hence Britain needed Palestine to protect the northeastern flank of this sea route to India and the East – the Suez Canal. Control of Palestine and the Fertile Crescent (Iraq/Mesopotamia) would make a land route to India possible. Thus, in his analysis, the Arabs were only temporary allies of Great Britain. A more permanent and safer client was the Zionist movement – a colonial movement in search of a patron. Herzl and his organization had actively engaged and sought out the Ottoman sultan in the late 1900s in efforts to persuade him of the benefits to the Ottoman Empire if he were to agree to their plan of establishing a Jewish state in Palestine. When Herzl and his group failed to persuade the sultan, he turned to Great Britain where he found sympathetic listeners. In fact as early

Between July 1915 and March 1916, Sir Henry McMahon began to correspond with the Sharif of Mecca (Antonius 1946). Their exchanges resulted in the McMahon/Hussein Treaty whereby Great Britain agreed to recognize and support the independence of the Arabs, should they revolt against the Ottomans. A few months later, Sir Mark Sykes (Secretary to the British War Cabinet) concluded a contradictory agreement with France and Russia to divide up the lands of the Arab Ottoman Empire so that France would take the territories that would emerge as Syria and Lebanon, Britain would take control of what would become Iraq and Transjordan, and Palestine would be placed under international administration with Russia agreeing to manage Jerusalem (Tannous 1988:62–63). After the Bolshevik Revolution in 1917, Russia withdrew from the agreement and also divulged the previously secret Sykes-Picot Agreement to the rest of the world, agreeing to a Franco-British division of the Arab provinces into zones of British (Palestine and Mesopotamia/Iraq) and French (Syria and Lebanon) control.

THE EMERGENCE OF EUROPEAN ZIONISM

Zionism emerged in the dying days of the nineteenth century as an irredentist political movement. It was, in some ways, a response to the growing anti-Semitism and racism that European and Russian Jews were facing at the time. It was also a movement which categorically turned away from earlier Jewish efforts at assimilation in Europe and Russia. In Russia, this assimilation movement led by wealthy merchants and educated Jews had a respectable following.[7] In 1897, the World Zionist Organization was established in Basel, Switzerland, as the brainchild of Theodor Herzl, who became its first head. In his book *Der Judenstaat* (1896), he proposed the establishment of a Jewish state in Palestine or Argentina, as a means of solving what was then known as the 'Jewish question'; the lack of a state for Jewish people in an era of nation-states, and in the context of the

as 1876, Lord Shaftesbury was to say 'Syria and Palestine will before long become very important ... The country wants capital and population. The Jews can give it both. Has not England a special interest in promoting such restoration? .... To England, then, naturally belongs the role of favouring the settlement of Jews in Palestine' (Zogby 1974).

[7] For example, in 1863, Jewish financier Baron Joseph Grunzberg, who had built the Russian railway system, established the Society for the Spread of Enlightenment among Jews in Russia. Its purpose was the assimilation of Jews into Russian culture. That same year, however, Czar Alexander, for a variety of political reasons, initiated a period of particular oppression of minorities, of which the Jews suffered most. At the time, the persecution of the Jews in Russia contrasted sharply with the tolerance and protection accorded them by the Ottoman government (Karpat 1972).

growing discrimination and persecution of Jews in Europe. After some internal debate Palestine, through its close association with the Old Testament, became the focus of this colonial or pioneering effort. It was Herzl's argument to Western powers that such a Jewish state would be like a 'rampart of Europe against Asia, an outpost of civilization as opposed to barbarism' (1896: chapter 2). The objective of this initiative was to settle Palestine with Jewish immigrants. But in order to ensure a majority (European) Jewish population in the predominantly Muslim and Christian Palestine, space would have to be made and some transfer, forced or otherwise, of the indigenous population would have to occur. Most of the nineteenth-century Jewish immigration to Palestine had been unsystematic and largely financed by wealthy Jewish bankers and merchants such as the French banker Baron Edmund de Rothschild.[8] Between 1882 and 1899, nineteen Jewish agricultural colonies were founded of which at least nine were financially and morally supported by the Baron (Margalith 1957:144). A second better-organized phase of Jewish immigration emerged, however, when the financing of settlements was turned over to the Jewish Colonization Association (a spin-off of the World Zionist Organization) and when Lord Rothschild (Lionel Walter Rothschild, the second Baron Rothschild) persuaded James Balfour and the British political establishment to support the establishment of a home for the Jewish people in Palestine.

In 1917 – less than a year after the Sykes-Picot Agreement had been signed – setting out the Anglo-French post-World War I division of spoils – the Balfour Declaration was revealed. On 2 November 1917, British Foreign Secretary Lord James Balfour sent Lord Rothschild, a British leader of the Zionist movement in London, a letter pledging support for the establishment in Palestine of a 'national home for the Jewish people'.

> Foreign office
> November 2,
> Dear Lord Rothschild,
>
> I have much pleasure in conveying to you, on behalf of His Majesty's government, the following declaration of sympathy with Jewish Zionist aspirations which have been submitted to, and approved by, the Cabinet. "His Majesty's Government view with favour the establishment in Palestine of a national home for the Jewish people, and will use their best endeavours to facilitate the achievement of this object, it being clearly

---

[8] Margalith is a good source for details of the settlements in Palestine, which were funded by the Rothschild family in the nineteenth century (Margalith 1957).

understood that nothing shall be done which may prejudice the civil and religious rights of existing non-Jewish communities in Palestine, or the rights and political status enjoyed by Jews in any other country." I should be grateful if you would bring this declaration to the knowledge of the Zionist Federation.

Yours sincerely,
Arthur James Balfour

With the close of World War I, the League of Nations was established and in its covenant signed in 1919, the Palestinian people were recognized as an independent nation placed 'provisionally' under British mandate. Other peoples in the former Arab Ottoman provinces were also placed under mandate(s), some British and others French. In 1922, the League of Nations issued the British mandate and incorporated the Balfour Declaration in its articles, perhaps not recognizing that a fundamental inconsistency now existed in its articles of incorporation. On the one hand, the British mandate required Great Britain to act as 'custodian' (in Article 22 of the Covenant) to the Palestinian people who were 'not yet able to stand by themselves' as an independent state. At the same time, the incorporation of the Balfour Declaration into the League of Nations mandate for Palestine (articles 2, 4, 6, and 7) clearly contradicted significant parts of the original covenant. These articles allowed Great Britain to consult with the Jewish Agency (a powerful, autonomous para-state structure representing the World Zionist Organization, with international reach, which the mandate specifically enjoined the British to establish and assist under terms set out by the League of Nations) on matters pertaining to land, Jewish immigration to Palestine, and settlement, without referring to or consulting with the indigenous Palestinian people.[9] The outcome of World War I was then one of humiliation for the Arabs. Instead of attaining independence and being united as one Arab nation, the region was unnaturally divided into five sections (Lebanon, Syria, Iraq, Transjordan, and Palestine). The lines on the map were largely drawn by Sir Mark Sykes, a great supporter of both Zionism and Armenian nationalism. Ibn Saud and his Bedouin forces in Arabia were purposefully kept at bay by the extension of Iraq and Jordan into the Northern Syrian Badia, and the Hijaz of the Sharif of Mecca was given independence.

---

[9] Another example of the British disregard for the rights of the indigenous Arabs in Palestine comes from a further statement Lord Balfour had written in 1919: 'In Palestine we do not propose ever to go through the form of consulting the wishes of the present inhabitants ... Zionism is of far greater importance than the desires and prejudices of the 700,000 Arabs who now inhabit the land' (Khalidi 1971).

The Arab response

By 1919 Arab nationalists feared the promises made by their ally, Great Britain, were about to give way to a carving-up of their lands; they were also concerned by the Balfour Declaration and the declared Zionist intent to take over part of their homeland. Thus in July of that year they convened the General Syrian Congress in Damascus, with delegates from the entire East representing Muslim, Christian, and Jewish communities of the area, and expressed their desire for unity and independent statehood. These delegates met to put forward the aspirations of the Arabic-speaking people of Syria and demanded 'full and absolute political independence for Syria and a rejection of its dismemberment, a desire for a constitutional monarch, disapproval of any tutelage of a mandatory power and rejection of the claims of the Zionists for the establishment of a Jewish commonwealth in that part of southern Syria known as Palestine'. These demands were presented to the King–Crane Commission, which had begun its inquiry just the month before.

American President Woodrow Wilson had sent Henry Churchill King and Charles R. Crane on a mission to Syria. Originally this visit was intended to be an inter-Allied fact-finding mission to determine whether the region was ready for self-determination and what, if any, nation(s) the local peoples wished to see take on a mandatory role. However, France refused to take part and Great Britain withdrew its nominated representative. In the end it was an official American commission into the circumstances and conditions in the Arab provinces of the former Ottoman Empire. It quickly became clear to this commission that, perhaps as a reaction to the last decades of the Ottoman Empire and the impending French and British mandates over them, a new Arab nation had come into being, one which had widespread popular support and which was based on a common history, language, territory and culture. The desire of the people in this state for independence and unity was clear to the commission. It was also clear to King and Crane that the people of Palestine – that coastal region of southwestern Syria – clearly identified themselves as part of this Arab nation. They also saw that the majority of the people in this Arab state of 'Syria' were against the formation of a Jewish state. The only way to establish a viable Jewish state, they reported, would be with armed force.[10] They advised that Syria be recognized as one state and that the

---

[10] The commission estimated that a force of at least 50,000 would be needed initially in order to set up the proposed Jewish state (King & Crane 1922).

League of Nations mandate be over the entire Arab region (contemporary Syria, Lebanon, Jordan, Israel, the West Bank, and Gaza). They also recommended that Emir Faisal be appointed head of such a constitutional monarchy and that America be the mandatory power for a specified period of time.

Needless to say, the recommendations of the King–Crane Commission, filed in August 1919, were rejected. In April 1920 at San Remo, the Allies proclaimed the establishment of the French (Syria and Lebanon) and British (Iraq, Transjordan and Palestine) mandates. As British and French troops entered the mandated territories, they were met with riots, mass demonstrations, prolonged nationwide strikes, and armed insurrections.[11] Initially these demonstrations and struggles were of a pan-Arab character with support for Palestine as part of the Arab nation. Volunteers from throughout the Arab world entered into British-mandated Palestine to aid fellow Arabs in their fight for independence. Even though this struggle in Palestine was originally part of the general Arab struggle for national liberation, it wasn't long before the weight of the British occupation and the intensity of the Zionist land and settler project began to isolate Palestine from the rest of the Arab world. In some ways, after 1920 Palestinian Arabs found themselves – for the first time in history – a distinct unit shut off from their Arab brothers (Barbour 1969:94). Although hostility to the European Zionist settlement schemes in Palestine had been expressed before the announcement of the Balfour Declaration and its incorporation into the League of Nations, there was no organized Palestinian response to this perceived threat until 1919. Muslim and Christian Palestinian leaders who had attended the first two meetings of the General Syrian Congress in Damascus of 1919 agreed to hold a third meeting in Haifa once the British mandate had been imposed.

The Third Palestine Arab Congress of December 1920 was the first independent Palestinian political event.[12] As a result of this congress, the first Palestinian organization – the Arab Executive, which consisted of

---

[11] See Antonius for greater detail on this struggle (Antonius 1938).

[12] The 'debate' over when Palestinian identity emerged is in some ways an artifice of the Zionist ideology, which has presented a version to the West that there was no Palestinian national identity until after the creation of the State of Israel. In other words, the nationalist struggle to create the State of Israel did not have any Palestinian opposition until late in the British mandate period. However, as Rashid Khalidi demonstrates in his influential book, *Palestinian identity: The construction of modern national consciousness*, a Palestinian national consciousness had it origins near the beginning of the twentieth century at a time when the Arab populations of the late Ottoman period and early British Mandatory Palestine had 'overlapping identities,' with some or many expressing loyalties to villages,

twenty-four Muslim and Christian leaders – was formed: an alliance of sects as well as the major tribal and familial factions of Palestine. According to Zogby, this traditional, largely feudal, leadership was only able to move hesitantly in a nationalist direction. They were unable to entirely separate their interests from the British Mandated Authority; nor were they able to totally support a truly popular revolution (which would have undermined their land holdings). They separated out Zionism from British policy and were unable to see that the two were, in fact, inextricably tied to each other (Zogby 1974). Over the next ten years, the Palestinian Arab Congress issued renewed demands for the British to halt Jewish immigration and slow down or prohibit the transfer of property from Arabs to Jews as well as to establish a democratic government with proportional representation – the largest proportion naturally going to Arabs in accordance with their greater numbers (Waines 1971b:225–226). But beyond making such pronouncements, the Arab Congress seemed paralysed by the growing political and economic chaos in the country. Finally in August 1929, the Arab population rose up and attacked a number of Jewish settlements, killing many and burning their synagogues. Rather than take up this popular rebellion, the Arab Executive appealed to the masses to return to their homes and to assist in restoring order. The gap between this traditional leadership and the direction of protest among the masses of Palestinians was now increasingly clear.

Over the next three decades, the Jewish percentage of the population of mandated Palestine was to alter dramatically. In 1918, the Arab population of Palestine was estimated at 700,000 people, of whom 574,000 were Muslim, 70,000 Christian, and 56,000 Jews. Growing anti-Semitism in Europe in the 1930s pushed ever-increasing numbers of Jews to immigrate to Palestine. From 1932 to 1935, for example, the Jewish population of Palestine doubled.[13] By 1944, the number of Jews in Palestine was as much as 400,000 out of a total population of 1,700,000. Between 1946 and 1948, this number increased to 700,000 – around a third of the total population of about 2,115,000 (Farsoun & Zacharia 1997:79; Hadawi 1979:4).

This tremendous and rapid influx of Jewish immigrants into Palestine caused considerable pressure on the Arab population as well as serious

---

regions, a projected Arab national project, a nation of Palestine, and an alternative of inclusion in a Greater Syria (Khalidi 1997).

[13] In 1935, 72,000 Jews arrived in Palestine. With a total population of slightly more than one million, this was a very significant immigration. The total number of Jewish immigrants by this time is contested with Khalidi, R. (1997; Khalidi 1971) indicating a figure near 300,000, and Farsoun and Zacharia (1997) a figure nearer to 150,000.

local economic dislocation.[14] The large sums of Jewish capital flowing into the country brought about inflation and at the same time higher pay scales for Jewish workers. In 1936, Jewish workers averaged 140 per cent higher wages than those of Arabs doing identical jobs. In some trades the salaries for Jewish workers were 400 per cent higher (Waines 1971a:225). These problems were made worse by the rising rural urban migration of peasants being forced off their lands. In the past, the feudal nature of landholding had been such that as absentee landlords sold off land to others, the peasants historically carried on working for the new owners. But with land sales to Zionist organizations, Palestinian peasants were forced off the land. By 1931, 20,000 peasant families had been uprooted in this way and by 1941, 30 per cent of all Arab families employed in agriculture were landless. Many of these landless peasants flocked to the cities to look for work (Kanafani 1972:51–52).

Much of the land purchase in Palestine during this period was not by individuals, but by political agencies of the Zionist movement, such as the Jewish National Fund and the Jewish Colonization Association, and took the form of land acquisition from mostly absentee Arab landowners. The land was inhabited mainly by Palestinian tenant farmers, however, and this constituted a problem for the Jewish Agency. Clearing the land for newly arriving Jewish settlers became an important goal of the agency. Josef Weitz, for example, the director of the Jewish National Fund's Land Department, wrote in his diary on 20 December 1937:

Among ourselves it must be clear there is no room for both peoples in this country .... And the only solution is the land of Israel, or at least the Western land of Israel (Palestine), without Arabs. There is no room for compromise on this point. (Weitz, quoted in Morris 1987:27)

A few years later, in 1940, Weitz was to add in his diary:

We shall not achieve our goal of being an independent people with the Arabs in this small country. The only solution is a Palestine ... without Arabs ... and there is no other way than to transfer the Arabs from here to the neighbouring countries, to transfer all of them: Not one village, not one tribe should be left ... Only after this

---

[14] Jewish capital was seizing the economic initiative in the country and the Arab economic order was in ruins. The fledgling Arab bourgeoisie could not compete with the much better financed and more modern Zionist enterprises. In the years 1933–6, an average of 20 per cent of the total number of Jewish immigrants were listed as 'capitalists' – immigrants who brought with them enough capital to start a modest enterprise (at least £1,000 at that time). In addition, over £77 million had been set aside for the exclusive use of developing the Jewish economy in Palestine (Barbour 1969; Peel 1937).

transfer will the country be able to absorb millions of our brethren. There is no other way out. (Bober 1972:13; quoted in Zogby 1974:104)

The 1936–1939 Palestinian rebellion

The long-simmering Palestinian resistance marked by the 1929 uprising and the 1933 national strike finally erupted into a peasant-based national rebellion between 1936–9. One of the first acts of the British forces was to cut communication wires between Palestine and the other Arab regions (Kalkas 1971:244). By 1938 the British were so concerned with this pan-Arab support that 'Jewish labourers were employed by the Government at the cost of 100,000 pounds Sterling to build a barbed-wire fence around the northern and north-eastern frontier of Palestine. This fence was intended to separate the Arabs of Palestine from the Arabs of Lebanon and Syria' (Barbour 1969:192).

The rapid rate at which land was being purchased by the Jewish National Fund and other agencies along with the increasing rate of Jewish immigration and settlement, were two important factors in the rising alarm among Palestinians for their political future and their live-lihood (Khalidi 1984:86). As important was the dawning realization among Palestinians that British military institutions were cooperating with paramilitary Jewish organizations such as the Haganah, the Irgun, and the Stern Gang by providing them with military training and arms. The main purpose of the Haganah (defence, in Hebrew) at that time had been to protect the Jewish colonies and enclaves sprouting up in Palestine. One British officer in particular, Orde Charles Wingate, was responsible for turning the Haganah into an efficient military organization. Wingate began his career in Sudan, where he was particularly successful in developing an ambush policy against slave traders. In 1936 he was assigned to Palestine, where 'he quickly became enchanted by the Zionist dream. He decided actively to encourage the Jewish settlers and started teaching their troops more effective combat tactics and retaliation methods against the local population' (Pappé 2006:16).

Under the tutelage of Wingate, the Haganah became a supremely efficient military arm for the Jewish Agency, the Zionist government body in Palestine. He succeeded in attaching the Haganah to the British forces during the Arab revolt so that they could better learn what a 'punitive mission' to an Arab village should entail. For example, in June 1938, a Haganah unit and a British company jointly attacked a village on the border between Palestine and Lebanon and held it for a number of hours

(Hagana Archives file 0014 1938; quoted in Pappé 2006:16). The Haganah militia had its first taste of what it meant to occupy a Palestinian village.

During this same period, Palestinian Arabs recognized they were being prevented from arming themselves or developing self-defence mechanisms against Jewish attacks. Palestinian resistance to what they regarded as a colonization of their land was being met with British Mandate Authority abolishment of civil law, whereby Palestinians but not Jews were subjected to emergency law and military courts and the discharge of arms or carrying of weapons was punishable by death (Tannous 1988:230). They also gradually came to feel that the British Mandate Authority was not providing them with any assistance in creating civil and political institutions for self-government.

At this time, Shaykh Izzedine al-Qassam had come to Palestine to organize the Palestinian fight for independence against the British. He had made overtures to the traditional leaders in the Arab Executive, but had been turned down. Nevertheless he proceeded to organize the people of the countryside into guerrilla bands. On 2 November 1935, in the first organized operation he led near Haifa – in response to what Palestinians regarded as efforts to dispossess them – he was killed. Shaykh Izzedine's death sparked a protracted Palestinian rebellion, which was to last three years. Qassamite armed bands began their offensive against British and Zionist colonists in April 1936. The Jews rose in anger and Tel Aviv was filled with violent anti-Arab demonstrators who demanded the formation of an all-Jewish army. This in turn outraged the Arab community and the violence spread to Jaffa. Arab national committees were set up in nearly every city and village and calls were made for a nationwide strike. In an effort to salvage their leadership, the Arab Executive merged with representatives of the local strike committees to form the Arab Higher Committee (AHC). This Committee met then in May 1936 and called on all Palestinian organizations to continue the national strike until the British allowed Palestinians to form a national government based on democratic representative governance.[15]

This resistance to what Palestinians saw as the colonization of their land was met with repression and the abolition of civil law by the British. The British Mandate Authority tried to intimidate the Arab population

---

[15] Mayors of most Arab cities, the Arab national guard, the Arab police, 137 Arab senior officials in the mandate government, and 1,200 other Arab officials in government all publicly supported these demands and the strike (Zogby 1974).

into submission by using mass arrests, forced opening of businesses closed by the strike, collective fines, and confiscations against villages suspected of harbouring 'guerrillas' and widespread demolition. By June of 1936 they had arrested 2,600 strikers. Most of the old city in Jaffa had been levelled. The British army of occupation was also increased to 20,000 men. But the strike continued. Palestinians were subjected to emergency laws and military courts. The emergency laws declared all Palestinian political organizations 'illegal'. At the same time, the British continued to arm and train Zionist Jewish settlers and paramilitary organizations (Tannous 1988:238). In a desperate effort to end the strike as well as the violence and bloodshed, the son and grandson of the Sharif of Mecca – King Abdullah and King Ghazi, respectively – entered into the fray along with Ibn Saud and attempted to establish an atmosphere for negotiations. As part of the deal, Britain sent a commission to Palestine to study the Arab grievances, report on the causes of the revolt, and make recommendations that might solve the problems. This was the Palestine Royal Commission headed by Lord Peel (known popularly as the Peel Commission).

Lord Peel arrived in Palestine in November 1936. After two months, he returned to Britain and released his report in July 1937. The Arabs had hoped it would affirm their call for representative, democratic government, and a halt to Jewish immigration. Instead, the Peel Commission reaffirmed the League of Nations' British mandate and 'national home for Jews' policy. The commission suggested a solution to the violence would be the creation of a partitioned, racially divided state (see 1937). The north of Palestine would go to the Jewish state, with an international corridor around Jerusalem. The Arab state was to include the south mideastern Palestine. The report recommended that 'sooner or later there should be a transfer of land and as far as possible an exchange of populations' on the model of the Greek–Turkish exchange at the close of the Greco-Turkish War of 1922.

The Arabs regarded the report as a deep betrayal and the national strike and violence continued, particularly in Galilee. The British responded initially by outlawing the Arab High Council and the other national committees, arresting, sentencing to death, or sending into exile the Arab leadership. However, the rural revolt continued to grow. By mid- 1938, the rebels were in control of 80 per cent of the countryside as well as the older parts of Jerusalem, Nabulus, and Hebron (Kalkas 1971:247–248). Not prepared to allow the rebellion to succeed, the British unleashed a massive campaign of repression against the Palestinians. In addition to a

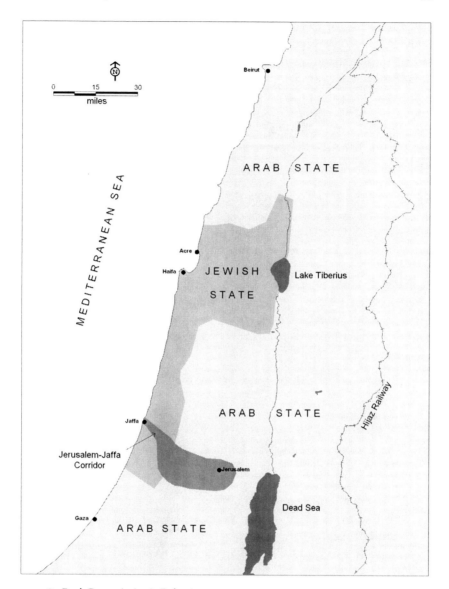

MAP 8. Peel Commission's Palestine

20,000-member occupation force, the British brought in squadrons of the
Royal Air Force from Cyprus and Egypt to quell this serious uprising.
Furthermore, hundreds of Jewish settlers were supplied with further arms
and organized into 'night squads' to attack Arab villages – their training

having been completed in the years before by Orde Wingate.[16] By 1939, the British were able to restore order along with 6,000 Jewish auxiliary police helping to suppress the last embers of the Arab revolt (Khalidi 2001:26).

Following the 1936–9 rebellion, the British called for a conference of Arabs and Jews to discuss how to proceed in Palestine. The St James Conference or Round Table Conference of 1939 brought together Arab representatives from Palestine, Egypt, Iraq, Saudi Arabia, Transjordan, and Yemen. The Arab delegates, however, refused to meet directly with the Jewish representatives, as they did not recognize the legitimacy of the Jewish Agency. Whatever affront the Jewish Agency may have felt at this refusal to directly negotiate with them, the 1936–9 rebellion had clearly benefited the Zionists; they now had 'demographic weight, control of strategic areas of land, and much of the weaponry and military organization that would be needed as a springboard for taking over the country within less than a decade' (Khalidi 2001:27).

The McDonald White Paper of 1939, which emerged at the end of the St James Conference, set out key provisions that appeased the Arabs of Palestine but severely compromised the British commitment to the Balfour Declaration of 1917. The key provisions of the white paper of 1939 were:

1. It was not British policy that Palestine should become a Jewish State (contrary to the fundamental principle of the Balfour Declaration).
2. Neither was it British policy that Palestine should become an Arab State (contrary to the McMahon Correspondence of 1915).
3. The establishment of an independent Palestine state in which Arabs and Jews have a government within ten years.
4. Jewish immigration to be limited to 75,000 over the next five years, so that the number of Jews in the country would not exceed one-third of the total population.
5. Transfers of land from Arabs to Jews to be severely restricted.

The Arab High Commission rejected the white paper because it did not explicitly include a commitment to the independence of the Palestinian people. The Jews of Palestine and in the rest of the world were outraged at what was seen as British betrayal. With the outbreak of World War II, the report and the League of Nations became irrelevant. Though the basis of British policy until the end of the mandate, the white paper never was

---

[16] See 'Orde Wingate' in Khalidi (1971).

effectively implemented and rescinding its decrees was the first action of the Israeli Provisional Council of State (formerly the Jewish Agency, headed by David Ben-Gurion), on 15 May 1948 when the State of Israel was declared.

In 1942, six hundred Jewish delegates met in New York to express their opposition to the white paper, demanding the establishment of a Jewish army, their own flag, and untrammelled immigration to Palestine. The white paper also prompted a change of policy within the Jewish Agency and the Haganah. Zionist armed attacks now focused on British targets as well as Arab ones. The most infamous of these included, in November 1944, the assassination of the British Minister of State in Cairo, Lord Moyne, by the Stern Gang led by Yitzhak Shamir as well as in 1946, the blowing up of the King David Hotel in Jerusalem by the Irgun, under the leadership of Menachim Begin. Before long, the British came to perceive the conflict in Palestine as an economic and political burden, and early in 1947, the government declared the mandate unworkable and announced the imminent withdrawal of its troops, handing the conflict back to the United Nations to find a solution.

The UN Partition Plan of 1947 the declaration of the State of Israel 1948

In 1947, the United Nations dispatched a Commission of Inquiry [UNSCOP] to Palestine. After the commission proposed the partition of Palestine, the United Nations General Assembly on 29 November 1947 passed Resolution 181, or what was also known as the UN Partition Plan. According to the plan, the Jewish state was to comprise 56.4 per cent of the territory while the area allocated to the Palestinian Arab state was 42.8 per cent. Jerusalem was to become an international zone. At the time the resolution was passed, Jews owned only 7 per cent of the total land area in Palestine; Palestinian Arabs owned the rest. Jews constituted nearly one-third of Palestine's population and Palestinians, two-thirds. Palestinians and other Arabs were outraged and rejected the United Nations resolution (Farsoun & Zacharia 1997:110–111).

The day following the rejection of the UN Partition Plan, armed conflict spread throughout Palestine. The Palestinians entered the fighting with a deeply divided and ineffective leadership, exceedingly limited finances, no centrally organized military forces or administrative organs, and no reliable allies. The Jewish population, on the other hand, though smaller relative to the Palestinians, was politically unified, had centralized para-state institutions, and was exceedingly well led and well armed. The outcome of the 1947–8 war was a foregone conclusion. The Palestinians had larger numbers, but the Jews had more important advantages. As Khalidi succinctly summed up the situation, the Jews had a 'larger and more diversified economy, better finances, greater firepower, superior organization, and considerable support from the United States and the Soviet Union' (2001:30).

Zionist paramilitary organizations – especially the Haganah and the international volunteers who came to assist them – engaged in a system of what Ben-Gurion called aggressive defence; that is, every Arab attack would be met with decisive counteraction, destruction of the site, expulsion of its residents, and seizure of the location. In March 1948, Ben-Gurion put into effect Plan Dalet with the aim of capturing, evacuating, and 'cleansing' Arab villages, neighbourhoods, and towns.[17] The following month, two events sent shockwaves throughout Palestine and the rest of the Arab world: the death of the charismatic Palestinian leader, Abd al-Qader al-Husseini, while defending the Arab village of al-Qastal; and the Irgun and Stern Gang massacre at Deir Yassin village. It led the Arab states, assembled in an Arab League, to consider intervention in Palestine with their regular armies (Farsoun & Zacharia 1997:114). The Arab League agreed to intervene, but only after the British mandate had officially ended. A volunteer force was quickly put together with Syrian, Iraqi, and Lebanese individual volunteers and small military units. Only the Jordanians had a professional army with a serious capacity to defend Palestinians.[18] Once the largely small and irregular Arab armies decided

---

[17] According to Pappé, when Plan Dalet went into effect in April 1948, a month before the end of the British mandate, the Haganah had more than 50,000 troops at its disposal, half of which had been trained by the British Army during World War II. The Plan D was to capture, cleanse, and destroy. 'As Arab villages fell, they were surrounded, attacked, occupied, their people expelled and their homes and buildings demolished'. In some cases the expulsion was accompanied by massacres, the most notorious of which was Deir Yassin (Pappé 2006:43).

[18] Many historians believe that King Abdullah of Jordan had agreed in secret talks with the Jewish Agency to limit the Jordanian Arab Legion to defending the West Bank for the Arabs. Recognizing that the only serious army they would have to face was Jordanian, the Jewish leadership fully expected the future State of Israel to stretch over 80 per cent of British-mandated Palestine: the 56 per cent promised to the Jews by the UN with an additional 24 per cent taken from the Arab state the UN had allocated to the Palestinians. The remaining 20 per cent would be picked up by Jordan as agreed in the secret Jordanian–Jewish Agency negotiations. One of the few triumphs in the Arab military history of 1948 was the Jordanians (with the help of an Iraqi contingent) successfully repelling repeated Jewish attempts to occupy parts of the West Bank throughout the second half of 1948 (Pappé 2006:92–97).

to intervene, most of the major cities and towns in Palestine had already fallen to the Haganah and other Jewish militias.[19] The Jewish fighting force included 52,000 men in the Haganah, 14,000 in the Jewish Settlement Police (which had been trained and armed by the British), and 27,000 World War II veterans as well as numerous paramilitary groups. Benny Morris described the emergence of the Haganah:

In the course of that year [1948], it [Haganah] emerged and efficiently functioned as a large conventional force, beating first the Palestinian Arab militias and then the combined irregular and regular armies of the Arab states. By April–May 1948, it was conducting brigade-size offensives, by July, multi-brigade operations; and by October, divisional, multi-front offensive (Morris 1987:22).

The Haganah, soon to be renamed the Israeli Defence Force, and other Jewish militias were superior in training, armament, and numbers to the local Palestinian forces and the Arab armies combined. Most of these Arab states had only just snatched their independence from French or British mandate and were not prepared for international campaigns. Egypt was still in a semicolonial relationship with Great Britain. Only recently had France grudgingly granted Lebanon and Syria their independence, in 1946 and 1943, respectively. And Jordan's King Abdullah was alleged to have given orders to his British-commanded Arab legion to secure only the part of Palestine – the West Bank – allotted to him in secret talks with the Zionist leadership.

The Palestinians were defeated by the Jews in the struggle to keep their homeland and, on Friday 15 May 1948, Ben-Gurion declared the establishment of the State of Israel. Henceforth, 1948 marked two contrasting historical experiences. For the Zionists, it was the culmination of the dream of creating a Jewish state, as a means to put an end to European anti-Semitism. For Palestinians it was the time of expulsion, exodus, and destruction of their land and society.

---

[19] The Zionist campaign to clear Palestine of Arabs had begun months earlier. After a pronounced campaign of intimidation and terror in Haifa in December 1947, for example, between 15,000 and 20,00 Palestinian elite left their residences in Lebanon and Egypt to await the return of calm to their city. They never came back. Safad reflected a more typical upheaval, if anything about war can be called typical. It was a town with a long-established and integrated Jewish community. It had 9,500 Arabs and 2,400 mostly ultra-Orthodox Jews who were not interested in Zionism or in fighting their Arab neighbours. It was attacked by a highly organized Haganah commando unit of 1,000 Palmach who confronted 400 Arab volunteers. As Ilan Pappé writes, Safad was 'one of many local imbalances that show the falsity of the myth of a Jewish David facing an Arab Goliath in 1948' (Pappé 2006).

Palestinian expulsion and the humanitarian emergency

Within a few short months in the spring of 1948, nearly three-quarters of a million people in Palestine were forced from their homes by armed Jewish militias and pushed to neighbouring states. It was an exercise in ethnic cleansing which had begun nearly a half-century earlier and which was now culminating in *al-Nakbah* (The Catastrophe), as Palestinians called this dramatic upheaval (Pappé 2006). This huge number of people took refuge in camps hastily set up by the Red Cross and other humanitarian agencies in the West Bank, Gaza, Lebanon, Syria, and Jordan. An estimated 5,000 Palestinian refugees followed the retreating Iraqi army back to Iraq.[20] Others fled to Egypt and carried on to wherever they could find shelter across North Africa.[21]

Unusually, instead of bringing this humanitarian emergency under the mandate of the existing International Refugee Organization (IRO), which held the dual protection and humanitarian relief mandate,[22] the United Nations set up a special agency in December 1949 in Resolution 302, the United Nations Relief and Works Agency (UNRWA), to manage Palestinian refugee camps and provide health, education, and humanitarian aid. The year before, the UN had set up a special commission, the United Nations Conciliation Commission for Palestine (UNCCP). Created by the General Assembly in Resolution 194(III) in December 1948, the commission was assigned to oversee the legal and political protection of Palestinian refugees. The UNCCP was composed of representatives of the United States, France, and Turkey. Its goal was to provide protection and facilitate durable solutions for persons displaced as a result of the 1947–8 conflict and war in Palestine.

---

[20] These refugees were mainly from Haifa and Jaffa and had taken refuge behind the Iraqi army lines. Upon their retreat they decided to return with them to Iraq. Later waves of Palestinians came to Iraq after the June 1967 war. Their descendants make up the majority of the 30–40,000 Palestinians who fled Iraq after the 2003 Anglo-American invasion of the country (Amnesty International 2007).

[21] The number of Palestinian refugees in Egypt is estimated at about 100,000 by Oroub Obeid. In the late 1990s and early 2000s she conducted the first large-scale study of this largely forgotten refugee community in Egypt (El-Abed 2003; El-Abed 2004; El Abed 2009).

[22] The International Refugee Organization (IRO) was established in 1946 as a temporary agency of the United Nations to assist refugees and displaced persons in many countries of Europe and Asia who either could not return to their countries of origin or were unwilling to return for political reasons. By 1952 it had resettled about one million persons. It was superseded by the Office of the United Nations High Commissioner for Refugees (UNHCR).

TABLE 4. *Palestinian refugees in UNRWA camps*

Field of Operations	Official Camps	Registered Families in Camps	Registered Refugees in Camps	Registered Refugees
Jordan	10	63,591	335,307	1,930,703
Lebanon	12	50,806	220,908	416,608
Syria	9	26,645	123,646	452,983
West Bank	19	39,895	161,408	754,263
Gaza Strip	8	93,074	492,299	1,059,584
Agency total	58	274,011	1,363,496	4,618,141

Figures derived from UNRWA as of 30 June 2008.

However, after four years of effort, the UNCCP proved it was incapable of providing Palestinian refugees with the basic international protection accorded all other refugees. The commission claimed it was unable to fulfil its mandate due to the lack of international political will to ensure the right of Palestinian refugees wishing to go back to their homes and villages. Today the commission has no budget and no staff. The secretary of the UNCCP is a staff member of the UN Department of Political Affairs.

The largest number of Palestinian refugees in the Middle East is found in Jordan, with more than 1.6 million registered with UNRWA today. Syria acknowledges 391,651 registered Palestinian refugees. In Lebanon, 382,973 Palestinian refugees are registered with UNRWA. Fifty-six per cent of them live in official refugee camps. In the West Bank, 37 per cent of the population – 607,770 Palestinians – comprises refugees and in Gaza, 852,626 Palestinian refugees, making up 75 per cent of the total population.

THE PALESTINIAN EXODUS: STATELESS REFUGEES WITHOUT PROTECTION OR RIGHTS OF RETURN

I was born in Safad, Galilee in 1941. It was a town built on a hill. I remember that we lived near the Jewish quarter. My mother used to take us to the Jewish physicians because she trusted them … One day there was a quarrel between an Arab and Jew about some clothes in a shop. The Jew was killed. Then instead of cooperation which used to distinguish the relations between the Jews and the Arabs in the town, everybody took care of themselves, they didn't mingle. Of course the war began outside Safad and in other villages. But when these villages were controlled [by the Jews] we were protected by Jordanian troops and some Syrian volunteers. Then, one day the Jordanian troops pulled out without telling any of the inhabitants they were leaving. The local defenders were very poorly armed and realized they couldn't put off an attack. There was no defence ... So we left. My sisters who were older carried me and my younger brother. It was the month of May, but it was raining and I remember that groups of people were walking with us. We moved north, not to Syria. There was no cover, nothing. There were soldiers walking with us. Syrian soldiers. We just walked and walked maybe 300 kilometres until we reached Bint il-Jbeil [south Lebanon]. We didn't stay long, maybe one night. Then we were put on a train for Tripoli. We went from one end of the country to the other. We didn't stay long there either. Maybe one night and then they took us to Homs where we started our life in Syria ... We thought we were going to go back to Safad in one week's time. We were promised, just get out of town until the Arabs regain it. When we left the fighting in Safad we thought that after one week we could come back. I remember I left in short trousers. We took no papers, not even our birth certificates. Nothing! Because we were promised that we were going back home soon. (Ali 2005, Damascus)

The official Israeli historiography claims that the Palestinian refugees fled due to enticement and encouragement by Arab governments. This claim has been refuted by the new Israeli historians who have found no evidence to show that either the leaders of the Arab states or the Mufti (religious leader) ordered or encouraged the mass exodus of April 1948 (Gelvin 1998; Gelvin 2005). The dramatic and abrupt dispossession and displacement of Palestinians in 1948 attracted significant international attention. In June 1948, Josef Weitz, Director of the Jewish National Fund, met with Ben-Gurion and put forward a plan for preventing the return of refugees to their homes. This plan was formalized and adopted by the Israeli Cabinet on 16 June 1948. Arab governments, at the same time, refused to integrate Palestinian refugees in their host countries, maintaining that this would threaten their right of return to their homes in Palestine.

For similar reasons the Arab states were generally opposed to having the International Refugee Organization (IRO) – the existing UN agency set up for refugees and displaced people after World War II – take on the needs and interests of Palestinian refugees. The Arab states did not want Palestinian refugees resettled and assimilated in new countries, a policy which at the time was the IRO's preferred durable solution. Instead, the Arab states wanted Palestinians to be repatriated and allowed to return to their homes. Thus, they pressed for the formation of a separate specialized organization to meet the short- and long-term economic relief of Palestinian refugees in occupied territory and in countries bordering on the former mandatory Palestine.

Politically, the establishment of the State of Israel and the flight of the majority of the Christian and Muslim Palestinians radically changed the face of Palestinian politics. The common experience of loss of homeland may have strengthened a Palestinian particularism, but the trauma of the loss seems to have muted any significant political activity. For the first decade in exile, Palestinians relied on the efforts of neighbouring states to keep their agenda public: the abolishment of the Zionist Jewish state; independence in a Palestinian state; and the right of Palestinian refugees to return to pre-1948 Palestine.

On 16 September 1948, Count Folke Bernadotte, the UN mediator in Palestine, submitted his recommendations to the UN General Assembly. His report reaffirmed Palestinians' right to return to their homes, to restitution, and to compensation. A day after this submission, he was assassinated by the Stern Gang. Nevertheless, the widely quoted UN resolution 194, based on his recommendations, was passed on 11 December 1948. This resolution established the UNCCP, whose early activities included intervention with Israeli authorities to permit the return of certain categories of refugees, reunification of separated families, recommendations to safeguard the rights and properties of refugees, intervention to abrogate discriminatory property laws, and facilitation of refugee access to blocked savings accounts and assets in banks inside Israel. The Economic Survey Mission, one of the sub-organs of the UNCCP, called for the establishment of short- and long-term economic relief for Palestinian refugees, which included the creation of the United Nations Relief and Works Agency. Six months later, in May 1950, the UNRWA took over humanitarian relief operations in the Jordanian-controlled West Bank, the Egyptian-controlled Gaza Strip, and in Jordan, Syria, and Lebanon. UNRWA's mandate was short: all relief and works operations were to be terminated by the middle of 1951 as it was expected that those refugees wishing to do so would soon be able to return to their homes in accordance with the General Assembly Resolution 194 (III). Those not willing to do so were entitled to resettlement assistance. In fact, because of the absence of durable solutions for these refugees, UNRWA's mandate has been extended on a regular basis year after year.[23]

---

[23] The definition which UNRWA employs of a refugee is different from that set out by the UNHCR. For UNRWA, to qualify as a Palestinian refugee means proving that you resided in Palestine at least two years prior to the establishment of the State of Israel on 15 May, 1948, and 'who lost both his home and means of livelihood as a result of the 1948 War'. Many Palestinians could not fit this description. Some lost homes and not livelihoods, others livelihoods but not homes. Some could not supply the documentation to prove physical residence, while others were displaced in the new Israeli state. For deeper analysis of Palestinian refugee numbers and the various categories of Palestinians who are excluded see Zureik (2001).

Palestinian refugees are a creation of the League of Nations and its successor, the United Nations. That is, their plight, their statelessness, and their liminality are the direct result of the misinterpretation of the covenant of the League of Nations, the misadministration of the British mandate, and the UN's decision to partition the Palestinian homeland and create two states. Palestinians are also hostage to the political positioning of Israeli politicians and within Israel and the occupied territories. Furthermore, through on-going 'legal' evictions, house demolitions, and more recently the Separation Wall, the numbers of Palestinian refugees continue to grow. Unlike many other refugee situations, the Palestinian case is crowded with numerous UN resolutions and recommendations relating to them. The three most important such resolutions are 181, 194, and 242.[24]

Although the Israeli state accepted UN Resolution 181 dividing Palestine into one Jewish and one Arab state, it refused to accept UN Resolution 194 'resolving that the refugees wishing to return to their homes and live at peace with their neighbours should be permitted to do so at the earliest practicable date, and that compensation should be paid for the property of those choosing not to return and for loss of or damage to property which, under principles of international law or in equity, should be made good by the Governments or authorities responsible.' In direct refutation to UN GA Resolution 194, the Israeli state moved quickly to consolidate legislation hindering Palestinians from returning and reclaiming their confiscated property. This included the Nationality Law of 1952, which placed many restrictions on non-Jews, namely Palestinian Arabs, for the purpose of excluding as many 1948 refugees as possible from eligibility for Israeli citizenship; and numerous laws regarding property rights such as the Absentees Property Law, which allowed the transfer of property of displaced Palestinians to Jewish citizens. This law also applied to Palestinians who were internally displaced and had fled their homes and villages temporarily during the armed conflicts. Others were forcibly evicted. These Palestinians in the State of Israel became the

---

[24] UN General Assembly Resolution 181 proposed the partition of mandated Palestine into a Jewish state side by side with a Palestinian state. UN General Assembly Resolution 194 resolved that Palestinian refugees wishing to return to their homes and live in peace with their neighbours should be permitted to do so. Furthermore it was resolved that a commission (the UNCCP) be set up to facilitate repatriation, resettlement, and economic and social rehabilitation of the Palestinian refugees and the payment of compensation. UN Security Council Resolution 242 called for the withdrawal of Israeli armed forces from territories occupied in 1967 (the West Bank and the Gaza Strip) and the termination of all claims or states of belligerency.

'Present Absentees'. Those who managed to remain in the Palestinian territories that became Israel in 1948 numbered approximately 150,000 and 25 per cent of them became internally displaced persons.

After their initial expulsion during and consequent to the 1947–8 war, Palestinians were subjected to further displacement. During the Arab–Israeli War in 1967, Israel occupied the remaining 22 per cent of mandated Palestine, namely the West Bank and Gaza, as well as other Arab territory. As a result, approximately 350,000 Palestinians were uprooted from the West Bank and Gaza – more than half of them for the second time. Most of these refugees and displaced persons found shelter in Jordan. The Israeli invasion into Lebanon in 1982 resulted in the death and displacement of thousands of Palestinians in refugee camps, which were targeted by Israeli forces for attack both by air and later by proxy land forces. The Gulf War of 1990–1, when Saddam Hussein of Iraq attacked and occupied Kuwait, caused another mass forced migration of Palestinians. An estimated 350,000 largely middle-class Palestinians who had been residents in Kuwait, sometimes for decades, were thrown out of the country with no opportunity to return. Most of them went to Jordan to join close relatives or other more distant kin. With the end of the Gulf War in 1991, none of these Palestinians were allowed to return to Kuwait, as both the PLO and, surprisingly, King Hussein had taken sides with Iraq in the early stages of the conflict.

In the middle of the 1990s, Libya evicted its Palestinian community of some 30,000; many of them straddled the Libyan–Egyptian border for months and some remained for more than a year, unable to return to Palestine or find a country that would allow them entry. With no legal protection – that having been assigned to the UNCCP, which had ceased to function effectively after 1952 – these people were at the mercy of the humanitarian impulse of the world. Then, and also now, the main refugee agency of the United Nations – the United Nations High Commission for Refugees (UNHCR), with a clear protection role for refugees – stepped in to help these stateless people who had been specifically excluded from its mandate in the region. Then, in the aftermath of the Anglo-American invasion of Iraq, the 50,000 Palestinian refugees in that country began to flee, seeking protection mainly in Syria and Jordan. Most of them were trapped in hastily erected UNHCR temporary camps, some on the 'no-man's land' between states, unable to go forward and afraid to go back. After lengthy negotiations between the UNHCR and neighbouring states, a few selected categories of Palestinians have been allowed entry into Jordan and Syria; most are awaiting third country settlement.

PALESTINIANS IN DIASPORA

After their expulsion, Palestinian refugees sought shelter in neighbouring countries, primarily in the West Bank and Gaza (which had fallen under the control of Jordan and Egypt, respectively) Lebanon, and Syria. Others managed to find refuge in North Africa, in the Arabian Gulf (particularly Kuwait), Europe, and North America. Those who remained in the new Israeli state often found themselves 'permanently' internally displaced and declared 'Absent Present'.[25] The majority of Palestinians believed their expulsion would end in a matter of days – at most, a few weeks. Most had not carried their belongings with them and many had left their doors open, while others took their keys and house deeds. To this day, many hold on to the keys to their homes as a symbol of hope and resistance to exile, while others dream of returning to their villages and towns of origin. In some cases – particularly in Lebanon and Jordan – Palestinian refugees can see the lights of their villages at night from their current places of residence in refugee camps, middle-class urban neighbourhoods, and poor squatter settlements on the edges of Arab cities. Most Palestinian refugees settled unwillingly into particular sites in the adjacent countries in the 1950s along with fellow refugees from the same villages, towns, and cities in Palestine. Many remain in these places today.

By the late 1950s Palestinians in exile began to see themselves as capable of accomplishing some of the goals of their Palestinian national movement. In 1959 Yasser Arafat and others established the 'Palestinian Liberation Movement' (*Fateh*) (Gelvin 2005). This was followed closely by the establishment of a number of other 'guerrilla' organizations whose 'Fedayeen' fighters increasingly engaged in small-scale attacks and skirmishes on Israel. These included the Popular Front for the Liberation of Palestine (PFLP), the Democratic Front for the Liberation of Palestine (DFLP), and many others. In 1964, following an earlier decision of the Arab League, 422 Palestinian national figures met in Jerusalem and founded the Palestinian Liberation Organization (PLO) with the goal of liberating Palestine through armed

---

[25] Palestinians in the immediate region of the Arab Middle East, the five UNRWA field sites, are the focus of this study. However, those who went further afield make up the other half of the estimated nine million Palestinians in diaspora. The significance of their contribution to Palestinian national identity cannot be overestimated. Ties to Palestinians in the Arab Gulf have been significant in maintaining systems of remittances; Palestinians in the USA holding American passports have been instrumental in manipulating important legal channels for Palestinian family reunification in the face of increasing Israeli obstruction and hostility (Ashkar 2006).

struggle. After the humiliating defeat of the Arab states by Israel in 1967 (which brought the West Bank and the Gaza Strip and East Jerusalem under Israeli rule), Fateh and numerous other liberation organizations saw a huge increase in membership. Many of these organizations also gained support from Egypt and Syria as a means of maintaining indirect warfare against Israel. By the 1970s the PLO was effectively an umbrella group of eight organizations (many with political as well as military wings) with head-quarters in Damascus and Beirut, having the common aim of armed resistance to Zionism, or Israeli occupation. After 1970, and after Black September in Jordan, the PLO established itself in Lebanon in accordance with the Cairo Agreement of 1969.[26] After 1982, the PLO was defeated in the Israeli invasion of Lebanon and its leadership was permitted safe passage to move to Tunis. During this decade the PLO suffered a period of disarray, and splinter groups (the Rejection Front) emerged. A major shift occurred after the first Intifada in the West Bank and the Gaza Strip (1987–93), and it was the Palestinian refugees of the occupied territories who came to the forefront of the nationalist struggle. The concerns of these populations were somewhat different from those Palestinians in Jordan, Syria, and Lebanon, in that they were primarily interested in independence rather than in refugee return (Sayigh 1997).

The historical timeline, social and political conditions, civil rights, and proportion of Palestinians to the population differ from country to country in UNRWA field sites. Palestinians form a politically, socially, and economically disadvantaged group within the region and within the countries they live in; many of them live in poverty and in their populations, the young predominate numerically. With the exception of those living in Jordan, none of them had citizenship rights until 1995, when Palestinians living in the Gaza Strip and the West Bank had the right to Palestinian passports issued by the Palestinian Authority. Given that each location has experienced a unique set of historical and demographic realities, it is useful to briefly contextualize each country or territory.[27] For

---

[26] After the defeat of the Arab states in the 1967 war, many Palestinian guerrilla movements increased their activities in Lebanon with the backing of a number of Arab states. In November 1969, a Lebanese delegation headed by army commander Emile al Bustani met with Yasser Arafat, chairman of the PLO, and agreed an effective endorsement of PLO freedom of action in Lebanon to recruit, arm, train, and employ fighters against Israel. The Lebanese Army was to protect their bases and supply lines. In effect, the Cairo Agreement permitted the PLO to bear arms and use Lebanon as a launching pad for its 'war' on Israel.

[27] Detailed socioeconomic survey results are regularly available through various studies of the Institute of Palestine Studies (www.palestine-studies.org); since 1993 with the first

Palestinian refugees in Syria, for example, their presence and political experience in the country is perhaps the most stable and least affected by the continuous crises and armed conflicts in the region. In Lebanon, on the other hand, continuous armed conflict since the 1960s has intimately shaped the unending displacement and forced migration imposed on Palestinian refugees in that country and reinforced their marginalization. Governance in the West Bank and the Gaza Strip has changed dramatically over the past sixty years. The West Bank was governed by Jordan between 1948 and 1967, by Israel between 1967 and 1994, and by the Palestinian National Authority after 1994. The Gaza Strip moved from Egyptian to Israeli control and finally after 1994 to the Palestinian National Authority. The changes in central authority dramatically affected the lives of the Palestinians and Palestinian refugees in the occupied territories of the West Bank and the Gaza Strip.

Historical timeline, socio-political conditions and civil rights

Lebanon

Approximately 100,000 Palestinians fled to Lebanon in 1948 during the Nakbah from the Galilee region and northern Palestine (including Acre, Beisan, Safad, Tiberias, and Haifa) when the State of Israel was established. During 1948 and 1949, the International Red Cross offered Palestinian refugees relief services, especially food rations. In 1950, UNRWA took over from the Red Cross providing only shelter, food rations, education, and health care. Fifteen areas were set aside in Lebanon and designated to temporarily settle Palestinians. These sites eventually became officially recognized UNRWA camps. During these early years, Palestinians were considered temporary guests in Lebanon awaiting the international community's settlement of their problem. They received great support and sympathy from the public and about 30,000 Christian Palestinian refugees were granted Lebanese citizenship. However, once it became evident that there would be no early return, the Lebanese authorities imposed strict measures on the refugees, especially those resident in refugee camps. Between 1965 and 1982, the relations of Palestinians in Lebanon entered a second phase,

survey of living conditions presented to the Oslo Refugee Working Group, FAFO (Institute of Applied International Studies, www.fafo.org) has conducted living condition surveys among Palestinian refugees in Lebanon, Syria Jordan, the West Bank and the Gaza Strip; and in 2006, UNRWA contracted the University of Geneva and the Catholic University of Louvain to conduct a comprehensive socioeconomic survey of all UNRWA-registered Palestinian refugees (www.UNRWA.org).

which Hudson calls the ascendancy of the PLO.[28] This period precedes and encompasses the early years of the Lebanese civil war in 1975. Even before the civil war broke out, the relationship between Palestinian refugees and the Lebanese authorities was highly coloured with tension. By 1976, the PLO and Palestinian militias were seen by some as important actors in Lebanon's instability. In June of that year, Syrian troops crossed the border to defend the Christian Lebanese Maronite community from what was generally feared would be a Palestinian coalition victory. Then, in 1982, Israel invaded the country, determined to rid Lebanon of its Palestinian fighters. This was the third phase of Palestinian history in Lebanon, the decline of the PLO (1982–1991). The entry of Israel was supported by some Christian groups who were ready to see the Palestinian Muslim refugees cleaned out of the country.

Since 1991, Palestinian history in Lebanon has entered into its fourth phase, the 'era of the peace processes'. But the relationship between the Lebanese government and its Palestinian refugees has never recovered from the civil war years (Halabi 2004).[29] Lebanon has the worst human rights record of all the UNRWA countries with regard to its treatment of Palestinians (Weighill 1997).[30] The highest ratio of Palestinians in refugee camps is in Lebanon at 56 percent, which gives evidence of the state's resistance to integrating these refugees into the fabric of the country (whereas in Jordan, Syria, and the West Bank, the ratio of Palestinians in refugee camps is 17.6 per cent, 28 per cent, and 27 per cent, respectively; Gaza is a different matter, with refugees an overwhelming majority of the total population). The Lebanese government severely limits camp expansion and reconstructions. Most camps in the country have suffered massive destruction during one of the many conflicts of the past half-century and the government has prohibited their reconstruction or replacement.[31]

[28] Hudson succeeds in elegantly describing the tortured barriers which have impacted on so many Palestinian families spread out between Jerusalem, Haifa, Beirut, and Amman (Hudson 1997).

[29] Simon Haddad examines the root causes of Lebanon's poor treatment of Palestinian refugees (Haddad 2004). Souheil Al-Natour addresses the Lebanese laws and implementing structures that have impacted on the status, lives, and freedom of Palestinian refugees in Lebanon (Al-Natour 1997).

[30] Weighill and Shehadi edited a special issue of the *Journal of Refugee Studies* in 1997 which included the work of Anthony Parsons on the diplomatic history of the United Nations and Palestinian Refugees and Abbas Shiblak on Palestinians and the PLO in Lebanon (Weighill & Shehadi 1997).

[31] The exception here may well be the Lebanese government-backed UNRWA programme to rebuild the severely damaged Nahr al-Bared Palestinian refugee camp in the north of the country. After intense fighting in the summer of 2007 between the Islamic militant group Fatah al-Islam and the Lebanese Army, the camp was nearly flattened. The political

Palestinians in Lebanon have few rights; they may not own property, and are severely restricted in the occupations they may pursue.[32]

Syria

The majority of Palestinians who came to Syria were poor, illiterate peasants who fled their villages and towns in the northern part of Palestine. Due to the geography of the region, they entered into the southern parts of Lebanon where the International Red Cross received them and set them up in temporary camps. Within a very short time, they were moved on into Syria and were redistributed around all the major Syrian urban centres. The refugees were first given shelter in mosques, schools, and tents; later the Syrian government offered them parcels of land, constituting the beginning of the establishment of the UNRWA Palestinian camps in Syria (Brand 1988a; UNRWA 1992).

Unlike their counterparts in Lebanon, Palestinian refugees in Syria enjoy civil rights similar to that of a Syrian citizen, including equal access to employment in the public and private sector, and health and education services. In July 1956, the government issued Law number 260 to integrate Palestinian refugees into Syrian civil life. Palestinians residing in Syria have the same rights as Syrians in all things covered by the law and connected with the right to employment, commerce, and national service while preserving their original nationality (Brand 1988a; UNRWA 1992). However, despite this 'Law of Integration', most Palestinians are not permitted to vote in Syrian elections, and they are not eligible for Syrian citizenship 'passports'. The argument generally made for this position is so as not to undermine their Palestinian nationality and their 'Right to

---

deadlock in Lebanon with regards to the civil and political status of the largely Sunni Muslim Palestinian refugees was a major hurdle to the camp's reconstruction. However, the continuing media focus on the personal tragedies in the camp battles has impacted on the successful drive by UNRWA to rebuild the camp.

[32] In June 2005, the Ministry of Labour (MOL) partially repealed restrictions prohibiting Palestinian refugees from working in seventy types of jobs. The edict covered about two-thirds of the occupations previously restricted, generally the low- to medium-skilled ones. However, the edict did not change a 1964 law that also imposed a reciprocity condition on membership in professional syndicates – a precondition for employment in professions such as law, medicine, engineering, and journalism.

Numerous books detail the lived experience of Palestinian refugees in Lebanon. The classic 'people's history' built up from interviews with Palestinians living in refugee camps is Rosemary Sayigh's *Palestinians: From peasants to revolutionaries* (1979). A more recent anthropological study of Palestinians in Lebanon is Julie Peteet's *Landscape of hope and despair: Palestinian refugee camps* (2005). There is also the book chapter, Palestinian Refugee Children and Caregivers in Lebanon by Bassem Serhan (2005) and the oral history project, *Nakbah Archives*, founded by Diana Allan.

Return'. They have a legal status, however (as intended in the Casablanca Protocol), which provides them with a modicum of civil and legal rights and is referred to by some in international law as equivalent to 'temporary protection'.[33]

Beginning in the 1960s, many Palestinians, especially refugees, actively participated in Palestinian resistance movements. Thousand of Palestinians were killed in the *Fedaayeen* (freedom fighters) activities against Israel, in the Black September campaigns in Jordan in the 1970s, and in the Lebanese civil war during the 1980s. These activities did result in some further flight of Palestinians from Jordan and Lebanon to Syria, but by and large, the Palestinian refugee population was not uprooted during this period. Today the Palestinian refugee community in Syria is a young population.[34] UNRWA statistics show that nearly half of the refugee population (46 per cent) consists of children under age 15. Recent UNRWA reports show that 68 per cent of the Palestinian refugees in Syria were originally from Galilee and 22 per cent from Haifa and other coastal areas in British-mandated Palestine. Currently Palestinian refugees in Syria live in ten UNRWA refugee camps and three residential areas. The largest Palestinian settlement, known as Yarmouk camp, is located near Damascus and hosts one of the largest numbers of Palestinian refugees but is not recognized as an official UNRWA camp.

Jordan

Close to one million Palestinians found themselves abruptly acquiring refugee status following al-Nakbah in 1948. Two years later in 1950, Transjordan annexed the West Bank and renamed itself the Hashemite Kingdom of Jordan. Following this annexation, Jordan extended full citizenship rights to the majority of Palestinian refugees living on the east and west banks of the Jordan River. This included the refugees who had been uprooted

---

[33] The Protocol for the Treatment of Palestinians in Arab States (Casablanca Protocol) was agreed in September 1965 and was designed to give Palestinians legal and civil rights, a form of temporary protection, in the Arab states which had largely not signed up to the 1951 Convention Relating to the Status of Refugees (1951 Refugee Convention).

[34] Compared to the other UNRWA sites in the Middle East, Syria has been little studied. UNRWA is an important source of basic socioeconomic information on this population as are the FAFO reports; a number of unpublished reports from various diplomatic missions are also important such as the Canadian Mission Report of 1999. There are some general references to Palestinians in Syria but very little focusing on the lived experience of Palestinian refugees (Brand 1988b; Cattan 1988). Adnan Abdul-Rahim's chapter, 'Palestinian Refugee Children and Caregivers in Syria' is a recent qualitative study which addresses this gap for Palestinian youth (2005).

during the 1947–8 war. Today Palestinians with Jordanian passports represent the majority of the Jordanian population. This fact is a politically sensitive issue to the extent that statistics revealing the number of Jordanian citizens with Palestinian origins are unavailable to the public; government officials rationalise the inaccessibility of such data on the basis that such a revelation might incite ethnic conflict (Zureik 1996). Palestinian identity and Jordanian citizenship sit uncomfortably on many Palestinian shoulders; citizenship was granted to some Palestinian refugees but not others.

Three major armed conflicts led to the waves of refugees entering Jordan. The first, the 1947–8 war, resulted in approximately 100,000 people fleeing Palestine for Transjordan. In the 6 June 1967 war, an estimated 400,000 people flooded into Jordan from the West Bank and Gaza Strip. The third exodus occurred during the 1990–1 Gulf War, when approximately 400,000 Palestinian expatriates were expelled from Kuwait. The latter were Palestinians carrying Jordanian passports and classified as 'Returnees' even though most of them had never lived in Jordan, having been born and having spent most of their lives in Gulf countries. Each wave was assigned a different category and status. For example, those whose refugee status originated in the 1947–8 war were regarded as refugees and largely acquired Jordanian citizenship. Those uprooted in 1967 were largely regarded as displaced and were not granted citizenship, nor were those who fled from the Gaza Strip. In addition to the three major wars, other conflicts also resulted in forced migration and internal displacement, such as the 1968 al-Karameh battle and the armed clashes around Black September in 1970–1, which led to the ousting of the Palestine Resistance Movement by the Jordanian government, mainly to Lebanon.[35] All these different relocations, categories, and differentiated political statuses as well as variable access to UNRWA services has meant that in Jordan the sense of identity and belonging is more fractured and influenced by personal exodus history.[36] The displaced Palestinians from 1967 are not eligible for all UNRWA services – in fact, their descendents do

---

[35] Al-Karameh was the site of the first organized Palestinian resistance moment clash with the Israeli army. Although the Palestinians were defeated, their ability to fight and inflict losses on the enemy boosted morale among Palestinians and in the Arab world especially since it followed closely the Arab defeat in 1967.

[36] A number of researchers have treated the theme of identity in their work; none more so than Randa Farah whose work, based on her dissertation from the University of Toronto in 1999, focuses on the themes of popular memory and identity reconstruction (1999). Other research looking at elements of the lived experience include the project led by Riccardo Bocco analyzing UNRWA in popular memory in Jordan, the West Bank, and Gaza Strip (1999). Jason Hart has also written on Palestinian identity and youth in Jordan

not even appear in the agency's statistical records. Those displaced from the Gaza Strip in 1967 – many of them also 1948 refugees – are not eligible for Jordanian citizenship. Although the sense of belonging to Jordan varies by factors such as class, generation, and legal status, Palestinians have maintained a sense of 'people-hood' and separate national identity. However, Jordanian policies, mainly those that provide for preferential recruitment of Transjordanians in the public sector, aggravate the schism between the two communities. Around 18 per cent of Palestinian refugees live in ten UNRWA camps. If the percentages of refugees living in the immediate vicinity of designated legal boundaries of camps were included, the figure would rise to 65 per cent.

West Bank

The war to establish the State of Israel in 1948 resulted in the dispossession of two-thirds of the Palestinian people, some of whom ended up in emergency humanitarian aid camps in the West Bank. The Israeli army prevented the return of any of these 'internally' displaced Palestinians to their homes for security reasons (Morris 1987). When Jordan annexed the West Bank, it granted Jordanian citizenship to refugees and residents alike. Following the June 1967 war, the Israeli military occupied the West Bank and the Gaza Strip and another massive wave of Palestinians fled. About 500,000 refugees comprising 37 per cent of the West Bank's total inhabitants remained and became subjects of the occupying Israeli power between 1967 and 1994. After 1994, with the Oslo Accords, their governance was transferred to the Palestinian National Authority.

The West Bank covers an area of 5,500 square kilometres. Its refugee camps are overcrowded, but many of the original UNRWA concrete shelters have been replaced by multi-floor private homes. The refugees who live outside the camps form 74 per cent of the total refugees of the territory. Following the Oslo Definition of Accords, refugee camps are located in areas A (under Palestinian control), B, C (under Israeli control – 75 per cent of the West Bank) as well as in occupied east Jerusalem. This means that while some refugee camps are located in areas fully controlled by the Palestinian Authority, other camps are still directly exposed to Israeli military rule and yet others are placed under Israeli Civil Administration (Area C) with all civil and security affairs governed by the Israeli state. Israeli soldiers guard the adjacent roads, patrol the camps,

(2004) while Joseph Massad (2001) has addressed the issue of Palestinian identity in the context of Jordanian national identity.

and continue to chase after stone-throwing children (Rosenfeld 2004b; Zaroo 2005). Refugees in the West Bank are deeply affected by the waves of forced migration and prolonged conflict of the past half-century. They are devastated by the Separation Barrier which is resulting in further dispossession, loss of livelihood, and displacement on a slow but steady and incremental scale. The consequences of these events are ever present and include the expropriation of lands, loss of water resources, home demolitions, on-going construction of illegal Israeli settlements and bypass roads, violence, imprisonment, emigration, deportation, and imposed closures.[37] One consequence of these measures is the growth and transformation of a highly politicized society; political parties and organizations that dominated the scenes in the 1980s and 1990s are giving way to community-oriented institutions focused on the development of social services and cultural activities (Thabet 2005; Thabet et al. 2002; Thabet & Vostanis 2000). Those Palestinians active in this shift are the public figures, mainly veteran activists and former leaders in the camps. Their search for new directions coincides with an ever growing population frustrated by the lack of real improvement in their economic and political conditions and the inability of the Palestinian National Authority to protect them (Rosenfeld 2004b).

The Gaza Strip

Prior to 1948 the Gaza Strip was part of the southern district of British-mandated Palestine. Within a very short time after the creation of the State of Israel, 250,000 Palestinian refugees fled their homes and took refuge in the Gaza Strip. Its population tripled almost overnight, and the internal dynamics of the territory were transformed forever. Between 1948 and 1967, the Egyptian government administered Gaza, which it set aside as an administrative territory and people from Gaza did not have Egyptian citizenship; on the contrary, they kept their nationality as Palestinians (Tamari 1992). After June 1967, Israel occupied the Gaza Strip. During

---

[37] The experience of imprisonment, interrogation, and torture of young Palestinian activists in the West Bank and the Gaza Strip in an attempt to break them down and turn them into informers for the Israeli military/civil occupation is well documented by numerous NGOs such as *Al-Haq* (International Commission of Jurists and Law in the Service of Man), *B'tselem*, and the Palestinian Human Rights Information Centre (PHRIC). The first detailed report regarding the physical and mental torture of youth in Israeli detention was produced in 1984 by *Al-Haq*. These experiences impacted heavily on the community as a whole and turned an entire cohort from its public activism into an edgy and wary socially responsible generation.

the years of the Israeli occupation, the Palestinian economy was very dependent on that of Israel. Twenty years later in December 1987, four residents of Gaza were killed in a traffic accident involving an Israeli military vehicle. Civilian protests over the deaths quickly escalated onto the streets. Within a week, the protests had spread throughout the Gaza Strip and the West Bank and were being referred to as the *Intifada* (Uprising). The Intifada lasted for seven years and ended with the signing of the Oslo Accords, a partial withdrawal of the Israeli military occupation forces from the West Bank and Gaza, and the handing over of government administration to the Palestinian National Authority in 1994. With the election of Hamas to office in the Gaza Strip, a serious rift has emerged in the governing of the Palestinian National Authority with Gaza increasingly isolated and squeezed economically, socially, and politically by the Israeli government as well as the PLO-backed government of the West Bank. The inhabitants of Gaza – en masse – face enormous mental and physical hardships not unlike that suffered by the Palestinian nationalists and revolutionaries incarcerated in the Sarafand detention centre (now Tsrifin) set up by the British during their mandate over Palestine (Thabet 2005; Thabet et al. 2002; Thabet & Vostanis 2000).

According to the UNRWA (2009) there are now more than one million registered refugees in the Gaza Strip out of a total population of nearly 1.5 million people,[38] and about half the refugee population (478,272) live in overcrowded refugee camps. The economy has always been totally dependent upon Israel and each closure or shutdown by Israel profoundly affects the mental and physical health and well-being of the Palestinian refugees. For nearly the last sixty years, Palestinians living in the Gaza Strip were exposed to a variety of harmful and stressful situations, including repeated displacement, imprisonment, beatings, collective punishment, house demolitions, land confiscation and clearing for military purposes, targeted assassinations, and constant social and economic pressure.

DISCUSSION

Given the protracted nature of the Palestinian dispossession, the unique historical timelines in the places of exile, and the frequent dispersal of close family and kin across zones of armed conflict, one must wonder what

---

[38] In the Gaza Strip, there were 1,016,964 registered refugees as of 31 December 2006 (UNRWA 2009). Estimates of the Gaza Strip population for mid-2006 and mid-2007 were 1,443,814 and 1,499,369, respectively (UNRWA 2009).

mechanisms operate to keep a sense of 'people-hood' alive among Palestinians. The narrative histories that follow are abridged from interviews conducted by my research teams in the early 2000s in Damascus. I have selected them to give a sense of the range of experiences of dispossession, disappointment, and crushing humiliation as modulated by wealth as well as extreme poverty.

Josephine's story

Josephine was born in al-Ramleh in Palestine in 1926. She was married when she was 14 years old to a Palestinian with business interest in Syria who was chosen by her stepfather. She had nine children; four were born in Palestine and five in Syria. In al-Ramleh, her husband owned two big houses, one was rented and the other was used as a family house. When the Nakbah of 1948 occurred, her husband was in Damascus while she was resident in the family home in al-Ramleh. Her husband was supposed to be returning within a short time, but the war started and she was alone in the house without news of him. She heard that soldiers had attacked the Allad Mosque. She was very frightened at this time because she did not have anybody to protect her family. The Jewish militia who took over the town announced that all men and women should gather in the town's square. She was confused because her husband was away and her children were young, so she decided to hide with her children at home. One morning in early June, she heard somebody knocking at her door. Her children started to cry. She looked out of the window and saw more than 20 soldiers carrying guns, she did not know if the soldiers were British or Jewish militia. She opened the door and their leader approached her aggressively asking her what she was doing in the house. The other soldiers pulled her from the shoulders and forced her out of the house. She started to scream and her children ran and stood besides her crying while the soldiers stood laughing. She was very upset, lonely and confused. She didn't know what to do, where to go and who to turn to. The soldiers told her that they would return the next day.

She had a sleepless night. She hid the little money that her husband had left for house expenses. At about five o'clock the next morning the soldiers returned with a lorry full of Palestinian women and children all crying and praying to God and to Jesus Christ to help them. She saw the Star of Zion on the doors and the sides of the vehicle. The soldiers pushed her and her children violently into the vehicle. They drove them away; she did not know where they going. After a few hours of horror driving, they were dropped off in the mountains. She spent the night in the mountain and the next morning they walked till they reached an area called al-Bira, where they stayed for a month trying to find a way to leave Palestine. She later learned that her husband had been arrested. She could not cross the border because her husband had their passports. After a month, they left al-Bira and fled to Amman with many other Palestinian refugees. In Amman, they were given shelter in a church where they remained for some time. One of her sons died after a fall there when they failed to get him emergency medical treatment.

She crossed the Jordanian/Syrian border illegally and went to find her relatives in al-Midan district of Damascus. She stayed there for a while and then rented a house in the old city. Her life outside Palestine was difficult and stressful; she could not answer her children questions about their father's whereabouts. She prayed day and night for God to bring her husband back safe and sound. After two years her husband came back to Damascus and the family was at last reunited.

Once her husband was settled they moved into a much larger house in al-Joura quarter in old Damascus. Although the family was happy in this new house, still they considered that their stay in Syria was temporary and that they would soon be returning to Palestine. Some of her children did not attend the Syrian schools, because the family assumed that children could waste their time as they would very shortly be returning to Palestine and studying the Palestinian curricula. Recently, her husband died and now most of her children are married and live near her. A year ago, one of her sons died leaving her to look after his family. Although Josephine is well off, she still dreams of going back to Palestine.

Josephine, abridged narrative history, narrated and recorded in Damascus, 2000. (Josephine, quoted in Chatty & Lewando Hundt 2005:65)

Josephine's story throws up the difficult question of identity and the way in which it is inhabited. Josephine was born in Palestine and was unquestionably Palestinian. Her husband was a Palestinian Arab living in Damascus but upon marriage chose to live in Palestine and bring up his family there. Even in exile, both Josephine and her husband held their children back from school for two years awaiting the opportunity to return to Palestine. Convinced that their exile was temporary, they did not see the value of their children studying a Syrian curriculum. As time passed, pragmatism resulted in their registering their children in schools in Damascus, but the desire to return remained.

Sa'ada's story

Sa'ada was born in Palestine in 1914; she was brought up and lived in Al Qabba'a, near Safad. She was married at the age of 14 years, and she gave birth to three children. She divorced her husband when he was jailed; her brother-in-law then took the custody of the children. Then she worked as an agricultural labourer and sold green thyme. A year later she married Khalil who was already married with five children and a sick [paralyzed] wife. She lived with her new husband's family and gave birth to two children.

In 1948 the Zionist forces attacked her village (al-Dallatah), many people were killed and injured and hundreds of men were arrested. Sa'ada fled the fighting in her village. She left behind everything she owned and sought refuge in the Hauran in Syria. In 1952 her husband died leaving her with two young children. She found work again as an agricultural labourer. In time she left the Hauran and went to Damascus to search for people from her village. She managed to get work in the agricultural gardens of the Ghouta on the edge of the city before it turns into desert.

She had then only a one-room shelter at the very top of Mount Kassoun. After the end of her working day on the farm, she would gather some discarded onion, radish and marrow in a bag and sell them in the market in order to have money to buy some cheese and bread and candles to feed her children and to light their room.

Her children were provided with schooling by UNRWA. The school gave her children free education but she had to provide them with clothing and stationery. She could not afford the clothing and had to rely on some wealthy Damascene residents to provide her with second-hand shoes and clothes. In time, she saved some money and bought a room and made it habitable. Her children had to work during the school summer holiday in order to support their studies. One of her sons finished school while the other became involved in the Palestinian resistance movement.

Her eldest son has died and left behind a wife and six children. Her second son is married with six children. He works as a casual labourer in a restaurant. He also rents a small shop to sell Falafel. Sa'ada shares her one-room house with her children and grandchildren. Today, they have electricity and water and the house is not so remote and isolated as it was in the past, Now, when her grandchildren make their way to school in the morning, they buy bread and sell it on in the neighbourhoods they pass to earn money to support the family.

Although she has lived in Syria for many years and her children are grown up, she still feels alienated and she hopes to die and be buried in Palestine.

Sa'ada, abridged narrative history, narrated and recorded in Damascus, 2001 (Sa'ada, quoted in Chatty & Lewando Hundt 2005:65–66)

Every refugee and forced migrant has a unique story to tell; some, like Josephine, are cushioned by wealth while others, like Sa'ada, are engulfed in poverty so extreme that there is no escape. And other stories, like Ali's, reflect the significance of family, education, and the Palestinian national movement in shaping their lives. Of course, poverty and forced migration do not need to remain insurmountable conditions. Many Palestinian refugees have managed to use the education provided them by UNRWA to break out of the cycle of despair and loss. But the sense of having been wronged, of wishing to return to their homes and villages, of taking up the livelihoods left behind under dire circumstances does not necessarily pass away.

Walid's story

I am Palestinian from Safad which is about 90 kilometres from Damascus. I was born in 1931. My family, the al-Asadi family, was one of the largest in Safad. I had 11 brothers and 2 sisters. My father was wealthy and we had a big house. All the al-Asadis lived like a community in one street. Strangers had to get permission to enter our streets or else they had to be accompanied by a member of the family. Safad had a population of 12,000 Muslims, 4,000 Jews and about 2,000 Christians.

I grew up with the Palestinian Revolution [of 1936–39]. But I was always quarrelling with the Jews. My father, my uncle, the police chief and the head of

Safad Municipality decided they had to keep me away from Safad. There was a complaint about me every day. So, they sent me to the Ibrahimi College in Jerusalem when I was 12 years old [1943]. I spent 5 years in Jerusalem. But in 1948 I came back. There were battles between the Arabs and the Jews. I wanted to mount an operation against the Jewish quarter in Safad. Already one Jew had been killed by an Arab over a quarrel about laundry ... We had many battles. But we were mainly irregular forces with different kinds of arms, British, Belgian, German, Italian and Greek. The Jordanians said they would send us ammunition according to the types of arms we had. But they distributed ammunition to the wrong fighters. So our weapons ceased to function. Then the Jews asked the fighters to surrender using loudspeakers. The Safad population feared that the Jews would revenge the massacres against them from 1927, so most of them began fleeing. I was able to get cars to transport the family and take us directly to Damascus. Because of my fighter status I was able to get an introduction to Al Shishakli [Syrian commander of the voluntary Arab Army at one point and later elected president of the Syrian Arab Republic]. Then, when Safad fell, my parents came to Damascus as well. We rented an apartment at first. We were given 22 mattresses and blankets as well as kitchen utensils from the Red Crescent to start our new life. We were 11 brothers and we all went out and got jobs. I got a job distributing gas to Palestinians for cooking. Then I got a second job as a physical education teacher in a school and also a third job with a magazine called 'al-Waad'. I had three jobs. Eventually my father bought many pieces of land in Mezza where he settled with many of my brothers ... I married my cousin in 1953 and had four sons and four daughters. They are doctors. One is in now Paris, one in Kuwait, another in Jordan. We are spread out. But it is not possible for a human being to forget his homeland. We were told when we fled that we could go back in 10 days. We never thought the Jews would be so strong. When the United Nations decided to divide Palestine between Arabs and Jews, establish two states for two nations, we Arabs refused. But the Jews accepted, knowing that they would take Palestine and more. (Walid 2005, Damascus)

Walid and many like him never lived in a refugee camp, although he eventually registered as a refugee with UNRWA and also worked for it over a number of years. He and his family exemplified the resilience of Palestinian society as well as the longevity of the desire to return to his home and homeland in Safad, a town less than 60 miles away from where he has lived ever since fleeing his hometown at the age of 17. Like many middle-class Palestinians, he lives in a neighbourhood largely made up of other Palestinians. His successes in life are closely linked to his family ties and his children's education as well as to UNRWA provisions in the early years of exile. But his 'refugeeness' remains the main quality of his identity tied up as it is with the fall of Safad and the almost mythical status of those battles between poorly armed Arab irregular militia, and the well trained and armed Jewish militias. That the political status of Palestinian refugees and their 'Right of Return' is still the subject of international debate and power politics after the passage of nearly sixty years contributes to his life-long struggle with closure related to his dispossession from his homeland and his personal conflict regarding his lack of rootedness common to many Palestinian refugees.

Ali's story

My father and mother were very young when they married. They were 16 and 14, but my father had a very intelligent older sister who never married and she used to look after the household. She had to take care of her brother, my father. She was, even at that time, the decision-maker, and she stayed the decision-maker in the house even after we left Palestine.

We were two boys, and one girl. There was me and my younger brother, because my older brother had moved to be with our uncle a few days before we fled Safad. So we were just two brothers and one sister. My older sister stayed in Tyre because she was a nurse and she decided to work in a hospital in Tyre. My other two sisters with us too, but the oldest of these two was married and went to Jordan with her husband. So we were six; three children, my mother, my aunt and my father.

Our first home was a barracks [in Homs]. Yes, it was small about the space of this room [six by nine square metres]. And it had no real privacy because it was divided up into living areas for other families by blankets. But we didn't stay for long here; soon we moved to a small Christian village nearby. It was called Mishirfe. I remember it was a Christian village because I often used to go to the church there. The priest found me intelligent and used to treat me with respect. So I used to go there often; my family thought I was turning into a Christian, but I wasn't turning into anything. Then after a year, there were the UNRWA people who were also generous. Everything was very hard; living, coping with new circumstances instead of living in your own house, moving from one place to another.

After two years we moved to Damascus. My older brother found a job in a cement factory in Damascus. He wrote to us and said, 'Come to Dumar just outside of Damascus, I have enough resources to take care of you.' So he brought us to Damascus and he took care of us. And we managed to bring our oldest sister from Tyre to join us in Damascus. It was shameful that she should be all alone in a foreign country. And so she came and she worked as a nurse in UNRWA. So, both of them worked in order to give us a living. Now we were eight. In Dumar, conditions were most interesting. This is where I grew up and became what I am. It was a small village, nice small village, not spoiled by urbanization, with forest, with trees, with everything. It was very nice. I joined the UNRWA school there to level 6; then I had to come to Damascus to carry on my education at the Port Said School in Afiif in Muhajiriin. It took about 20–25 minutes every day each way and then I had to take a tram each way. There was a tram line from Victoria Station to Afiif. It was a hellish journey, but I liked it, because I liked my friends in the Port Said school. They were mainly Syrians, not Palestinians. I enjoyed being there. So I stayed in Damascus all day and went back home at 6 o'clock. I stayed there until level 10 and then I moved to the famous Lycée, Ibn Khaldun.

My father was not working during this time because he had no skills. He was illiterate. He was from a notable family but he had no skill and he couldn't manage to find any work. That was why my mother was always angry with him. He was illiterate and he never worked. In Safad he was a land owner. He was from a rich family.

After the Lycée Ibn Khaldun I went to University; at the same time I was employed as an UNRWA teacher. The quicker you passed examinations the more money you earned. So in four years I passed a lot of exams and became a teacher (which I hated). But I had to do it to earn a living for my family. So this is the kind of life we had. It was comfortable but it was also poor with modest contribution by my brother and sister. So we enjoyed our life in the village of Dumar. It was simple. Eventually, I wanted to move to Damascus. My sister bought a flat in Qusour (Damascus). As usual, my sister was very independent. She left us. And then we took a three room flat in Baramki. By then my older brother got married so there were then just six of us. But my brother used to still offer us financial assistance.

Then my father died. He died very young, well not so young, but young. He was 65. I was in Beirut at the time. I was working with the LAHAM Centre. I worked there for six months. I had taken a leave of absence from UNRWA and worked in Beirut. This is when my mother died as well. No, first my aunt died, and then two years later, my father died. We were all still there in Baramki. Our conditions continued to improve because I was working too. We led a normal life in Baramki. Then I finished my Master's Degree and I waited for ten years before I got the chance to travel and go to Budapest. I got a scholarship from the PLO representative to study in Hungary. There you had to know two languages besides your own mother tongue to do a PhD. So I got a certificate to state I knew French with English. So I was able to do my degree in three years in English. I wanted to know about Hungary and the people. I learned conversational Hungarian. I took my degree in Social Reality and Educational Goals of the Palestinian People .... All the time there was this pulling of me back to my family, to Palestine, to my friends. But it was a point of great conflict. I wanted to stay in Hungary, but I had to see my family. After one year I developed high blood pressure [so I went back]. I still had high blood pressure back in Damascus. In order to get rid of it [the high blood pressure], I used to go back to Hungary every summer for one month or two. I used to be able to do this because I was on the PLO Delegation. They used to send me outside the Middle East and I always found a way of travelling via Budapest coming or going. So if there was a conference in Casablanca, I would come back via Budapest ...

For ten years I was in the Fateh moment and then I moved to Budapest. When I finished my PhD, I was picked to go to Paris as the representative of the PLO. I refused to go for political reasons. When I came back to Damascus from Budapest I noticed that politically things were boiling here. There was a split in the PLO. There were many factions. I joined one of the factions, but not for long just for three years. But I didn't stop being active in the main unit. I didn't go to the Popular Front, the Democratic Front or the A'idoon group. I was always in the main part of the PLO. But eventually I stopped believing in any value of being affiliated to any one of them. The problem was that the things we felt at the beginning of our exile, they do not exist any more. Even now, our children, they don't feel it anymore. I don't think they suffer in the same way that we did. They don't have the same obstacles that we had.

I tried hard to organize my life, but it wasn't always under my control; it was not always in my hands. Not my decisions about my future; but I always held on to the thought that I must keep on studying because at that time most Palestinians thought that through education they could improve their situation; through education they could regain Palestine. They believed that education created miracles. It didn't happen of course, but this was the aim. You know, education was the only way to improve your life. I was convinced that education was the only way. Of course I would have preferred to be a citizen of a country somewhere in the world. And since I was born in Palestine I would have preferred to be a citizen of Palestine. But since I succeeded in making a life for myself here, I don't have a lot of things to complain about and I don't blame anybody, especially not the Syrians. They did not stop me from improving my life. I am satisfied now. I mean, I got what I was struggling for within the realm of what was possible. Even if I came back as a child in Palestine, I don't think I could have done more with my life.

Ali's story of arriving in Syria and the journey of his family from abject destitution to a comfortable but modest lifestyle clearly demonstrates the importance of family and the way in which siblings and kin worked together to rebuild their shattered lives. It also throws into sharp relief the significance of education, and of UNRWA services and employment in creating opportunities in the struggle for survival and, in some cases, modest economic success. Ali's story brings to the fore the Palestinian nationalist movement. Though described obliquely, it is clear that for him as well as for many other men of his generation, the PLO was a source of identity, support, and succour.

Although the political and social situation of Palestinian refugees varies broadly from one host state to another, there remain certain fundamental features in the development of individual and social identity that mark the Palestinians as unique. They are a people with a distinctive unassimilated Arab culture, dispersed over a wide region, variously discriminated against, yet on individual and family levels often well integrated into their host society.

CONCLUSION: PALESTINIAN NOTIONS OF IDENTITY, OF PLACE AND SPACE

My name is Ra'isa. I was born in Gaza in 1909. But I come from Safad. My father was an accountant for the Hijaz railway. He started his job in 1914. At that time, Bilad al-Sham [the Syrian provinces of the Ottoman Empire] was one country. My father moved us back to Safad when I was very young. Then, he developed a high fever and died. We were surrounded by family, the Khadra family. I studied at Safad until I finished elementary school and then I went to the Scottish College in Safad directed by Miss Mackintosh. In 1948 we were forced to leave Safad. As you know Safad is a mountainous city. We climbed down the valley and up the mountains until we got to Al Safsaf village, where we had some relatives. We arrived at nine in the evening. They offered us some yoghurt. We stayed for the night and early in the morning, we took a truck that was used to move sheep and headed to the Lebanese border – to Bint il-Jbeil and then to Alma village where we stayed for a few days. Then we continued on until we got to Homs. We arrived at 2:00 a.m. We found a house to rent and stayed there for 10 years. I was with my brother. He was a Law School graduate and found work with UNRWA as an official in charge of a district. In 1958 he was transferred to Damascus. The whole family moved to Damascus and we rented this house. I got a job as a headmistress of an UNRWA school in the Jewish Quarter. Then I retired in 1972. I was always comfortable. As a director of a school for Palestinians, I was well known and was committed to serving those whom I considered to be like my own daughters. I never felt as an immigrant. I always felt I was among my own people of Bilad al-Sham. It is, and has always been, one and the same country ... At my age, and with all the Khadra family members around me, I would not go back to live in Palestine. I would say, no I wouldn't [Sister-in-law interjects: 'Auntie, what the hell are you saying? If they allowed us to go back, we would; even if we have to live in a tent, it is our home country']. Not me. Not at this age. My house is no more there, and the neighbourhood is not the one I knew. I would only get back to bad and bitter memories. I would never forget the experience of the exodus – how we walked down the mountain and all the way to the Tawaheen valley, and then up to the border village and finally the ride in a sheep truck. (Ra'isa 2006, Damascus)

Identity, status, and kinship ties are the themes that emerge from these narratives. The land is also important, perhaps even primordial to Palestinian refugees, as they have all been abruptly severed from their roots. But between the generation which had to flee and the following generations born in exile, a difference is emerging: one that distinguishes between space and place accepting notions of identity that are more fluid and constructed around immediate social and cultural ties. For many of the oldest generation who fled their homes in Palestine to reach safety away from the armed conflict, the physical space is no longer the place where their identity is grounded and nurtured. As Ra'isa states, her house is no longer there, the neighbourhood is not the one she knew. Going back would only bring back sad and bitter memories. For her and many of the oldest survivors, identity and well-being are created and maintained by immediate family and friends, by Palestinian social networks and cultural ties in places of exile. The first generation remembers the physical spaces where their homes and communities were located. Some also have vivid memories of early challenges to those spaces by Jewish settlers during the British mandate period in Palestine. The second and third generation do not have original memories. Nor do they have experiences of contestation regarding their beings as Palestinians in the mandated territory. But they do have the recollected histories and stories of their caregivers. As one Palestinian youth in Jordan said:

My grandmother tells me about Palestine, she is like a dictionary; she has many stories to tell about Palestine. She always tells us about Palestine ... I wish I could visit Palestine. There is no one in the camps who does not wish to visit Palestine, my grandmother tells me we are from 48, and there is also 64 [he makes a mistake, meaning 1967] she says those from the 67 territories are going to return but the people from 48 are not. My grandmother is from Marj Ibn Amer from Haifa, my grandmother always tells me about Marj Ibn Amer, and Haifa ... (Yaser, Generation 2 quoted in Chatty & Lewando Hundt 2005:101).

The older Palestinians, I suggest, draw on their memories of belonging to an Arab nation or to Bilad al-Sham in which Palestine was an integral part, while the young hold on to the images and recollections of their original villages and homes as described by their caregivers. These narratives and descriptions are not that hard to construct into 'remembered memories', as the described landscape is often similar to that which surrounds the Palestinian refugee camps or the neighbourhoods some Palestinian refugees live in. The physical separation is often tens of miles rather than hundreds of miles. In some cases, refugees can see their original villages; at night, the lights in the distant darkness are assumed to be emanating from their villages of origin.

For the second generation – that group of Palestinians generally born in the first few years after al-Nakbah – identity, I suggest, is more problematic. Exposure to significant hardships while the camps were largely still of cloth tents, exposed variably to pity and discrimination, the second generation is most adamant that the return to the homeland is fundamental to developing a sense of worth and dignity by ending the exile into which they were born.

I never visited Palestine; I yearn to return to my Homeland, because a human being far from his Homeland feels like a stranger. The stranger without his Homeland feels disgraced and people ostracise him from society. To live in dignity we must work on our land and build our country. (Latifa, Generation 2 quoted in Chatty 2007:101).

This generation was the first to become active and be part of the struggle to return to the homeland. Many men and women joined the Palestinian national movement. Though not strictly divided by gender, men became active in Palestinian political organizations, working in PLO offices in the Middle East and sometimes reaching positions of representation in Europe; women were also active in the PLO as well as in the numerous unions, charities, and local NGOs that came under its umbrella and which provided non-formal education, and services in the camps and Palestinian neighbourhoods.

The third and fourth generations shared more than age or youthfulness. Many of them linked their status as refugees to a sense of marginality and exclusion from their original homelands and also, at times, from full legal, social, and civil participation in the communities that host them. They have learned to speak of 'their human rights' and through the active use of websites, blogs, social networking sites, and twitters, they keep themselves up-to-date, informed, and involved. For many of these youth, the composite collective memory of their parents' and grandparents' forced migration merged in internal contradictions with their own narratives. The past was as their parents had told them, but the present and their place in it was contested and showed clear elements of multivocal social memory.

I feel I belong to Yarmouk camp [in Damascus], even if I am asked in the future to choose between staying in Yarmouk or any other place [in Palestine], I would say that I prefer to stay here. (Omar, Generation 3, quoted in Chatty & Lewando Hundt 2005:76).

They belonged to the past, but they also belonged to the country that hosted them. Yet their identity as Palestinians remained fundamental. For many of these youth, education was the key to the future, the weapon with which they could fight for their 'Right to Return'.

I know that our enemy is highly educated and well skilled. Therefore, we must use the same technique and knowledge while fighting them. I am convinced that we can win the war because we have the right on our side. I miss Palestine and I can visualise my return to it. I can achieve this dream by studying and working hard to serve the cause of Palestine. (Mohammed, Generation 3 quoted in Chatty & Lewando Hundt 2005:78)

We are used to being called poor and not good enough. However, many refugees are successful students, many managed to continue their higher education. Some became doctors, engineers and teachers in spite of their families' experiences of poverty, homelessness, violence and wars. (Manar, Generation 3, quoted in Chatty & Lewando Hundt 2005:77)

Education for me was not easy, I had some difficulties in my schooling. I had a fight with the school director. The headmistress and some students laughed at me when I said that I am a Palestinian, and originally from Gjzem village in Palestine. I asked them why they are laughing and what is so amusing about being Palestinian. Many of my schoolmates told me that being a Palestinian means being a refugee and being a refugee indicated poverty, homelessness, being stupid and not good enough to study. But I know I had to stay in school and prove to them that I am not stupid and they were wrong. (Samia, Generation 3, quoted in Chatty & Lewando Hundt 2005:77)

Whether rich or poor, whether living in refugee camps or in the middle-class neighbourhoods of the major cities of the Arab world, Palestinian refugees have found a medium to express their cultural coherence and their social reality. That medium is education, formal state-sponsored and often UNRWA-delivered. Formal education for Palestinian youth has long been promoted as the weapon of the future generation. At the same time, the recognition that UNRWA schools must follow the curriculum of the country in which it operates has meant that Palestinian refugee youth learn of their history not in school but after school.[39] Non-formal education is very much in the hands of the Palestinian national movement and is executed in after-school clubs, youth camps, and other cultural activities organized by the PLO and associated NGOs and Palestinian charities; and informal education is absorbed in individual Palestinian households in which common language and dialect, common history, and common culture both as Palestinians and as Arabs is reaffirmed. As Fasheh stresses in his work, ending the occupation of Palestinian lands means also ending the occupation of Palestinian minds through the schoolroom, through conversations, dialogue, social activities, and cultural expression. It means '… feeling happy and proud of being Arabs, disregarding the racist and poisonous messages that the Western TV, journalists, academics and experts try to spread around the world against Arabs and Muslims. It also means defining ourselves as Palestinians, as Arabs, and not as underdeveloped or as developing' (Fasheh 1995:68–69).

Wherever Palestinian refugees are found and whatever generation they represent, there are Palestinian cultural clubs and charities, Palestinian women's unions, Palestinian writers' unions, and other professional bodies. For children and youth, there are Palestinian kindergartens and nurseries as well as after-school clubs teaching Palestinian history, music, and dance [*dabkah*]. The camps and the neighbourhoods are generally physically organized and named so as to remind their occupants of the villages and urban quarters left behind. Surrounded by kin and neighbours who fled together, making daily social contact with others like them, there is a physical reinforcement of 'Palestinianness' in the places they occupy today. And although identity has become multi-layered particularly for youth, the engagements in education and in supporting the family remain important features of Palestinian refugee society.

---

[39] Under agreements made with the host authorities, UNRWA has to use the curricula and textbooks of the countries/territories where it operates. However, the agency also creates educational enrichment materials to supplement the local curriculum. www.un/unrwa/programmes/education/basic.html).

6

Kurds: Dispossessed and Made Stateless

I was born in 1920 in Turkey in a village near Mardin. My father's family included 400–500 young men. We came here [to Syria] in 1925. The French were in Syria. They offered us shelter and were very good to us. We were tyrannized by the Turks who were against all Islamic teachings. The Turks were not true Muslims. They wanted us to assimilate. They wanted to force all the people in the villages to wear hats [this is a reference to Mustafa Kemal's efforts to get Western dress adopted by all Turks]. We fled after the revolution led by Shaykh Said in 1920. The Kurds revolted against the Turks. They demanded a self-governed Kurdish state in Turkey. When Shaykh Said was hung by the Turks, many Kurds fled Turkey and came to Syria. I remember we all travelled in big groups, seven or eight families and all of their sheep and cattle which they sold on the way at Ras al-'Ain. We all walked to Dayr al-Zor and then to Al-Sham [Damascus]. We had relatives here who received us and helped us to settle. This quarter had only Kurds who spoke Kurdish. What is funny was that when my father left Turkey, he had no idea there were other people than Kurds in the world. He was quite shocked when he got to Dayr al-Zor and heard people talking other languages. He used to say that he almost turned back there to return to Turkey. When we had been in Syria for six or five years we were granted citizenship [by the French mandate authority]. Citizenship was granted to anyone who resided in the country for five years.

I have been back to my town in Turkey twice once with my mother, to visit our relatives and friends. But I would not consider going back there to live. Life there is quite different from life here. There, life is still controlled by tribal norms. They are continuously fighting followed by endless acts of taking revenge. I told them when I was there that they are a hopeless case and that nothing good will come out of them. The reason they are like this is because of the Turks. The Turks have not allowed them to get good education. They even encourage conflicts between families. The Kurdish areas [in Turkey] suffer severe neglect in all respects. It is just like the situation in northern Iraq and Iran.

Mohammed (2006), Harat al-Akrad, Damascus

TABLE 5. *Kurdish population in the Middle East*

Country	Population	Percentage of Country's Population
Turkey	13 million	20%
Iraq	4 million	23%
Iran	5.7 million	10%
Syria	2 million	11%

Total: 25 million

There are today somewhere in the region of 25 million Kurds living in the Middle East. About 13 million live in modern-day Turkey and make up about 20 per cent of the population.[1] Four million live in Iraq and make up about 23 per cent of the population of that country. In Iran, Kurds number about 5.7 million and represent abut 10 per cent of the population; and in Syria they are about two million, mainly living along the northern border with Turkey and Syria and representing about 11 per cent of the population.

Many of the Kurds in Syria have been there for centuries; but in the 1920s, a wave of refugees arrived, escaping Turkish repression after their failed bid for independence during the Shaykh Said rebellion. Although the Syrian Kurds represent the smallest minority of this largely mountainous tribal people, the forced migrations in the past century into Syria most clearly illustrate the struggle of the Kurds for recognition as a nation. Turkey, Iraq, and Iran have similar mixes of indigenous as well as refugee Kurdish populations as a result of numerous intra-tribal power struggles and conflicts followed by group expulsions and abortive efforts to establish a Kurdish state.[2] Similar power struggles among the Kurdish tribal leadership as well as periodic nationalist uprisings have left the border regions with Kurdish exiles, refugees, and forced migrants living among long-settled and variously resident kin. Their failed bids for recognition as a nation-state

---

[1] An estimate made by Van Bruinessen (Van Bruinessen 1992:15). This is about the same as the percentage of Arabs in the state of Israel.

[2] In January 1946, a Kurdish republic of Mahabad was declared in the remote mountainous northern corner of Iran. In September of that year Archie Roosevelt Jr, then assistant US Military Attaché in Tehran, visited Mahabad. He was one of the few Westerners to ever visit during the republic's short existence. The Kurdish government sought to convince the American representative that the Kurds wished to form a democratic province under a federal system similar to the American model (Roosevelt Jr 1947). They sought American government support for Kurdish aspirations, or at least no opposition. All efforts were made to keep evidence of Russian influence out of sight. This, according to Eagleton, was not difficult as there was only one Soviet official in the town (1963:63). By December of 1946, the Kurdish state had collapsed and many Kurds involved in this venture took refuge in the Soviet Union and Iraq.

beginning in the 1920s and continuing, off and on, during the 1930s, 1940s, and 1960s have resulted in many thousands of Kurds taking refuge in Syria, Iran, Turkey, and neighbouring Caucasian states as part of the general international and regional power politics of the day. Seen alternatively as valiant nationalist struggles or as treacherous separatist revolts, these events in our modern era have displaced and dispossessed hundreds of thousands of Kurds, leaving many of them without citizenship and some acknowledged as stateless in their places of refuge. It is their story this chapter will address.

The homeland of the Kurds is the Zagros Mountain range. For centuries it has served as a fluid and permeable frontier region between great empires; the border between Iran and its western neighbours has been fairly constant for more than four hundred years. This fluidity has been of value to the Kurdish people. Being largely a pastoral tribal people, the open border regions provided the Kurds with economic opportunity for movement unrestrained by international frontiers until the 1920s. Much of the migration has been seasonal between spring upland pastures and winter villages. These migrations were important sources for trade, for example, salt in one direction and returning with wheat. The regions also afforded Kurdish tribal leadership with refuge and sanctuary when they tried to exploit border tensions. In more recent times, borders and frontiers have become less permeable. Wire mesh fencing, minefields, and air surveillance make it more difficult for people to cross frontiers other than at official border crossings.

The international borders, drawn up by the Western powers in 1919 (by Sir Mark Sykes), define the modern states of Turkey, Iran, Iraq, and Syria. Furthermore, these recently created formal borders cut across the major Kurdish linguistic and cultural groupings in Kurdish society. In each of these states – with the exception of the Kurdish refugees of the 1920s in Syria – Kurds are being increasingly drawn into the national fabric. As McDowall points out, there is now a tension between the 'imagined community' of the Kurdish nation and the practical requirements of economic survival that pushes large numbers of Kurds to seek employment in Istanbul, Tehran, Baghdad, and Aleppo (2004:8). Like other pastoral tribes in the Middle East, many Kurds have been dislocated and dispossessed not only from their homes but also from their communal grazing lands by the creation of borders. Kurds, Bedouin, and Turcoman, for example, had previously managed the permeable borders between empires to their advantage and together provided most of the livestock/meat requirements of the region. Like the Bedouin, the Kurds have largely given up their international migrations and succumbed to pressure to become more settled. Even so, many continue to keep livestock, making herding along with language and cultural traditions (but not necessarily religion) important markers of identity.[3] In each country where they seek safety or asylum, the Kurds slip into a remote 'paperless' existence. Their official documentation does not give them permission to be in the country and generally there are no mechanisms to become correctly documented. Some Kurds, such as those who took shelter in Syria in the 1920s, were granted citizenship by the French Mandate Authority, but that status was withdrawn during the Syrian union with Egypt in 1962. Male Kurds who received citizenship during the mandate period were stripped of their status, then selectively granted official documentation by the local government officials, or *mukhtars*. Many Kurds from the 1920s wave of immigrants live without documentation or hold government papers that declare them stateless, or *bidoon*.[4]

BACKGROUND (GEOGRAPHY AND HISTORY)

The region generally referred to as Kurdistan is centred on the Zagros Mountain range, which runs in ridges northwest to southeast along Iran, Iraq, and Turkey's common frontier. To the west, the mountains give way to rolling hills and the Mesopotamian plain of Iraq and Syria. To the northwest, the mountains give way to the Anatolian plateau (Turkey) and to the east they level out onto agricultural lands in Iran. The region

---

[3] The Kurds are predominantly Sunni Muslim, as are the majority of the populations of Turkey and Syria. In Iraq they are part of a sizeable Sunni minority (40–45 per cent) and in Iran they are a clear minority (McDowall 2004:10–12).

[4] *Bidoon* is a term in Arabic meaning 'without [citizenship]'. It is largely used to refer to those Bedouin whose common lands are within the Kuwait nation, but who refused to register in either 1925 or later in the 1960s when the government of Kuwait attempted to register its nationals. Perhaps as a hangover from the Ottoman era, such registration was regarded with suspicion by the Bedouin, who feared that it might be a prelude to taxation or government fines. During the first Gulf War many of these Bedouin fled as their common lands were targeted by allied troops. At the end of the fighting, when they attempted to return to their traditional grazing areas in Kuwait, they were prevented from doing so. As they had no papers, they were assigned the label of Bidoon and denied permission to enter Kuwait. The term has since been applied to anyone without citizenship papers, for example, the children of Kuwaiti women married to non-Kuwaiti men. The term Bidoon is commonly used among the 'stateless' Kurds in Syria to describe their condition.

Many Kurds came to the northern Syrian regions in the 1920s and were granted full citizenship under the French mandate. However, in the 1960s, after the Union with Egypt, the government stripped men of the opportunity to pass on their citizenship. Hence today in Syria, Kurdish women of the twentieth century wave of forced migrants may have Syrian citizenship, but, by and large, the men do not.

is important for agriculture and animal husbandry. It accounts for nearly 15 per cent of total cereal production in Turkey and 35 and 30 per cent, respectively, in Iran and Iraq. Until the early twentieth century, animal husbandry was the most important economic activity in Kurdistan, providing much of the meat for Anatolia, Mesopotamia, and Syria. Large flocks were driven annually to Istanbul, Baghdad, Aleppo, and Damascus (McDowall 2004:6).

The term *Kurdistan* was first used in the twelfth century by the Seljuks to describe the mountainous area and its people lying along the geopolitical fault line of three power centres: Ottoman, Qajar (Persian), and Russian. Until the late nineteenth century no power deemed it necessary to define Kurdistan's boundaries. Only when the European powers became concerned about Russian intents in the East did sensitivity emerge as to how many Muslims (largely Kurds) lived in the region compared with Christians (largely Armenian and Assyrian). As long as the Muslim population was the majority, there was the hope that Russia would not use religion as a pretext to seize these eastern lands, which would give it access to the Mesopotamian plain as a natural extension of Christian Russia or in order to protect the Armenian Christians of the Ottoman Empire. Apart from this issue, Europe seemed to have little interest in how generously terms such as Kurdistan or Armenia were drawn across a map. That changed in the twentieth century, as each of the empires crumbled and was replaced by a state, anxious to impose its homogenous identity on all the people in its territory.[5]

The Kurds speak an Indo-European language which, like Afghan and Farsi, is part of the Iranian group of languages. There is some doubt from linguistic evidence that the Kurds are descendants of a single common ancestor. Two major dialects or languages exist today in Kurdistan: Kurmanji, spoken by most northern Kurds and Surani, spoken by most southern Kurds. These differ from each other as English to German or German to Dutch. There are three other distinct dialects spoken by sizeable Kurdish minorities. In southeast Kurdistan, the dialect spoken is closer to Farsi than Surani. In some enclaves in southern Kurdistan, Gurani is spoken and in small pockets in northwestern Kurdistan, Zaza is spoken by both Sunni and Alevi Kurds. Zaza and Gurani belong to the

---

[5] Since World War II another reason for taking control of Kurdistan has become important and that is related to oil. No government will willingly give up control of its oilfields in the Kurdish region: Rumaylan (Syria), Batman and Silvan (Turkey), or Kirkuk and Khaniqin (Iraq) (McDowall 2004:7).

northwestern group of Iranian languages, whereas Kurmanji and Surani belong to the southwestern group. It is likely that Zaza and Gurani speakers were already in the Zagros region when Kurmanji and Surani speakers entered. During this population movement, it is thought that Zaza speakers may have been pushed westwards into Anatolia while the Gurani speakers – who may have been indigenous inhabitants – were surrounded, becoming a distinct subgroup with their own dialect (McDowall 2004:10).

Most Kurds are Sunni Muslim. But there is some religious differentiation (following linguistic lines), which may also indicate some differences in origins. Many Zaza speakers are also Alevi Muslims, a Shi'ite sect with strong elements of pre-Islamic religious beliefs, Zoroastrianism, and Turcoman shamanism. In southern Kurdistan, many Gurani speakers are also Ahl il-Haqq believers. This religion is similar to Alevi Islam but without the veneration of the Imam Ali. Both Alevi Islam and Ahl il-Haqq believers are found among non-Kurdish populations. In the Jabal Sanjar and around Shaykan and Mosul, among the Kurmanji speakers are the Yazidis. This religion is a synthesis of old pagan elements, Zoroastrian dualism, and Manichaean gnosis with Jewish, Christian, and Muslim elements.[6] About 15 per cent of Kurds, like most Iranians, follow Shi'a Islam (Ithna' Ashari Shi'ite or Twelvers), and live in the Kirmanshah Province of Iran. Kurdish religious distinctiveness has also been expressed in the strength of religious mysticism. Sufi brotherhoods (*tariqas*) are common among the Kurds and important markers of social organization, although the Turkish state has tried to control their membership.

Other religious communities existed in Kurdistan.[7] Small Jewish groups, mainly in the urban centres and towns, date back at least 2,000 years and their people tended to be traders and artisans. Although there was an exodus to Israel between 1948 and 1952, still some remained and probably affiliated themselves to certain tribes. There was a sizeable community of Christians of various sects in Kurdistan; the Gregorian Christian Armenians of eastern Anatolia, the Nestorian Christians or Assyrians

---

[6] A substantial number of Yazidis used to live in the Mardin area of Turkey. Many migrated to Russia at the end of the nineteenth century to escape the growing Islamization of the region. More recently many have migrated to Germany to escape religious oppression in modern Turkey.

[7] Kurdistan came to be generally referred to in the nineteenth century as an area encompassing the Zagros Mountains and beyond where a high density of the population spoke Kurdish. It was not a province within the Ottoman Empire although from the sixteenth century the Ottoman sultan recognized sixteen Kurdish principalities or feudal states in this mountainous region.

(sometimes referred to as the Assyro-Chaldeans), and the Suryani or Syrian Orthodox.[8]

It is likely that an indigenous population lived in the Zagros Mountains and was reinvigorated by wave after wave of migratory peoples settling in the region. The majority of the Kurds are probably descended from Indo-European tribes moving across Iran in the middle of the second millennium B.C. In the second century B.C., there are references to the Kurds as 'Cyrtii', Seleucid, or Parthian mercenaries dwelling in the Zagros Mountains. Semitic tribes may also have inhabited the region at this time. By A.D. 900s at the time of the Islamic conquests, the term *Kurd* referred to the nomads on the western edge of the Iranian plateau and probably included Arab and Turcoman tribes. Within several hundred years the latter came to be recognized as Kurdish, although their Arab and/or Turcoman roots were generally recognized. Likewise, numerous Kurds who left Kurdistan to become professional soldiers with Muslim armies or in groups as herders or farmers or merchants lost some of the cultural attributes of Kurdishness over time (McDowall 2004:1–18).

From about the twelfth century, the term *Kurd*, as with the term *Bedouin* in Arabia, came to mean 'nomad'. Over the centuries both Bedouin and Kurdish tribes consolidated their presence in agricultural areas adjacent to their migrations and commonly held grazing lands. A pejorative sense of 'outlaw' or 'bandit' also came to be attached to the term and gained widespread usage in the late seventeenth, eighteenth, and early nineteenth centuries. This was a time of particularly weak Ottoman central government, when the state establishment either could not manage or had no interest in controlling its Anatolian and Arab provinces. Kurdish raids and demands for tribute payment from peasants and villagers – in exchange for protection from the depredations of other tribes – were widespread.

By the nineteenth century, 'Kurd' had taken on the meaning of tribes-people who spoke the Kurdish language. Although there were Kurdish peasants and urban dwellers who did not claim tribal affiliation, most did. The dominant ideology of Kurdish society was kin-based and rooted in a myth of common ancestry. Most Kurdish tribal groups have their own real or imagined ancestor going back either to the time of Mohammed in the eighth century or to a hero in early Islam such as Khalid ibn al-Walid or in

---

[8] The Assyrian or Nestorian Church broke with the Western church in 413. At one time it extended as far as China, Siberia, Turkestan, and Eastern Iran. It was badly undermined by the Mongols at the end of the fourteenth century and shrank to a small community around the towns of Hakkari and the Urumiyah. There were also Syrian Orthodox or Suryani Christians (also known as Jacobite), mainly in the area of Tur Abdin and Mosul.

the later period to Salahadin al-Ayoubi. The Kurds, as with the Bedouin, have a range of terms to describe descending orders of social organization of the tribe. Many of these are the same in Kurdish and in Arabic. The highest order of organization was the confederations of tribes descending down to the tented encampment.[9] Each tribe had a strong sense of common origin as well as a sense of territorial identity but not necessarily ownership. This applied not only to common lands held by the tribe for pasture and grazing of their livestock, but also the villages and towns within their territorial domain and from which they could exact tribute. Among the tribes there was a sense of responsibility to maintain order and control, but also an assumed right to exact payment for that social and political management. This territorial universe was never entirely static and could accommodate other tribes' needs or requirements. For example, in the northern Jazirah of Syria, both the Arab Shammar Bedouin and the Kurdish Milli tribe – supposed enemies – shared certain pastoral grazing areas; the latter in winter and the former in summer (McDowall 2004:15).

Among the Kurds, as with the Bedouin, leadership is instilled in particular individuals at all levels of tribal organization: – the confederation, the tribe, sub-tribe, lineage, and the extended family. These chiefs (*agha*, pl. *aghawat*) are expected to take on certain functions. They act as arbitrators of disputes and allocators of resources, benefits, and duties. The chief of the tribe or confederation is also expected to act as a mediator with other tribes or with the state. These roles clearly give the leaders significant status and power, the monopoly of which is jealously guarded. Leadership is often dynastic and passed down from father to son, but a poor successor will be quickly challenged and the leadership will pass onto another family. In relations with the state, the role of the chief in such primarily pastoral societies works well. The flexibility and latitude accorded the tribal leaders to negotiate access, to mediate conflict, and to represent interests is far more successful than rigid and inflexible state mechanisms of state 'control'.[10]

---

[9] Among the Bedouin the terms are Al, Qabila, Ashira, Fakhad, and Bayt. Among the Kurds they are Ashira, Qabila, Taifa, Tira, Oba, and Haqwz.

[10] In some cases, a tribe may be no more than a ruling family that has attracted a large number of clients. The Barzani family in the nineteenth century attracted a large following of non-tribal peasantry escaping the repressive regime of neighbouring tribes. It could be said that the Barzani shaykhs created a tribe, thus 'tribalizing' non-tribal people. Such movement of people from settled to nomadic and back again is well documented (see Lancaster & Lancaster 1995). It may well be that the same movement among tribal and non-tribal people has occurred throughout Kurdish history (McDowall 2004:16).

Again as with the Bedouin of Arabia, the Kurds maintain an oppositional dichotomy, which extends back to their imagined origins. Whereas the Bedouin trace their origins to two mythical brothers Qais and Yemen – founders of their two tribal confederations, the Aneza and the Shammar – the Kurds regard Zilan and Milan as the equivalent. This dichotomy is expressed today in the opposition of the Talabani and the Barzani and it extends to the two political allegiances of the Kurds between the Patriotic Union of Kurdistan (PUK) and the Kurdish Democratic Party (KDP). They constitute a contemporary neotribal confederation.

Kurdish social organization had a fully developed hierarchy based on acquired and achieved status both among settled and pastoral folk. At the highest level was the chief or agha who generally held both economic and political power. In agrarian areas, the local landowner held enormous power over the peasantry, often controlling land, water, livestock, equipment, seeds, and labour itself. Peasants were often unable to move at will.[11] The agha was chief or leader of a community and the title was generally granted by the Ottoman state. An example of how the title of agha was awarded can be found in eighteenth-century Damascus. This was a period of general decline and significant in-migration of peasants, Bedouin and Kurds from areas in eastern Anatolia and the desert steppe where insecurity from tribal raiding as well as famine was pronounced. Local scholars from the religious establishment frequently mentioned their disdain for the aghawat who were moving in on the periphery of the city and setting up their own system of management and governance. Khoury describes this growing independent power base in the city, which threatened the old guard. 'In a section of the sparsely settled suburb of al-Salahiyyah, to the northwest of Damascus ... Kurdish immigrants unable to penetrate the old city set up home there. Their chiefs created paramilitary forces composed of their tribesmen and the state awarded them the title of agha for policing the countryside' (Khoury 1983:22),[12] In some cases these newcomers managed to become part of the urban ruling class. The Kurdish Yusuf family and the Shamdins, for example, came to

---

The Barzani case is interesting as well as it is evidence of the important role which religion can play in reinforcing group solidarity. The Barzani were originally religious leaders who then also acquired the role of tribal leader. But it does not necessarily follow that members of one tribal confederation belong to the same religion. Among the Kurds, Yazidis, Suryani, and Assyrian tribes have been known to belong to predominantly Sunni confederations.

[11] According to McDowell, until the 1960s, Iranian Kurdish peasants had to obtain permission from the landlord or his agent to even leave their village (2004:17).

[12] Khoury (1983:23) cites Rafeq (1966) and Baer (1982:49–100).

prominence in the second half of the nineteenth century in Damascus where they were competitors for the same Kurdish clientele in al-Salahiyyah. One of the offspring of a marriage between these two families was known to be among the richest men in Damascus and held one of the most prestigious posts in the Empire, the Commander of the Pilgrimage (Emir il-Hajj) in the late 1890s.[13]

The Ottoman state's ambiguous relationship with Kurdish tribal leaders (and later urban aghawat) and intellectuals has its origins in Kurdish–Ottoman relations dating back to the early sixteenth century. At that time, Kurdistan with all its tribal principalities and fiefdoms was threatened by the rulers of Persia, who sought to annex the region. In 1514, during the battle of Tchaldyran (north of Kurdistan), Kurdish tribal leaders fought alongside the Ottoman Sultan Selim and contributed to his victory. As a result, Sultan Selim concluded a pact with the main Kurdish tribal leaders. This Kurdish–Ottoman pact formally recognized sixteen independent Kurdish principalities, about fifty Kurdish *sanjak*s (fiefdoms) and a number of Ottoman sanjaks (Kendal [Nezan] 1980:22).[14] The Kurdish tribal leaders of southern Kurdistan were given significant independent status; they could strike coinage and have the Friday public prayer recite their name; they did not have to pay tribute nor were they accountable to the sultan. However, they were not permitted to change the frontiers of their principalities or fiefdoms. This was perhaps so as to protect the rights of adjoining principalities as much as it was to prevent the emergence of a centralized state in Kurdistan (Kendal [Nezan] 1980:22). These tribal chiefs (termed *Beys* and sometimes *Pashas* by the Ottomans) in effect became vassals of the Ottoman sultan.

---

[13] The Yusuf family is traced back to Diyarbakir where they had been livestock merchants until the early nineteenth century. In 1830 Ahmad Agha was an agent for the Emir Shihab of Mount Lebanon and received from him land in the Beqaa Valley for his services. Later, he was appointed Emir al-Hajj (Commander of the Pilgrimage) and governor of the Hauran. The Shamdin family origins are more obscure. A Kurdish tribal shaykh who was living in Acre, Palestine had a son named Shamdin. In the early nineteenth century, Shamdin came to settle in the al-Salahiyyah suburb of Damascus and rapidly built up a powerbase among immigrant Kurds by commanding a local garrison. A small family setback occurred in 1860 when Shamdin's son, Muhammed, failed to prevent Kurdish gangs from entering Bab Tuma and massacring Christians. He was exiled to Mosul, where, after restoring order to the chaotic town, he was returned from exile by the Sultan and rewarded with the governorship of the Hauran in the late 1860s (Khoury 1983:39–40).

[14] These principalities are cited in a number of works including Turan (1963:205–207) and von Hammer-Purgstall (1835). The latter mentions the province of Diyarbakir, which was 'divided into 11 Ottoman sanjaks, 8 Kurdish sanjaks, and 5 hereditary fiefs'.

They were free to manage their fiefdoms as they pleased; their power was generally absolute and hereditary, but they were expected to fight for the sultan in the empire's campaigns, particularly against the Persians. These sanjaks covered about a third of the territory of Ottoman Kurdistan and included important centres such as Diyarbakir, Siirt, Mardin, and Kharput.

This feudal and imperial relationship was respected by both sides until the beginning of the nineteenth century. As a result of this general independence, a specifically Kurdish literature and culture bloomed particularly in Bitlis and Hakkari, the capitals of the most powerful Kurdish tribal leaders. Yet during this period, sometimes referred to as the golden age of Kurdish feudalism, Kurdish society was practically cut off from the outside world. Each tribal leader's horizon extended no further than his own frontier. Quarrels over supremacy and precedence set one tribal ruler against another and hindered any unity among the principalities (McDowall 2004:38–48).

At the beginning of the nineteenth century, as the Ottomans' grip on its European provinces began to slip, it sought to recruit ever more troops to bolster its failing campaigns. It turned then to Kurdistan as an important source of manpower. This move, however, began to be regarded by some Kurdish princes as an infringement of their privileges. Kurdish territory also became the theatre for the Russian–Ottoman wars (1823–30, 1877–8) and the Ottoman–Turkish wars, bringing a level of death and destruction that fuelled Kurdish hostility and outrage towards the Ottomans. In addition, outside influences such as Western penetration into Kurdistan in the form of missions, consulates, and schools began to impact negatively on the Kurdish tribal leadership's sense of privilege. In the course of the nineteenth century, more than fifty insurrections broke out during which Kurdish feudal leaders defended their centuries-old privileges by refusing to pay tribute or to furnish the sultan with soldiers for his military campaigns. These uprisings were mainly aimed at preserving and extending their age-old privileges. They failed because they were disjointed and because the sultan, with greater ingenuity, was able to play one Kurdish leader off against another. These revolts included:

THE BABAN REVOLT IN 1806

This revolt took place in 1806 in Baban under the leadership of Abdurrahman Pasha. The principality had been established under Sulayman the Magnificent following his annexation of southern (Iraqi)

Kurdistan. Early in the nineteenth century, the Ottoman authorities began to worry about the power of Baban and so attempted to impose a member of a rival Kurdish tribe as the Emir. Affronted, Abdurrahman Pasha led an offensive against the Ottoman armies and Kurdish tribes who had allied themselves with the Ottomans. In 1808 he was defeated and took refuge in Iran.

In the north of Kurdistan, Ottoman troops had reinforced their presence as a measure to contain expected Russian aggression. The military occupation itself along with taxation and pillage in the region provoked a number of uprisings in the provinces of Erzurum and Van starting in 1815. Kurds and Armenians took part in these revolts, which were mainly attempts by the population to defend themselves or maintain the status quo. In 1828–9, another wave of rebellion occurred during the Russian–Ottoman war, which was fought in this part of Kurdistan and which again brought misery, pillage, and death to the people.

MIR MOHAMMED'S UPRISING IN SORAN

Several years after the Baban revolt, Mir Mohammed, sovereign of the principality of Soran, endeavoured to take advantage of Ottoman difficulties with the Russians as well as with Mohammed Ali in Egypt. A descendant of Saladin, Mir Mohammed attempted to create an independent Kurdistan. He set out to establish a regular army and also established armaments factories in his capital, Rawanduz. By May 1833, he had put together an army of 10,000 cavalry and 20,000 infantry, bringing much of southern Kurdistan under his control. His objective was to unite all the Kurdish tribal leaders who resented the influence of the Ottomans and not to extend his own sphere of influence by force. He invited his neighbouring tribal leader to join him, but this was rejected (Kendal [Nezan] 1980:45; Safrastrian 1948:52). The Ottoman Sultan sent his army supported with troops from the governors of Mosul and Baghdad to put down this insurrection. This Kurdish–Ottoman war raged throughout the summer of 1834 and the Ottoman troops eventually withdrew exhausted and demoralised. Mir Mohammed continued his campaign and set about 'liberating' Iranian Kurdistan. In 1836 fighting broke out again and this time, armed with 40,000 men, he was able to force the Ottoman army into retreat. The religious leaderships, at the behest of the Ottomans, called for an end to the internecine fighting of Muslim against Muslim and this eventually turned the tide against Mir Mohammed. He was sent to Constantinople where he spent six months in exile. Upon his release he was assassinated by the sultan's men in Trabzon. The uprising, however, had set off sparks of revolt and resistance throughout Kurdistan. The Bedir Khan Revolt of the mid-1840s had all the elements of hereditary rule, genuine popular support, family intrigue, and religious meddling before a significant feudal principality was brought under the Ottoman yoke.[15]

YEZDAN SHER REVOLT

In the spring of 1855, Yezdan Sher launched an attack on Bitlis and then on Mosul, which he captured and then went on to liberate Siirt, the administrative and military centre of the Ottoman occupation in Kurdistan. Within months he had brought together under his control a vast area from Baghdad to Lake Van and Diyarbakir. By the end of the summer of 1855 he had more than 100,000 men under his command. However, Britain and France, allies of the Ottoman Empire in the Crimean War against Russia, had no interest in seeing the emergence of an independent Kurdistan, particularly as it might then fall under Russian influence. British emissary Nimrud Rassam was sent to Mosul in 1855 with a great deal of cash and demanded to be received as a mediator at the headquarters of the Kurdish movement. After some time he was able to persuade Yezdan Sher to settle the question of independence through Kurdish–Ottoman negotiations with Britain as the mediator. Yezdan Sher believed in Rassam's promises and in the good intentions of 'civilized Britain'. Furthermore as was the case for Greece and Egypt, he believed that an independent state could be set up only with the support of a European power. He travelled with Rassam to Constantinople to begin the British-sponsored negotiations with the Ottoman court. The moment he arrived in the capital, he was arrested and put into prison. His troops carried out a few skirmishes in his absence and eventually dispersed (Kendal [Nezan] 1980:31).

---

[15] According to Arshak Safrastian, Bedir Khan was a just ruler not only to the Kurds, but also towards the Armenians and the Assyrians living in his principality. A Russian traveller of the time wrote that Christians enjoyed freedom of religion, were allowed their places of worship in Jazirah as elsewhere and suffered no discrimination. He praised the order, justice, and peacefulness that prevailed in the territories controlled by Bedir Khan, in marked contrast to the disorder, injustice, and corruption he found in the places in the Ottoman and Persian Empires he visited (direct quote in Kendal [Nezan] 1980:45).

SHAYKH OBEIDULLAH'S REVOLT OF 1880

The last important Kurdish revolt of the nineteenth century involved both Ottoman Kurds and Kurds in Persia. In 1872 the Persian government demanded payment of taxes from the Kurds along their northwestern frontier. The Kurds refused and declared that they regularly paid their taxes to Shaykh Obeidullah, both an important spiritual leader (of the Naqishbendi Sufi movement) as well as their feudal prince. The Shaykh appealed to the Ottoman government for support, which they gave in the form of a mission by the Wali of Erzurum to plead the case in Tehran. Perhaps hoping to secure support from the Ottomans in the future, the Shaykh sent a small fighting force to participate in the Russian–Ottoman War of 1877–8, which was being fought in Northern Kurdistan. This war was followed by one of the worst famines the Kurds had experienced for centuries. Ottoman soldiers and officials who were no longer being paid were terrorizing the local population, extorting supplies and money. Revolts broke out in towns and cities such as Dersim, Mardin, and Hakkari. The Shaykh sent an emissary to Constantinople to ask for an end to the persecution of his people and for damages to be paid for the havoc the Ottoman soldiers had wrought. At the same time, he established contact with the Sherif of Mecca and the Khedive of Egypt, hoping to gain their support. In the end, he received support from the British, but only in the form of weapons and ammunition (Kendal [Nezan] 1980:31). In October 1880 Shaykh Obeidullah launched an attack on Persia with 80,000 men. He took over Mahabad and drew near to Tabriz, then the capital of Azerbaijan. The Shaykh's successes worried the Persian shah who protested to the Ottoman sultan to better 'control' this Kurdish prince. The sultan, at the same time, began to worry about these military successes as well as the shaykh's intention of setting up an independent Kurdistan. Both Persian and Ottoman troops then encircled Kurdish forces and Shaykh Obeidullah stood down and agreed to go to Constantinople for discussions with the sultan. After two years of diplomatic wrangling, Shaykh Obeidullah attempted to slip away and return to Kurdistan. He was caught and sent into exile to Mecca, where he died a few years later.

After nearly a century of feudal revolts, the Ottoman court changed its approach and sought to control and integrate the Kurdish ruling class into the broad system of rule. Many of the sons or nephews of those Kurdish leaders who had led revolts were appointed to government. The son of Bedir Khan, for example, was appointed aide-de-camp to the sultan himself and the son of Shaykh Obeidullah became president of the Ottoman

Senate in 1908 and was later appointed president of the Council of State. In addition, the sultan created a special Kurdish cavalry force drawn on a tribal basis. These regiments, the Hamidiyyah, were originally set up in areas bordering on the Russian Caucasus (Erzurum, Bitlis and Van) where the Kurds had not systematically rebelled and where the Armenian nationalist movement was in full swing. Finally, in 1892 Sultan Abdul Hamid set up two special schools in Baghdad and in Constantinople for the children of tribal leaders among the Kurds and the Arab Bedouin. Although these schools were short-lived, they were to have an enormous impact on the formation of a limited but effective Kurdish and Arab tribal intellectual growth in future generations.[16]

The policies of Abdul Hamid regarding the Kurdish secessionist and nationalist aspirations were successful. His various measures guaranteed that Kurdish nationalism, which could easily have flourished alongside other Ottoman millet nationalisms, was restricted to the activity of a few intellectual circles. Kurdistan's intelligentsia began to emerge only at the end of the nineteenth century. Almost all of its intellectuals had aristocratic backgrounds. Some were the sons of exiled princes or tribal leaders; some were educated in the tribal schools of Constantinople and Baghdad and others had emerged from training and education in the Ottoman Empire's military academies which, after 1870, admitted young Kurds. Until the Young Turk revolution, which subdued and eventually overthrew Abdul Hamid II in 1908–9, Kurdish nationalism was largely restricted to a few intellectual circles.[17] After 1908, numerous Kurdish associations sprang up in Constantinople and Kurdistan. These included the Recovery and Progress of Kurdistan Association, under the direction of Shaykh Abdul Qadir (Shaykh Obeidullah's son), which published a Turkish language journal entitled *Kurdish Mutual Aid and Progress Gazette*. This publication was the first legally circulated Kurdish journal. Other committees were formed in Constantinople, as well as in Kurdistan itself, where young intellectuals and militants set up Kurdish clubs in the main urban centres of Bitlis, Diyarbakir, Mus Erzurum, and Mosul. In 1912 a secret

[16] Children of Kurdish and Arab tribal leaders as far as the Negev and the Hijaz were sent to these schools. They returned to their territories and often became important government functionaries as well as the leaders of the various movements for independence and self-determination. See Rogan (1996) and Abu Rabia (2001) for more details.

[17] The first bilingual Kurdish–Turkish journal, *Kurdistan*, had been established in 1898 as a cultural and educational magazine but over time became an outlet for Kurdish nationalism. Eventually, as political circumstances changed, the journal was forced to move its offices first to Geneva, then London and finally Cairo. See Chirguh (1930:50).

society, Kurdish Hope, created in 1910, was legalized. This seems to have been the first centralized and structured Kurdish political organization and was led by a member of the Ottoman Parliament, Dr Chukri Sekban.[18] At the end of the same year, an Association of the Friends of Kurdistan had been formed in Constantinople to inform public opinion about the Kurdish 'question'.

Kurdish identity evolved dramatically during the nineteenth century. Up to the very end of the century and early into the twentieth century, when nationalist and secessionist movements generally gripped the Ottoman Empire, few Kurds regarded themselves as anything other than members of their particular religious community or millet. The Kurdish peasantry continued to struggle with the demands of feudal landlords or pastoral tribal leaders. In many urban settings, local Kurdish workers and artisans had to deal with the demands of their aghawat, the local Kurdish power brokers and leaders. The latter, in turn, had to show respect and pay taxes to their hereditary princes (*Beys* or *Pashas*). The struggle to maintain distance and independence and remain outside of state control, which had been part of Kurdish (and Bedouin) tribal ideology and activity, gradually came to be integrated into the nationalist movements emerging from the urban power centres. These struggles highly coloured the way in which Kurds and their militias responded to the end of empire.

With the exception of the Arabian provinces, no other part of the Ottoman state was as weak and poorly managed as Ottoman Asia, that part of southeastern Anatolia and northern Iraq which was home to the Armenians, Assyrians, and other syncretic religious communities as well as the Kurds. The mountainous terrain as well as the general unwillingness of its nomadic peoples to submit to central authority made anything other than local governance in this region very difficult.

Although there were numerous Christian groups in the region, the Muslim population was largely Kurdish. They formed a distinct group in the Dersim region (southwest of Erzincan) and in the provinces of Van, Diyarbakir, and Mosul. There were settled farmers and city-dwellers, but the large majority were nomadic and semi-nomadic pastoral tribes. The Kurdish tribes, as with the Bedouin, saw themselves in opposition to central authority. They were unaccustomed to following any orders

---

[18] Dr Sekban was to later recant and become an advocate of Kurdish assimilation in Turkey. In a pamphlet published in 1933 on the Kurdish question, he was to write 'later events have shown that the emergence of an independent Kurdish state would have been a calamity a disaster for the Kurdish people's real interests' (quoted in Kendal [Nezan] 1980:46).

other than those of their leadership. They were part of an alternative system of social organization based on mobility and fluidity of boundaries between tribes. From the time of the Ottoman Golden Age of Sulayman the Magnificent (1520–66), the Ottomans struggled, not so much to control the Kurds, but to keep them from causing trouble. As long as they did not disrupt trade or attack settled regions, the Ottoman authority often were content to leave them alone. The Kurdish (and Bedouin) tribal practice of demanding tribute from settled villagers did not raise pronounced objection from the Ottomans until late in the nineteenth century when tax was desperately needed by the state and the Kurdish practice of collecting tribute was undermining official state tax collection. The Ottoman army was generally only used to control the Kurds when they disrupted the region by significant raiding of settled areas or their leaders attempted a revolt.[19] Various interpretations of the Ottoman efforts to curb Kurdish tribal activity suggest that Kurdish tribes were the main factor in civil unrest. These interpretations regard local Armenians and settled Kurds as the primary victims of Kurdish tribesmen, while Kurdish landlords were viewed as oppressing the local Muslim and Armenian agrarian population in southeast Anatolia (McCarthy 1995; Shaw & Shaw 1977). Other historians consider the general lack of control of Ottoman troops posted in the region, without pay and without effective leadership, as the instigators of Kurdish tribal activity (Chaliand 1980).

After the lessons of the 1877–8 Russian–Ottoman war, the Ottoman state attempted to impose its authority over these traditionally rather autonomous Kurdish regions (see Chapter Two for similar activities in the Syrian provinces to control the Bedouin). Sultan Abdul Hamid II attempted to bring the Kurdish tribes under his control by using their strengths to his advantage. For example, the creation of the Hamidiyyah Cavalry in 1891 was made up of units of mounted tribal Kurds. He provided them with arms, uniforms and some training. They were used for the first time in the repression of the Armenians between 1894 and 1896 and this ended in a series of massacres in which tens of thousands of Armenians were killed. These same troops were used against the Kurds of Dersim when they rose up against the sultan. They were also put into

---

[19] Raiding of settled populations and exacting tribute had long been practiced by Kurdish and Bedouin tribes. It was only when the raiding was long and sustained or in the case of the Syrian provinces, there was the additional threat of *Ikhwan* takeover under the leadership of Ibn Saud in the Nejd of Arabia, that Ottoman troops were brought into play. Alternatively, the Ottomans played at 'divide and rule' and often armed one group of tribes so as to support their attacks on another (Toth 2005).

action against Arab nationals under the command of Ibrahim Pasha (Kendal [Nezan] 1980:34). When Abdul Hamid was deposed fifteen years later, the Hamidiyyah Cavalry was renamed, reuniformed, and more centrally integrated into the formal standing army as the tribal regiments of light cavalry.[20] The new government, the Committee of Union and Progress (CUP), adopted a more practical approach, bringing these Kurdish regiments under regular military control. But the home region, southeast Anatolia, was never controlled. The lack of even an effective police or gendarmerie meant that Kurdish tribes were able to continue to exact tribute from settled society and Armenian revolutionaries were able to organize themselves and manage smuggling networks to move weapons and ammunition into the region (McCarthy 2001:66).

Only in the last decades of the Ottoman Empire did an extension of some control over eastern and southern Anatolia and the southern Syrian provinces emerge. Telegraph lines and new roads brought Ottoman administrative authority to areas such as Van and Diyarbakir. For the first time in recent history, Ottoman officials were able to reach remote villages and identify the inhabitants for census and conscription records (McCarthy 1983:163–181). However, with the advent of World War I, Ottoman troops were sent from their garrisons in southeastern Anatolia to fight the Russians on the Caucasian border. Only a minimal gendarmerie was kept back to undertake public security. With most of the gendarmerie absent and the Ottoman troops (including Kurdish units) fighting on the Russian front, Kurdish pastoral tribes were able to renew their traditional tribute collecting and raiding on civilian populations.[21]

Despite the exhortations of the Ottoman sultan and the Grand Mufti to 'Holy War', many pastoral Kurdish tribal leaders took a neutral position during World War I (Ahmad 1994). Other leaders took advantage of the

---

[20] McCarthy is quite scathing of the Hamidiyyah Cavalry and likens the process as 'equivalent to a city mayor today arming a local street gang and giving them colourful clothes in the hopes that they would become good citizens' (2001:66). However, a later 'experiment' in Transjordan in the 1920s to transform the tribal Bedouin into an effective fighting force was successful and was the basis of the Arab Legion created for Emir Abdullah by John Glubb. Here, perhaps, the training was long and sustained, and the cause to defend the state from the depredations of Ibn Saud and his Ikhwan Bedouin fighters was more critical to the very survival of the Bedouin of Jordan.

[21] In theory, Kurdish tribesmen should have been conscripted into the Ottoman army. But in practice, it was largely the settled and agricultural Kurds as well as Kurds in eastern cities who went off to war. In order to conscript a large number of Kurds, the tribes would first have to have been subdued or pacified by the Ottoman army. For both the Kurds and the Bedouin, this is a measure which was not attempted until the time of the British and French mandate over the former Arab provinces after World War I (McCarthy 1995:184).

situation to make a break for secession or to be on the winning side. Some Kurdish tribal sections found themselves in conflict with Ottoman forces. A number from the region of Dersim had joined the Ottoman army at the beginning of the war, but later switched sides, joining Armenian, other Kurds, and Russian forces in attacking Ottoman convoys and pillaging local villages. In Van, one Kurdish leader, Bedirham Abdurrezzak, attempted to set up a major Kurdish revolt during this period. In order to quell the uprising, the Ottomans called up an entire gendarmerie battalion to fight his Kurdish fighters.

The Kurdish people could not have stayed aloof, as Kurdistan was the scene of a devastating struggle between three armies: Ottoman, Russian, and British. These armies clashed from 1914 to 1918 in many Kurdish districts, engaging in fierce battles that shifted the balance of power between combatants and caused huge disruption, death, and homelessness in many parts of Kurdistan. Many Kurds became war casualties as the vast majority of the Ottoman 9th Army deployed in Erzurum, the 10th Army in Sivas, the 11th Army in Elazig, and the 12th Army in Mosul consisted of Kurds (Zaki 1947:274). After a few months of fighting in the Caucasus, more than 15,000 Kurdish horsemen had deserted the ranks of the 3rd Army. In border regions, it was not unusual for Kurdish soldiers, tribesmen, and their leaders to go over with their arms to the Russians (Ahmad 1994:91). In other areas, Kurdish tribesmen mounted surprise attacks on Ottoman troops, sometimes looking for arms and ammunition for themselves or in cooperation with the British.[22] In the territories initially conquered by the Russians in northeast Anatolia, Kurdish pastoral tribes generally made peace quickly with the occupiers. However, skirmishes between Armenian militia and Kurdish tribesmen continued throughout the war. In the general state of anarchy which prevailed in this region of Anatolia, some significant depredations by Kurdish tribal elements against Armenians, settled Kurds, and Turks took place (McCarthy 1995). Many of the Kurdish tribesmen, who were fighting alongside the Ottoman army in the campaign against Persia in 1915, deserted and joined in the general pillage and rampage being carried out by the tribes in the region between Van and Urumiyah (Allen & Muratoff 1953:426–438).

---

[22] German sources make reference to successive attacks by 'Kurds and Arabs' from the spring of 1914 to the end of 1915 against convoys heading for the battlefields in southern Iraq, forcing the Ottoman–German joint commands to bring in additional forces to protect the routes taken by these convoys (quoted in Ahmad 1994:114; comment attributed to Carsoon).

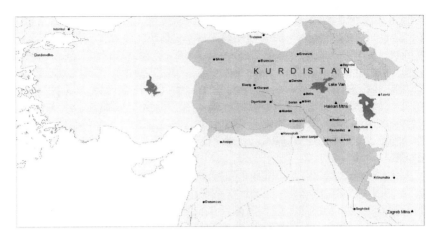

MAP 9. Kurdistan

Along the Russian front, Kurdish tribesmen and their leaders were being alternatively wooed and chased away while the Armenians and other Christian groups were by turns victorious or victims of massacres. The Russians never developed a coherent policy towards the Kurds, probably because Kurdish aspirations were bound to clash with those of the Armenians. As McDowell writes: 'it suited Russia in its policy with both Kurds and Armenians to encourage dissidence in order to weaken the Ottoman hold on the region, but not in order to permit either Armenian or Kurdish independence. Russia wanted eastern Anatolia for itself' (2004:102). The war plunged Kurdistan into chaos as armies marched and countermarched across the land. With this came a form of ethnic cleansing. When the Russians advanced at the end of 1914 to Bayazid, they generally garrisoned Armenian troops, many of whom were ex-Ottoman citizens. By the time they withdrew, very few if any of the Muslim (and largely Kurdish) population were reported to have survived. Most Armenians and Assyrians then fled northwards in the wake of the Russian army.[23] Those who remained were subjected to terrible treatment by the remaining Ottoman troops, especially the Kurdish Hamidiyyah cavalry. In Russia, Kurdish leaders who had changed sides were reported to have been treated

---

[23] The Assyrians were also the focus of a campaign of ethnic cleansing by the Ottomans. Probably motivated by fear of a Russian advance into the area and knowing the Assyrians' desire for Russian protection, the Ottomans mounted a preemptive attack on the Assyrians of Hakkari. This resulted in the evacuation of the entire population of 15,000 people to Urumiyah under Russian protection.

dishonourably by some of the Russian commanders resulting in these Kurds realigning themselves with the British who seemed to have adopted a more intelligent policy towards them.[24] The Russians, however, had a continuing and serious interest in the Kurds both hidden and declared. Their long-standing imperial goal was to push south into Ottoman Armenia and Kurdistan towards the Persian/Arabian Gulf as well as to gain access to the Mediterranean through the Dardanelles Straits.

The British, on the other hand, were determined to push as far north and east as possible from the mouth of the Shatt il-Arab to meet up with Russian forces and squeeze the Ottoman armies between them.[25] The day after the Ottoman Empire became an official combatant in World War I, British forces attacked southern Iraq and occupied Basra. After this rapid occupation, and perhaps as a result of it, the Ottomans were able to raise a force of 10,000 men, including many Kurds, to fight against the British invaders. In April of 1915, Ottoman units battled the British at Shu'aiba, where the Ottomans were badly defeated and suffered serious losses. Many Arab and Kurdish fighters left the battlefield then and returned to their homes. By March 1917, the British entered Baghdad. After the Russian October Revolution of 1918, the British sped up their northward drive beyond Baghdad and later engaged in fierce battles to take Mosul and then Kirkuk before the signing of the Armistice of Mudros on 30 October 1918. The British were seeking to consolidate and protect their oil interests, which had been negotiated and agreed several years earlier in the secret Sykes-Picot Agreement.[26]

As early as a year into World War I, in the autumn of 1915, secret talks had begun between Britain and France regarding the division of the Ottoman Empire. Sir Mark Sykes, the British Foreign Minister, and his French counterpart, George Picot, were determined that the Arab provinces of the empire as well as other areas would be partitioned. Early in

[24] The memoirs of Boris Shakhovski mention that some of the Kurdish leaders such as Rasul Beg and Khaled Beg, both of whom fought on the Russian front were arrested by the Russians after inviting them to a military ceremony and then dispatching them under escort to Siberia (quoted in Ahmad 1994:114; Kurd-Oghlu 1932:108).

[25] In March 1915 the Russians and the British signed a secret agreement to split Persia between the two, thus ignoring Persian Kurdish nationalist aspirations but putting these Kurds again in a frontier position between two major armies (Ahmad 1994:92–97).

[26] Oil had been discovered in the Mesopotamian region in 1908. The Turkish Petroleum Company (TPC) was set up in 1912, followed by the Anglo Persian Oil Company in 1913. The Sykes-Picot secret agreements assigned the British and the French direct control and spheres of influence over this region with an eye to oil claims as well as the development of railways (Mirak-Weissbach 2006; Yergin 1991).

1916, Sykes and Picot travelled to St Petersburg, where they sought the cooperation of the Russian czar. After some modification of their original plan to accommodate Russian demands, they obtained approval from the Russian Foreign Ministry and returned to London. By September Britain, France, and Russia had all endorsed the plan (Ahmad 1994:186–187).

At the start of the negotiations, Russia made it clear that, in addition to its desire to control the Dardanelles and Constantinople, it wanted all of Ottoman Kurdistan and Ottoman Armenia. After lengthy bargaining with the French – who also had strong interests in the same area – an agreement was reached whereby Russia would have the northernmost Armenian regions of Erzurum, Trabzon, Van, and Bitlis up to a point on the Black Sea to the west of Trabzon. It would also control the Kurdish regions to the west of Van and Bitlis. The British had established claims to Mosul province as part of its plan for control of the oilfields and the outlets in the Middle East. It also pushed to acquire parts of Persian Kurdistan, even though Persia had remained neutral throughout the war years. The French, however, wanted some of the southern Ottoman Kurdish areas to protect its interests in the railway concession in Anatolia.[27] After further delicate negotiations whereby France guaranteed full recognition of British 'rights' to Mosul province, it was permitted a section of southern Kurdistan, almost as a buffer zone between the Russian and British zones of interest.[28] The Sykes-Picot Agreement was followed by another round of negotiations and secret agreements. Italy, which had been excluded from these discussions, lodged a protest to its allies and managed to join in the division of spoils in November 1916. Early in 1917, Russia and France reached another secret agreement whereby, among other conditions related to Europe, France pledged to support Russia's claims to Constantinople and the Dardanelles. These secret agreements – many of them contradictory – were setting the stage for one of the most dramatic land claims

[27] Ahmad notes that Russia was initially firmly opposed to giving any Kurdish parts of the Ottoman Empire to France, because it wanted the whole of Ottoman Armenia and Kurdistan for itself. However, after lengthy bargaining and coaxing, it agreed to let large Kurdish regions fall within the zone of French influence. Great Britain, which had no intention of giving up any of southern Kurdistan did eventually decide there was some advantage to letting France realize its goal and thus avoid direct friction with the Russians in their zones of influence (Ahmad 1994:206).

[28] After the signing of the Sykes-Picot Agreement, Sir Edward Grey called the French ambassador Paul Cambon several times to secure France's full recognition of British rights to Mosul province. Cambon declared, 'France is ready to recognize all the privileges that Britain had [in Mosul province] before the war' (quoted in Ahmad 1994:206; see Gofman 1920:81).

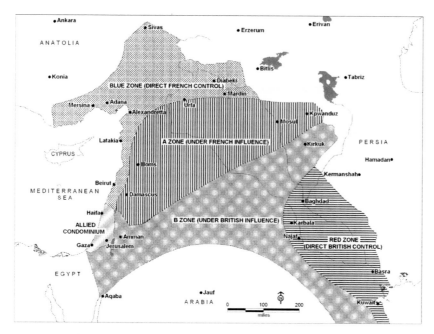

MAP 10. Sykes-Picot Agreement Relevant to Kurdistan

in colonial history, dismissing and at the same time toying with the aspirations and destinies of the Arabs, Armenians, and Kurdish people.[29]

Before the war ended, however, czarist Russia had come to an end with the October Revolution of 1917. The new Soviet state withdrew from the Allied consortium and disassociated itself from the public and secret treaties of the previous regime. It recalled its troops from the battlefields and abandoned every area they had conquered. Great Britain, previously happy to have France insert a buffer area between it and Russia, now urgently tried to impose its presence as close as possible to the new state border fearing the Bolshevik system represented a serious menace. British forces in southern Iraq then prepared to occupy the largest portion of Kurdistan that they could before the war ended (Churchill 1933:1395). On 8 November 1917, the new Soviet government denounced the colonialist

[29] The Allied forces, in particular the British, were at the same time courting the leaders of these peoples and signing agreements with some of them, providing assurances of independence for their countries as soon as the war ended, in exchange for their support in the war effort. This is nowhere more clearly evident than in the 1915 Hussein-McMahon Correspondence guaranteeing the Arab nation independence from the Ottomans – as long as it sided with the British in this war effort.

secret diplomacy and pledged to publish the texts of the Great Power treaties in its possession. After six weeks, it released a number of these publications in the daily Soviet press. One of these included clauses of the Sykes-Picot accord along with all the communications and letters exchanged relating to the quibbling, bartering, and horse-trading that had taken place. These revelations caused consternation throughout the Middle East and in Europe. The Sherif of Mecca, still trusting British loyalty and friendship, asked for clarification from the British government as these revelations completely undermined his own correspondence with Henry McMahon, the British High Commissioner of Egypt, regarding the status of the Arab provinces after the war. In an official letter sent by the Foreign Office via Cairo to Sherif Hussein, the British tried to dismiss the matter as a mere 'Bolshevik game' aimed at corrupting relations between the Arabs and the Allies. For a time, it seemed Sherif Hussein was mollified (Ahmad 1994:191).

The Kurdish intellectual response was relatively muted, as was that of the Armenians and Assyrians. Many of the region's political leaders believed the British Foreign Office assertion that the 'Bolshevik game' was aimed at destroying the relationship between the Allies and them-selves. The Allies quickly altered their political statements sometimes in direct contradiction of the contents of the secret agreements. In January 1918, British Prime Minister Lloyd George asserted his country had been forced to participate in the war 'in defence of the rights of the peoples'. In the same speech, he told of the importance of 'principles of self-determination' and about 'Arabia, Armenia, Mesopotamia, and Syria being entitled to a recognition of their separate national conditions' (Lloyd George 1933:2515–2527). Three days later, US President Woodrow Wilson announced his famous Fourteen Points before Congress. Point 5 recalled: ... *the necessity for free, open-minded and absolutely impartial adjustment of all colonial claims based upon ... the interest of the populations concerned .... [having] equal weight with the equitable claims of the government whose title is to be determined*. Point 12 related specifically to the Ottoman Empire and stipulated that: *The Turkish portions of the present Ottoman empire should be assured a secure sovereignty, but the other nationalities which are now under Turkish rule should be assured an undoubted security of life and an absolutely unmolested opportunity of autonomous development* (Wilson 1918). For their part, the British put considerable energy into bringing the Kurds round to their 'side' by promises of liberating oppressed peoples and granting them the rights of self-determination. In Kurdistan and in Mesopotamia, the British forces of occupation invested significant time and energy in the publication of two newspapers, *Al-Arab* and *Tigeyashteni Raste* which carried much of what was written by Lloyd George as well as Woodrow Wilson to the Kurdish- and Arabic-speaking world. Many Kurdish intellectuals pinned their hopes on Wilson's Fourteen Points and wanted the USA to be more actively involved in determining their destiny at the end of the war.

The British had shouldered most of the burden of war on the part of the Triple Entente in the Ottoman domains. It had about one million troops on the war fronts, of whom nearly 125,000 were casualties, while the French forces in the Middle East were very small in comparison. The United States had no troops in the area as it never actually declared war on the Ottoman Empire (Eisenhower 2001). Thus, it was British troops in Palestine, Syria, and Iraq during the war with permanent bases in Cyprus, Egypt, Aden, and Kuwait. Given this extraordinary presence, the British were convinced that their claims were greater than others to be the 'legitimate' heirs to czarist Russian claims under the Sykes-Picot Agreement as well as other secret agreements. Nowhere was this more pronounced than with regard to Russia's former claims to Kurdistan. In total disregard of the 25 clauses of the Mudros armistice of 1918, ending the fighting between the Allies and the Ottoman Empire, the British forces advanced and took over several Ottoman Kurdish districts after the armistice had been declared. In what many read as a blatant provocation, the British flag was raised above the Ottoman governor's office building in Mosul, drawing a strong protest from the Sublime Porte in Constantinople.

Kurdish interests at the Paris Peace Conference, which lasted for more than a year (January 1919–January 1920), were represented by a small delegation led by Sherif Pasha, a Kurdish high-ranking Ottoman military figure and diplomat.[30] Other potential delegates of Kurds living in the Kurdish territories occupied by the British, who may have had a dissident opinion, were alleged to have been prevented from joining their colleagues in Paris (Ahmad 1994:20). For many at the Paris Peace Conference, the Kurdish question was connected to the Armenian question. Some time was spent discussing Armenia and which mandate it would come under. President Wilson sent a special commission, led by James Harboard, to study the Armenian question. Harboard visited Asia Minor and also some

---

[30] The exact number of members of the delegation is not known. They were probably Kurdish politicians in exile who were opposed to the Ottoman CUP. Sherif Pasha, himself, had gone into exile and settled in Paris after the CUP takeover in 1908 (Ahmad 1994:209). See also Pearly (1946:6).

Kurdish regions. His recommendation, made in October 1919, was that one state should have mandate over all of Turkey and the trans-Caucasus. The British exerted pressure on the Americans to accept the mandate over the whole of Armenia, Constantinople, the Dardanelles, and the Caucasus. However, the USA rejected these proposals and renewed deliberations ensued between Great Britain and France. British interests in Kurdistan were particularly focused. They considered the Kurds to be a vital element in creating a strong British military border zone to the north of Baghdad,[31] and were unwilling to see Kurdistan shared with the French. These opposing positions among the Allies resulted in the inclusion of a number of awkward and contradictory articles regarding the Kurds into the Treaty of Sèvres.

The treaty was signed on 10 August 1920 in Sèvres, near Paris. The signatories included Britain, France, Italy, Japan, Belgium, Greece, Romania, Poland, Portugal, Czechoslovakia, Yugoslavia, Hijaz, and Armenia on the one hand and the Ottoman Empire on the other. It consisted of 13 sections and 433 articles prepared by five special committees formed during the Paris Peace Conference. It included the 'just causes' of both the Armenian and the Kurdish peoples. Part III of Section III was devoted to the Kurdish question and consisted of three articles (62–64). These set out a timetable first for local Kurdish autonomy followed, a year later, by the right of petition to the League of Nations for an independent Kurdish state.[32] However, the ambiguity of the language in many of these articles relating to the Kurds, as well as the recognition of the overlapping interests of the French, British, and Italians in Kurdistan, meant that whatever optimism there may have been regarding Kurdish rights of self-determination was unfounded. The Treaty of Sèvres was, to use the words of William Eagleton,

---

[31] In December 1919 the British and French held a special conference to study the situation, in particular the situation in Kurdistan and the Caucasus. Lord Curzon, the British representative rejected the idea of dividing Kurdistan between Britain and France and instead talked of Kurdish 'autonomy', 'independence', and guaranteeing secure borders for Mesopotamia in the north (Ahmed 1994:201).

[32] Article 62 called for the setting up of a special committee within six months to set out a scheme of local autonomy for the Kurdish areas lying east of the Euphrates, south of the southern boundary of Armenia (as was to be determined by President Woodrow Wilson), and north of the frontier of Turkey with Syria and Mesopotamia. Article 63 stipulated that the Turkish government would accept these decisions within three months. Furthermore, Article 64 set a one-year limit for the provision of Article 62; thereafter, the Kurdish people granted local autonomy could address the Council of the League of Nations to show that they desired independence from Turkey. Should the League of Nations agree, there would be no objection for the Mosul vilayet to become part of the new Kurdish state (quoted in Ahmed 1994:212; Temperley 1920–1924:83–91).

'a dead letter from the moment it was signed for history was written otherwise by Mustafa Kemal and finally by the Treaty of Lausanne in 1923. By then, it was clear that within Ataturk's Turkey there was no place for an Armenian or Kurdish nation' (Eagleton Jr 1963:12).

The treaty proposed to strip the Ottoman Empire down and confine it to just the northwestern and north-central Anatolia with Constantinople remaining as its capital, which would have excluded more of the Turkish population than it included. Although the representative of the sultan signed the treaty, the remnants of the Ottoman army regrouped under the command of Mustafa Kemal, who refused. The terms of the treaty were such as to reinforce their will to resist and to fight for their own independent Turkish state over all of Anatolia. After the signing of the armistice of Mudros in 1918, the Ottoman army had kept to the terms of the armistice and moved out of Cilicia towards Konya and awaited further orders. The French had then moved into Cilicia in violation of the armistice. With too few men to replace Ottoman authority, they sent in 5,000 Armenian soldiers and officers as well as French colonial troops from Africa to hold the territory. Inappropriate behaviour on the part of the Armenian soldiers and reports of the massacre of Muslim civilians in the region resulted in the development of an active local resistance to the French occupation, aided by former Ottoman soldiers under the command of Mustafa Kemal (McCarthy 2001:138–141). On 21 October 1921, the French abandoned their claims to Anatolia and signed a treaty with Mustafa Kemal's government. The French left Anatolia in December of that year, taking 30,000 Armenians with them to Syria and Lebanon which were under their mandate. This agreement broke the united stand of the Allied powers. Although Britain supported Greece's prize of western Anatolia under the terms of the Treaty of Sèvres, it was not prepared to act without the backing of France. By August 1922, the Turks had retaken most of western Anatolia occupied by Greek forces and in September of the same year, they entered Izmir on the Mediterranean coast. In eastern Anatolia, Ottoman troops which had earlier defeated the Armenian republic withdrew to the west in 1918, obeying the requirements of the armistice of Mudros. McCarthy estimates that at least 400,000 Muslim refugees fled Armenia during this period (2001:143). Spurred on by reports of massacres of Muslims, this former Ottoman army, which included many Kurdish soldiers, was mobilized under the command of Kazim Karabekir (McCarthy 2001:143). On 30 October 1920, Karabekir defeated the Armenians once again, and reestablished the 1877 borders between Russia and the Ottoman Empire. At the peace treaty signed two months later, Armenia gave up all claims to eastern Anatolia.

In October 1923, the nationalist government of Mustafa Kemal agreed a new treaty at Lausanne. Three bitter years of fighting on the heels of World War I had left the young government weak. In the negotiations at Lausanne, the Turkish nationalist government representative, Ismet Pasha, had little choice but to accept Allied demands on matters that did not touch directly on the heart of Turkish independence in Anatolia. Thus, he accepted British and French rule in Palestine, Syria, and Iraq. He also begrudgingly agreed that the status of the Kurdish province of Mosul, which the Turks viewed as an integral part of Anatolia, could be decided by the Council of the League of Nations.[33] The Treaty of Lausanne completed the expulsion of populations with a final exchange of Greeks and Turks between Greece and Anatolia. Kurdistan was divided between four newly created states carved out of the Old Ottoman Empire: Turkey, Iran, Iraq, and Syria.

For the Kurds living in their largely mountain villages, these new lines defining the postwar territorial states made little difference to daily life. However, in Turkey, from a prewar population of 17.5 million, four million people had been lost between 1914 and 1922. The religious and ethnic character of the state had also changed massively with the flight and expulsion of Christians (mainly Greeks and Armenians) and the in-migration of Muslim refugees (mainly Bulgarians, Muslim Greeks, Albanians, Kosovars, Tatars, Circassians, and other Transcaucasians). The Kurds largely remained in their homelands, although much of Kurdistan was now divided and occupied by the British and their allies. In the British-mandated Iraq, the British first depended upon Kurdish and Assyrian levies to support their occupation. The Assyrians were refugees from Kurdish southeastern Anatolia who had lost their support in Russia when the October 1917 Revolution had toppled the czar.[34] This auxiliary

---

[33] The Council of the League of Nations later gave Mosul to British-mandated Iraq. See the decision of the XXXVII session of the Council of the League of Nations, 16 December 1925 (Vanly 1980:161–162).

[34] After the Russian October 1917 revolution, the Assyrians found themselves with no support and unable to return to their original homes in Kurdistan. British agents made contact with them with a view to recruiting them to help in the war effort. 50,000 Assyrians were given refuge at the British headquarters in northern Iraq. At the Paris Peace Conference, Assyrian delegates demanded 'An Assyrian state under the protection of some mandatory power in order that the Assyrian people might be freed from the repetition of the former barbarities to which they have been subjected for centuries' (Al-Rasheed 1995:244). The British attempted to resettle the Assyrians into their villages in Kurdistan. In 1920, with the support of 6,000 armed Assyrian men, their attempt to move north failed due mainly to Kurdish opposition. Instead, the British enlisted the Assyrians into a gendarmerie force to protect the refugees as well as the Mosul frontier. By 1928, the levies were almost entirely Assyrian. Eventually, the Assyrians were moved to

army of nearly 7,500 Kurdish and Assyrian men became almost entirely Assyrian by the late 1920s as the Kurds grew increasingly restive.

After the defeat of the French and the Greeks in Anatolia, Mustafa Kemal and his nationalist government set up the radical restructuring of Ottoman society and state in order to create the Turkish republic. Although many Kurdish intellectuals worked alongside him in this effort, many other Kurds, mainly tribal, were uncomfortable with the reforms he was to institute. Mustafa Kemal 'Ataturk' was determined to alter the language, education, form of government, clothing, place of religion, and even 'self-identification' or citizenship of the people in this new state. In order to do so, he needed to wipe out any persisting beliefs in Ottomanism – the concept that the state could be a multiethnic order. With nearly one-fourth of the population of Anatolia dead during these war years, and a massive Muslim in-migration of refugees, Mustafa Kemal decided to focus on reform and the creation of a homogenous Turkish citizen.

The greatest breaks with Ottoman tradition were religious and cultural. Ever since the Tanzimat era of the mid-nineteenth century, the Ottoman Empire had set itself on the path to Europeanized reform. Now, however, Mustafa Kemal would break with the past. In 1922 he abolished the Ottoman sultanate and in 1924 the Islamic caliphate. Religious groups continued to provide welfare and education, but the millet structure was abolished. The Sufi brotherhoods were outlawed, and oriental symbols, such as Muslim religious clothing, veils for women, old-style peasant clothing, and the fez, were discouraged. In addition, a European calendar was adopted, polygamy abolished, the Arabic alphabet was replaced by Roman characters, and the surname, in the tradition of Europe, was adopted by all.[35] In the place of the millets and Islam came the state (McCarthy 2001:210–211).

The 1919–22 War of Independence had forged the first mass Turkish nationalism. Kemal Ataturk believed it was essential to develop this nationalism. No thought was given to continuing with the Ottoman tradition of ethno-religious identity. The difficulties, however, were that although many of the current inhabitants of Anatolia were descendants of Turks who arrived long ago from Central Asia (or who joined with the Turks in some earlier era and had become Turks linguistically and ethnically), others had been added to this mix more recently and were not

---

Habaniyyah, a British Royal Air Force base, and were increasingly used to suppress Arab and Kurdish revolts (Al-Rasheed 1995:244).

[35] Mustafa Kemal was given the surname of Ataturk, 'Father Turk' by the parliament (McCarthy 2001:211).

linguistically or ethnically assimilated: Circassians, Abkhazians, Laz, Kurds, Arabs, Bulgarian and Greek Pomaks, and Sephardic Jewish. Mustafa Kemal Ataturk needed to formulate an inclusive nationalism to integrate all these peoples. For Ataturk, there was no room for minorities; all the population of Anatolia had to assimilate, speak Turkish, and accept the secular state (McCarthy 2001:212–213). Non-Turkish ethnic expression was suppressed. For most of those who did not have Turkish heritage, this was a problem. The main antagonists were the Kurds. Some Kurds accepted this ideology, became 'ethnic' Turks, and went on to be full partners in the governing of the Turkish republic. However, for many Kurds, this assimilationist nationalism was repugnant and became the focus for building solidarity for Kurdish separatism and rebellion.

KURDISH SEPARATISM AND NATIONALISM

In 1922, Mustafa Kemal was finally able to defeat the government of Constantinople which, as heirs to the Ottomans, had signed the Treaty of Sèvres. He then set about proclaiming his intention to create a modern republic of Turkey in which the Kurdish and Turkish peoples would live as equals and with full 'ethnic rights'. In the name of that fraternity between Kurds and Turks, which the new government had adopted as one of its slogans, the Turkish republic called on the British to hand back the old Vilayet of Mosul.[36] The British, however, issued a declaration that solemnly recognized the rights of the Kurds in British-mandated Iraq to form an autonomous Kurdish government within the frontiers of Iraq.[37] The British hoped to obtain international confirmation of the control of Mosul within the Iraqi frontiers and thus secure the rights to exploit the oil fields of southern Kurdistan.

Although Kurdish delegates were present at the negotiations leading up to the Treaty of Sèvres, none were present at the negotiations in Lausanne in 1922–3 to replace the now-defunct Treaty of Sèvres. At the negotiations, Ismet Inonu and Lord Curzon, as heads of the two countries' respective delegations, each claimed deep concern for the interests of the Kurds. But in fact, the real bone of contention was simply a border dispute between the republic of Turkey and the Arab kingdom of Iraq (represented by the

[36] During the Turkish War for Independence 1919–22, Kemal Ataturk felt it was important to keep Kurds fighting with him rather than in opposition. Thus he paid lip service to a state where Kurds and Turks could live side by side (Kendal [Nezan] 1980).
[37] This was the Anglo-Iraqi Joint Declaration communicated to the Council of the League of Nations on 24 December 1922.

British Colonial Office). The negotiations were inconclusive on the issue of the Kurds other than a few articles insisting on respect for the linguistic and national rights of Turkey's non-Turkish minorities. More significantly, the Treaty of Lausanne recognized Turkey as a new power and furthermore stipulated that the Turkish–Iraqi frontier was to be fixed along 'a line to be determined in conformity with the decision of the Council of the League of Nations' (Article 3 note 2 of the Treaty of Lausanne).

Throughout the Independence War years, military officers under the command of Mustafa Kemal took pains to stamp out any emergent attempts at forming specifically Kurdish organizations or associations. The Kurdish club at Diyarbakir, for example, was closed down in 1919. The Kurds who had contributed heavily to the fighting forces on both the eastern and western fronts thought they were building a state in which 'Turks and Kurds would live as brothers and equals', as Mustafa Kemal had promised (Kendal [Nezan] 1980:57). However, within three months of the successful conclusion of the Turkish War for Independence, on 1 November 1922, Mustafa Kemal declared to the National Assembly that 'the state which we have just created is a Turkish State' (Kendal [Nezan] 1980:57).[38] The Kurds were quick to rise up in protest and the next two decades witnessed scenes of constant revolts in Kurdistan.

SHAYKH SAID REVOLT

The first such rebellion began fomenting towards the end of 1922 when a few Kurdish deputies founded a Committee for Kurdish Independence in Erzurum with links to the main towns in Kurdistan. A number of Kurdish religious leaders joined the movement the following year. On 2 March 1924, on the very day that the Islamic caliphate was abolished,[39] a government decree was issued banning all Kurdish schools, associations, publications, religious fraternities, and schools in a determination to assimilate the Kurds into the Turkish state. The break between the government of Mustafa Kemal and most of the population in Kurdistan was complete.

---

[38] This contrasted directly with the speech of the Turkish representative at the Treaty of Lausanne negotiations who stated that 'Turks and Kurds are equal partners in the government of Turkey' and that 'although Turks and Kurds may speak different languages, these two peoples are not significantly different and form a single block from the point of view of race, faith and custom' (Ismet Pasha's speech to the 23 January 1923 session of the Conference of Lausanne).

[39] The Islamic caliphate is a form of government representing the political unity and leadership of the Muslim world. From the time of Mohammed until 1924, successive caliphates were held by the Umayyad, the Abbasid, and finally the Ottoman dynasties.

From 1925 to 1939, there were constant revolts and peasant uprisings in Kurdistan. The first major revolt or insurrection was that of Shaykh Said who was determined to create an independent Kurdish state. Within the space of a few months he and his partisans were able to take control of one-third of Kurdistan in Turkey and besiege the city of Diyarbakir while other Kurdish units were liberating the region north of Lake Van. The Turkish government sent the bulk of its armed forces, 80,000 men, into the region and, with the approval of the French government in Syria, was able to send fresh troops along the northern Syrian railroad and thus encircle the Kurdish forces besieging Diyarbakir. The uprising was eventually put down in April of 1925, some of its leaders were taken prisoner, and others sought refuge among the followers of powerful Kurdish tribal leaders such as Simko in Iran or among the Kurds of Iraq and Syria. In September 1925 Shaykh Said and fifty-two of his followers were hung in Diyarbakir (Kendal [Nezan] 1980:62–63). Thousands of Kurdish peasants were killed and hundreds of villages were burnt to the ground. This wave of repression resulted in tens of thousands of Kurds fleeing to Syria, Iraq and Iran.

MOUNT ARARAT REVOLT

Many of the Kurds who had fled to Iran and Iraq in 1925 began to regroup around Mount Ararat in response to efforts of the National Kurdish League (*Hoyboun*) which had been formed somewhat earlier in Lebanon by some Kurdish intellectuals and tribal leaders. Its founding conference, held in August 1927 in the mountain resort of Bhamdun, Lebanon, brought together representatives of all Kurdish parties and political organizations. An Armenian leader of the Dashnak Party also attended. As a result of the agreement between the Kurdish and Armenian leaders, the Ararat region, not far from Soviet Armenia, was chosen as the centre for a new uprising. In addition, the Shah of Iran saw cooperation with this group as a way of forestalling a Kurdish revolt in Iran under the leadership of Simko. In 1929 the Kurdish forces had seized control of an area stretching from Mount Ararat to the northern parts of Van and Bitlis. By June of 1930, the Kurds had taken 1,700 prisoners and seized 600 machine guns and 24 canons. They had shot down 132 aircraft. By then, the Turkish government had managed to come to an agreement with the Shah of Iran who agreed to cut off his aid to the Kurds. The Kurdish rebels were surrounded and the rebellion was put down at the end of the summer of 1930. The ensuing government violence against the Kurdish community was fierce, sending thousands more Kurdish families into exile. By 1932, the Turkish government had passed a law ordering the deportation and dispersion of the Kurds throughout Anatolia, while Kurdistan itself was to be partially repopulated by Turkish immigrants.[40] Towards the end of 1935, the mass deportation of Kurds was stopped, in response to a new revolt in the Dersim region.

POPULAR RESISTANCE IN DERSIM

Dersim was a particularly mountainous region of Kurdistan that had always retained some autonomy. Its people had not joined the *Hamidiyyah* Cavalry, had not participated in the Russian–Ottoman wars, World War I, or the Turkish War of Independence. It was the last pocket of Kurdish resistance. The Turkish government began a determined campaign to pacify this region in the spring of 1937. By the end of the summer, despite massive artillery and air bombardments and the use of poison gas, the Turkish army still had made no tangible gains. By the middle of 1938, the government sent in three Army corps and most of its air force to batter the region. Finally in October 1938, the people of Dersim were defeated. The region was devastated. Some reported that during the decade-long struggle, more than one and a half million Kurds had been deported and massacred (Kendal [Nezan] 1980:68). The whole affair had reflected so badly on the Turkish government that for the next thirty years the region was kept out of bounds to foreigners. After the fall of Dersim, there were no more major armed uprisings in Kurdistan. The massacres, the massive deportations, the militarization, and the systematic surveillance of the Kurdish territories had greatly intimidated the population. Open revolt ceased to be a credible avenue towards self-determination and liberty.

Over the years, the Kurdish national movement's centre of gravity has shifted. It first emerged in Turkish Kurdistan between 1925 and 1938. Then it moved to Iraqi Kurdistan from 1943 to 1945 when Mustafa Barzani led a revolt in Barzan. His fighters managed to overrun the Iraqi army in the area of Arbil. In 1945 the British Royal Air Force pushed these Kurdish rebels into retreat in Iranian Kurdistan. This was followed by a brief Kurdish flourishing in 1946 when an autonomous democratic republic was set up in Mahabad, Iran. A year later, the small Kurdish republic had collapsed and Barzani and his best fighters forced their way through northern Kurdistan and took refuge in the Soviet Union where they stayed for eleven years (Vanly 1980:163). Between 1961 and 1975, the centre of

---

[40] The full text of this law can be found in Bedirhan and Yayınları (1997).

Kurdish resistance was once again in Iraq. In the wake of the overthrow of the Iraqi monarchy in 1958, Abdul Karim Kassem had promulgated a provisional constitution which recognized the rights of the Kurdish people and welcomed Mustafa Barzani back from the Soviet Union as a hero. However, within two years, these promising beginnings had come to nothing. Kassem specifically rejected Kurdish demands for autonomy and started a campaign to assimilate the Kurdish people. In September 1961, he entered into a programme of air bombardments against the Kurds designed to bring them to their knees. The Kurdish 1961 revolution then began as a movement seeking to secure the autonomy of the Kurds within the framework of the new Iraqi Republic.

In 1963, after the Baathist takeover, the campaign against the Kurds was renewed with important support from the Syrian Baath Party (Vanly 1980:167). Several years of 'peaceful accommodation' of Kurdish demands for self-determination in Iraq followed before the government launched a new offensive against them in 1965.[41] In 1970, after long and laborious negotiations, a truce was announced between the government of Iraq and the Kurds as represented by Mustafa Barzani and his Kurdish Democratic Party (KDP). Among numerous articles in the truce pertaining to the rights of Kurds to self-determination and to share in the national government was the recognition of the Kurdish nation, recognition of the linguistic and cultural rights of the Kurdish nation, and a general amnesty for all civilians and soldiers. This truce – like those before – was very short-lived as the Iraqi government embarked on a campaign to 'Arabize' significant parts of Iraqi Kurdistan. Along with attempts to assassinate Mustafa Barzani, Iraqi military units began a campaign to force an exodus of Kurds from the region, and to introduce Arab tribes to take over their lands. In 1973, the attack on Sanjar, where particularly brutal house-to-house searches took place, resulted in thousands of Yazidi Kurds fleeing and seeking refuge elsewhere. In February 1974, Kurdish workers in the Kirkuk oil industry were expelled and replaced by Arabs. Hundreds of Kurdish families had to leave, many taking refuge in Syria. This policy of door-to-door harassment, aerial bombardment, and the use of poison gas as well as the occupation of villages continued throughout the next two decades sending more refugees across the borders with Iran, Syria, and Turkey and elevating the level of Kurdish guerrilla warfare against the Iraqi Baath government of Saddam Hussein.

[41] Michel Aflaq, the Greek Orthodox Syrian founder of the Baath Party, had been aware that some could interpret Arab nationalism as excluding non-Arab minorities. For him, the socialist dimension of Baathism included national minorities.

TABLE 6. *Timeline of Kurdish revolts*

Date	Events
1919–1920	Shaykh Mahmoud Kurdish revolt against British occupation. South Kurdistan (Iraq). Quelled by British.
1920–1930	Simko revolt against Iranian domination (Iran). Assassinated in Tehran 1930.
1923	Shaykh Mahmoud second revolt against British occupation. Exiled to India.
1925	Shaykh Said revolt in Turkish Kurdistan. Arrested and hung. Followers go into exile in Syria.
1930	Hoyboun (Kurdish National League) Mount Ararat insurrection against Turkey and Iran. Quelled.
1931	Jafar Sultan revolt in Iranian Kurdistan (after assassination of Simko in Tehran). Quelled.
1931	Sheikh Mahmoud third revolt in Iraqi Kurdistan. Put under house arrest in Baghdad.
1933	Barzani led uprising in Iraq. Quelled.
1936–1938	Guerrilla war by Kurds in Dersim, Turkish Kurdistan.
1943–1945	Barzani uprising in Iraq; flees into Iran.
1946	First Kurdish Republic at Mahabad destroyed in 1947. Barzani flees to USSR.
1956	Kurds in Iran rebel; put down by joint Iranian and Iraqi forces.
1961	Kurdish insurrection in Iraq.
1963	New offensive against Kurdish insurrection Iraqi Baathi with Syrian Baathi support. USSR warns Iraq, Iran, Turkey, and Syria not to launch joint offensive in Iraqi Kurdistan.
1964	Kurdish movement splits Talabani PUK (Patriotic Union of Kurdistan) and Barzani KDP (Kurdish Democratic Party).
1965	Renewed fighting in Iraqi Kurdistan.
1967–1868	Kurdish guerrilla war in Iran.
1967	Iraqi war against Kurdish partisans relaunched.
1974	Iraqi war against Kurds stepped up.
1977–1978	Hundreds of Kurdish villages on the Turkey, Iran, and Syrian frontiers destroyed in Iraq; many Kurds flee into Syria.
1979	After the fall of the Shah, violent clashes between Kurdish fighters and Iranian supporters of Ayatollah Khomeini, guerrilla operations; Peshmergas regain control of Kurdish cities in Iran.
1980–1990	Iraqi programme to disperse Kurds and Arabize Kurdistan; Saddam Hussein launches chemical warfare after failed Kurdish assassination attempt.
1990–2003	Iraqi Kurdistan becomes safe haven for Kurds fleeing Saddam Hussein to prevent their crossing Iraqi border; Kurdish refugees enter into Syria.
2003–present	Iraqi Kurdistan becomes Regional Kurdish Government in Iraq. Repression in Turkey results in new wave of Kurdish refugees to Syria.

Sources: Chaliand, 1980; O'Balance, 1973; Fuccaro, 1999; Van Bruinessen; McDowall, 2005.

Then in 1990, with the misjudged and misguided attack on Kuwait, the Iraqi government was put on a back foot. The north of Iraq was taken over by the Allied Western powers and declared a no-fly zone; the region was put under international protection as a 'safe haven' for Kurds. This was as much to protect Kurds from reprisals by the government of Iraq as to prevent them from crossing the frontier and seeking refuge in Turkey – where the government had made clear they would not be welcomed.

The twentieth century has been one long series of Kurdish revolts and uprisings in an effort for self-determination – if not actual separatism.[42] During and after each uprising in Turkish, Iranian, and Iraqi Kurdistan, Kurds fled cross the frontiers of these nation-states to reach safety and to regroup among close kin or other Kurds. Movement back and forth, clandestine but carefully regulated by Kurdish fighters or *Peshmergas* across the little patrolled Turkish, Syrian, Iranian, and Iraqi border was common. Only in Syria was there no uprising or revolt. Instead, Syria became a place of exile as well as a political refuge for its leaders and political parties such as the Kurdish Democratic Party (KDP), the Patriotic Union of Kurdistan (PUK) and between 1980–98 the Partya Karkari Kurdistan (PKK).[43]

Beginning in the 1920s and continuing throughout the century, Kurdish forced migrants have entered Syria to seek asylum among Syrian Kurds. The following section focuses on the integration of Kurdish refugees and exiles among Syria's indigenous Kurdish population over the past century, beginning with the 1925 Shaykh Said revolt. It examines the way in which these forced migrants found new places to live and regroup. It examines the factors which gave Kurds in Syria space to integrate yet maintain their Kurdish language and culture. Despite the vagaries of recent political fortunes in Syria, many Kurds, even those who have recently become stateless (bidoon) have managed to keep their cultural and linguistic

---

[42] Self-determination is not always the same as separatism. During the mandate period, the French attempted to set up a number of separate states along different ethnic community lines in Syria; Druze, Alawite, and so on. However, this was rejected by these communities, who were determined to remain part of the greater whole. This was also the case with the Kurdish movements. Some were focused on self-determination within the framework of a larger state, while others were based on separatist agendas.

[43] The Kurdish political parties were largely neo-tribal confederations. The Kurdistan Democratic Party (KDP) was generally aligned with the Barzani tribe; the Patriotic Union of Kurdistan (PUK) was associated with the Talabani tribe and had a more distinct Marxist-Leninist leaning. Between 1980 and 1998 the Kurdish Worker's Party (PKK), led by Abdallah Ocalan operated largely out of Syria and Lebanon and had a clear socialist, revolutionary, and irreligious outlook (McDowall 2004:462–463).

heritage alive. The discrimination they face is, in part, discretionary and can be overcome by using social and political networks as well as local patronage systems. As a country that has been receiving Kurds for most of the past century, Syria offers an opportunity to examine the notion of migrant integration without assimilation.

KURDS IN SYRIA: STATELESS AMONG CITIZENS

Kurds are found throughout the Syrian Arab republic, although their greatest concentration is along the northern borders shared with Turkey and Iraq – those parts of Kurdistan ceded to the French-mandated Syrian state in 1920. Damascus alone has a population of 300,000 Kurds, most of whom live in Salahiyyah and the *Harat al-Akrad* (the Kurdish quarter) in the foothills above Damascus. This area was first settled in the twelfth century by the families of the Kurdish soldiers under the command of Salahadin during the Crusades. A similarly large Kurdish population lives in Aleppo. The most densely populated Kurdish area of Syria is in the 'Mountain of the Kurds' (Kurd-Dagh) to the north and west of Aleppo. Most of these inhabitants trace their lineage back even further than the Kurds of Damascus. Here, some 360 prosperous Kurdish villages represent the westernmost region of Kurdistan. Further east, where the Euphrates River enters Syrian territory, there are 120 Kurdish villages in the Ain al-Arab region. However, the largest Kurdish population in Syria is found in the Jazirah, which shares a long – 280 kilometres – border with both Turkish and Iraqi Kurdistan. During the Ottoman era, this region was nearly devoid of permanent settlement and was shared by competing, and at times, hostile Bedouin and Kurdish pastoral tribes. Today, this region is made up of predominantly Kurdish villages – more than 700 – and Christian towns, most of which were settled during the French mandate period between 1920 and 1946. Most of the Arab population in this area was once nomadic, though many have since settled and practice seasonal and mobile animal husbandry interspersed with limited cultivation. The Kurds in the Jazirah are largely descended from refugees who fled across the borders from Turkey in the 1920s and early 1930s and also from Iraq during its many Kurdish insurrections and upheavals. Large groups of Christian refugees (Assyrian and other Eastern Church refugees from Kurdistan) also settled in the region. Qamishli, created by the French on the railway line, became an important settlement point as did Hassakah, which became the provincial capital of the region; Mosul, which had been the accepted provisional capital, was now separated from the Jazirah by an international border.

These three major regions of Kurdish settlement are separated from each other by pockets of heavily populated Arab concentrations. Thus, 'Kurdistan' in Syria is essentially a fractured territory, a noncontiguous area, where language, customs, and culture are well defined. The old generation Kurds generally speak Arabic in public though many retain their language in their homes and communities, while the 'new generation' Kurds tend to speak Kurmanji in public and maintain greater adherence to Kurdish traditional dress and customs. There are no official statistics on the number of Kurds in Syria. The likely current population is about two million, representing roughly 10 or 11 per cent of the population (Gambill 2004; Lowe 2006).

The Kurds today are the largest ethnic minority in Syria. They speak Kurmanji and are, by and large, Sunni. Many Kurdish refugees fleeing the failed Shaykh Said insurrection (1925) in Turkey, the military revolt around Ararat also in Turkey (1927–31), and other similar upheavals in Iraq were granted citizenship and became 'Syrian' during the French mandate (Nouri Pasha 1986; Tejel 2009). This process continued into the early years of the independent Syrian republic after 1946. In 1957, a group of Kurdish intellectuals, workers, and peasants founded the Kurdish Democratic Party in Syria on the model of the Iraqi KDP. Its aim was to obtain recognition for the Kurds as an ethnic group entitled to its own culture rather than as a separatist movement. It continues to exist but periodic crackdowns on all opposition parties in Syria have meant that the Kurdish leadership has faced frequent imprisonment,[44]

National identity in Syria has always been pliable and multi-layered. Partially as a heritage of the millet structure of the former Ottoman Empire and also as a legacy of the French-mandated state borders, contemporary Syria is a multi-ethnic and plural religious state, where pan-Arabism and the notion of a single national identity has not been straightforward. When France acquired the League of Nations mandate for Syria after World War I, it adopted a policy of promoting minority identity in order to weaken the Sunni majority. In its first few years, the French attempted to 'divide and

---

[44] Syrian political space during the mandate era was particularly tolerant of ethnic pluralism. Post-mandate politics was less tolerant with anti-imperialist and pan-Arab aspirations. A growing mainstream ideological unanimism encouraged a strategy of 'dissimulation' among the Kurds and other minority groups (Scott 1990). Under certain conditions, Kurds chose to cultivate their differences in order to challenge official ideology and at other times, like all Syrian citizens, they acted as though they adhered to the regime, its leaders, and its principles (Wedeen 1999). Kurdish elites and the fifteen political parties they represented had to find a political terrain which lay somewhere between submission and revolt (Tejel 2009). In that search, they often ran afoul of the government and thus periods of repression and crackdown on political parties were frequent.

rule' along a series of geographical and sectarian divisions by setting up separate administrations, for example, for the Maronites, the Alawites, and the Druze. These efforts were resisted by the people of Syria in the Great Revolt of 1925 (Provence 2005:14–20). Here, in Syria's diverse regions, ethnic, and sectarian groups – Arabs and the non-Arab Kurds alike, Muslims, Christians, Druze, and Jews – united for the common goal of the formation of the Syrian Arab nation (Provence 2005:13).

The Kurdish ruling aghawat class, however, in the early decades of the twentieth century was deeply tied with the former Ottoman system, and generally did not welcome the Arab revolt against the Ottomans led by the Sherif of Mecca nor the arrival of his son, Faysal, as the new ruler of Syria in 1918. As a member of the Syrian Congress of 1919, Abd al-Rahman al-Yusuf, the leader of the Damascus Kurds, opposed Syrian independence and quietly strengthened his contacts with the French before they had actually overthrown the kingdom of Syria in the summer of 1920 (McDowall 2004:468). A few years later, when the French needed troops to put down the Great Arab Revolt of 1925 led by Arab and Druze fighters, France deliberately recruited auxiliaries from the Kurds, Armenians, and Circassians to crush this uprising. Many of these Kurds were recent arrivals fleeing oppression in Turkey, but others were commissioned by their local leader and patron in the Kurdish Quarter, Omar Agha Shamdin.

The connection of Agha Shamdin and the French authorities has entered into local myth and even in 2006 he is mentioned in the narratives of the Kurds. One of my elderly Kurdish interviewees in the old Kurdish Quarter of Damascus told me:

There is an old proverb which says: 'An Arab can never be stingy; A Kurd can never be subservient; and a Cherkess can never be generous'. A Kurd is known for never being weak or compromising. That is why the Kurds were so appreciated by the French. They knew that Kurds are straight, honest people. Omar, Agha Shamdin, a most important Kurdish public figure from this quarter, used to be visited often by high-ranking French officers. They knew that he was held in greatest respect by the whole community. His requests of the community were met as one. The French knew that the loyalty of the community to Agha Shamdin could be also loyalty to them. (Yusuf 2006, Harat al-Akrad, Damascus)

When the Pan-Kurdish Independence Party, *Hoyboun*, was founded in 1927, it seems the French allowed it to operate as it caused Arab nationalists some disquiet. Before its first year had ended, however, the French curtailed its activities following a protest from Ankara concerning its anti-Turkish activities. The following year, one of Hoyboun's leading members, Prince Jaladat Badr Khan, published a Kurmanji Kurdish journal *Hawar* and developed the use of Latin script instead of the Arabic alphabet as the former was better suited linguistically to this Indo-European language. Also in 1928, a petition was submitted to the Constituent Assembly of Syria seeking official permission to use the Kurdish language alongside other languages and to permit the Kurdish language to be taught in the three Kurdish regions of Syria. These demands were no more than those required by the League of Nations when it awarded the Vilayet of Mosul to British-mandated Iraq in 1926. However, the French refused to accept this petition. Some Kurds continued to embrace a Kurdish nationalist agenda, but most Kurds in Syria worked within the broad movement for Syrian independence.

Today, other than the 'bidoon', most of Syria's Kurds have full citizenship and the same rights and opportunities as any other Syrian national. They are very aware of being Kurdish, and fully understand the complexity of their relation with the state. Some urban and affluent Kurds are in positions of power or influence and speak Arabic in public rather than Kurmanji. Other Kurds, however, particularly those more recent migrants, do face distinct discrimination. The latter group represent perhaps 1 per cent of the total population of Syria. However, since 2004 international political scrutiny has focused on this section of the Syrian Kurdish population. As Gambill remarks, the events of 2004 involving Kurds in Syria were 'a politically-timed initiative to pressure the Assad regime in the face of heightened Syrian-US tensions and Iraqi Kurdish political gains' (Gambill 2004; also see Lowe 2006; Montgomery 2005:80).

I was born in a Christian village in Jazirah. My mother was originally Christian. She was born in a village in Turkey. After the trouble and famine of the 1920s her family fled with others. A Turkish Muslim family took her in and brought her up. They married her to a son of theirs, but she couldn't stand it. She met my father and they both came to the Jazirah where they got married. My father was born in Turkey. His father had been an officer in the Turkish army. After Shaykh Said was executed, he didn't want to continue serving in the Turkish army and left for Syria. He came with the brother of Shaykh Said, Abdul Rahim. After first arriving in Jazirah he settled in Harat il-Akrad, in Damascus and stayed for 18 years. Then he moved back to Jazirah to be able to encourage Kurds to be aware of their national identity. He was concerned to create and reinforce strong national feelings in Kurdish youth telling them that when they have their own state, they would become public figures and ministers. The Syrian authorities did not approve of my father's activities he was arrested and subjected to great humiliation.

I have six daughters and one son. We all speak Kurdish at home, but in school all my children learn Arabic. Some of my children speak it so well that no one would guess that they are Kurds. But it is forbidden to learn Kurdish in schools. Teaching Kurdish is carried out by political parties and involves only adults. We are not members of any party. But my son can read Kurdish. He studied French literature at the University of Aleppo. So he can read Kurdish because it is written in Latin and he can write it. My father-in-law advises us not to be affiliated with any party Kurdish or Arabic. He believes that parties will destroy the unity of the Kurdish nation. There are now 14 to 15 Kurdish political parties in Syria. (Um Lorens 2006, Aleppo)

Official Syrian government discrimination against the Kurds did not emerge until the late 1950s and was partially in response to the instability and uncertainty faced by neighbouring governments in Turkey and Iraq with their own Kurdish populations.[45] Paranoia took hold, perhaps fuelled by the growing Kurdish separatist movement in Iraq as well as the discovery of oil at Karachukin in 1956 and at Suwaydiyah in 1959 in the Kurdish heartland of Syria. Tensions were heightened between 1958 and 1961, when Syria joined Egypt to form the United Arab Republic. Kurds were accused of undermining Nasserite pan-Arabism and a number of leaders of the Syrian KDP were arrested on the orders of President Nasser (Nazdar 1980:215). Furthermore, the large representation of Kurdish intellectuals in the Communist Party of Syria (CPS), led by the Kurd, Khalid Bakdash, did little to assuage the concerns of the Syrian government. The year following the end of the union of the United Arab Republic, Syria turned inward and took a decided look at its northernmost province, where so many non-Arabs lived. Its concerns about growing Kurdish 'foreign' elements possibly disrupting the country led to the study of existing population figures. Official numbers between 1954 and 1961 were indicating a 25–30 per cent increase in the population of Hassakah over the seven-year period. This province, once a lawless area controlled by Kurdish and Bedouin tribes, became, after French mandate pacification, a fertile agricultural region with great potential as the country's next breadbasket. The Syrian government was understandably concerned by its rapid population growth. Indeed, as one British diplomat put it: 'It seems doubtful if the Damascus government could easily control the area if Kurdish dissidence from within Syria's borders or an irruption by Kurdish tribesmen from without, should disturb the uneasy tranquillity' (FO 371/164413 1962).

---

[45] Under the umbrella of Great Britain and the United States, Turkey, Iran, and Iraq signed the Baghdad Pact. One of the clauses of this agreement envisaged the coordinated repression of any revolts in any one of the states. This was carried out in Iran to put down the rebellious Kurds of Juanroj (Iranian Kurdistan) by combined Iraqi and Iranian armed forces. Such activity could only cause alarm in Syrian government circles where Kurdish political activity had recently come into play with the formation of the Syrian branch of the Kurdish Democratic Party (Chaliand 1980:236).

In August 1962, the government promulgated a special decree author-
izing an exceptional population census in the governorate of Hassakah. All
non-Arab inhabitants had to prove, by documentation, that they had been
resident in Syria prior to 1945. As a result of that census, some 120,000
Kurds were stripped of their citizenship.[46] The official justification for the
enactment of this measure was that these were 'alien infiltrators' from
Turkey who had recently crossed 'illegally' into Syria and hence had no
entitlement to citizenship. Many of these now stateless (or bidoon) people
had actually fled into Syria from Turkey in the 1920s and 1930s and had
bona fide citizenship papers granted during the French mandate. The local
designation for these peoples stripped of their citizenship papers was
ajanib (non-citizen foreigners) on their new, red identity cards. They
could not vote, own property, or hold government jobs, but the men
were still expected to do military service. Those who failed to take part
in the 1962 census or who were born from marriages between the ajanib
and Syrian citizens were in a worse situation as they could not even be
registered. These unregistered persons or *maktoumeen* (those who are
muted) do not exist in official records and face even greater discrimination
and hardship than the ajanib. Sources estimate that there are currently
200,000 ajanib and maktoumeen in Syria.[47] Others put the figure higher,
with 200,000 ajanib and 100,000 maktoumeen (Montgomery 2005:80).
Not only can these stateless (bidoon) Kurds not vote, as is the case for
Palestinian refugees; they are not allowed passports and have no travel
documents thus they cannot leave the country. Their entitlement to education and health care is discretionary; the local village or urban neighbourhood mukhtar (mayor) has the power to grant or deny such access. As
individuals without a standard Syrian identity card, they have difficulty
travelling internally on public transport and cannot even stay in a hotel.

We are quite comfortable. Our children all went to school; we have made a lot of
Arab friends. I am proud of my Kurdish nationality, but this has not interfered with
my respectful relations with the Arab community in which I live. I do wish to see my
people liberated from any kind of colonialism. I would like to feel free to do what I
feel like doing without fear of being questioned. For example, I would like to feel

---

[46] A number of my informants told me a similar story to the effect that Jamal Abdul Nasser,
    on a visit to the *Jazirah*, was reported to have noted that the region was being overrun by
    Kurds. His advice to the Syrian president was to be careful to monitor the situation
    otherwise the sheer number of Kurds could cause the security services trouble. This,
    then, was the common Kurdish narrative regarding the rise of discrimination in Syria.

[47] Both ajanib and maktoumeen are official designations. *Bidoon* is the local term or collo-
    quialism employed by Kurds themselves to refer to their 'statelessness'.

free to speak my language and hang the Barzani picture on the wall of my home. Also I would like to see all Kurds have identity cards ... The husband of my daughter doesn't have one and their children are not registered. He [Um Lorens's son-in-law] was born here. The identity cards held by the Kurds were taken away from them in the census of 1962. They were withdrawn from them in order to deny the existence of Kurds in Syria. For example, I have six sisters. They all have identity cards but their husbands don't. My son-in-law doesn't have one although he was born here and his parents came about the same time as mine. Some cards have been restored. It is completely up to the mukhtars (mayor) of the village to determine who would have his identity card restored. The mukhtars – some are Arab and some are Kurds – are like feudal lords. Some feel it is not in their interest to grant citizenship to Kurds in their village for fear that one day the Kurds might ask for a share of the land. This is why some were given their identity cards back and some were not. The husbands of my six sisters have the red identity cards. They are a kind of refugee. They have no right to own property, to travel outside of Syria or to hold a government job. (Um Lorens 2006, Aleppo)

In the fifty years since such discrimination became widespread in Syria, there has been little organized Kurdish political agitation to address this inequitable and discriminatory policy. Part of the reason may be due to the disunity among Kurds in Syria where traditional ties of loyalty to family and tribe are paramount and where political parties are cautious and take careful measures to curry favour rather than antagonize the government. A considerable number of Kurds in Syria have fought in Kurdish uprisings in Iraq and Turkey. Such activity parallels Syrian government support for the Turkish and Iraqi Kurdish nationalist movements (Kurdish Democratic Parties of Turkey and Iraq)[48]. Furthermore, a substantial number of Syria's Kurds see themselves as part of a multiethnic Syrian nation. Many live and work in the major Syrian cities, serve in the Syrian army, and feel an attachment to the wider Syrian community. Amongst the most celebrated contemporary Kurds in Syria are Ahmad Kuftaro, the mufti of Syria between 1964 and 2004, and Khalid Bakdash, the renowned leader of Syria's Communist Party. Other Kurdish religious leaders are author-ized by the state to follow public careers, such as Shaykh Muhammad Said Ramadan al-Bouti, who has a popular religious TV programme and pub-lishes books in Kurdish (Pinto 2007:265). Thus, any Kurdish campaigns for restoring the citizenship of stateless Kurds in Syria (many of whom are probably recent migrants with strong links to family in Turkish or Iraqi Kurdistan) needs to be negotiated in such a way as not to undermine either

---

[48] The Syrian Kurdish Democratic Party, which was formed in 1957, had a number of its leaders arrested in 1959 at the time of the union with Egypt.

their own sense of Kurdishness in the Syrian 'Arab' Republic or the Syrian state's support for Turkish and Iraqi Kurds.

I was born in Qamishli in 1969. My father was born in Turkey, but it was my grandfather who brought him here when he was five or six years old. My grandfather had to leave Turkey on a personal matter, escaping a revenge crime. He chose to go to Qamishli because it was close to the border and there was a Kurdish community already there. He was the first member of the family to come. That was in the 1950s. He settled in a mixed Kurdish and Arab village where the community gave him mattresses and such things to get started. He had three sons with him and they all stayed here and got married. My father worked on the farm. I went to school until Grade 9. I could have taken the official Grade 9 certificate but I felt it was useless. There is no chance for the 'Bidoon' to get a government job. We don't have Syrian identification cards. My little boy who is doing very well at school has started to consider leaving school because he knows that he will not be able to get a job. He will not be able to travel outside Syria. The 'red identification card' we have states bluntly: 'Not valid for obtaining travel documents for travelling outside the country'.

I was born here in 1969. My family was in Syria when the census was conducted. But the census was not done properly. My grandfather's uncle and his family, for example, who came to Syria later than my grandfather, were granted Syrian citizenship and Syrian identification cards, but we were not. This was because documentation of who lived here and how long they had been here was based on the mukhtar's whims and interests rather than on actual facts. When asked ... about a person, it was his [the Kurd's] personal connection to that person [the mukhtar] that determined his ability [the Kurd's] to gain citizenship. If he said that a certain person had been in the country long enough to be eligible for citizenship, that person would then be considered as such. If not, he wouldn't. The mukhtars cheat and the data they provide is not fact-based. Because my birth was actually registered in 1969, I got my 'red' identification card. But my children are not registered and cannot get even a 'red' card. This is because their mother is a Syrian citizen and holds a Syrian identification card. In such cases, marriage between a Syrian and an ajanib, ['red card' holder] the marriages may not be registered and neither are the children. They say this year there may be a new law allowing registration of marriage between a Syrian and an ajanib. This will in turn make it possible to register the children. (Abu Alaa 2006, Damascus)

In the wake of the 2003 Anglo-American invasion of Iraq and the Iraqi Kurdish political gains in the territory adjacent to the Syrian Jazirah, Kurds in Syria – citizens, ajanib, and maktoumeen– have become restive. In 2004, Kurdish riots erupted throughout the country. This outbreak of ethnic violence was the worst the country had seen in several decades. Some sources recognized that although the disturbances were fuelled by popular frustration in the Kurdish community, the riots 'were not an entirely spontaneous eruption, but a politically timed initiative' designed to put internal pressure on the Syrian regime to match the international isolation it was facing in its refusal to support the Anglo-American invasion of Iraq (Gambill 2004).[49]

It is clear that the Syrian Kurdish community has begun to experience a political reawakening after the Syrian government, pressured by Turkey, agreed to end its specific support for Abdallah Ocalan's Kurdistan Worker's party, the PKK.[50] In 1998, Turkey massed 10,000 troops on Syria's northern border and demanded that the PKK be expelled and Abdullah Ocalan be handed over. Syria and Lebanon had been the home base of the PKK since at least the 1980s. Within a very short time after the PKK's formal withdrawal, Kurdish activists in Syria began to be more open in their criticism of the regime's policy regarding Kurdish assimilationist aspirations. After the death of the Syrian president Hafez Assad in June 2000, Kurdish activists felt particularly emboldened, as did many other civil rights advocates. It was the time of the 'Syrian spring' when a liberal ambiance, fuelled by the American push for 'democracy and human rights', pervaded the country. Political organizations met openly and stores began to openly distribute Kurdish books and music. Private Kurdish language classes proliferated. In 2002, Bashar Assad, the new president, visited the predominantly Kurdish province of Hassakah. This was the first time a Syrian president had done so in more than forty years. In December of that year, a new, younger generation of Kurds and their sympathizers emerged as the Yekiti (or Unity) Party, a pro-KDP group, and staged a sit-in demonstration outside the parliament building. They delivered a statement calling on the Syrian regime to remove the barriers imposed on the Kurdish language and culture and recognize the existence of the Kurdish nationality within the unity of the country' (Agence France Presse 2002; Gorgas 2007:269–276). Slogans like 'citizenship for Kurds' and 'end the ban on the Kurdish language and culture' were prominently displayed and captured on Syrian television. Security forces broke up this gathering and arrested a number of the activists. However, Kurdish books, newspapers, and music tapes and CDs continued to circulate freely. The Kurds and other social groups, striving for greater civil liberties, continued their agitation for several

---

[49] Syria supported the US-led invasion in the Gulf War of 1991 to liberate Kuwait from Iraqi occupation. However in 2003, Syria opposed the Anglo-American invasion of Iraq.

[50] Ocalan founded this Marxist-Leninist Kurdish national liberation movement in 1975. Operating largely from the frontier regions, PKK activities are reported to have led to an estimated 12,000 deaths between 1984 and 1994. In response, the Turkish government admitted to emptying out 2,000 Kurdish villages in an attempt to undermine and defeat the PKK (McDowall 2004:420).

months. At times this was permitted and at others, the activists were arrested.

On 8 March 2004, after the approval of an interim Iraqi constitution that recognized the KUP/KDP administrative and military control over Iraqi Kurdistan, the Syrian regime anticipated a resurgence of Kurdish activism in Syria. Less than a week later, on 12 March 2004, in Qamishli, fans of a visiting Arab soccer team arrived at a stadium and began shouting ethnic slurs and chanting pro-Saddam Hussein slogans. When fans of the Kurdish team responded with chants praising President Bush, the two sides began to scuffle. Security forces opened fire on the Kurdish crowd, killing six people and setting off a mass panic. This sparked a riot by Kurdish residents of the city. The unrest quickly spread to nearby towns where protestors torched the offices of the Baath Party and vandalized photos of the Syrian president and his late father. In the days that followed, the violence spread to Ain al-Arab, Aleppo, and Afrin in the Kurd-Dagh region. Protests also reached the Kurdish neighbour-hoods of Damascus. In an eight-day period, forty people were killed, four hundred injured, and more than 2,000 Kurds were arrested,[51]

The outbreaks of violence among Kurdish communities in 2004 and the typically heavy-handed Syrian security response have shaken many Kurds as well as the regime. For nearly fifty years, Kurds in Syria, newly arrived and long settled, have accepted the intransigence of government with regard to their community aspirations. These swings in official tolerance of difference or insistence on unanimous ideology were a reflection of internal politics in the Syrian state. The rise of the communist parties in the 1950s (with strong Kurdish membership), their demise with the take-over of the Baath Party, and the Correctionist movement of Hafez Assad after 1970 all impacted on how the Kurds and other minority groups fared (Hinnebusch 2001; Perthes 1995). The Syrian government's support for the three separatist movements – the KDP, KUP, and PKK, which was provided with a home base as well as refuge – meant that Syrian Kurds, in their 'gratefulness' for Syrian support for their struggle against Turkey, were largely muted from further agitation for cultural and linguistic rights in Syria (Scott 1990). Yet all the while, many Kurdish youth organizations ran informal courses teaching the Kurdish language as well as literature (Pinto 2007:261–2). However, once the PKK had been closed down in

---

[51] In the summer of 2005, the Syrian government announced that it was considering award-ing nationality to 120,000 Kurds. There have been further reports of officials visiting ajanib and carrying out a census in preparation for this (Lowe 2006:6).

Syria and, furthermore, after a Kurdish Regional Authority had been established in Iraqi Kurdistan, many Syrian Kurds, particularly the youth, began an active, and at times violent, agitation for the rights of all Kurds in Syria to be recognized as citizens. At the same time, the Syrian government, concerned with the Anglo-American occupation of Iraq and disconcerted by the 'separatist' presence of the Kurdish Regional Government in the north of that country, began to view its own Kurds with suspicion as possible enemy collaborators in the event of an American-led attack on Syria. Given such political positioning, it is not surprising that Kurdish youth in Syria have begun to take a militant and uncharacteristic violent stance.

Despite the recent flare-up of violence, Kurds have managed to maintain and keep alive their language and culture, poetry and prose, and songs and music through family efforts as well as community projects and associations. Their interests in Syria are not separatist, but rather to advance their own political, cultural, and social agenda to formalize their integration in the country by having the citizenship claims of all who entered the country prior to 1945 be recognized. They also seek to establish a reasonable process for acquiring citizenship for those who entered the country more recently. Citizenship, as well as the right to formally and publicly maintain their own language and cultural traditions through private education if not public school, is a key priority for all Kurds and is especially promulgated by the more militant Kurdish organizations. Not having to constantly adjust to the shifting Syrian political landscape, which at times aggressively outlaws Kurdish language and culture and at other times tolerates it, is now being demanded as a basic civil and human right. The unpredictable but regular closing down of Kurdish bookshops in Damascus and Aleppo between the 1950s and 1970s and the concurrent destruction of their publicly sold music cassettes and records need not be part of the future of Kurds in Syria (Pinto 2007:262).

I work in the construction business here in Damascus and live in a village where I rent a house from an Arab acquaintance. My sisters live with me and we all speak Kurdish at home but we don't know how to write it. It was forbidden to teach Kurdish in schools. Recently, I heard that Kurdish schools have been allowed in Turkey and Iraq. For me (and for my father), citizenship is vital for the future of our children. Even if they finish their studies as lawyers or doctors they cannot get government work. The 'red' identification card, which I can get for them after the registration of my marriage will [still] not allow them to work or to travel or to own property. I am doing all I can to encourage my son to finish his studies. I even promised him to smuggle him out of Syria, if necessary, when he gets his Baccalaureate. If I had two wishes, I would ask for Syrian citizenship and the teaching of Kurdish language in the schools. It is not much to ask to learn to speak, read and write one's own national language. (Abu Alaa 2006, Damascus)

Like the efforts to promote multiethnic nationhood in the last decades of the Ottoman Empire, the Kurds in Syria are struggling for recognition as Syrians and as Kurds in a state that is unofficially multiethnic but formally pan-Arab. As before, the future lies not only on what happens internally, but also on the regional and international scene. After decades of either subduing or ignoring Kurds in Syria while at the same time supporting Kurds in Turkey and in Iraq, the Syrian regime is at a crossroads, divided by both hard-line nationalists and pragmatic realists. It appears to be uncertain how to proceed. The Kurds in Syria, however, have found a voice and strength from these same international uncertainties. They are not imagining a homeland, they are living it. Their homeland is in the places where their communities live, in their strong kinship ties and patronage networks, in their language and culture. For many, the Kurdish homeland is in part of Syria and Syria is part of Kurdistan. The pivotal issue for most of my informants was the desire to be recognized as Syrian but with the right to speak their Kurdish language in public, to teach it to their children, and to listen to it on TV as well as to promote and play Kurdish music. It is a rejection of the periodic Syrian assimilationist policies while at the same time a common calling for the basic human and cultural rights of all Kurds in whichever state they choose to live.

7

Liminality and Belonging: Social Cohesion in Impermanent Landscapes

As the three great empires of Europe and the Middle East fell, the movement of people into and within the Middle East far surpassed that of those fleeing the region. The history of Ottoman tolerance for minorities is part of the explanation of this great inflow. However, the fact that Muslim refugees from the borderlands of the three empires were unwelcome both in Europe and in the new Soviet Union also determined that the first – or perhaps only – choice of movement was south and then west. Four such groups have been the focus of this book: the Muslim Circassians and related peoples; the Armenians and other Eastern Christian peoples; the Palestinians; and the Kurds. They represent a significant range of the ethno-religious communities who were dispossessed, uprooted, and made liminal. Eventually – and largely through their own efforts – these groups reestablished socially cohesive identities in the Arab Middle East assisted perhaps by the cultural memory of the Ottoman millet, which tolerated and encouraged ethno-religious 'otherness' and in some ways respected a local 'cosmopolitanism'.

This book has aimed to contextualize the experience of dispossession among these forced migrants within the international and regional political arena of its time. Furthermore, by highlighting the individual experiences of forced migration within the dispossessed populations, it has set out to understand the mechanisms whereby individuals and family members have created new communities, often without contiguous territorial bases. Understanding the context of these dispossessions and forced migrations permits us to grasp the immense individual and social price which such upheavals have demanded. It also permits us to comprehend and admire the capacity of the human being to survive, overcome indescribable suffering, and reconstruct social networks based on trust, moral faith, and empathy. This process has been described for refugee groups in Western contexts and been variously defined as processes of social incorporation, social cohesion, and social capital formation or the building of social relationships (Hudson et al. 2006; Zetter et al. 2007). However, little attention has been given to such processes in the Middle East, perhaps because the Western debate around refugee integration and the value of assimilation or multiculturalism is an extravagance that most practitioners, policymakers, and researchers in the region have had little opportunity in which to engage.

Most of the dispossessed groups which entered the Arab Middle East have succeeded in physically and socially integrating and creating new identities for themselves as minorities in one or a number of modern states (e.g., Armenian, Circassian, and Chechnyan). Some others have become stateless (Palestinian and Kurds); among them a smaller number occupy informal, shadowy places where they are socially and economically constrained, if not discriminated against. Some individuals and families belonging to these groups have left the region altogether, joining the ranks of refugees and émigrés resettled in Europe and North America (Palestinian, Armenian, Assyrian, Yazidis, and Kurds). Those who have remained have created real, virtual, and imagined coherent communities despite the often deterritorialized nature of their 'homeland' and cultural ideology. This dichotomy between those who leave and those who remain is not irreversible; nor do I mean to suggest a clean break between the two as movement between these far-flung places is ongoing in the form of family visits, transfer of resources, Internet connections, and other activity. That said, the minority communities re-created in the region – though not entirely self-contained – have a material and symbolic importance that overcomes their modern liminality and contributes to building a social cohesion from a number of factors as the quote below suggests.

My father was born in Yozghak, Turkey. His father had been killed (burnt alive with lime water) in the town and his mother had left Turkey with him and his older sister. His mother and older sister were both kidnapped by Muslims and he knew nothing more about their whereabouts. He arrived in Deir-ez-Zor by himself in 1915. He must have been 6 or 7 years old. He stayed there for a while and then was taken to Aleppo where he was put into an Armenian Church boarding school until he was 14. Then he was asked to leave the school and manage on his own because they needed the space for younger children. He knew nobody. First he went to Banias in the hope of joining some relatives there, but they couldn't support themselves so he had to leave. Then he went to Latakiyyah. There he slept in the street and managed to get small jobs as a porter. Sometimes he was paid and sometimes he wasn't. He used to eat the peel of the fruits left behind in restaurants. Later, he left with a couple of other Armenians and went to Beirut. There he managed to get a job with an electricity company. After a few more years he came to Damascus looking for an Armenian family he had known back in Turkey who had a girl he still remembered [early 1930s]. Her grandmother had a little money which meant she was able to smuggle her granddaughter and her son into Syria. The girl was only five years old when her father brought her to Damascus. Her father was an upholsterer and was able to find a job in Damascus in no time. My father found this girl. He married her and took her back to Beirut. He lived and worked there until 1957, when the Camille Chamoun revolution [sic] started. Then he left Lebanon and moved his family to Damascus to live in Bab Touma with three or four other Armenian families in one house.

I went to a private Armenian school in Beirut. My younger brother also went to the same school. My father could not afford to keep us both there, so I had to leave after grade 10 and start working. My brother finished and got the Baccalaureate. We studied in Armenian and also French. The school was sponsored by an Armenian charitable association, but we still had to pay something ... I got married in 1956. My wife's family was also from Turkey. They came to Deir-ez-Zor and then to Beirut. She had three brothers. They were my friends. Then they all died suddenly, one after the other, in just a few months. I felt so sorry for the family. I started to visit them frequently and bring them food. They were very poor. That is how I got to know her. We got married and lived together for forty years.

After two years, I got an offer to establish a furniture factory in Damascus. We came here and when I had made some money I bought an apartment. My wife used to work with the Armenian Charitable Association. She raised funds for them. She was a strong, intelligent woman. She was educated with a high school certificate and was the director of an Armenian school. Her school is supported by the Armenian Church. We have a certain number of poor students. We cannot afford to offer free education to all. Instead we take 2000 SP [$40] from an Armenian family and from an Arab who wants his child to attend we take 5000 SP [$100]. The number of non-Arab students in the school is increasing. It is the reputation of the school that counts. We have 400 students in our school and the numbers are increasing.

We had three sons and a daughter. My oldest is an engineer. The second, who is smarter, attended college for a year then dropped out. He preferred to work in our furniture factory. The third was not interested in studying. He dropped out at grade six. He worked in the factory for a while and then immigrated to Canada. He has been there for 20 years. He is doing very well. He established a very reputable furniture factory. He got married to an Armenian there. When my daughter finished high school and got the Baccalaureate, a young man from Lebanon proposed, I did not hesitate to accept. All our children speak Armenian at home and Arabic in public. Two of my sons married Arab women. When they are present, we have to speak Arabic whether we like it or not. But their children speak Arabic and Armenian. I sent them to a course to learn Armenian. When they come to visit, I insist that the grandchildren speak Armenian ....

I have more Arab friends than Armenians. I have a couple of Armenian friends with whom I get along well. On the other hand I have 20 Arab friends who keep visiting me and with whom I go out and have good times. I thought to visit the place where my father was born. But when I went to Turkey they warned me not to go there. They told me that the people there are monsters. If they knew you were Armenian they would kill you. Would I consider going to Armenia? That depends on the political situation there. That is what I care for most of all. So far, I don't approve of what is going on in Armenia. It has a 'mafia', so going to settle there is out of the question. (Hagop 2006, Damascus)

What are the prominent features of this narrative? It is the story of an Armenian orphan in the closing years of the Ottoman Empire, dispossessed and forced from his homeland. It is the tale of death and immense suffering with a grandfather murdered and a grandmother 'disappeared'. It is the story of exceptional resilience as a small child is forced to march hundreds of miles along the Euphrates River until he reaches Deir-ez-Zor where he is picked up and given care by a church charity. After an upbringing in an Armenian Church orphanage, it tells of the survival strategies of a young adolescent and then a youth who searches for and finds social links back to his village of origin and Armenian community. It is a snapshot of survival and refuge in both Syria and Lebanon during the French mandate period followed by gradual success in reestablishing links to a similar community of Armenian survivors both in Beirut and in Damascus. The Church-based education with its priority on Armenian history and language becomes the central core of the new family as it knits together, with the next generation entering the same profession established by the first generation survivor, not only in Syria but also in Canada. Marriage is both from within the refugee community and from the host community of Arabs. Yet the Armenian language and culture is perpetuated by the rise of charitable associations providing language lessons for both the young Armenian children and adults who have married into the community. This is not a family 'Arabizing' but rather one that is incorporating local women. There is no animosity toward local Arabs; quite the reverse, the link to the Arab community is strong.

The actual homeland is lived within the family and its networks and in the focus on perpetuating Armenian language and culture. It is not the same as the imagined homeland, nor is the Armenian republic the mythical home. The latter is run by 'mafia' and is not the idealized place to which he might one day return. He is settled in Syria where his identity is as a member of a minority, but the country has given refuge and provided him with the opportunity to flourish economically and socially. He is both a Syrian and an Armenian. His liminality is overcome by the strength of religious charities, educational establishments, and other faith based-organizations; his economic successes and social networks have gradually created a cohesive social network for himself and other families in the Armenian community. The history of his family's exile and dispossession assumes heroic proportions. The nearly unbearable pain and neglect which the orphaned young boy, the narrator's grandfather, endured enters into family lore; cleansed of the dirt, grime, and pain of forced migration, it becomes a tale of personal courage, strength, and dignity.

As with so many others interviewed for this study, the relations with the host community are consistently reported as strong. This is not to suggest an assimilation of the minority but rather a form of local cosmopolitanism.[1] Here, the minority maintains constant relations with other minorities and the majority culture. This extends beyond a recognition of being the 'Other', and at the level of the individual and family, describes the ways in which ordinary members of these ethno-religious and minority groups mix, mingle, and intensely interact with other groups sharing some practices such as the cultures of food, fashion, languages, and symbols in history and memory (Bayat 2008; Hannerz 1990). It is a cosmopolitanism from below, an almost silent process of cultural, religious and communal interaction reminiscent of inter-millet relations in the Ottoman period. It is what Rabo suggests for Aleppo, an 'everyday civility and co-existence' (Rabo 2008). This is the down-to-earth way in which ordinary men and women from different 'cosmos' in the Arab Middle East engage, associate, and live together at the level of the every day with an acceptance, even a celebration and curiosity of the 'Others' with no suggestion of competition or fear of a limited good.

---

[1] The terms *cosmopolitan* and *cosmopolitanism* are originally derived from ancient Greek Stoic ideals of man as rooted in a narrow *polis* with the *cosmopolis,* a city of the world in which all people were equal, independent of race and class. In contemporary discourse, cosmopolitanism and globalization have become keywords but with diverse and shifting meanings (Benhabib 2006:17; Zubaida 1999:15). Bauman, Benhabib, and others see a philosophical debt to Immanuel Kant and his ideas of the right of the world citizen or cosmopolitan right based on a duty of hospitality (c.f. Bauman 2006; Benhabib 2006). This hospitality is a right for all human beings and thus, in Hannah Arendt's terms, it is the basis for a right to have rights and the contemporary international discourse of human rights which she played such an important part in developing (1973:296). In the social sciences, the cosmopolitan discourse has shed some light on contemporary concepts such as multiculturalism and hybridity (Rapport & Stade 2007:223–235). Most relevant to this study is the distinction made between cosmopolitanism as an everyday practice and as a social-scientific ethos. It is the latter, the everyday cosmopolitanism, which I am addressing here (Bayat 2008:5).

DISPOSSESSION, DESTRUCTION AND RECONSTRUCTION

Most human beings reside somewhere near their places of birth. Willingly leaving home to live and work elsewhere or being dispossessed and evicted is more the exception than the rule. Yet, migration is the story of human life. The Fertile Crescent of the Middle East has been the focus of centuries, if not millennia, of largely involuntary movements of people; the terrified flight of some groups, and the opportunistic entrance of others to fill the unoccupied spaces left behind. For much of the last five hundred years, this largely forced movement of people was absorbed by a system of government which encouraged and tolerated variations among people, drawing out subtle differences between similar peoples and encouraging the formation of unique identities based on religious, linguistic, and cultural commonalities. The state that encouraged such minority status and limited self-governance – the Ottoman Empire – came to an end with World War I, which saw the Russian and Austro-Hungarian empires crumble as well. In the new states which emerged in the former European provinces, the violent displacement of people – often through 'voluntary' as well as compulsory exchange – was generally accompanied by a variety of state and international (Western) assistance which included the granting of citizenship, housing aid, the provisions of land, and sometimes financial packages as well as employment. Thus, for example, Asia Minor Greeks were taken and given space to live by the Greek state. The League of Nations' Refugee Settlement Commission (RSC, the effective predecessor of the United Nations High Commission for Refugees), financed by high-interest international loans, assisted with land allocations and agricultural start-up packages for the Asia Minor Greeks; but no similar League of Nations' packages were offered to the Greek Muslims sent into Asia Minor. Between 1923 and 1930, some 2,000 villages were created (at the Greek state's direction) in the newly conquered zones from which Muslims had been forced 'voluntarily' to leave (Hirschon 1998; Loizos 1999). One such settlement was in Nea Kokkinia, a then little occupied zone near the port of Piraeus. There, a heterogeneous mix of Christians from Asia Minor arrived in 1923 and were assisted by the RSC to construct durable temporary housing. Surveyed in 1930, they were found to be the poorest of the refugees. Forty per cent described themselves as labourers and many others as peddlers and craftsmen (Mazower 1991). By 1972, when Hirschon conducted her research, these refugees were no longer in dire poverty; they were however, structurally disadvantaged, earning only 70 per cent of the national average wage. But there was great pride in the way in which they had turned their original government-subsidized housing into permanent homes. They had also created a distinctive neighbourhood, which had become a morally integrated, in-marrying community (Hirschon 1998). This was not state-led social transformation or 'social inclusion', but a spontaneous neighbourhood initiative. At its foundation was the continued use of Asia Minor origins as a mark of distinctiveness based on the conviction that what they had in Asia Minor before their deportation was superior to the ways of life they found in Athens. This mythologizing of the past, the cleaning or erasure of the trauma and suffering of the deportations was not rooted in any hope of return – there was no such option; it was turned towards the Greek political system in the hopes of improving their economic disadvantage one day.

Those dispossessed, uprooted, and deported from the Ottoman European provinces, who struggled to build new lives and re-create communities among the rubble of the dead empire, were rarely provided with much national or international assistance. They were often left to their own devices to survive and reconstruct their social and economic networks and communities. Not having international support was balanced, however, by being in the midst of supportive social environments made up of discrete communities of people sharing common beliefs about their identities based on ideas of religion and, also, ethnicity (Barth 1969; Eriksen 1993). Here, in the Arab provinces of the Ottoman Empire, belonging was based not on a physical birthplace alone, but specifically included the social community of origin (Humphrey 1993; Kedourie 1984). As migration within the empire had long been tolerated and even in some cases encouraged, for religious and economic purposes, belonging was rooted in the connections and links between and among a specific group of people as much as, if not more so than, in a physical space or territory. Thus, when the Muslims from Crete arrived on the Asia Minor coast, they had been informed that they would be resettled on abandoned properties. Their transport had been arranged by the new Turkish republic and there was some very limited financial support (Ladas 1932:705–719).[2] On their arrival they often found that the formerly Greek Orthodox-owned lands and houses which should have been available to them had been appropriated by local people or government officials (Loizos 1999:245). Overall,

---

[2] The financial assistance offered by the Turkish state is given as one-twentieth the value provided by the Greek state from its international loans. Loizos, citing Onur Yıldırım, maintains that this was not because the Turkish government refused to seek foreign help but because Turkey could not get European credits when it requested them at the Treaty of Lausanne negotiations (Loizos 1999).

the Turkish government had no systematic plans for settling these refugees (or any others), nor was there any outside international aid. Once the initial determination of destination had been made and the small start-up packages for farmers distributed, the Muslim Cretans were on their own. In the struggle to create a new homeland for themselves, they largely re-created Crete in their new physical space. In the process, they maintained their 'otherness' while at the same time successfully integrating economically and socially into the Turkish republic. Without any assistance from the new republic, they transcended the isolation of their dispersal both with help from their immediate social surroundings as well as from within the new social group. Essentially they healed each other and built new communities based on trust, exchange, and mutuality. They, too, consciously retained a separate identity from the rest of their surroundings and thus actively sought to mark themselves out as an unassimilated minority.

One recent study among those Muslim refugees from Crete who settled in Cunda, an island north of Izmir, noted that the similarity in topography of this region with Crete allowed many to re-create the past in their present condition. The similarity of the terrain meant that many were able to carry on cultivating olives, raising sheep, and dairy farming as they had in Crete. Furthermore, as a result of the pre-1920s economic prosperity in both areas, there were many beautiful houses and buildings constructed in the neoclassical style (Koufopoulou 2003:209–219). These physical and ecological similarities made complete assimilation less likely. As Koufopoulou suggests, '[g]iven the recurrent visual reminders of their former residence and the similarities in landscape between their old and new communities, Cretans did not have to change their attitudes and lifestyles dramatically as they would have done if they had been relocated to a completely different environment. This similarity allowed them to live and identify themselves much as they had done in the past (Koufopoulou 2003:212–213). The Cretan Muslims in Turkey re-created their past by retaining certain selected key elements of their culture while other parts diminished in importance (cf. Hirschon 1998).

The process of re-creation, however, was not straightforward. Cretan Muslims who arrived at Cunda – the Kritiki, as they preferred to be called – found that they also had to create new economic links; they could not simply take up those abandoned by the Christians who had been expelled. A vibrant economic network between the island and Izmir had come to an end with the expulsion of the Greek Orthodox Rum bourgeoisie – but not the workers and farmers – as they had taken with them their specialized knowledge of trade links to Europe. These incoming Muslim Cretans lacked any trade networks or 'social capital' connections. So, rather than pick up where they had left off in Crete, there was an intense period of scrambling to make a living until these 'exchangees' (they preferred to differentiate themselves from 'refugees') were able to re-create and accentuate specific identities and social networks in order to recover from the trauma of their uprooting and liminality. Unlike many of the dispossessed peoples who gravitated to Europe, these Cretans chose to emphasize their distinctiveness and set themselves out as ethnic Cretans, while at the same time as Sunni Muslims and Turkish nationals. In Crete they had emphasized their 'Muslimness' in contrast to the Christians of the island, but here in their new homeland, they emphasized their origins from Crete as an identity which set them apart from those around them. Government assistance to these people had been minimal. Even the official state process of 'assimilation' – which included a brief period when in education and in the mass media the Cretan language could not be spoken in public or in the presence of Turkish officials – was soon dropped or loosely applied (Koufopoulou 2003:218).

The centrality of the Kritiki re-creation of their home and homeland is also emphasized by the fact that they lived and operated in a border area. Research has shown that borders have a significant impact on community life in terms of preserving double or multiple national and ethnic identities (Donnan & Wilson 1999; O'Dowd & Wilson 1996; Wilson & Donnan 1998). In the case of Cunda, from the earliest years of their uprooting and relocation, there has been considerable smuggling activity across the Greek–Turkish border. This activity began in the 1930s and was instrumental in establishing new economic networks for these 'exchangees'. It continues to this day and involves regular and sustained, if clandestine, contact between the two border communities (quoted in Hirschon 2003:218; Koufopoulou & Papageorgiou 1997). Thus, after seventy-five years, a distinctive Cretan identity has been maintained where language, cuisine, and a flair for commerce, trades, and crafts has emerged to set the Cretans apart from Turks. Although sharing the same religion with the Turks around them – the justification for their expulsion from Crete – their emphasis on their ethnic Cretan identity is a statement of what Loizos calls the 'maintenance of memory' (1999:246). They are Turkish, but they are also Kritiki, and it is their Kritikiness, expressed in language, food, and crafts, which makes them special and forms the basis of their social cohesion in a new physical space. In contrast with such Greek 'new villages' as Nea Kokkinia, where the conscious retention of a separate identity linked with their past in Asia Minor is expressed in their memory of difference, the Kritiki have set themselves apart physically, economically, and socially as integrated Turks but non-assimilated, socially cohesive Kritiki.

The nineteenth and twentieth centuries have seen a startling array of movements of communities once rooted in the frontier zones of the Austro-Hungarian, Russian, and Ottoman empires into the heartland of the former Arab provinces. Unlike the refugees who found asylum in Europe and America and were heavily assisted by humanitarian agencies, the dispossessed and displaced in the former Ottoman Empire had little help.[3] They included individual and family groups on the Russian–Ottoman border lands such as the Circassians, the Abkhazi, the Chechnyan, the Armenians, and other Northern Caucasus peoples such as the Ossetians, and the Laz (Barkey & Von Hagen 1997; Brubaker 1995). Other dispossessions had their origins in the lines drawn on maps by the Great Western Powers to create the new proto-nation states of Iraq, Syria, Jordan, Lebanon, and Egypt (Chatty 1986; Gelvin 1998; Helms 1981; Wilkinson 1983). The dispossessed from these board room and battlefield exercises included the Palestinians, Kurds, and the pastoral Bedouin. Some forced migrations, such as those of the largely Kurdish Yazidis and the Eastern Christian Assyrians, were closely linked to various efforts to create a pan-Arab, socialist, or Islamic state, thus driving out those peoples who were not seen to fit or who had allied themselves with a retreating or inferior Western power (Al-Rasheed 1994; Khalidi 1997). These refugees found new homes and built or created new communities without much attention or assistance from either the new Turkish republic or the international order.

---

[3] The League of Nation's Refugee Settlement Commission specifically set up to assist the Greek government in the resettlement of Christians from Asia Minor, Bulgaria, and Russia was a massive effort. A 'Marshall Plan' of its time, it involved more than 1.2 million people for integration and assimilation in Macedonia, Thrace, and the Greek mainland. The consequences of the settlement of these refugees were so dramatic that it literally changed the character of the land (Kontogiorgi 2006). The Armenians fleeing the massacres and forced marches as well as the general war zone were assisted by the American Committee for Armenian and Syrian Relief, which was founded in 1915 (after 1918 it was renamed the American Committee for Relief in the Near East, ACRNE) or Near East Relief. Its primary aim was to alleviate the suffering of the Armenian people. At first it was set up under the chairmanship of the US Department of State and operated by making direct transfers to Armenian missionaries and US consuls without Ottoman government involvement. By 1919, ACRNE had been incorporated into the USA by an act of Congress. That same year it raised more than $16 million for Armenian refugees, delivering food, clothing, and material for shelters as well as placing thousands of Armenian orphans in mission facilities within the USA.

They established themselves on new soil, but managed their memories so as not to lay down new roots, but rather to keep alive the past in such a manner as to strengthen the commonality and trust in their immediate social network. They were creating 'horizontal' moral communities with social capital that fuelled internal social cohesion; they were becoming integrated in the new states, but remaining separate and non-assimilated in important aspects.

DISSOLUTION OF THE OTTOMAN EMPIRE, THE 'UNMIXING OF PEOPLES' AND THE RE-CREATION OF DERACINATED 'COMMUNITIES'

The mid-nineteenth and early twentieth centuries marked the beginnings of modern, large-scale involuntary population movements across the Eurasian continent as the European, Russian, and Ottoman empires faced pressures to transform themselves into nation-states. The first such modern nation-state to emerge from the Ottoman Empire was Greece in 1832, which became a client state of Russia and Britain. Greece then steadily encroached on Ottoman territory and each of these gains precipitated the flight of part of the local Muslim population.[4] There followed the establishment of Bulgaria, Serbia, and Montenegro. Each new state sought to unmix their nationalities as their minorities came to be regarded as obstacles to state building.[5] As a result of the nationalist movements of the nineteenth century and the unmixing of peoples, Greek, Bulgarian, Romanian, and Turkish minorities generally sought to move from an area

---

[4] Greece acquired Thessaly in 1881, Crete in 1908, and Macedonia in 1913. These locations were largely evenly divided between Greek Orthodox and Muslims resulting in a massive flight of the Muslims to the remaining Ottoman territories. Those Muslims who chose to remain were later forced to move under both the voluntary and compulsory exchange of populations negotiated between Greece and Turkey at Lausanne in 1923.

[5] The term *unmixing of peoples* was attributed to Lord Curzon in his reflections on the Balkan wars (Marrus 1985:41). It later became a political slogan for negotiations at the Lausanne Treaty. This unmixing was regarded by some as a human rights disaster, and by others as a move which saved thousands of people seriously at risk of massacre. A few exceptions to this unmixing were permitted for political expediency and also to allow each party a 'toe-hold' in each other's state. Thus 1.3 million Asia Minor Turkish-speaking Christians were to be received by Greece, and Muslims in the new states of Bulgaria and Greece were sent to Asia Minor. Two exceptions were made to this compulsory exchange: the Greeks of Constantinople were allowed to stay as were the Muslims of western Thrace. This had little to do with sympathy for the individuals but rather rested on Greece's wish to see the Greek Orthodox patriarchate maintain its presence in Constantinople. In return for this concession, Greece agreed to permit an equal number of Muslims to remain in Greece.

where they had once constituted a minority, to another where their nationality was dominant. Consequent to the establishment of these nation-states, millions of people fled or were expelled, many of them Muslims and Jews who moved south seeking refuge in Asia Minor and the Ottoman heartlands (Kulischer 1948). At the same time, the European Zionist movement, also part of the Western penetration of the Middle East, was establishing settler communities in the southern Ottoman provinces, setting the stage for the dispossession and exile of indigenous Palestinians.

Circassian and Chechnyan Muslim refugees from the frontiers of the empire

It was the Russian imperial expansionist agenda which caused the most damage to the Ottoman Empire. It forced the creation of an independent Bulgaria, Serbia, and Romania by defeating the Ottomans in wars it had initiated. As detailed by Justin McCarthy, Russia dispossessed and ejected the native populations of Circassia and Abkhazia in the Caucasus, forcing the Ottomans to take in more than 800,000 Caucasian peoples at great human and civil costs. A further 900,000 Turks were also forced by the Russians to take refuge in the Ottoman Empire (McCarthy 2001:21). By the beginning of the twentieth century, at least 1.8 million Tatars had been evicted from the Crimea and into the Middle East (Karpat 1985:66). These forced migrations of Muslim groups from the Caucasus regions carried on throughout the 1880s and 1900s and increasingly included Chechnyan and Daghestani refugees from new areas of Russian conquests in the Caucasus. This last wave of forced migrants was estimated at another 500,000 people (Karpat 1985:67–70). The total movement of Muslim refugees from these Russo-Ottoman wars was more than two million.[6]

Armenians and other Christian refugees on the Russian–Ottoman borders

This tight ethno-religious community was recognized by the Ottoman state and had its own patriarchate and millet. By the 1850s two more millets had been established, in recognition of the growing number of Catholic

---

[6] Some historians have pointed to the return migration of Russian Muslims and have seen this process as cyclical rather than a one-way movement. Meyer argues that, except for the 1877/78 mass expulsions, return migration of Russian Muslims was also typical (Meyer 2007). He documents for the close of the nineteenth century a certain regularity of cyclical migration as Ottoman Muslims of Russian origin sought family reunion or trade.

and Protestant converts. After the withdrawal of Ottoman Orthodox Christians from Anatolia to become part of the newly created kingdom of Greece, many Armenians moved in to fill the high government administrative positions left open by the departing Orthodox Greeks. As Russia expanded into Transcaucasia, it annexed Georgia in 1800 and then, between 1804 and 1829, it occupied areas that today are the Azerbaijan and Armenian republics. Local Armenian nationalist militias aided these campaigns. However, when European powers forced Russia to withdraw and return some of these areas to the Ottoman Empire, their Armenian allies fled with them to Russia. In 1914, war erupted again between Russia and the Ottomans along the eastern Anatolian frontier. In 1915, the Ottoman government – worried about the loyalty of the Armenian community – ordered the deportation of the entire Armenian population of eastern Anatolia southward into the Syrian Desert. Between 1.5 and 2 million Armenians were forced from their homes and sent out on death marches along the Euphrates River towards Deir-ez-Zor and Mosul. At least half that number perished. The remaining 750,000 dispersed into Syria, Lebanon, Jordan, Palestine, and Egypt or found asylum abroad in France, Canada, and the United States.

Palestinians

Palestine was an integral part of the Ottoman Empire. Towards the end of the nineteenth century, Europe began to look to Palestine as a potential market for its Industrial Revolution as well as a source of raw materials. In addition, wealthy European Jewish entrepreneurs, later followed by Zionist organizations, looked to it as a potential bulwark of Europe against Asia, 'a vanguard of culture against barbarism' (see Herzl 1896). In 1915, Great Britain approached the Sherif of Mecca, Emir Hussein, to secure his support in opening a southern front in its war against the Axis powers. Once the British agreed to support an Arab state at the end of the war, Emir Hussein called on the Arabs to revolt against the Ottomans and to fight on the side of France and Britain.[7] A few months later, the Secretary to the British War Cabinet revealed a contradictory agreement with France and Russia which would have the lands of the Arab Ottoman Empire divided up between France and Great Britain, with Palestine placed

---

[7] Eight months earlier, Great Britain had reported to be 'prepared to recognize and uphold the independence of the Arabs in all regions (with some noted modifications) lying in the frontiers proposed by the Sherif of Mecca' (Antonius 1938:413).

under international administration and Russia managing Jerusalem (Tannous 1988:62–63).[8] A year later, in 1917, the Balfour Declaration was announced pledging support for the establishment in Palestine of a 'national home for the Jewish people'. For the next thirty years, the Arabs of Palestine fought against this declaration which undermined the entire spirit of the British League of Nations mandate to bring Arab Palestine to full independence. By 1947 the British had given up its League of Nations mandate and handed Palestine over to the United Nations. Within a few short months in 1948, nearly 750,000 Palestinians were forced from their homes and pushed into neighbouring states. It was an exercise in ethnic cleansing culminating in the dramatic upheaval called the *Nakbah* (Pappé 2006). Sixty years on, more than four million Palestinian refugees in the Middle East alone remain in exile.

Kurds

At the beginning of the nineteenth century, the Ottoman government began to regularly turn to Kurdistan to recruit troops to bolster its failing campaigns against the Russian and Austro-Hungarian empires. This move was regarded by many Kurdish traditional leaders as an infringement of their privileges. Kurdish territory also became the theatre for a number of Russo-Turkish and Persian wars. These campaigns brought a level of destruction which evoked strong Kurdish hostility towards the Ottomans. In the course of the nineteenth century, more than fifty insurrections broke out during which Kurdish feudal leaders either refused to pay long-established tribute or denied the Ottoman sultan Kurdish soldiers for his military campaigns. These uprisings were mainly aimed at maintaining and extending their age-old privileges. Up to the early twentieth century, when nationalist and secessionist movements generally gripped

---

[8] Zogby regards this move as a reflection of the need of Great Britain to maintain access to the ever-increasing volume of raw materials to fuel its industrial growth. It needed to protect these resources and markets from its rivals and hence Britain needed Palestine to protect the northeastern flank of this sea route to India and the East – the Suez Canal. Control of Palestine and the Fertile Crescent (Iraq/Mesopotamia) would make a land route to India possible. Thus, in his analysis, the Arabs were only temporary allies of Great Britain. A more permanent and safer client was the Zionist movement – a colonial movement in search of a patron. Herzl and his organization had actively engaged and sought out the Ottoman sultan in the late 1800s in efforts to persuade him of the benefits to the Ottoman Empire if he were to agree to their plan of establishing a Jewish state in Palestine. When Herzl and his group failed to persuade the sultan, he turned to Great Britain where he found sympathetic listeners (Zogby 1974:96).

the Ottoman Empire, few Kurds regarded themselves as anything other than members of their particular millet. In the Sykes-Picot Agreement, Russia made it clear that it wanted all of Ottoman Kurdistan and Ottoman Armenia. But Britain also set out claims to Mosul province as part of its plan for control of the recently discovered oilfields and the outlets in the Middle East. The French, however, wanted some of the southern Ottoman Kurdish areas to protect its interests in the railway concession in Anatolia.[9] These secret agreements – many of them contradictory – were setting the stage for one of the most dramatic land grabs in colonial history. In October 1923, the nationalist government of Mustafa Kemal agreed a new treaty at Lausanne accepting Allied demands on matters that did not touch directly on the heart of Turkish independence in Anatolia. Thus, he accepted British and French rule in Palestine, Syria, and Iraq. He also begrudgingly agreed that the status of the Kurdish province of Mosul (which the Turks viewed as an integral part of Anatolia) would be decided by the Council of the League of Nations.[10] The terms of this treaty divided Kurdistan between four newly created states carved out of the old Ottoman Empire (Turkey, Iran, Iraq, and Syria). Sixty years later nearly 23 million Kurds remain without a state divided among these four countries as well as in exile in Europe and elsewhere.

FROM LIMINALITY TO SOCIAL COHESION IN IMPERMANENT LANDSCAPES

Over the past 150 years the Middle East has provided refuge and asylum to numerous groups of people dispossessed of their property, their livelihoods, their neighbourhoods, and their community as a result of the upheaval leading to and including the end of empire and ensuing neocolonial enterprises endorsed by the League of Nations. Perhaps as a residual trait of the tolerance towards multiethnic and plural society that

[9] Ahmad notes that Russia was initially firmly opposed to giving any Kurdish parts of the Ottoman Empire to France, because it wanted the whole of Ottoman Armenia and Kurdistan for itself. However, after lengthy bargaining and coaxing, it agreed to let large Kurdish regions fall within the zone of French influence. Great Britain, which had no intention of giving up any of southern Kurdistan, did eventually decide there was some advantage to letting France realize its goal and thus avoid direct friction with the Russians in their zones of influence (Ahmad 1994:20).

[10] The Council of the League of Nations later gave Mosul to British-mandated Iraq. See the decision of the XXXVII session of the Council of the League of Nations, 16 December 1925 (Vanly 1980:161–162).

the Ottoman Empire had enshrined, the Arab Middle East has successfully hosted refugee and exiled minority cultures; the states themselves, while sometimes formally seeking to create homogeneous subjects, have tolerated, if not actively endorsed, the rise and establishment of these minority cultures.

The nostalgic wish to return to the imagined homeland while at the same time accepting the emergence of a substitute place with social networks and connections reminiscent of the Ottoman millet are clearly evident in this short excerpt from an interview with an Iraqi exile from Saddam Hussein's Iraq.[11] Currently he is officially a permanent resident in Denmark with his wife, two ex-wives, and children. Yet he repeatedly returns to Damascus for months at a time each year, seeking out his fellow Iraqi exiles, musician colleagues, and others in the cafés and private homes of the city.

I was born in Babel in 1944. I was exiled from Iraq in 1974. The irony, the satire or the black comedy, if you want to call it, was the fact that I enjoyed a good reputation as a composer [in Iraq]. While teaching in Basra, they wanted me to compose something for the regime (in praise of the regime). I tried to explain to them that, as a politically-oriented person, if I had been convinced of the principles of the party, I would have done something without being asked to. But since I was not, any music I would write would be vulgar, and would neither be good for them or for me. They couldn't accept this as an answer and they started placing a lot of pressure on me. I was first transferred from the position of a university teacher to the job of a clerk. Then they sent me home on open leave. Later I was transferred to Baghdad. Once I was moved to Baghdad, things got a bit better, but I am a 'bad' guy and I soon got affiliated with another [political] party. One day, a friend who was a party member dropped by at midnight and advised me to leave the country. Do you remember the movie 'Z'? That was exactly what was going to happen. I have a 'long tongue'. I tried to trim it but no luck. I was a member of the Communist party. I turned to the party and explained that it was urgent that I should leave the country. They gave me the option to go and study in Czechoslovakia. I did not do well in my study in Czechoslovakia and left for the Soviet Union. ... Now I am a permanent resident of Denmark. But since I am homesick for al-Sham [refers to Damascus], since I have a sickness called al-Sham you eventually find me here .... I have no family left in Iraq. Some were killed, some were exiled and others fled the country after the 1961 agreement. They went to

---

[11] Although Iraq has been producing political exiles for decades as individuals have fled for fear of their lives from the Baath Party of Saddam Hussein, they have dispersed widely throughout the Middle East, Europe, and North America (Chatelard 2009). As such, they do not form discrete social communities in the Arab Middle East as do the Kurds, Armenians, Palestinians, and Circassians. Since 2006, a wave of 1–2 million Iraqis has flooded into Syria and Jordan. If they do not return to Iraq in the coming few years, they may in time form discrete integrated but unassimilated minorities as well. But it is too early in this case of dispossession to predict.

Saudi Arabia and most of them are now with me in Denmark. The Red Cross in Denmark helped me bring them from the camp including my ex-wife ... But still I am homesick for al-Sham (Damascus). Damascus is the only place where I have never felt a stranger for one single minute. It is here that I have made such great close friends I can never do without. Al-Sham is my life breath, my "lungs". Through all my travels away from Iraq, my life's dream and the only justification for my existence has been to return to Iraq and be able to offer something that would contribute to its well-being and joy. I went there after the fall of the regime [of Saddam Hussein] with the intention of staying permanently. But I could not stand the amount of rubbish left over by the regime: the Ama'ems (Men's religious head wear) the pencils (spying and internal reporting) and all manifestations and forms of backwardness. I left Iraq when I was 29 and have had the dream of returning ever since. It didn't work. It is OK. Damascus is offering a fair compensation. (Kais 2008)

For Kais and many others like him, the reference to *al-Sham* is a complex association with the imagined past of the Ottoman Empire, of belonging to a millet rather than a piece of land. It is also the recognition of the sophistication of the local cosmopolitan, those ordinary men and women with whom the 'Other' is accepted, even celebrated. It is a reaffirmation of the commonality of cultural differences in this region where cultures, languages, and religions are not rooted in particular spaces but are carried in kinship and social networks and have a virtual and symbolic presence which is recognized and respected by insiders and outsiders alike.

Each of the narratives I collected over the past two years from among the oldest surviving generation of migrants whose families were dispossessed of their homelands and set onto a journey of real or metaphysical exile tells a similar story of extraordinary courage and resilience as well as luck. Among the Muslim Caucasians, the Christian Armenians and Assyrians, the Palestinians, and the Kurds driven out from Turkey and Iraq, the tales of the journeys to escape death or forced religious conversion are all similar. They describe traumatic physical hardship, accompanied by disease, starvation, and death. Generally these journeys were made by familial groups or small bands of orphans. The recollections are transformed by the imaginations of the listeners. In the telling, the stories are 'cleaned up' and made more bearable by the games which memory plays on human minds. They become heroic stories of exile, the backdrop to contemporary homelands, both imagined and re-created. These narratives bring the lived experience of exile and dispossession to the fore and provide glimpses of the social mechanisms which contribute to the successful integration without assimilation of these social groups into the states in which they have found themselves.

LIMINALITY AND BELONGING

In much recent scholarship on forced migration, the place of the refugee in the systems of nation-states has come to be examined. For some scholars, the refugee represents a liminal or interstitial node within the natural order of nations (Malkki 1990:34). Along with the displaced and stateless, refugees represent a challenge to the powerful, hegemonic system of nations (Anderson 1983; Herzfeld 1987:13; Soguk 1999). The nation-state system is increasingly regarded as belonging to an order of some antiquity even though it hardly emerged as a historical category much before the end of the eighteenth century in Europe and the twentieth century in the Middle East. Because refugees and forced migrants generally are viewed as outside the contemporary order of things, states have developed a system or routine for dealing with such categories of peoples. Prior to World War II, particularly in the Arab Middle East, central governments sought to transform the displaced and dispossessed into subjects and/or citizens as quickly as possible, regarding their liminality as a temporary physical condition to be overcome. Thus, each major wave of dispossession was accompanied by national or international responses of humanitarian aid and sometimes resettlement. Beginning with the 1859 Ottoman Refugee Act and including the American Committee for Relief in the Near East (Near East Relief) and the League of Nations Greek Refugee Settlement Commission, attention was focused on efforts to 're-place' people in space.

In the years immediately before and after World War II, a different instrument for managing and ordering the displaced and disposed emerged – the refugee camp. Here, a system of control and standardized routine became the principal tool for managing large numbers of displaced and refugee populations around the world. In the Middle East, the United Nations Relief and Works Agency, established in 1949, was set up to deal with nearly one million Palestinians displaced by the 1947–8 war. Here, the Agency provided the basics of life – food, shelter, health care, and primary education – but did not address the interstitial nature of the lives of the individual refugee. Refugee camps gradually became the focus of a surge in consciousness which set out to manage the liminality of the lives of the inhabitants in the form of the national liberation movement (Brand 1988b; Farsoun & Zacharia 1997; Peteet 2005; Rosenfeld 2004a). Based on her research among the Hutu, who fled Burundi in 1972 and who have lived as refugees in rural Tanzania since then, Malkki has identified what she regards as a widespread explanatory tool to understand this phenomenon. Refugees in camps, she maintains, live in conditions which promote an 'extremely historicized form of social existence' (Malkki 1990:34). Those who self-settle – in this case, those Hutu who made their way to the towns and set themselves up with little outside help – have a less well-articulated historical consciousness or collective narrative of their past to set them apart as a distinct people with their own historical trajectory. Following the definition of an imagined community as set out by Anderson, the Hutu camp refugees, then, would have a more highly developed sense of themselves as a moral community than would the self-settled Hutu (Anderson 1983:15). Although these ideas are highly pertinent to contemporary discourses about refugees and displaced people in general and the utility and significance of refugee camps in particular, the specific context of forced migration in the Middle East does not easily lend itself to such conclusions.[12] Palestinians, for example, both the self-settled and those within refugee camps, form a single 'imagined' community with a notion of a collective past and a sense of nationness and belonging to a particular place (Chatty & Lewando Hundt 2005; Farah 1999; Khalidi 1997). Whether in a refugee camp or living in a middle-class or poor urban or suburban settlement, Palestinians have a clear sense of their common belonging and community. In most refugee camps, the original homeland has been re-imagined and re-created, the neighbourhoods and villages reconstructed in the imagination as well as in the physical proximity of original inhabitants. The liminality or interstitial aspects of their lives are physically shared by those in camps and those who are self-settled. Both have created in the physical space around them a moral community drawn together by the common demand of the 'Right to Return'. Both incorporate and accentuate an aspect of liminality in their continued demand for their right to return to their original homes and villages. This stance both historicizes and mythologizes the homeland; the past is re-created and relived in new kinship ties and social networks in exile.

For the dispossessed and involuntary migrants of the Middle East, return to the homelands of origin is a hope, a nostalgic dream, or a unifying myth. Those early Muslim refugees of the nineteenth and early twentieth centuries knew they could not look back. They had to create their homelands on new spaces. None of the populations exchanged after the 1923 Treaty of

---

[12] Malkki makes clear that she is not implying that the Hutu were previously without consciousness or history. What she suggests is that in the specific setting of the refugee camp, a transformation in the production of historical and national consciousness emerges distinct from the forms which emerge in a self-settled context. Notwithstanding this conclusion, she also suggests that 'a heterogeneity of forms of consciousness can exist at once among particular groups of actors' (Malkki 1990:34).

Lausanne had any ambiguity about their condition. They knew they were not going to be allowed to return, and they had to get on with their survival and adjustment. The liminality might have been physical, but there was no question of their future. They had to create a new community, both imagined and moral, in which new ties or kinship and trade could emerge. Perhaps more than any other group, the Kurds alternated between a realistic hope and a nostalgic dream. Their homeland remains divided between four modern states, it can be accessed and visited, but it remains outside the contemporary order of nation-states. It is a place which no longer exists. It is now taken up by a frontier zone between states, thus offering those who so wish, a locality upon which to build a nostalgic aspiration.

Place and space

Most Palestinians living in refugee camps in the Gaza Strip, the West Bank, Jordan, and southern Lebanon are within a hundred miles of their original villages and urban neighbourhoods. Many Armenians have travelled back to visit their 'homeland' – both in Turkey and in the republic of Armenia. So, too, have the Circassians and other Caucasians. Some Kurds, particularly those who arrived in Syria in the 1920s, have managed to smuggle themselves across the border, sometimes on the backs of Peshmerga fighters, to visit their mountainous place of birth. Few have remained for more than a brief period of time. Some recognize that the locations they visit are the spaces where their imagined homelands once existed, but they are not the same; they no longer contain the social ties and networks that made the space a location, homeland, or a 'neighbourhood' (as defined by Appadurai), and so they return to their contemporary homes with new memories of their imagined homeland. Some are happy with their visits, with the discovery of long-lost social and kinship ties and, for a few, the discovery of a deep sense of belonging and peace. Although some of the younger generation of the displaced are now marrying back from the original community and building a further hybridity, for the most part the middle aged and, particularly, the elderly recognize that they carry their homelands within. It exists in their memories and in their relationships with their moral community.

Maintaining a moral community is hard work, as is the maintenance of the places that ground the social forms of that expression. These places are the localities and neighbourhoods of the social community. Turton, following Appadurai, distinguishes between locality as a phenomenological quality or dimension of social life and neighbourhoods as the actual existing social forms in which the locality is realized. It is, Turton continues, an 'inherently fragile social achievement'. Even in the most intimate spatially confined, geographically isolated situations, locality must be maintained carefully against various kinds of odds (Appadurai 1996:178–179; Turton 2004:22). In situations of dispossession and forced migration that re-creating and maintaining of a sense of place needs extraordinary work, everything from building a simple shelter or constructing a house or settlement to the reassertion of rituals, traditions, and institutions in order to bind a community of kin, neighbours, acquaintances, friends, and even foes together. The work of producing and reproducing such a community is a struggle in the best of times, entered into in order to keep at bay an endemic sense of anxiety and instability in social life (Appadurai 1996:179). In the context of dispossession, displacement, and dispersal, it is all the more difficult, stripping back existing connections and networks to minimal nodal cores. The effort to reverse the misfortune of displacement and dispossession and to em-place then becomes a strategy for survival and its success is a measure of the resilience of the forced migrant as exhibited by the new communities established by Circassians, Armenians, Palestinians, and Kurds in the Arab Middle East.

How successful forced migrants are in re-creating and re-placing themselves depends on the nature of the displacement, and dispossession itself. As both Kibreab (1999:406) and Parkin (1999:309) make clear, the way people experience movement to a new place and the extent to which this is a shocking and disruptive experience is determined by the conditions under which they move and whether they can extend their notions of territorial attachment to new areas not necessarily adjacent to each other. Thus the Cretan Muslims were able to re-create their identity in several new locations outside of Crete, on the northern coast of Lebanon and Syria as well as on an island off the coast of Izmir in Turkey.

For most forced migrants, however, the move is generally conducted in more traumatic conditions. The task of re-creating a place, home, or neighbourhood, of 'producing a locality' is dominated by the effort to reestablish some continuity with the past places of origin (Turton 2004:22). This work of continuity maintenance and management of memory is clearly articulated in the writings of Hirschon (1999), Parkin (1999), Malkki (1995), and Loizos (1999). Each of these authors describes the way in which forced migrants set about making new places through the telling and retelling of stories about former homes and places of origin, re-creating familiar aspects of the lost landscape and environment and its social networks. The tragedy of the displacement is thus transformed;

it both recognizes the experience of the loss of place and the pain that entails while at the same time recognizes the struggle to make a new place in a new world. The latter is conducted in a context in which others are also maintaining their 'differentness' in their own localities and neighbourhoods. The nature of post-Ottoman Arab society – as separate from its politics – has been such that it has tolerated and acknowledged multiple layers of belonging in the struggle to make new places in the world. Although not physically displaced, the peoples of the Arab provinces of the post-Ottoman Empire have spent most of the twentieth century creating new identities, and em-placing themselves in a new social order. Those dispossessed and entering the region during the late nineteenth and twentieth centuries, a time of widespread regional upheaval and destruction, found social environments conducive to the task of rebuilding, re-placing, and re-creating homes, neighbourhoods, and attachments to place.

Survival required individuals and family groups to knit together and re-create kinship and trade networks, as well as moral and nurturing support groups. These social relations then became resources used by the dispossessed and refugee groups to help them realize their goals of survival and social sustainability. Loizos (Loizos 2000) has elaborated on how refugees, in recognizing their shared values and norms of trust, expectations, and reciprocity, become 'social capitalists'[13] (this is drawn from the work of Coleman, 1988). He recognized that refugees and forced migrants use these ties to work together to reconstruct their social networks in exile and also to reinvigorate and reimagine their sense of shared social life and identity. It is, he has pointed out, the package of customs, beliefs, and practices from before their displacement which continue to serve them in their diasporic adjustments (Loizos 2000:132). Resilience to further adversity means that any social capital that had been stored and saved had to be directed at developing human capital for long-term survival. In the context

---

[13] James Coleman, developing his ideas from a theory of rational action, sees social capital like other forms of capital (physical and human) as being defined by its function. He sees social capital as productive, making possible the achievement of certain ends. Whereas human capital is created by the changes in persons that bring about skills and compatibles that make them able to act in new ways, social capital comes about through changes in the relations among persons that facilitate action. While physical capital is wholly tangible, human capital is less so. Social capital, however, is even less tangible as it exists in the relations among persons: in the trust and trustworthiness, responsibilities, obligations, expectations, norms, and sanctions that tie people together. Drawing on the example of family life, he demonstrates how the effect of social capital in the family and in the community aides in the formation of human capital in the next generation (Coleman 1988:100–104).

of the Arab Middle East, where the Circassians, Armenians, Palestinians, Kurds, and other minorities have struggled to survive and thrive, the social capital which has been created has also functioned in a defensive and protective role, essentially an internal coherence in a fragmented and at times exclusionary wider social environment. Following in a similar manner the argument made by Zetter in contemporary Britain, these newly established social communities, of often ancient ethnic stock, have pulled together into cohesive units or communities to create social capital both for their betterment and sustainability but also for their protection (Zetter et al. 2007).[14] The environment in which they have rehomed and relocated themselves remains preternaturally politically unstable. Thus the creation of social capital amongst these groups is a vehicle for intracommunity social cohesion in a landscape in which differentiation from the larger society is both a defensive mechanism against real and potential exclusion as well as a protective distancing tool for collective action.[15] The greater the self-reliance of the group, the stronger the supporting networks, norms and values, trust, and the sense of belonging in the face of an unpredictable and impermanent political landscape.

Identity and language

After numerous individual and family moves over the decades, these dispossessed peoples generally managed to find accommodation in close quarters with others from the same background. And in this manner they set about creating the social capital necessary to survive. These cohesive social communities were nearly all close knit, but not exclusively so. When the immediate blood family could not be established, fictive kinship was created. From within, they set up social and cultural associations where

[14] Community is a notoriously 'fuzzy' concept with many meanings. Some are place-based, as much of the policy-related work in the UK on refugee integration and assimilation suggests. Others are more imagined or virtual, linking people through their contacts and relationships (Pahl & Spencer 2003). This volume has regarded 'community' as much more in the latter deterritorialized category, although some communities in the Arab Middle East are physically coherent and contiguous entities.

[15] Kearns and Forrest develop this idea further by examining the ways in which the coherence of neighbourhoods can be argued to have developed a social cohesion as much for stability and harmony as for defence and potential conflict. The coherence of neighbourhoods (and in our case communities) is as much a product of how they are seen by external agencies and those living outside as by the social characteristics of the residents themselves. The acquired reputations of neighbourhoods can set them apart as places to avoid or attack. Thus social cohesion within can also exist in broader differentiated and unassimilated contexts (Kearns & Forrest 2000:1013).

their languages, social traditions, and transitional youth-to-adult activities could be conducted without external criticism or public depreciation. The relative separateness and isolation of these communities from the wider society meant that they had time and space to develop their human capital. The mechanisms of state control in nearly all the Arab Middle East also promoted this inward-looking community management and development. As long as individuals kept quiet and made little trouble, the state – reminiscent of the Ottoman era – managed its relations with the community through its traditional leadership or religious authorities. Charities, even among the poorest of these communities, were often funded from within to look after the less fortunate of their group. The state played almost no role in the welfare of the poor. Regularly, these communities invested in their religious institutions and hence the church or the mosque became an important source of respite and education. When marriage occurred from outside the community, the religious institutions generally made language classes and other related activities widely available for the outsider spouse.

It is the transmission of the language which most of these groups see as the link to the past, the imagined homeland and contemporary spaces they occupy today. In Amman, certain parts of the city are known to be Circassian or Chechnyan, the same in Damascus and in certain outlying Syrian towns. For the Armenians, parts of Cairo, Jerusalem, Beirut, Damascus, and Aleppo are closely associated with them; road signs and shop fronts accommodate both Arabic and Armenian script. The languages spoken on the street also support the otherness of the cultural identity of the community. So, too, for the Palestinians. Although many Palestinians are physically integrated into the cities and towns that gave them refuge in 1948 and 1967, others remain in the UN refugee camps dispersed throughout Lebanon, Syria, Jordan, the West Bank, and Gaza. Yet, even here, the camps have been framed by the Palestinian villages of origin, families often living adjacent to their village neighbours. Their village dialects are reinforced and passed down the generations, as are the particular recipes for foods and spices.

CONCLUSION

Although the Caucasian refugees of the nineteenth century were in many ways the pioneers for later forced migration of their Transcaucasian brethren, the Palestinians, Kurds, and Armenians were already present in the region. The history of migration within the Ottoman Empire in previous centuries was such that movement for trade or family reunion was common, and small communities of urban Armenians, Palestinians, and

Kurds were spread out throughout the region. Armenian communities had existed for centuries in Egypt, Palestine, and Syria as had the Kurds, who often delighted in tracing their origins back to at least the twelfth century and the troops of Salahadin and occupied well-defined quarters in the major cities.

These communities have absorbed the stories of origin and generally accepted a multiplicity of identities to accommodate both the past and the present. The language or dialect and the culture of these forced migrants is clung to and passed down from one generation to the next. It is rarely reinforced in the state education curriculum, but it comes alive in non-formal education as exemplified in the after-school clubs, social centres, and charitable associations which promote their language and particular customs that differentiate them from others. The Armenians in Egypt are Egyptian and Armenian; those in Lebanon, Lebanese Armenians; and in Syria, both Syrian nationalists and Armenians. Palestinians maintain their nationality and their right to return to their ancestral homes even when they take on citizenship, such as Jordanian. Similarly, the Kurds in Syria maintain their language, music, literature, and customs and live in close quarters to each other. Many are Syrian citizens, but a small minority are stateless and protest at being denied Syrian citizenship. Yet that protest does not diminish their Kurdishness.

These ethnic minority communities in the Middle East have found a way to physically and socially integrate themselves in their new surroundings, but at the same time have resisted the common phenomenon of assimilation over the long term. Although discrimination in one form or another exists in each of the states in which these forced migrants have created a new homeland, the pull to remain different, to maintain their otherness is more powerful. Patronage and real as well as fictive kinship networks are powerful positive forces; so too are the religious and charitable associations which these groups have set up to help those less fortunate in their community. These are people assured of whom they are and how they fit into the broader picture. There is no sense of liminality or marginality. They are confident in their language, their education, and their culture. They know they are at home and occasionally are specific in their rejection of the post-colonial created state that is meant to replace their imagined or mythical homeland, such as the republic of Armenia, the Palestinian National Authority, or the Kurdish Regional Authority in Iraq. These are people who are more postmodern than many of us. They are living in places where their imagined homelands can thrive. This allows them to integrate into the physical spaces they occupy, but not to culturally assimilate or lose their deterritorialized roots.

Bibliography

Abdul-Rahim, Adnan. 2005. Palestinian Refugee Children and Caregivers in Syria. In *Children of Palestine: Experiencing forced migration in the Middle East* (eds) D. Chatty & G. Lewando Hundt. Oxford and New York: Berghahn Books.

Abdul-Salam. 2005. *Interview 8 (October 25)*.

Abu-Rabia, Aref. 2001. *A Bedouin century: Education and development among the Negev tribes in the 20th century*. Oxford: Berghahn.

Abu Alaa. 2006. Interview 18, April 24. Damascus, Syria.

ACSHSS. 2003. Armenian Church timeline: Armenian Church Sourp Hagop Sunday School (ACSHSS).

Adel. 2006. Interview 15, April 7. Marj al-Sultan, Syria.

Agamben, Giorgio. 1994. *The Open: man and animal* (trans.) K. Attell. Stanford: Stanford University Press.

Agence France Presse. 2002. Kurds protest outside Syrian parliament against discrimination.

Ahmad, Kamal Madhar. 1994. *Kurdistan during the First World War* (trans.) A. M. Ibrahim. London: Saqi.

Ahmed, Sénia. 1994. *Letter from National Union of Saharawi Women*. National Union of Saharawi Women Letter.

Al-Natour, Souheil. 1997. The Legal Status of Palestinians in Lebanon. *Journal of Refugee Studies* 10, 360–377.

Al-Rasheed, Madawi. 1994. The myth of return: Iraqi Arab and Assyrian refugees in London. *Journal of Refugee Studies* 7, 199–219.

   1995. Iraqi Assyrians in London: Beyond the 'immigrant/refugee' divide. *Journal of the Anthropological Society of Oxford* 26, 241–255.

Ali. 2005. Interview 1, October 12. Damascus, Syria.

Allen, William E. & Paul Muratoff. 1953. *Caucasian battlefields: A history of the wars on the Turco-Caucasian border, 1828–1921*. Cambridge: Cambridge University Press.

Amnesty International. 2007. *Iraq: Human rights abuses against Palestinian refugees*.

Anderson, Benedict. 1983. *Imagined communities: Reflections on the origin and spread of nationalism*. London: Verso.

   1991. *Imagined communities: Reflections on the origin and spread of nationalism*. London: Verso.

Anonymous. 1909. Days of horror described: American missionary an eyewitness of murder and rapine. In *New York Times*.

   1977. Armenians in America (Special Issue). *Ararat* 18, 1–149.

Antonius, George. 1938. *The Arab awakening: The story of the Arab National Movement.* London: Hamish Hamilton.

———. 1946. *The Arab Awakening.* New York: Capricorn.

APJSO. 1997. Armenians in the Holy Land: The Patriarchate: Armenian Patriarchate of Jerusalem Support Organization (APJSO).

Appadurai, Arjun. 1996. *Modernity at large: Cultural dimensions of globalization.* Minneapolis: University of Minnesota Press.

Arberry, Arthur. 1969. *Religion in the Middle East.* Cambridge: Cambridge University Press.

Arendt, Hannah. 1973. *The origins of totalitarianism.* New York: Harcourt Brace Jovanovich.

Armenian Delegation. 1919. Réponse au mémoire de la Sublime-Porte en date du 12 février, 1919. Constantinople.

Ashkar, Antigona. 2006. *Perpetual limbo: Israel's freeze on unification of Palestinian families in the occupied territories.* B'Tselem.

Baer, Gabriel. 1982. *Fellah and townsman in the Middle East: Studies in social history.* London: Cass.

Barakat. 2005. Interview 6, October 18. Arnaout, Damascus, Syria.

Barber, Brian K. 2002. Politics, politics, and more politics: Youth life experiences in the Gaza Strip. In *Everyday life in the Muslim Middle East* (eds) D. Bowen & E. A. Early. Bloomington: Indiana University Press.

Barbir, Karl. 1980. *Ottoman rule in Damascus, 1708–1758.* Princeton: Princeton University Press.

Barbour, Neville. 1969. *Nisi Dominus.* Beirut: Institute for Palestine Studies.

Barkey, Karen & Mark Von Hagen (eds) 1997. *After empire: Multiethnic societies and nation-building: The Soviet Union and the Russian, Ottoman, and Habsburg Empires.* Boulder: Westview.

Barsoumian, Hagop. 1997. The Eastern Question and the Tanzimat Era. In *The Armenian people from ancient to modern times: Foreign dominion to statehood: The fifteenth century to the twentieth century: Vol. II* (ed.) R. G. Hovannisian. The Armenian people from ancient to modern times. London: Macmillan.

Barth, Fredrik (ed.) 1969. *Ethnic groups and boundaries: The social organization of culture difference.* Oslo: Scandinavian University Press.

Barton, James. 1930. *Story of Near East relief (1915–1930).* New York: Macmillan.

Baum, Wilhelm & Dietmar, Winkler. 2003. *The church of the East: A concise history.* London: Routledge Curzon.

Bauman, Zygmunt. 2006. The Fate of Humanity in the Post-Trinitarian World. In *Cosmopolitanism: Perspectives from the Engelsberg Seminar 2003* (eds) K. Almqvist & E. Wallrup. Varnamo: Axel and Margaret Ax:son Johnson Foundation.

Bayat, Asef. 2008. Everyday Cosmopolitanism. *ISIM Review* 22, 5.

Bedirhan, Celadet Ali & Avesta Yayınları. 1997. *De la question Kurde: La loi de deportation et de dispersion des Kurdes.* Istanbul: Avesta Yayınları.

Beinin, Joel. 1998. *The dispersion of Egyptian Jewry: Culture, politics, and the formation of a modern diaspora* (Contraversions). Berkeley: University of California Press.

Bell, Gertrude. 1902. Turkish Rule East of the Jordan. *The Nineteenth Century and After* 52, 226–238.

Benhabib, Seyla (ed.) 2006. *Another Cosmopolitanism* (The Berkeley Tanner Lectures). Oxford: Oxford University Press.

Bertier de Sauvigny, Guy de & David Pinkney. 1983. *The history of France*. Arlington Heights, IL: Forum Press.

Bhabha, Homi K. (ed.) 1990. *Nation and narration*. London: Routledge.

Bober, Arie (ed.) 1972. *The other Israel*. New York: Doubleday.

Bocco, Riccardo, Jaber, Hala, Al Husseini, Jamal, & Latte-Abdallah, Stephanie, 1999. The Palestinian Refugees and UNRWA in Jordan, the West Bank and Gaza 1949–1999 Amman, 1999.

Bocco, Riccardo, Ronald Jaubert, & Françoise Métral (eds) 1993. *Steppes d'Arabies, états, pasteurs, agriculteurs et commerçants: Le devenir des zones sèches* (Cahiers de l'I.U.E.D). Paris: Presses universitaires de France.

Brand, Laurie A. 1988a. Palestinians in Syria: The Politics of Integration. *Middle East Journal* 4, 621–637.

   1988b. *Palestinians in the Arab world: Institution building and the search for state*. New York: Columbia University Press.

Brandell, Inga & Annika Rabo. 2003. Nations and Nationalism: Dangers and Virtues of Transgressing Disciplines. *Orientalia Suecana* LI-LII, 35–46.

Brubaker, Rogers. 1995. Aftermaths of Empire and the Unmixing of Peoples: Historical and Comparative Perspectives. *Ethnic and Racial Studies* 18, 189–218.

Bryce, Viscount (ed.) 1916. *The treatment of the Armenians in the Ottoman Empire: Documents presented to Viscount Grey of Fallodon, Secretary of State for Foreign Affairs*. London: Her Majesty's Stationery Office (HMSO).

Castles, Stephen. 2000. *Ethnicity and globalization: From migrant worker to transnational citizen*. London: SAGE.

Castles, Stephen & Mark J. Miller. 2003. *The age of migration*. Basingstoke: Palgrave Macmillan.

Cattan, Henry. 1988. *The Palestine Question*. New York: Croom Helm Ltd.

Cernea, Michael M. 1993. Disaster-Related Refugee Flows and Development-Caused Population Displacement. In *Anthropological approaches to resettlement: Policy, practice, and theory* (eds) M. M. Cernea & S. E. Guggenheim. Boulder, CO: Westview.

Chaliand, Gerard (ed.) 1980. *People without a country: The Kurds and Kurdistan*. London: Zed.

Chatelard, Geraldine. 2009. What Visibility Conceals: Re-embedding Refugee Migration from iraq. Paper presented to the Dispossession and Forced Migration in the Middle East and North Africa. London, 2009.

Chatty, Dawn. 1986. *From camel to truck: The Bedouin in the modern world*. New York: Vantage Press.

   2007. Researching Refugee Youth in the Middle East: Reflections on the Importance of Comparative Research. *Journal of Refugee Studies* 20, 265–280.

Chatty, Dawn & Gillian Lewando Hundt (eds) 2005. *Children of Palestine: Experiencing forced migration in the Middle East*. Oxford: Berghahn Books.

Chirguh, Bletch. 1930. *La question Kurde* (Publ., Ligue nat. kurde Hoyboun), no. 6. Cairo: Paul Barbey Publisher.

Chorbajian, Leon. 1982. Armenians and Middle Eastern Americans. In *America's ethnic politics* (eds) J. Roncek & B. Eisenberg. Westport, CN: Greenwood Press.

Choucair, Julia. 2006. Lebanon: Finding a Path from Deadlock to Democracy. In *Carnegie Papers Middle East Series, 64*: Democracy and Rule of Law Project, Carnegie Endowment for International Peace.

Churchill, Winston. 1933. *The Great War*. London: George Newnes.

Clark, Bruce. 2006. *Twice a stranger: How mass expulsion forged modern Greece and Turkey*. London: Granta.

Clifford, James. 1988. *The predicament of culture: Twentieth-century ethnography, literature, and art*. Cambridge, MA: Harvard University Press.

Cohen, Anthony P. 1985. *The symbolic construction of community* (Key ideas. Chichester: Ellis Horwood.

Cohen, Robin. 1995. *The Cambridge Survey of World Migration*. Cambridge; New York: Cambridge University Press.

    1997. *Global diasporas: An introduction* (Global diasporas). London: Routledge.

Coleman, James S. 1988. Social Capital in the Creation of Human Capital. *American Journal of Sociology* **94**, 95–120.

Collier, Joseph (ed.) 1978. *American ethnics and minorities*. Los Alamitos: Hwong Publishing Company.

Condor, C. R. 1892. *Heth and Moab*. London.

Crivello, Gina. 2003. *Dreams of passage: Negotiating gender, status and migration in the Moroccan Rif*. PhD dissertation: University of California.

Dadrian, Vahakn N. 1997. *The history of the Armenian genocide: Ethnic conflict from the Balkans to Anatolia to the Caucasus*. Oxford: Berghahn.

Davison, Roderic H. 1954. Turkish Attitudes Concerning Christian-Muslim Equality in the Nineteenth Century. *American Historical Review* **59**, 844–864.

    1963. *Reform in the Ottoman Empire, 1856–1876*. Princeton: Princeton University Press.

    2003. Turkish Attitudes Concerning Christian-Muslim Equality in the Nineteenth Century. In *The Modern Middle East* (eds) A. Hourani, P. S. Khoury, & M. C. Wilson. London: I. B. Tauris.

Des Pres, Terrence. 1988. *Praises and dispraises: Poetry and politics, the 20th century*. New York: Viking.

Donnan, Hastings & Thomas M. Wilson. 1999. *Borders: Frontiers of identity, nation and state*. Oxford: Berg.

Doumani, Beshara. 1992. Rediscovering Ottoman Palestine: Writing Palestinians into history. *Journal of Palestine Studies* 21.

Dowty, Alan. 1987. *Closed borders: The contemporary assault on freedom of movement*. New Haven: Yale University Press.

Eagleton Jr, William. 1963. *The Kurdish Republic of 1946* (Middle Eastern Monographs, no. 5). London: Oxford University Press.

Eisenhower, John S. D. 2001. *Yanks: The epic story of the American Army in World War I*. New York: Free.

El-Abed, Oroub. 2003. *The Palestinians in Egypt: An investigation of livelihoods and coping strategies*. The American University in Cairo Executive Summary.

    2004. *Unprotected in Egypt: Living and coping as a Palestinian*. Cairo.

    2009. *Unprotected Palestinians in Egypt since 1948*. Jerusalem: Institute of Palestine Studies.

El-Hamamsy, Laila. 1975. The Assertion of Egyptian Identity. In *Ethnic identity: Cultural continuities and change* (ed.) G. D. Vos. Palo Alto: Mayfield.

Eriksen, Thomas Hylland. 1993. *Ethnicity and nationalism: Anthropological perspectives* (Anthropology, culture, and society). London: Pluto.

Erikson, Erik. 1968. *Identity: Youth and crisis*. New York: W.W. Norton.

Fairchild, Henry Pratt. 1925. *Immigration: A world movement and its American significance*. New York: Macmillan.

Falk, Richard & Asli Bâli. 2006. International Law at the Vanishing Point. In *Middle East Report*.

Farah, Randa. 1999. *Popular memory and reconstruction of Palestinian identity: Al-Baq'a Refugee Camp*, Jordan. Ph.D.: University of Toronto.

Farsoun, Samih K. & Christina E. Zacharia. 1997. *Palestine and the Palestinians*. Boulder: Westview.

Fasheh, Munir. 1995. The Reading Campaign Experience within the Palestinian Society: Innovative Strategies for Learning and Building Community. *Harvard Educational Review* **65**, 66–92.

Fletcher, Richard. 1992. *Moorish Spain*. London: Weidenfeld and Nicolson.

FO 78/2847. 1878.

FO 78/2848. 1878.

FO 195/1201. 1878.

FO 195/1202. 1878.

FO 195/1368. 1881. Stewart, July 14.

FO 195/1886. 1883. Damascus consular report.

FO 195/1932. 1895–6. Damascus consular report.

FO 371/164413. 1962. Report on the census taken in the province of al Hassakah, 8 November.

FO 424/70. 1878. Layard to Salisbury (confidential report 585/600), May 10.

FO 424/210. 1906a. Lloyd, Constantinople, April 16.

424/210. 1906b. O'Connor to Grey (enclosure no. 28), April 16.

Freeman, Edward Augustus. 1877. *The Ottoman power in Europe: Its nature, its growth, and its decline*. London: Macmillan.

Freer, Goodrich. 1905. In *A Syrian saddle*. London.

Gambill, Gary C. 2004. The Kurdish Reawakening in Syria. *Middle East Intelligence Bulletin* **6**, 1–8.

Gauld, W. A. 1927. The 'Dreikaiserbundnis' and the Eastern Question, 1877–8. *The English Historical Review* **XLII**, 560–568.

Geertz, Clifford. 1963. The Integrative Revolution: Primordial Sentiments and Civil Politics in the New States. In *Old societies and new states: The quest for modernity in Asia and Africa* (ed.) C. Geertz. New York: Free Press of Glencoe.

Gellner, Ernest. 1983. *Nations and nationalism (New perspectives on the past) (Basil Blackwell Publisher)*. Oxford: Basil Blackwell.

Gelvin, James L. 1998. *Divided loyalties: Nationalism and mass politics in Syria at the close of Empire*. Berkeley: University of California Press.

2005. *The Israel-Palestine Confict: One hundred years of war*. Cambridge: Cambridge University Press.

Gibney, Matthew J. 2004. *The ethics and politics of asylum: Liberal democracy and the response to refugees*. Cambridge: Cambridge University Press.

Giddens, Anthony. 1984. *The constitution of society: Outline of the theory of structuration*. Cambridge: Polity.

Gofman, K. 1920. *Petroleum policy and Anglo-Saxon colonialism*. Moscow.

Goldson, Edward. 1996. The Effect of War on Children. *Child Abuse and Neglect* 20, 809–819.

Goodwin-Gill, Guy. 1996. *The refugee in international law*. Oxford: Clarendon.

Gorgas, Jordi Tejel. 2007. La jeunesse Kurde entre rupture et engagement militant. In *La Syrie au présent: Reflets d'une société* (eds) B. Dupret, Z. Ghazzal, Y. Courbage, & M. Al-Dbiyat. Paris: Actes Sud.

Grabill, Joseph. 1971. *Protestant diplomacy and the Near East*. Minneapolis: University of Minnesota Press.

Great Britain. 1895. Parliament. Sessional papers. Vol. 109, c. 7894, Turkey no. 1. 1896. Parliament. Sessional papers. Vol. 109, c. 7894, Turkey no. 1.

Gulizar. 2006. Interview 24, June19. Amman, Jordan.

Gupta, Akhil & James Ferguson. 1992. Beyond "culture": Space, identity, and the politics of difference. *Cultural Anthropology* 7, 6–23.

Habib, Rasha Tarek. 2002. *The Armenian community in Cairo: An ethnic minority by choice*. MSc thesis: American University of Cairo.

Hacker, Jane. 1960. Modern 'Amman: A social study: University of Durham.

Hadawi, Sami. 1979. *Bitter harvest: Palestine between 1914–1979*. Delmar, NY: Caravan Books.

Haddad, Simon. 2004. The Origins of Popular Opposition to Palestinian Resettlment in Lebanon. *International Migration review* 38, 470–492.

Hagana Archives file *0014*. 1938. June 19.

Hagop. 2006. Interview 21, April 27. Damascus, Syria.

Halabi, Zeina. 2004. Exclusion and Identity in Lebanon's Palestinian Refugee Camps: a Story of Sustained Conflict. *Environment and Urbanization* 16, 39–48.

Hampartsoum. 2006. Interview 12, January 17. Heliopolis, Cairo, Egypt.

Hannerz, Ulf. 1987. The World of Creolisation. *Africa: Journal of the International African Institute* 57, 546–559.
    1990. Cosmopolitans and Locals in World Culture. *Theory, Culture & Society* 7, 237–251.

Hansen, Art & Anthony Oliver-Smith (eds) 1982. *Involuntary migration and resettlement: The problems and responses of dislocated people* (Westview Special Studies). Boulder: Westview.

Haron, Yafa, Rivka Eisikovits, & Shai Linn. 2004. Traditional Beliefs Concerning Health and Illness among Members of the Circassian Community in Israel. *Journal of Religion and Health* 43, 59–72.

Harrell-Bond, Barbara E. 1986. *Imposing aid*. Oxford: Oxford University Press.

Hart, Jason. 2004. Beyond Struggle and Aid: Children's Identities in a Palestinian Refugee Camp in Jordan. In *Children and Youth on the Front Line* (eds) J. Boyden & J. de Berry. Oxford and New York: Berghahn Books.

Harvey, Leonard. 1990. *Islamic Spain, 1250–1500*. Chicago: University of Chicago Press.

Hathaway, James. 1991. *The law of refugee status*. Toronto: Butterworths.

Hein, Jeremy. 1993. Refugees, Immigrants and the State. *Annual Review of Sociology* 19, 43–59.

Helms, Christina. 1981. *The cohesion of Saudi Arabia*. London: Croom Helm.

Herzfeld, Michael. 1987. *Anthropology through the looking-glass: Critical ethnography in the margins of Europe*. Cambridge: Cambridge University Press.

Herzl, Theodor. 1896. *Der Judenstaat [The Jewish State]* (trans.) S. D'Avigdor. New York: American Zionist Emergency Council.

Hinnebusch, Raymond A. 2001. *Syria: Revolution from above*. London: Routledge.

Hirschon, Renée. 1998. *Heirs of the Greek catastrophe: The social life of Asia Minor refugees in Piraeus*. Oxford: Berghahn.

   (ed.) 2003. *Crossing the Aegean: An appraisal of the 1923 compulsory population exchange between Greece and Turkey* (Studies in Forced Migration, vol. 12). Oxford: Berghahn.

Hobsbawm, Eric J. 1962. *The age of revolution: Europe, 1789–1848*. London: Weidenfeld & Nicolson.

   1997. The End of Empire. In *After empire: Multiethnic societies and nation-building: The Soviet Union and the Russian, Ottoman, and Habsburg Empires* (eds) K. Barkey & M. Von Hagen. Boulder, CO: Westview.

Hopkins, MaryCarol & Nancy D. Donnelly (eds) 1993. *Selected papers on refugee issues (A publication of the Committee on Refugee Issues, a committee of the General Anthropology Division, a unit of the American Anthropological Association)* 2. Washington, DC: American Anthropological Association.

Horst, Cindy. 2005. *Transnational nomads: How Somalis cope with refugee life in the Dadaab camps of Kenya* (Studies in Forced Migration, vol. 19). Oxford: Berghahn.

Hourani, Albert. 1968. Ottoman Reform and the Politics of Notables. In *Beginnings of modernization in the Middle East: The nineteenth century* (eds) W. R. Polk & R. L. Chambers. Chicago: University of Chicago Press.

Hovannisian, Richard G. 1967. *Armenia on the road to independence, 1918*. Berkeley: University of California.

   1983. Causasian Armenia between Imperial and Soviet Rule: The Interlude of National Independence. In *Transcaucasia: Nationalism and socialism* (ed.) R. G. Suny. Ann Arbor: University of Michigan Press.

   (ed.) 1987. *The Armenian genocide in perspective*. New Brunswick and Oxford: Transaction Books.

   1992. *The Armenian genocide: History, politics, ethics*. New York: St Martin's Press.

   (ed.) 1997a. *The Armenian people from ancient to modern times: Foreign dominion to statehood: The fifteenth century to the twentieth century: Vol. II* (The Armenian people from ancient to modern times 2). London: Macmillan.

   1997b. The Armenian Question in the Ottoman Empire 1876 to 1914. In *The Armenian people from ancient to modern times: Foreign dominion to statehood: The fifteenth century to the twentieth century: Vol. II* (ed.) R. G. Hovannisian. The Armenian people from ancient to modern times. London: Macmillan.

   1997c. The Republic of Armenia. In *The Armenian people from ancient to modern times: Foreign dominion to statehood: The fifteenth century to the twentieth century: Vol. II* (ed.) R. G. Hovannisian. The Armenian people from ancient to modern times. London: Macmillan.

Hrant. 2006. Interview 13, January 17. Cairo, Egypt.

Hudson, Maria, Joan Phillips, Kathryn Ray, & Helen Barnes. 2006. *Social cohesion in diverse communities*. London: Joseph Rowntree Foundation.

Hudson, Michael C. 1997. Palestinians and Lebanon: The Common Story. *Journal of Refugee Studies* 10, 243–260.

Humphrey, Michael. 1993. Migrants, Workers and Refugees: The Political Economy of Population Movements in the Middle East. *Middle East Report* 23, 2–9.

Hütteroth, Wolfgang & Kamal Abdelfattah. 1977. *Historical geography of Palestine, Transjordan and Southern Syria in the late 16th century*. Nuremberg: Junge & Sons.

Ibn Khaldûn. 1958. *The Muqaddimah: An introduction to history* (trans.) F. Rosenthal (Bollingen Series). Princeton: Princeton University Press.

Issawi, Charles 1966a. *The Economic History of the Middle East, 1800–1914*. Chicago: University of Chicago Press.

Issawi, Charles (ed.) 1966b. *The economic history of the Middle East, 1800–1914*. Chicago: University of Chicago Press.

Johns, Jeremy. 1994. The Longue Duree: State and Settlement Strategies in Southern Transjordan across the Islamic Centuries. In *Village, steppe and state: The social origins of modern Jordan* (eds) E. Rogan & T. Tell. London: British Academic Press.

Kais. 2008. Interview 38, September 20. Damascus, Syria.

Kalkas, Barbara. 1971. The Revolt of 1936: A Chronicle of Events. In *The transformation of Palestine* (ed.) I. Abu-Lughod. Evanston: Northwestern University Press.

Kanafani, Ghassan. 1972. *The 1936–39 Revolt in Palestine*. New York: Committee for a Democratic Palestine.

Karal, Enver Ziya. 1982. Non-Muslim Representatives in the First Constitutional Assembly 1876–1877. In *Christians and Jews in the Ottoman Empire* (eds) B. Braude & B. Lewis. New York: Homles and Meier.

Karpat, Kemal H. 1972. The Transformation of the Ottoman State, 1789–1908. *International Journal of Middle East Studies* 3, 243–281.

———— 1974. Ottoman Immigration Policies and Settlement in Palestine. In *Settler regimes in Africa and the Arab world: The illusion of endurance* (eds) I. Abu-Lughod & B. Abu Laban. Wilmette: The Medina University Press International.

———— 1979. The Status of the Muslims under European Rule: The Eviction and Settlement of the Cerkes. *Journal of the Institute of Muslim Minority Affairs (JIMMA)* 1, 7–27.

———— 1985. *Ottoman population 1830–1914: Demographic and social characteristics*. Madison: University of Wisconsin Press.

Kearns, Ade & Ray Forrest. 2000. Social Cohesion and Multi-Cultural Urban Governance. *Urban Studies* 37, 995–1017.

Kedourie, Elie. 1984. Minorities and Majorities in the Middle East. *European Journal of Sociology* 25, 276–282.

Keith-Roach, E. 1934. Changing Palestine. *National Geogrpahic Magazine* 65, 491–527.

Kendal [Nezan]. 1980. The Kurds under the Ottoman Empire. In *A people without a country: The Kurds and Kurdistan* (ed.) G. Chaliand. London: Zed.

Kerr, Malcolm H. 1971. The Changing Political Status of Jerusalem. In *The transformation of Palestine: Essays on the origin and development of the Arab-Israeli conflict* (ed.) I. Abu-Lughod. Evanston, IL: Northwestern University Press.

Keyder, Çağlar. 1997. The Ottoman Empire. In *After Empire: Multiethnic societies and nation-building: The Soviet Union and the Russian, Ottoman and Habsburg Empires* (eds) K. Barkey & M. Von Hagen. Oxford: Westview.

Khalidi, Rashid. 2001. The Palestinians and 1948: The Underlying Causes of Failure. In *The war for Palestine: Rewriting the history of 1948* (eds) E. L. Rogan & A. Shlaim. Cambridge Middle East Studies, no. 15. Cambridge: Cambridge University Press.

Khalidi, Rashid. 1997. *Palestinian identity: The Construction of Modern National Consciousness.* New York: Columbia University Press.

Khalidi, Walid (ed.) 1971. *From haven to conquest: Readings in Zionism and the Palestine problem until 1948* (Anthology Series (Mu'assasat al-Dirasat al-Filastiniyah) 2). Beirut: Institute for Palestine Studies.

   1984. *Before their diaspora: A photographic history of the Palestinians 1876–1948.* Washington, DC: Institute for Palestine Studies.

Khoury, Philip S. 1983. *Urban notables and Arab nationalism.* Cambridge: Cambridge University Press.

   1984. Syrian Urban Politics in Transition: The Quarters of Damascus during the French Mandate. *International Journal of Middle East Studies* 16, 507–540.

Kibreab, Gaim. 1999. Revisiting the Debate on People, Place, Identity and Displacement. *Journal of Refugee Studies* 112, 384–410.

King, Henry Churchill & Charles Richard Crane. 1922. *First publication of King-Crane report on the Near East (Recommendation of the King-Crane Commission on Syria and Palestine, August 28, 1919)* 55. New York.

Kontogiorgi, Elisabeth. 2006. *Population exchange in Greek Macedonia: the forced settlement of refugees 1922–1930.* Oxford: Oxford University Press.

Koufopoulou, Sophia. 2003. Muslim Cretans in Turkey: The Reformulation of Ethnic Identity in an Aegean Community. In *Crossing the Aegean: An appraisal of the 1923 compulsory population exchange between Greece and Turkey* (ed.) R. Hirschon. Oxford: Berghahn.

Koufopoulou, Sophia & D Papageorgiou. 1997. Morphes kai Oria "Perithoriakon" Epikoinoniakon Dyktion ston Aigaiako Horo: I Praktiti tou Lathremporiou sto Aivali kai sti Lesvo [Borders and expressions of marginalised communicative networks: The practice of smuggling in Aivali and Lesvos]. In *Dytia Epikoinonias kai Politismou sto Aigaio [Communication networks and culture in the Aegean].* Athens: Pnevmatiko Idryma Samou.

Kouymjian, Dickran. 1997. Armenia from the fall of the Cilician kingdom (1375) to the forced emigration under Shah Abbas (1604). In *The Armenian people from ancient to modern times: Foreign dominion to statehood: The fifteenth century to the twentieth century: Vol. II* (ed.) R. Hovannisian. London: Macmillan.

Kulischer, Eugene Michel. 1948. *Europe on the move: War and population changes, 1917–47.* New York: Columbia University Press.

Kurd-Oghlu. 1932. Kurds and Imperialism. *Middle East News Bulletin [Tashkent]* 13–14.

Ladas, Stephen P. 1932. *The exchange of minorities. Bulgaria, Greece, and Turkey.* New York: Macmillan.

Lancaster, William & Fidelity Lancaster. 1995. Land use and population in the area north of Karak. *Levant* 27, 103–124.

Lane-Poole, Stanley & Arthur Gilman. 1888. *The Moors in Spain* (Story of the Nations). London: T. Fisher Unwin.

Langer, William. 1960. *The diplomacy of imperialism, 1890–1902.* New York: Knopf.

Le Petit Robert. 1978. Paris: Société du Nouveau Littré.

Lepsius, Johannes. 1897. *Armenia and Europe: An indictment.* London: Hodder and Stoughton.

Lerner, Daniel, Lucille W. Pevsner, & David Riesman. 1958. *The passing of traditional society: Modernizing the Middle East.* New York: Free Press; Collier-Macmillan.

Levy, Avigdor. 2000. Christians, Jews and Muslims in the Ottoman Empire: Lessons for contemporary coexistence: Brandeis University.

Lewis, Bernard. 1954. *Studies in the Ottoman Archives, no. 1.* School of Oriental and African Studies.

    1961. *The emergence of modern Turkey.* Oxford: University of Oxford Press.

Lewis, Ioan M. 1985. *Social anthropology in perspective.* Cambridge: Cambridge University Press.

Lewis, Norman. 1987. *Nomads and settlers in Syria and Jordan, 1800–1980.* Cambridge: Cambridge University Press.

Lindholm, Charles. 2002. *The Islamic Middle East: Tradition and change.* Oxford: Blackwell Pub.

Lloyd George, David. 1933. *War memoirs of David Lloyd George, vol. 5 (5).* London: I. Nicholson & Watson.

Lockman, Zachary. 2004. *Contending visions of the Middle East: The history and politics of Orientalism.* Cambridge: Cambridge University Press.

Loizos, Peter. 1999. Ottoman Half-Lives: Long Term Perspectives on Particular Forced Migrations. *Journal of Refugee Studies* 12, 237–263.

    2000. Are Refugees Social Capitalists? In *Social capital: Critical perspectives* (eds) S. Baron, J. Field, & T. Schuller. Oxford: Oxford University Press.

Lowe, Robert. 2006. *The Syrian Kurds: A people discovered.* Chatham House.

Luke, H. & Keith-Roach, E (ed.) 1930. *The Handbook of Palestine and Trans-Jordan.* London: Macmillan.

MacKay, Angus. 1992. The Jews in Spain during the Middle Ages. In *Spain and the Jews: The Sephardi experience 1492 and after* (ed.) E. Kedourie. London: Thames and Hudson.

Makdisi, Ussama. 2002. Ottoman Orientalism. *The American Historical Review* 107, 768–796.

Malkki, Liisa H. 1990. Context and Consciousness: Local Conditions for the Production of Historical and National Thought among Hutu Refugees in Tanzania. In *Nationalist ideologies and the production of national cultures* (ed.) R. Fox. Washington, DC: American Anthropological Association.

    1992. National Geographic: The Rooting of Peoples and the Territorialization of National Identity among Scholars and Refugees. *Cultural Anthropology* 7, 24–44.

    1995. *Purity and exile: Violence, memory, and national cosmology among Hutu refugees in Tanzania.* Chicago: University of Chicago Press.

Mandelstam, Andre. 1917. *Le sort de l'Empire Ottoman*. Paris, Lausanne.

Mardin, Şerif. 1962. *The genesis of young Ottoman thought: A study in the modernization of Turkish political ideas*. Princeton: Princeton University Press.

Margalith, Israel. 1957. *Le Baron de Rothschild et la colonisation juive en Palestine*. Paris: Libraire. M. Riviere.

Margolis, Max & Alexander Marx. 1969. *History of the Jewish people*. New York: Atheneum.

Marrus, Michael Robert. 1985. *The unwanted: European refugees in the Twentieth Century*. New York: Oxford University Press.

Marsot, Afaf Lutfi al-Sayyid. 1984. *Egypt in the reign of Muhammad Ali*. Cambridge: Cambridge University Press.

Massad, Joseph. 2001. *Colonial effects: The making of national identity in Jordan*. New York: Columbia University Press.

Mazower, Mark. 1991. *Greece and the inter-war economic crisis*. Oxford: Clarendon Press.

McCarthy, Justin. 1983. *Muslims and minorities: The population of Ottoman Anatolia and the end of the empire*. New York: New York University Press.

   1995. *Death and exile: The ethnic cleansing of Ottoman Muslims, 1821–1922*. Princeton, NJ: Darwin Press.

   2001. *The Ottoman peoples and the end of empire* (Historical Endings. London: Arnold.

McCarthy, Justin, Esat Arslan, Cemalettin Taşkıran, & Ömer Turan. 2006. *The Armenian rebellion at Van*. Salt Lake City: University of Utah Press.

McDowall, David. 2004. *A modern history of the Kurds*. London: I.B. Tauris.

Melson, Robert. 1996. *Revolution and genocide: On the origins of the Armenian genocide and the holocaust*. Chicago: Chicago University Press.

Meyer, James. 2007. Immigration, Return, and the Politics of Citizenship: Russian Muslims in the Ottoman Empire, 1860–1914. *International Journal of Middle East Studies* 39, 15–32.

Migliorino, Nicola. 2006. 'Kulna Suriyyin'? The Armenian Community and the State in Contemporary Syria. *Revue des mondes musulmans et de la Méditerranée* 115–116 (Special Issue on La Syrie au quotidien. Cultures et pratiques du changement), 97–115.

   2007. *(Re)constructing Armenia in Lebanon and Syria: Ethno-cultural diversity and the state in the aftermath of a refugee crisis* (Studies in Forced Migration, vol. 21). Oxford: Berghahn.

Miller, Donald E., & Lorna Touryan Miller. 1982. Armenian Survivors: A Typological Analysis of Victim Response. *Oral History Review* 10.

   1987. In *The Armenian genocide in perspective* (ed.) R. G. Hovannisian. New Brunswick and Oxford: Transaction Books.

Minority Rights Group. 2008. Who are minorities?: Minority Rights Group International.

Mirak, Robert. 1997. The Armenians in America. In *The Armenian people from ancient to modern times: Foreign dominion to statehood: The fifteenth century to the twentieth century: Vol. II* (ed.) R. G. Hovannisian. The Armenian people from ancient to modern times. London: Macmillan.

Mirak-Weissbach, Muriel. 2006. Shades of Sykes-Picot Accord Are Cast Over Southwest Asia *Executive Intelligence review* 6–15.

Mohammed. 2006. Interview 17, April 20. Harat al-Akrad, Damascus, Syria.

Montesquieu (Charles de Secondat). 1748. *De l'esprit des lois (The spirit of the laws)* (trans.) T. Nugent. Originally published anonymously. Online posting: constitution.org.

Montgomery, Harriet. 2005. *The Kurds of Syria: An existence denied*. Berlin: Europäisches Zentrum für Kurdische Studien.

Morgenthau, Henry. 1918. *Ambassador Morgenthau's story*. Garden City: Doubleday.

Morris, Benny. 1987. *The birth of the Palestinian refugee problem, 1947–1949*. Cambridge: Cambridge University Press.

Mr. Baladyan. 2005. *Personal communication*. Armenian Charitable Association, Heliopolis, Cairo.

Nalbandian, Louise. 1963. *The Armenian revolutionary movement*. Berkeley and Los Angeles: University of California Press.

Nazdar, Mustafa. 1980. The Kurds in Syria. In *People without a country: The Kurds and Kurdistan* (ed.) G. Chaliand. London: Zed.

Niles, Emory & Arthur Sutherland. 1919. *The report of Captain Emory H. Niles and Mr. Arthur E. Sutherland, Jr. on trip of investigation through Eastern Turkish Vilayets*.

Nisan, Mordechai. 1991. Assyrians: An Ancient People, a Perennial Struggle. In *Minorities of the Middle East*. Jefferson, NC: McFarland and Company.

Nouri Pasha, Ihsan 1986. *La revolte de l'agri dagh*. Geneva: Editions Kurde.

O'Dowd, Liam & M Wilson (eds) 1996. *Borders, nations and states: Frontiers of sovereignty in the new Europe*. Aldershot: Avebury.

Old Testament. Genesis 8:4.

Oliphant, Laurence. 1880. *The land of Gilead*. London.

Oliver-Smith, Anthony & Art Hansen. 1982. Introduction: Involuntary Migration and Resettlement: Causes and Contexts. In *Involuntary migration and resettlement: The problems and responses of dislocated people* (eds) A. Hansen & A. Oliver-Smith. Westview Special Studies. Boulder, CO: Westview.

Olwig, Karen Fog & Kirsten Hastrup (eds) 1997. *Siting culture: The shifting anthropological object*. London: Routledge.

Öncü, Edip. 2003. *The beginnings of Ottoman-German partnership: Diplomatic and military relations between Germany and the Ottoman Empire before the First World War*. Master's thesis: Bilkent University.

Ottoman Archives F.M. (I) 346 and 6078/183. 1891. November 16: Foreign Ministry (Idare).

Ottoman Archives F.M. (I) 47646/183. Foreign Ministry (Idare).

Owen, R. 1981a. *The Middle East in the World Economy: 1800–1914*. London: Methuen.

Owen, Roger. 1981b. *The Middle East in the world economy, 1800–1914*. London: Methuen. P.P. 1877. Vol. 91, 90, 143, 322.

Pahl, Ray & Liz Spencer. 2003. *Personal communities: Not simply families of 'fate' or 'choice'*. Institute of Social and Economic Research (ISER).

Palairet, Michael. 1997. *The Balkan economies c. 1800–1914: Evolution without development*. Cambridge: Cambridge University Press.

Pallis, Alexandros A. 1925. Racial Migrations in the Balkans during the Years 1912–1924. *The Geographical Journal* 66, 315–331.

Papikian, Hakob. 1919. *Adanayi Yegherne*. "*Teghekagir*" [The Adana Calamity. "Report"].

Pappé, Ilan. 2006. *The ethnic cleansing of Palestine*. Oxford: One World Publications.

Parkin, David. 1999. Mementoes as Transitional Objects in Human Displacement. *Journal of Material Culture* 4, 303–320.

Parsons, Talcott. [1937] 1964. *The structure of social action: A study in social theory with special reference to a group of recent European writers* (McGraw-Hill Publications in Sociology). New York: McGraw-Hill Book Company Inc.

Pearly, David. 1946. *Kurdistan: The Kurdish ideal and its reflections on Assyrian-Kurdish relations*. New Jersey.

Peel, Earl (Lord).1937. *Palestine Royal Commission Report*. London: Her Majesty's Stationery Office (HMSO).

Perthes, Volker. 1995. *The political economy of Syria under Asad*. London and New York: I.B. Tauris.

Peteet, Julia. 2005. *Landscape of hope and despair: Palestinian refugee camps*. Philadelphia: University of Pennsylvania Press.

Pinson, Mark. 1972. Ottoman colonization of the Circassians in Rumili after the Crimean War. *Etudes Balkaniques*, 71–85.

Pinto, Paulo G. 2007. Les Kurdes en Syrie. In *La Syrie au présent: Reflets d'une société* (eds) B. Dupret, Z. Ghazzal, Y. Courbage & M. Al-Dbiyat. Paris: Actes Sud.

Price, Charles. 1969. The Study of Assimilation. In *Migration* (ed.) J. A. Jackson. Sociologickâe studie; 2. London: Cambridge University Press.

Provence, Michael. 2005. *The Great Syrian Revolt and the rise of Arab nationalism* (CMES Modern Middle East Series, no. 22). Austin, TX: University of Texas Press.

Qahtan. 2006. Interview 20, April 24. Dummar, Damascus, Syria.

Quataert, Donald. 2000. *The Ottoman Empire, 1700–1922* (New Approaches to European History, 17. Cambridge: Cambridge University Press.

Rabo, Annika. 2008. Narrating Ethnic and Religious Heterogeneity in Contemporary Aleppo. In *9th Mediterranean Research Meeting, Robert Shuman Centre* Montecatini European University Institute.

Rabo, Annika & Bo Utas (eds) 2005. *The role of the state in West Asia* (Transactions). Stockholm: Swedish Research Institute in Istanbul.

Rafeq, Abdul Karim. 1966. *The province of Damascus, 1723–1783*. Beirut: Khayats.

Ra'isa. 2006. Interview 16, April 19. Damascus, Syria.

Rapport, Nigel & Ronald Stade. 2007. Debate Section: A cosmopolitan turn – or return? *Social Anthropology* 15, 223–235.

Richmond, Anthony H. 1988. *Immigration and ethnic conflict*. Basingstoke: Macmillan.

1994. *Global apartheid: Refugees, racism, and the new world order.* Oxford: Oxford University Press.

Richter, Julius. 1910. *A history of protestant missions in the Near East.* Edinburgh: Oliphant, Anderson and Ferrier.

Robert, Le Petit. 1978. Paris: Société du Nouveau Littré.

Rogan, Eugene. 1996. Asiret Mektebi: Abdulhamid II's School for Tribes 1892–1907. *International Journal of Middle East Studies* 28, 83–107.

1999. *Frontiers of the state in the late Ottoman Empire.* Cambridge: Cambridge University Press.

Rogan, Eugene & Tariq Tell. 1994. *Village, steppe and state: The social origins of modern Jordan.* London: British Academy Press.

Roosevelt Jr, Archibald Bulloch. 1947. The Kurdish Republic of Mahabad. *Middle East Journal* 1, 247–269.

Rosel, Jakob. 1997. Nationalism and Ethnicity: Ethnic Nationalism and the Regulation of Ethnic Conflict (trans.) C. f. I. R. o. S. Stress. In *War and ethnicity: Global connections and local violence* (ed.) D. Turton. Studies on the Nature of War, v. 2. Rochester, NY: University of Rochester Press.

Rosenfeld, Maya. 2004a. *Confronting the Occupation: Work, education and political activism of Palestinian families in a refugee camp.* Stanford: Stanford University Press.

Rosenfeld, Maya. 2004b. *Confronting the occcupation: Work, education and political activism of Palestinian families in a refugee camp.* Stanford: Stanford University Press.

Rothschild, Joseph. 1974. *East Central Europe between the two World Wars.* Seattle: University of Washington Press.

Russell, Sharon Stanton. 1992. International migration and political turmoil in the Middle East. *Population and development review* 18, 719–727.

Safrastian, Arshak. 1948. *Kurds and Kurdistan.* London: Havril Press.

Salma. 2005. Interview 7, October 24. Damascus, Syria.

Salt, Jeremy. 2003. The narrative gap in Ottoman Armenian history. *Middle Eastern Studies* 39, 19–36.

Sarkis. 2005. Interview 10, November 2. Damascus, Syria.

Sauvaget, Jean. 1934. Esquisse d'une histoire de la ville de Damas. *Revue des Etudes Islamiques* 8, 421–480.

Sayigh, Rosemary. 1988. Palestinians in Lebanon: Status Ambiguity, Insecurity and Flux. *Race and Class* 30, 13–32.

1994. *Too many enemies: The Palestinian experience in Lebanon.* London: Zed.

1979. *Palestinians: From peasants to revolutionaries.* London: Zed Books

Sayigh, Yezid. 1997. *Armed struggle and the search for state: The Palestinian national movement, 1949–1993.* Oxford: Clarendon Press.

Scholch, A. 1982. European Penetration and the Economic Development of Palestine, 1856–1882. In *Studies in the economic and social history of Palestine in the nineteenth and twentieth centuries* (ed.) R. Owen. Carbondale: Southern Illinois University Press.

Schumacher, Gottleib. 1888. *The Jaulan.* London: Palestinian Exploration Fund.

Scott, James. 1990. *Domination and the arts of resistance: Hidden transcripts.* New Haven and London: Yale University Press.

Seremetakis, Constantina Nadia (ed.) 1994. *The senses still: Perception and memory as material culture in modernity.* Boulder: Westview.

Serhan, Bassem. 2005. Palestinian Refugee Children and Caregivers in Lebanon. In *Children of Palestine: Experiencing forced migration in the Middle East* (eds) D. Chatty & G. Lewando Hundt. Oxford and New York: Berghahn Books.

Shami, Seteney. 1982. *Ethnicity and leadership: The Circassians in Jordan. PhD dissertation:* University of California, Berkeley.

    1994. Mobility, Modernity and Misery: Population Displacement and Resettlement in the Middle East. In *Population displacement and resettlement: Development and conflict in the Middle East* (ed.) S. Shami. New York: Center for Migration Studies.

    1995. Disjuncture in Ethnicity: Negotiating Circassian Identity in Jordan, Turkey and the Caucasus. *New Perspectives on Turkey* 12, 79–95.

    2000. Prehistories of Globalization: Circassian Identity in Motion. *Public Culture* 12, 177–204.

Shaw, Stanford J. 1978. The Ottoman Census System and Population, 1831–1914. *International Journal of Middle East Studies* 9, 325–338.

    1980. Ottoman Population Movements during the Last Years of the Empire, 1885–1914. *Journal of Ottoman Studies,* 191–205.

Shaw, Stanford J. & Ezel Kural Shaw. 1977. *History of the Ottoman Empire and modern Turkey,* vol. 22. Cambridge: Cambridge University Press.

Sheshani. 2006. Interview 23, June 18. Jerash, Jordan.

Shorter, F. C. 1983. *The population of Turkey after the war of independence.* Population Council.

Şimşir, Bilâl N. 1968. *Rumeli'den Türk Göçleri.* Ankara: Türk Kültürünü Araraştırma Enstitüsü.

Singer, J. David & Melvin Small. 1972. *The wages of war 1816–1965: A statistical handbook.* New York: John Wiley and Sons.

Soguk, Nevzat. 1999. *States and strangers: Refugees and displacements of statecraft (Borderlines 11).* Minneapolis: University of Minnesota Press.

Sonia. 2006. Interview 11, January 6. Cairo, Egypt.

Stoianovich, Traian. 1960. The Conquering Balkan Orthodox Merchant. *Journal of Economic History* 20, 234–313.

Tamari, Salim. 1992. The Transformation of Palestinian Society: Fragmentation and Occupation. In *Palestinian society in Gaza, West Bank and Arab Jerusalem: A survey of living conditions* (ed.) K. Knudsen. Fafo Report 115. Oslo: Fafo – Norwegian Institute for Applied Social Science.

Tannous, Izzat. 1988. *The Palestinians: Eyewitness history of Palestine under the British Mandate.* New York: I.G.T. Company.

Tejel, Jordi. 2009. *Syria's Kurds: History, politics and society.* London and New York: Routledge.

Tekeli, Ilhan. 1994. Involuntary Displacement and the Problem of Resettlement in Turkey from the Ottoman Empire to the Present. In *Population displacement and resettlement: Development and conflict in the Middle East* (ed.) S. Shami. New York: Centre for Migration Studies.

Temperley, Harold. 1936. *England and the Near East: The Crimea.* London.

Temperley, Harold William Vazeille (ed.) 1920–1924. *A history of the peace conference of Paris*, vol. 66). London: H. Frowde, and Hodder & Stoughton.

Thabet, Abdel Aziz. 2005. Palestinian Refugee Children and Caregivers in the Gaza Strip. In *Children of Palestine: Experiencing forced migration in the Middle East* (eds) D. Chatty & G. Lewando Hundt. Oxford and New York: Berghahn Books.

Thabet, Abdel Aziz Mousa, Yehia Abed & Panos Vostanis. 2002. Emotional Problems in Palestinian Children Living in a War Zone: A Cross-Sectional Study. *The Lancet* 359, 1801–1804.

Thabet, Abdel Aziz & Panos Vostanis. 2000. Post Traumatic Stress Disorder Reactions in Children of War: A Longitudinal Study. *Child Abuse and Neglect* 24, 291–298.

Thompson, Elizabeth. 2000. *Colonial citizens: Republican rights, paternal privilege, and gender in French Syria and Lebanon* (History and Society of the Modern Middle East Series). New York: Columbia University Press.

Toledano, E. R. 1982. *The Ottoman slave trade and its suppression: 1840–1890*. Princeton: University of Princeton Press.

Toth, Anthony B. 2005. Tribes and Tribulations: Bedouin Losses in the Saudi and Iraqi Struggles over Kuwait's Frontiers, 1921–1943. *British Journal of Middle Eastern Studies* 32, 145–167.

Toynbee, Arnold. 1916. A Summary of Armenian History up to and Including 1915. In *The treatment of the Armenians in the Ottoman Empire: Documents presented to Viscount Grey of Fallodon, Secretary of State for Foreign Affairs* (ed.) V. Bryce. London: Her Majesty's Stationery Office (HMSO).

1967. *Acquaintances*. London: Oxford University Press.

Tsokalidou, Roula. 2006. Greek-speaking enclaves of Lebanon and Syria: Proceedings of the 2nd Simposio Internacional Bilingüismo.

Turan, Serafettin. 1963. *Administrative boundaries of the 17th century Ottoman Empire*. Ankara: Ataturk Universitesi.

Turton, David. 2004. The Meaning of Place in a World of Movement: Lessons from Long-Term Field Research in Southern Ethiopia. In *Annual Colson Lecture*. Refugee Studies Centre, Oxford University.

Um Lorens. 2006. Interview 22, April 28. Aleppo, Syria.

UNHCR. 1951. United Nations Convention on Refugees: United Nations High Commissioner for Refugees (UNHCR).

United States. 1943. Papers relating to the foreign relations of the United States, 1919: The Paris Peace Conference, vols. 3–2, 6: Department of State. Washington, DC.

UNRWA. 1992. *Basic data on Palestine refugees and UNRWA*. United Nations Relief and Works Agency for Palestine Refugees in the Near East (UNRWA). 2009. UNRWA Basic Education.

Valensi, Lucette. 1993. *The birth of the despot: Venice and the sublime Porte* (trans.) A. Denner. Ithaca, NY: Cornell University Press.

Van Bruinessen, Martin. 1992. *Agha, shaikh, and state: The social and political structures of Kurdistan*. London: Zed.

Van Hear, Nicholas. 1993. Mass Flight in the Middle East: Involuntary Migration and the Gulf Conflict, 1990–1991. In *Geography and refugees: Patterns and processes of change* (eds) R. Black & V. Robinson. London: Belhaven.

1998. *New diasporas: The mass exodus, dispersal, and regrouping of migrant communities*. Seattle, WA: University of Washington Press.

2000. People Abroad and People at Home in Societies under Strain. *Forced Migration Review* 7.

van Oord, Lodewikj. 2008. The Making of Primitive Palestine: Intellectual Origins of the Palestine-Israel Conflict. *History and Anthropology* 19, 209–228.

Vanly, Ismet Sheriff. 1980. Kurdistan in Iraq. In *People without a Country: The Kurds and Kurdistan* (ed.) G. Chaliand. London: Zed.

Varukan. 2005. Interview 9, November 1. Damascus, Syria.

Vatikiotis, P. J. 1967. *Politics and military in Jordan: A study of the Arab Legion, 1921–1957*. New York: Praeger Publishers.

Vlaykov, T. G. 1934–42. Prezhvyanoto (Experiences), 3 vol. Sofia.

von Hammer-Purgstall, Joseph. 1835. *Histoire de l'Empire Ottoman: Depuis son origine jusqu'à nos jours* (trans.) J. J. Hellert. Paris: Bellizard, Barthès, Dufour & Lowell.

Voutira, Eftihia. 1994. *Anthropology in international humanitarian emergencies*. European Community Humanitarian Office (ECHO).

2006. Post-Soviet Diaspora Politics: The Case of the Soviet Greeks. *Journal of Modern Greek Studies* 24, 379–414.

Waines, David. 1971a. The failure of the nationalist resistance. In *The transformation of Palestine: Essays on the origin and development of the Arab-Israeli conflict* (ed.) I. Abu-Lughod. Evanston: Northwestern University Press.

1971b. *The unholy war: Israel and Palestine, 1897–1971*. Wilmette: Medina University Press International.

Walid. 2005. Interview 5, October 15. Damascus, Syria.

Walker, Christopher J. 1980. *Armenia: The survival of a nation*. London: Croom Helm.

1997. World War I and the Armenian Genocide. In *The Armenian people from ancient to modern times: Foreign dominion to statehood: The fifteenth century to the twentieth century: Vol. II* (ed.) R. G. Hovannisian. The Armenian people from ancient to modern times. London: Macmillan.

Warriner, Doreen (ed.) 1965. *Contrasts in emerging societies: Readings in the social and economic history of south-eastern Europe in the nineteenth century*. Bloomington: Indiana University Press.

Weber, Max. 1968. Basic Concepts of Sociology. In *Economy and society: An outline of interpretive sociology* (eds) M. Weber, G. Roth & C. Wittich. New York: Bedminster Press.

Wedeen, Lisa. 1999. *Ambiguities of domination: Politics, rhetoric and symbols in contemporary Syria*. Chicago: University of Chicago Press.

Weighill, Marie-Louise. 1997. Palestinians in Lebanon: the Politics of Assistance. *Journal of Refugee Studies* 10, 294–313.

Weighill, Marie-Louise & Nadim Shehadi (eds) 1997. *Journal of Refugee Studies*, Vol. 10 no. 3).

Weightman, G. H. 1970. The Circassians. In *Readings in Arab Middle Eastern societies and cultures* (eds) A. Lutfiyya & C. Churchill. The Hague: Mouton.

Weiner, Myron. 1995. *The global migration crisis: Challenge to states and to human rights* (Harper Collins Series in Comparative Politics). New York: Longman.

Wilkinson, John. 1983. Traditional Concepts of Territory in South East Arabia. *The Geographical Journal* **149**, 201–315.

Wilson, Thomas M. & Hastings Donnan (eds) 1998. *Border identities: Nation and state at international frontiers*. Cambridge: Cambridge University Press.

Wilson, Woodrow. 1918. 65th Congress: Joint session: Program for world's peace, January 8.

Yergin, Daniel. 1991. *The Prize: The epic quest for oil, money and power*. New York: Simon and Schuster.

Yusuf. 2006. Interview 17, April 20. Harat al-Akrad, Damascus, Syria.

Zaki, Muhammad Amin. 1947. *A brief history of Kurds and Kurdistan, from antiquity to the present* (trans.) M. A. 'Awni. Cairo: Matba'at al-Sa'ada.

Zaroo, Salah. 2005. Palestinian Refugee Children and Caregivers in the West Bank. In *Children of Palestine: Experiencing forced migration in the Middle East* (eds) D. Chatty & G. Lewando Hundt. Oxford and New York: Berghahn Books.

Zetter, Roger, David Griffiths, Nando Sigona, Don Flynn, Tauhid Pasha & Rhian Beyon. 2007. *Immigration, social cohesion and social capital: What are the links?* London: Joseph Rowntree Foundation.

Zogby, James. 1974. The Palestinian Revolt of the 1930s. In *Settler regimes in Africa and the Arab world: The illusion of endurance* (eds) I. Abu-Lughod & B. Abu-Laban. Wilmette, IL: Medina University Press International.

Zolberg, Aristide R. 1982. State Formation and Its Victims: Refugee Movements in Early Modern Europe. *Paper presented to the Verhaegen Lecture*, Erasmus University, Rotterdam, 1982.

    1983. International Migrants in Political Perspective. In *Global trends in migration* (eds) M. M. Kritz, C. B. Keely, & S. M. Tomasi. New York: Center for Migration Studies.

Zolberg, Aristide R., Sergio Aguayo, & Astri Suhrke. 1989. *Escape from violence: Conflict and the refugee crisis in the developing world*. New York: Oxford University Press.

Zolberg, Aristide R., Astri Suhrke, & Sergio Aguayo. 1986. International Factors in the Formation of Refugee Movement. *International Migration Review* **20**, 151–169.

Zoryan Institute. Audio and video library of testimonies of survivors of the Armenian genocide.

Zoryan Institute. 1983. *Oral testimony*. Cambridge, MA.

Zoryan Institute. 1988. *Oral testimony*. San Francisco.

Zubaida, Sami. 1999. Cosmopolitanism in the Middle East. In *Cosmopolitanism, identity and authenticity in the Middle East* (ed.) R. Meijer. Richmond: Curzon.

Zürcher, Erik. 1993. *Turkey: A modern history*. London: I.B. Tauris.

Zureik, Elia. 1996. *Palestinian refugees and the peace process*. Washington, DC: Institute for Palestine Studies.

    2001. Constructing Palestine through Surveillance Practices. *British Journal of Middle Eastern Studies* **28**, 205–227.

Index

Abdul Hamid (Ottoman Empire sultan),
    74–75
  Bedouin and, 245
  Kurds and, 245–246
Abdul Hamid II (Ottoman Empire
    sultan), 139
  Armenians and, 143–144, 150
  Kurds and, 247
  Young Turks and, 150–151, 245
Abdul Majid I (Ottoman Empire sultan), 67
Abdul Rahman I (Ottoman Empire sultan), 39
Abdullah (king of Jordan), 119, 198
  Jewish Agency and, 202
Abkhazians, 4, 7
  Armenians and, 78
  Russia and, 61
Absentees Property Law, 208
ACRNE. *See* American Committee for Relief
    in the Near East
Adigye (Circassians), 92
Aeneid (Virgil), 8
agha (Kurd leaders), 238
aghawat (Kurd leaders), 238
AHC. *See* Arab Higher Committee
Ahl-il Kitab (People of the Book), 46
ajanib, 272
Albanian, 4
Albigensians, France and, 39
Alexandropol, Treaty of, 162
Alhambra Decree, 39
Altarass, Isaac, 74
American Committee for Relief in the Near
    East (ACRNE), 163, 288
  Near East Relief and, 164
American Congregationalists, 78
American Relief Administration, 164
  Asia Minor and, 164
Anatolia
  Armenians in, 139
  Circassians in, 103–108
  deaths in, 99–100
  Greece and, 85–86, 100

  Jews to, 7
  Muslims to, 7
  Refugee Code and, 98–99
  Russia and, 159–160
  Tatars and, 94
  Turkic and, 8
Anderson, Benedict, 21
Anglo Persian Oil Company, 251
anti-Semitism
  in Europe, 189, 194
  in Russia, 189
Anzor, Talustan, 110
Arab Executive, 193–194, 197
Arab Higher Committee (AHC), 197
  McDonald White Paper and, 200–201
Arabness, 32
Arabs
  Britain and, 191, 196–201, 290
  British Mandate and, 192–201
  nationalism of, 264
  Palestine population of, 194, 291–292
  Zionism and, 192–201
Arafat, Yasser, 210–211
Arendt, Hannah, 37
Armenakan Party, 78, 145
Armenian Assembly, 165
Armenian Church, 134, 164–165, 172. *See
    also* Gregorian Church
  in Egypt, 168–169
  Greek Orthodox Church and, 77
  in Syria, 175
Armenian Relief Committee. *See* American
    Committee for Relief in the Near East
Armenians, 5, 9
  Abdul Hamid II and, 143–144, 150
  Abkhazia and, 78
  in Anatolia, 139
  Bedouin and, 158
  Canada and, 163
  Chechnyans and, 109
  as Christians, 138
  in Cilicia, 138, 151–152